Five Films by Frederick Wiseman

FIVE FILMS BY
FREDERICK WISEMAN

Titicut Follies

High School

Welfare

High School II

Public Housing

TRANSCRIBED AND EDITED BY
BARRY KEITH GRANT

WITH A FOREWORD BY
FREDERICK WISEMAN

University of California Press   Berkeley Los Angeles London

University of California Press, one of the most
distinguished university presses in the United
States, enriches lives around the world by advancing
scholarship in the humanities, social sciences, and
natural sciences. Its activities are supported by
the UC Press Foundation and by philanthropic
contributions from individuals and institutions.
For more information, visit www.ucpress.edu.

University of California Press
Berkeley and Los Angeles, California

University of California Press, Ltd.
London, England

Library of Congress Cataloging-in-Publication Data

Grant, Barry Keith, 1947–
    Five films by Frederick Wiseman : Titicut follies,
    High school, Welfare, High school II, Public
    housing / transcribed and edited by Barry Keith
    Grant.
        p.   cm.
    Filmography: p.
    Includes bibliographical references.
    ISBN 0–520–24456–7 (cloth : alk. paper)— ISBN
    0–520–24457–5 (pbk. : alk. paper)
    I. Wiseman, Frederick.   II. Title.
    PN1998.3. W57 G72   2006
    070.1'8—dc22   2005006233

Manufactured in the United States of America

15 14 13 12 11 10 09 08 07 06
10 9 8 7 6 5 4 3 2 1

The paper used in this publication meets the
minimum requirements of ANSI/NISO Z39.48–1992
(R 1997) (*Permanence of Paper*).

Contents

Illustrations

Foreword

For me, the making of a documentary film is in some ways the reverse of making a fiction film. With fiction, the idea for the film is transformed into a script by the imagination and work of the writer and/or director, which obviously precedes the shooting of the film. In my documentaries the reverse is true: The film is finished when, after editing, I have found its "script." If a film of mine works, it does so because the verbal and pictorial elements have been fused into a dramatic structure. This is the result of the compression, condensation, reduction, and analysis that constitute the editing process for me.

Nothing in my films is staged for the camera. During shooting, which takes anywhere from four to twelve weeks, my goal is to accumulate material that interests me in the moment. I have no idea at the time which sequences, shots, and transitions will make it into the final film or what the themes or point of view will be. I generally use about three percent of the material shot. My work as editor, like that of the writer of a fiction film, is to try to figure out what is going on in the sequence I am watching on the editing machine. What is the significance of the words people use, the relevance of tone or changes of tone, pauses, interruptions, verbal associations, the movement of eyes, hands, and legs? Whereas the scriptwriter imagines a script, the documentary film editor, in contrast, has to understand and evaluate already existing sequences; their respective imaginative processes are totally different. The people whose behavior the editor is analyzing exist totally apart from his or her imagination. The sequences in a documentary are not staged but "found" during the process of shooting. Their importance for the film is determined by the editor, who initially evaluates them and then edits them into the form in which they will appear in the final film.

The shape of each sequence is important, but in addition the relationship of the sequences to each other must make it appear as if no other order were possible. There has to be a rhythm that implies that the final film represents the only possible form for the material. The structure must create the illusion, even if it is temporary, that the events seen in the film occurred in the order in which they are seen on the screen. In this way, the form of my documentaries can be called fictional because their structure is imagined and therefore may resemble plays or novels, the more traditional dramatic forms.

I am very pleased that Barry Grant has transcribed five of my documentaries. My hope is that reading these transcripts will help the viewer understand my process in making films.

Frederick Wiseman
Spring 2005

Acknowledgments

Many thanks to Karen Konicek at Zipporah Films for everything. Also at Zipporah, Victoria G. Davis gave me some invaluable help with textual matters. The Office of Research Services, Brock University, provided me with a Chancellor's Chair Award for Research Excellence, which funded the research for this book. At the University of California Press, Eric Smoodin, who first listened to the idea; Mary Francis, who saw it through to completion; and Kate Warne have been wonderfully supportive. Elizabeth Berg provided the careful copyediting the manuscript needed. Sarah Bradley and Olga Klimova, graduate students in the Interdisciplinary M.A. Program in Popular Culture at Brock, helped in preparing the transcriptions. Spanish translations are by Dr. Irene Blayer, professor of Spanish and Portuguese, Brock University. I am particularly indebted to Rob Macmorine, film and video technician at Brock; Divino Mucciante, of Brock's Photographic Services; and Dan Barnowski, student extraordinaire, for help in producing the frame enlargements from Wiseman's films.

And above all, of course and as always, I thank Frederick Wiseman, both for his cooperation with this project and for making such extraordinary films.

Illustrations are courtesy of Frederick Wiseman and Zipporah Films. All dialogue in the films is reprinted with the permission of Frederick Wiseman and Zipporah Films.

Introduction

This book, containing transcripts of five documentary films by Frederick Wiseman, represents, I believe, something of a first in the study of nonfiction film. These transcripts are not screenplays or shooting scripts, of course, since the films were shot in the observational manner, recording unrehearsed and unscripted events as they happened. But they do contain all the dialogue and description of other aspects of the soundtrack, along with notations about camera work and editing. The underlying assumption of this book is that, despite their unscripted origins, Wiseman's documentaries are of sufficient interest both as information (their "documentary value," as John Grierson would have said)[1] and as art to warrant such documentation. Wiseman's distinctive approach and style, as well as the complexity of the human interaction captured by his camera, make his films eminently worthy of transcription.

The few precedents for the present book are diverse. In 1967, Peter Watkins published *The War Game,* based on his controversial 1965 documentary about a nuclear attack on Great Britain. The book, which the back cover informs us was "adapted by Mr. Watkins for those who would further consider the deeply disturbing implications of *The War Game,*"[2] contains a collage of stills from the film, some of the film's dialogue and expository text, and additional text by Watkins, all presented in a bold graphic style meant to duplicate the raw power of the film. But while the book may succeed as a graphic equivalent of the film on the printed page, it is not a transcript in the conventional sense. The Maysles brothers' book of *Salesman,* a classic of American direct cinema, is a more straightforward transcript that includes all of the film's dialogue. Published in 1969, the same year as the film's release, this "post facto film scenario" also inserts "screenplay scene settings" credited to Paul Zimmerman and parenthetical descriptions of some of the actions that accompany the dialogue, reminiscent of stage directions in a play. Oddly, though, the book makes no mention whatever of the images or the film's construction, other than Harold Clurman's unexplained claim in his introduction that the editing functions to sharpen the film's narrative."[3] The Maysles' book of *Salesman* is focused almost exclusively on the soundtrack, a curiously reductive treatment that is even more pronounced in *Dont Look Back*, published as "A Film and Book by D. A. Pennebaker" in 1968, one year after the film. In his foreword to the book, Pennebaker explained, "This is not the script from which *Dont Look Back* was made. The film was made without a script. This is simply a transcript of what happened and what was said."[4] Pennebaker occasionally describes actions that occur in *Dont Look Back*—for example, "[Alan] Price gulps first from gin bottle, then from bottle of orange mixer"[5]—but says nothing of the shots that show them. Unlike these other books, the transcripts of Wiseman's documentaries here take into account, within certain limits explained below, the films' visual aspects and dialogue.

More than any other filmmaker associated with American observational documentary, Frederick Wiseman has established a distinctive style and personal vision. Pauline Kael once praised him as "the most sophisticated intelligence in documentary"[6]—an assessment of Wiseman's prominent place in American cinema that, I would argue, is as true today as when Kael offered her opinion almost forty years ago. Whereas Richard Leacock, himself a major figure in American observational cinema, asserts that in observational documentaries the filmmaker cannot be said to function as a director, Wiseman explicitly identifies himself as director in the end credits of all his documentaries. "When you're signing the film, you are saying it's your film, this is the way you see it," he has said, and in fact the designation *director* accurately conveys Wiseman's creative shaping of the material.[7] Wiseman has managed to retain complete creative control of his films, founding his own distribution company, Zipporah Films, in 1971.

Since 1967, Wiseman has directed an astonishing thirty-two feature-length documentaries, almost one every year (in addition to directing two fiction films and several works for the theater). His films have been broadcast on television in many European countries, and they have won many awards, including three Emmys.[8] This remarkable output rivals that of any other documentary filmmaker, especially considering the length of some of these films (*Near Death* [1989], for example, has a running time of almost six hours, *Belfast, Maine* [1999] just over four). Wiseman's ongoing relationship with the Public Broadcasting System (PBS) has allowed him to premiere his films on American national television (even if some unenthusiastic PBS affiliates insist on scheduling them at impossible hours), giving him access to an audience for which other documentary filmmakers, with the rare exception of someone like Michael Moore, can only wish.

Whereas so many observational documentaries focus on individuals, often famous or extraordinary, Wiseman's documentaries are about institutions and the people who represent them, as well as those the institutions are supposed to serve. With few exceptions (the worker Sam in *Welfare* [1975] or Mrs. Finner in *Public Housing* [1997]), Wiseman does not follow or return to particular individuals with whom viewers might identify in a sustained way. Wiseman has defined an institution as "a place that has certain kinds of geographical limitations and where at least some of the people have well-established roles," although the films' conception of an institution broadens over time from specific tax-supported organizations to wider, more general issues of ideology.[9] Of the films included in this book, *Titicut Follies* (1967) and *High School* (1968) are clear examples of the former, while *Public Housing* is perhaps more representative of the latter, even though it remains within one Chicago housing development. Like the work of the most fascinating auteurs (think of Peter Wollen's explanation of his preference for Ford's films over Hawks's because of the "richness of the shifting relations between antinomies" in Ford's films),[10] Wiseman's vision of institutions is dynamic.

Reminiscent of Jean Renoir's notion that the film artist repeatedly makes the same film, Wiseman has said that his documentaries "are always the same film, by and large," that they "are all one film that is fifty hours long."[11] This mammoth work-in-progress is "a natural history of the way we live,"[12] and Wiseman has shown on film more of American life—how Americans actually dress, behave, and most crucially, talk—than any other filmmaker. In 1974, Wiseman observed that a recurrent theme in his work has been the depiction of "a gap between the formal ideology and actual practice, between the rules and the way they are applied" in the different institutions he has filmed.[13] However, later films, such as *Meat* (1976) and *Missile* (1987), sometimes show an institution working so well that ideological gaps seem to have been entirely sutured. A further difference between Wiseman's earlier and later films, like the four-part *Deaf and Blind* series (1986), is that the more recent work tends to be more gently humanistic, less muckraking, in tone, and consequently takes a more balanced approach to the functioning of institutions. But whether the focus of the film is on a specifically bounded locale like New York's *Central Park* (1990) or more diffuse, such as the entire town of *Belfast, Maine*, Wiseman treats individual institutions as microcosms (in his words, "cultural spoors") reflecting larger aspects of American society. The films employ aesthetic strategies to encourage us to read *High School,* for example, as being not about just Northeast High School, but also about high school generally; or about the educational process, conformity, and the state; or about the alienation of youth; or more metaphysically, as "an essay on emptiness."[14]

Most practitioners of the Leacockian fly-on-the-wall style of direct cinema maintain, at least roughly, the chronology of events. Al Maysles has declared that "in the long run what works best—and we find ourselves coming back to it—is having it happen just the way it happened."[15] This is generally true of the work of American observational filmmakers, even though, as Stephen Mamber has astutely pointed out, the Drew Associates developed a "crisis structure" that combined chronology with a conventional dramatic structure involving a rising dramatic arc.[16] Wiseman's films, however, are considerably more complex in design, standing apart from those of Leacock, Pennebaker, and the Maysleses by avoiding individual protagonists and relying more on rhetorical argument than narrative logic. Bill Nichols has described Wiseman's distinctive approach as a mosaic structure, noting that while individual sequences—the facets or "tesserae" of the mosaic—are organized by narrative codes of construction, the relations between these facets are rhetorical.[17] Wiseman's rejection of chronological organization is apparent immediately in his first documentary, *Titicut Follies,* which begins and ends with parts of the same musical show, with over an hour of other footage sandwiched in between.

Wiseman edits his own films, spending considerably more time editing than shooting them. While he typically spends anywhere from four to six weeks shooting on location, Wiseman devotes at least as many months to sifting through and giving shape to the footage in the editing room. *High School* took Wiseman a relatively short four months to edit, *Primate* (1974) fourteen months. His shooting ratio is high, varying from 10:1 in the lengthy *Near Death* to 30:1 for *Missile,* which at two hours is only one-third as long. Apart from their reliance on editing for continuity within scenes, some of Wiseman's films, such as *Primate* and *Meat,* rely more heavily on editing for their expressiveness.[18] Of the films transcribed here, *Titicut Follies* contains a particularly powerful (albeit uncommon) instance of thematic montage involving parallel shots of an inmate being force-fed and of his corpse being prepared for burial. The intercutting of the two events ironically contrasts the care the dead body is given with the impersonal treatment of the live man, and suggests that death is the only way out of the entrapping world of Bridgewater, a state prison for the criminally insane.

In the editing process, Wiseman works out a "theory," as he describes it, of the events, which is reflected in the film's structure. His films are not objective accounts of institutions but, as he acknowledges, a "report on what I've found."[19] Aesthetic artifacts as well as documentary records, Wiseman's documentaries are instances of what Dziga Vertov called "film objects"—texts based on raw reality but given artistic shape. Thus, according to Wiseman, although his footage originates in the real world, individual shots "have no meaning except insofar as you impose a form on them."[20] For example, *High School* presents high school as an alienating experience, from the opening approach to Northeast High School—which emphasizes its resemblance to a factory—to the closing shot of the principal reading a letter from a former student who, about to parachute into Vietnam, defines himself as "only a body doing a job."

Shots in Wiseman's documentaries are connected by straight cuts rather than by transitional devices such as fades, wipes, or dissolves. (In *The Store*, shot in Neiman-Marcus's flagship store in Dallas, Texas, Wiseman humorously uses the opening and closing of elevator doors as the found equivalent of a wipe, but technically in this film too he relies, as always, on the basic cut.) Wiseman provides no clues to temporal or causal relations between the events shown (although such information may arise naturally in the dialogue); nor is there ever voice-over narration or a talking head addressing the spectator (with one notable exception in *Primate*, where a scientist explains the purpose of his experiment with animal locomotion directly to the camera). Consequently, as commentators on Wiseman's work have noted, his films require particular attention from the viewer to perceive meaning beyond the random presentation of a series of loosely related events. As Wiseman puts it, viewers "have to fight the film, they have to say, 'What the hell's he trying to say with this?'"[21]

Given the inclination of film criticism to attend to the image, the few critics who have written at length about Wiseman's documentary work, myself included, have predictably tended to focus on their visual and structural intricacies.[22] Yet Wiseman also pays considerable attention to the sound. There is no question that Wiseman is one of the greatest documentary filmmakers because of his ability to capture with the camera events both extraordinary and mundane, yet his ear is perhaps equally attuned. In fact, Wiseman operates the tape recorder and not the camera during shooting. (Since 1966, Wiseman has used a Nagra 3, 4.2, ISL, and more recently, a Fostex; his microphones are the Sennheiser 815, 416 and a Trans Radio Mic.) He directs the camera via hand signals worked out in advance with his cameraman or by leading him with the microphone. He used established ethnographic filmmaker John Marshall on *Titicut Follies* and Canadian cinematographer Richard Leiterman on *High School,* then worked with William Brayne for ten films, and with John Davey for all of his documentaries since *Manoeuvre* (1979). This continuity has allowed camera operators to develop a good sense of what Wiseman wants, and, according to Wiseman, doing the sound rather than looking through the viewfinder gives him greater freedom to see the details of the profilmic events he is filming, as well as allowing greater sensitivity to the auditory environment of his subjects. (The third member of his crew is an assistant who helps with the equipment and changes the film magazines.)

The importance of sound in Wiseman's films is dramatically clear even in *Titicut Follies'* montage sequence of the death of the inmate Malinowski. Accompanying the visual crosscutting between the face of the living and deceased inmate is a boldly expressionist manipulation of the soundtrack: the shots of the inmate being force-fed are thick with ambient noise (which contributes to a sense of the force-feeding procedure as insensitive and invasive), while the shots of his corpse are completely devoid of sound, evoking the stark reality of death. These brief moments of silence are powerful, and impossible to achieve during observational shooting unless the microphone was turned off during filming or the sound was eliminated during editing.

Although such pronounced manipulation is rare in Wiseman's work, Wiseman's sound editing is technically more varied than his editing of the images. Whereas he is content to create visual meaning through montage and mise-en-scène, always connecting shots by straight cuts, on the soundtrack he also uses audio fades (both in and out) and sound bridges. At one point in *Titicut Follies,* for example, an inmate, after being escorted to his cell, goes to the window and looks out. On the soundtrack we hear a trombone fade in, which carries over into a scene in the prison yard, where we see the inmate playing "My Blue Heaven" on a trombone. We are encouraged to perceive a (narrative) continuity by reading the scene in the prison yard as revealing what the inmate in his cell was looking at through his window—a visual construction aided by the sound editing.

A scene in *High School* where the camera follows a teacher patrolling the school hallways (reconstructed as a *nouvelle vague*–like homage in Wes Anderson's *Rushmore* [1998]) works similarly. After questioning students on the telephone about their hall passes, the teacher looks through the window in a door as the pop song "Simple Simon" fades in on the soundtrack. The song's authoritative commands—similar to much of what we hear throughout *High School*—reinforce the film's overall view of the education process as impersonal and authoritarian. The film cuts from the teacher in the hallway peering through the window of the door into the gym, where girls in uniform are exercising to the song, and again we are encouraged to make a connection: that the teacher was looking at this particular activity in the gym. Encouraged by both image and sound, viewers have often imputed a predatory sexuality to the teacher in the hallway, reading the camera's emphasis on the girls' buttocks as a point-of-view shot from the teacher's perspective.

Both of these scenes employ found music, which always carries a wider meaning in Wiseman's films. Although the music almost always originates in profilmic events, it usually has thematic significance. The first scene of his first documentary, *Titicut Follies*, which begins with George Gershwin's "Strike Up the Band" performed in the inmates' annual show, signals the importance of music for Wiseman. The film contains several songs, all with metaphorical implications. For example, following a hawks-and-doves debate by two inmates about American involvement in Vietnam, one inmate sings the "Ballad of the Green Berets" in the yard, a further expression of the political tensions within Bridgewater and, by extension, across America at the time (Bridgewater as "cultural spoor"), while there is an unavoidable irony in the hellish context in which an inmate plays "My Blue Heaven" on the trombone. Music also establishes a thematic perspective at the beginning of *High School*, when Otis Redding's "(Sittin' On) The Dock of the Bay," a song about alienation in contemporary America, is heard on the car radio as the camera approaches Northeast High School.

As already suggested, ambient sound also plays an important role in Wiseman's films. In *Welfare*, the constant din of office work underscores the administrative nightmare that is the welfare system, while in *Public Housing*, the unrelenting cry of babies while a birth control counselor tries to explain the use of condoms lends the scene an ironic urgency. Also in *Public Housing*, ambient sound and music come together in the recurrent police sirens and inane calliope music from the ice cream truck that recur throughout the film. These sounds describe the Chicago neighborhood where the film was shot, but the pervasive sirens also express the constant presence of danger and violence there. In addition, the two sounds mark the contrast between childhood innocence and adult experience that informs the film as a whole.

The most important element of Wiseman's soundtracks is, of course, human speech. In his films, the conversation of people is just as important and fascinating as the sights we are shown. Wiseman is attuned to the importance of language, on occasion using dialogue rather than visual logic to structure the film. Thus *High School* cuts from the fashion design teacher asking the class if they have any questions to the typing teacher asking the same question before beginning a typing test. Later, the film cuts to a close-up of girls swinging at T-balls in the gym as a teacher reading "Casey at the Bat" pronounces the last words, "Mighty Casey has struck out." Wiseman has spoken of rare moments of speech in his films as "found eloquence," a kind of auditory equivalent to Jean Rouch's notion of the privileged moment observational filmmakers seek to capture with the camera. Mr. Hirsch's reference at the end of *Welfare* to Samuel Beckett's absurdist drama *Waiting for Godot* is a perfect example, for the film itself, as Dan Armstrong has shown, works as an extended analogy to Beckett's play.[23]

Just as Wiseman has captured the way Americans look, so he captures the authentic talk of Americans, the rhythms of real speech that are so essential to observational cinema. His films are alive with American speech, with what Emerson called the "primal warblings" of the American people, like the vibrant *parole*, the colorful slang, that draws the linguist played by Gary Cooper in Howard Hawks's *Ball of Fire* (1941) away from the lackluster dictionary to the lively streets of America. People in Wiseman's documentaries use language in vivid, surprising, and individual ways. They use slang (the dreaded "gill" in *High School II* [1994]) and even make up words (in *Welfare*, one client complains that he is being pressured to move "instamatically," while the white racist talks of blacks "progenerating" and compares them to white people "biologically, and nomalogically, and pharmanology"). As Louis Marcorelles enthused, in this kind of filmmaking, "It is possible to forget the written word in favor of the living, lived word, flung out by man [*sic*] *en situation.*"[24]

Of course, the most common activity that Wiseman records in his films is conversation, people talking. Rarely does he hold his camera on people silently doing something, as he does so poignantly with the elderly Mrs. Cheatham slowly cleaning cabbage in her kitchen in *Public Housing*. With few exceptions, talk is incessant in Wiseman's films. One almost has the impression in *High School II* that talking is all students do. The social actors in Wiseman's films are often eloquent, even when they are not very articulate, as demonstrated by Dr. Weiss in *Near Death*, whose annoying habit of never finishing a sentence expresses the impossible psychological burden of caring for terminally ill patients. In *Welfare*, the stumbling and somewhat improbable answers by Larry and his girlfriend to a worker's questions say a good deal about the clients that the worker apparently fails to perceive. But the absence of dialogue also speaks volumes in Wiseman's films, as we see with the supervisor Sam in *Welfare*, who on more than one occasion rummages through his desk for nothing in particular, saying nothing, after a disturbing conversation. And sometimes, in the cinematic contexts established by Wiseman's editing, dialogue resonates with meaning beyond that intended by the speaker. While Mr. Hirsch may be aware that his reference to Beckett's play is a perfect metaphor for the Waverly Welfare Center, he is unaware of its relevance to the vision of Wiseman's film; and the earnest English teacher in *High School* who uses Simon and Garfunkel's song "The Dangling Conversation" in a poetry lesson hardly intends the poem to characterize the dynamic of Northeast High School, and by extension the overall school experience, as the film clearly does.

. . . . .

In early 2002, when I began working on this project, the five films included here were those most frequently rented or leased by Zipporah Films over the previous two-year period. (I cannot be more specific about numbers and types of clients because Zipporah divulges only that these include universities and a variety of other educational, social, and professional groups.) The transcripts are arranged chronologically, in order of their production and release. As a group, these five films provide a good sampling of Wiseman's work. Spanning almost the entirety of his career, with over thirty years separating the first (*Titicut Follies*) from the most recent (*Public Housing*), they show Wiseman's view of institutional dynamics evolving from a simpler dualistic model of workers and clients to a more complex view of institutional organization and behavior.

Zipporah has produced unofficial transcripts of these films, to which Wiseman has generously allowed me access. Although I consulted the Zipporah transcripts in the preparation of this book, I did not base my transcripts on them. The Zipporah transcripts are inconsistent in the terminology by which they designate scenes, sequences, and shots. These terms are problematic at the best of times, and too often are used loosely and interchangeably (not unlike the terms *direct cinema* and *cinema verité*). Apart from sorting through which segments of Wiseman's films might be scenes and which sequences, I examined the transitional montages (which Wiseman has called "medleys," emphasizing their rhythmic qualities as much as their visual aspect) that frequently occur between segments. Ranging from two brief shots to a dozen, it is unclear whether these medleys mark the beginning of a scene or sequence or the end of one, or whether they should be designated as sequences in their own right.

I watched videotapes of each film, provided by Zipporah Films, laptop computer at hand, as many times as were necessary for me to produce a rough version of a transcript. I then watched each film twice more with a graduate student research assistant under normal viewing conditions, together transcribing what we could. Then we both watched the films again independently, taking as much time as we needed to work through all the dialogue, replaying some parts dozens of times if necessary. I collated both sets of notes, and watched the films yet again, replaying particularly difficult parts as many times as I needed until all the audible dialogue was transcribed as accurately and fully as possible. With some words and phrases that were especially difficult to understand, I used standard quality earphones to listen more closely, and if I still could not understand what was said, I deemed them inaudible. These moments are indicated in the transcripts, and occur because the speaker is talking simultaneously with someone else, competing with ambient noise, speaking too far away from the microphone, or simply mumbling. Finally, another graduate research assistant double-checked the transcripts against the films, noting any errors that remained, which I checked and incorporated as required by watching the films several more times.

Overall, the sound quality is much better in the more recent films than in the earlier ones, largely because of improvements in technology. Nevertheless, I was amazed to discover how much dialogue I had missed when watching all the films under normal viewing conditions, despite the many times I had seen them. (I also discovered visual details I had never noticed before, the most profound being the frequency with which people fleetingly glanced at or acknowledged Wiseman's camera.) Since we are capable of listening fully to only one voice at a time, we cannot grasp all of what is said, let alone implied, in overlapping and animated discussions involving several participants, such as the one between the policemen and the two men accused of stealing a refrigerator in *Public Housing*. Some social actors, like the school coprincipal Debbie in *High School II*, talk too quickly and swallow their words, making it very hard to understand what they say.

The Zipporah transcripts contain only the dialogue and do not refer at all to the images or the camera work, whereas I have attempted to provide a sense of what is going on visually in the films, to help the reader appreciate, if not (re)visualize, the context of the dialogue. (I use the following abbreviations throughout: CU—close-up; MS—midshot; LS—long shot.) At the same time, I did not want to swamp the transcripts with the kind of annotation that one would find in a detailed shooting script. If it is true that a picture is worth a thousand words, then these transcripts would be much lengthier, not to mention considerably more cumbersome, depending on how much detail one chose to include. Even individual shots in many cases would require more copious annotation than a Eugene O'Neill play, for Wiseman's camera, as in most observational cinema, moves often as it follows events and records conversations. There is constant panning between speakers during conversations, tracking to follow events as they unfold and people as they move, tilting and more complex combinations of camera movements to search out significant visual details, even jarring motions when the camera operator moves suddenly. Impressions of movement result from the frequent adjustments of the telephoto lens, which change the framing as the camera zooms in and out, and because of rack focusing, or adjusting the depth of field—techniques typical of filming in what Mamber has called "uncontrolled" situations.

Another important issue is how to annotate in detail the temporal duration of shots. The question of shot length is important for a filmmaker like Wiseman, since each film has its own distinctive rhythm and pace, ranging from *Meat*, with its reliance on lengthy montages of relatively short shots to reflect the sense of unrelenting routine that characterizes the process of "animal fabrication," to the more leisurely *Deaf and Blind* films, with their many stunning long takes. In these transcripts I have tried to maintain this rhythmic quality as much as possible—allowing, of course, for the differences between cinema and print.

Thus, I have sought a style here that is factual without being scientific, or impressionistic or interpretive. I indicate where Wiseman cuts from one segment to the next, when there is a series of cutaways or inserts, when there are expressive montages, when there are transitional "medleys." But I do not point out every time a cutaway is used to maintain continuity, nor do I always specify the content of every shot in every medley. Moreover, I do not explain the significance of a shot's mise-en-scène or why it appears where it does. My annotations are less interpretive than descriptive, but not mechanically so. I have attempted to establish as much as possible a "neutral" tone and not to impute meaning, whether intended or imposed, to individual shots or sequences.

At the same time, I am fully aware that deciding what is description and what interpretation is itself an act of interpretation. Wiseman's films are certainly writerly texts in Roland Barthes's sense, both because they are observational documentaries in which the camera is literally set "before the infinite play of the world,"[25] and because they forsake coherent narrative structures for complex mosaics that require unravelling by the spectator ("What the hell's he trying to say with this?"). As noted above, Wiseman's films require active participation and allow for such interpretive play on the part of viewers; they have even been referred to as Rorschach blots where viewers are free to read into them what they wish.[26] Knowing that my reading would close off other possible readings, my aim in these transcripts has been to provide description without being "condemned to the adjective," as Barthes says.[27] To put this another way, I have tried throughout the transcripts to place my voice in the service of—to submerge it within—the voice of each of these five films.

In doing so, I have attempted to work out a system of notation that reflects as much as possible *how* the films' social actors say what they say, in addition to recording *what* they say. For example, since people often fail to speak in grammatically proper sentences or follow correct punctuation in their verbal rhythms, there are times when it is unclear where sentences start and stop. I have been guided throughout by common sense as well as by verbal delivery. In addition, the typical and frequent little "ums" and "ahs" that mark the hesitations of spoken discourse do not appear here, since they are so numerous that, uh, they would litter the transcript and halt the flow of the dialogue. Thus only significant pauses or hesitations in someone's speech are indicated. Dashes represent a change in the speaker's direction of thought, the abandonment of an idea or sentence, left incomplete, for the spontaneous embrace of a new one, but only when such a change is discernibly abrupt; more commonly, commas are used because the speaker had no disruption in the rhythm of his or her speech. Although the standard punctuation here would be an ellipsis, it would leave in doubt whether the speaker had in fact paused or hesitated. A dash at the beginning of a sentence indicates the speaker is continuing a statement that had been interrupted by someone else or, on a few occasions, that a shot is beginning with someone already in the act of saying something. Dialect and accent are another difficulty, and unless a speaker is clearly altering a word (as is often the case here with "'cause" for "because," for example), the transcripts use the proper spelling of words.

Of course, just as it is impossible to capture fully the images in print, so it is futile to attempt to convey all the expressive possibilities of language beyond denotation—intonation, gestural accompaniment, and all those slippery, perhaps ineffable qualities that Barthes calls "the grain of the voice"—that are part of common speech and that one hears while listening to Wiseman's films. In *High School*, a teacher tells Rhona's father, "It depends on the language," which is true not only of the dialogue in the film but also more generally to the extent that we understand language to mean both denotation and delivery. Just as a transcript can only approximate a film's images and visual style, no written record could ever fully capture the nuances and particulars of spoken language. Even as D. A. Pennebaker noted in his preface to the book of *Dont Look Back,* the book "is no substitute for the reality of the film." Regarding the importance of direct sound in observational documentary specifically, Louis Marcorelles has said that because it implies a new perception of reality, the recording of live speech will mean not only the reinvention of the cinema but also that we "invent a new dramaturgy."[28] Perhaps this book will mark one step in that direction.

These transcripts, then, can only be approximations, like annotations of improvisatory jazz, with its polyrhythms, syncopations, and blue notes. Inevitably, as a transcriber, I am like the observers in *Primate,* doomed to record complex activities of living beings with a system inadequate to the task. Yet, as limited as they necessarily are, by allowing for a leisurely examination of the dialogue and structure of Wiseman's documentaries, these transcripts will undoubtedly help viewers appreciate the depth and complexity of this filmmaker's work, as well as providing a tool for the further scholarly examination of the films. After making documentaries about American institutional life for over five decades now, Wiseman himself has become an institution. The publication of this book is one indication of Wiseman's prominence within American documentary film practice.

Notes

1. John Grierson, "Flaherty's Poetic *Moana,*" in *The Documentary Tradition,* 2d ed., ed. Lewis Jacobs (New York: Norton, 1979), p. 25. Grierson's review of *Moana* (1926) originally appeared in the *New York Sun* (February 8, 1926).

2. Peter Watkins, *The War Game* (New York: Avon Books, 1967). The book was first published in Great Britain the same year, jointly by Sphere Books and Andre Deutsch.

3. *Salesman: A Film by The Maysles Brothers and Charlotte Zwerin* (New York: Signet, 1969), pp. 6–7.

4. Bob Dylan, *Dont Look Back: A Film and Book by D. A. Pennebaker* (New York: Ballantine Books, 1968).

5. *Dont Look Back,* p. 32.

6. Pauline Kael, "The Current Cinema," *New Yorker,* October 18, 1969, p. 204.

7. Richard Leacock, quoted in Louis Marcorelles, *Living Cinema: New Directions in Contemporary Filmmaking,* trans. Isabel Quigly (London: George Allen & Unwin, 1973), p. 53. Wiseman, quoted in G. Roy Levin, *Documentary Explorations: 15 Interviews with Filmmakers* (Garden City, NY: Anchor Press, 1971), p. 321.

8. For a complete filmography and list of awards through 1990, see Appendix.

9. Eugenia Parry Janis and Wendy MacNeil, eds., *Photography within the Humanities* (Danbury, NH: Addison House, 1977), p. 67. See also Alan Rosenthal, *The New*

Documentary in Action: A Casebook in Film Making (Berkeley: University of California Press, 1972), p. 69.

10. Peter Wollen, *Signs and Meaning in the Cinema,* rev. ed. (Bloomington: Indiana University Press, 1972), p. 102.

11. Quoted in Anon., "Viewpoints: Shooting the Institution," *Time,* December 9, 1974, p. 95.

12. David Eames, "Watching Wiseman Watch," *New York Times Magazine,* October 2, 1977, p. 97.

13. Alan Westin, "'You Start Off with a Bromide': Conversation with Film Maker Frederick Wiseman," *Civil Liberties Review* 1, no. 2 (Winter/Spring 1974): 60.

14. Joseph Featherstone, "Documentary: *High School,*" *New Republic,* June 21, 1969, p. 28.

15. James Blue, "Thoughts on Cinéma Vérité and a Discussion with the Maysles Brothers," *Film Comment* 2 (Fall 1965): 27.

16. Stephen Mamber, *Cinema Verite in America: Studies in Uncontrolled Documentary* (Cambridge, MA: MIT Press, 1974), p. 115ff.

17. Bill Nichols, "Fred Wiseman's Documentaries: Theory and Structure," *Film Quarterly* 31, no. 3 (Spring 1978): 15–28; and *Ideology and the Image* (Bloomington: Indiana University Press, 1981), chap. 7.

18. For a detailed textual analysis of these films, see my *Voyages of Discovery: The Cinema of Frederick Wiseman* (Urbana: University of Illinois Press, 1992), pp. 235–39.

19. John Graham and George Garrett, "How Far Can You Go: A Conversation with Fred Wiseman," *Contempora* 1, no. 4 (October–November 1970): 31.

20. Ibid., p. 32.

21. Ibid., p. 33.

22. Thomas Benson and Carolyn Anderson, both of whom approach Wiseman's films from a communications rather than film studies background, are the notable exceptions. See their *Reality Fictions: The Films of Frederick Wiseman,* rev. ed. (Carbondale: Southern Illinois University Press, 2002).

23. Dan Armstrong, "Wiseman's Cinema of the Absurd: *Welfare,* or Waiting for the Dole," *Film Criticism* 12, no. 3 (Spring 1989): 2–19.

24. Louis Marcorelles, *Living Cinema: New Directions in Contemporary Film-Making* (London: George Allen & Unwin, 1970), p. 123.

25. Roland Barthes, *S/Z: An Essay,* trans. Richard Miller (New York: Hill and Wang, 1974), p. 5.

26. For a discussion of Wiseman's films as Rorschachs, see my *Voyages of Discovery,* pp. 32–33.

27. Roland Barthes, "The Grain of the Voice," *Image/Music/Text,* trans. Stephen Heath (New York: Hill and Wang, 1977), p. 180.

28. Marcorelles, *Living Cinema,* p. 155.

Titicut Follies (1967)

Titicut Follies was filmed over four weeks in April and May 1966, at the Bridgewater State Prison for the Criminally Insane in Massachusetts, which is run by the state's Department of Corrections. Wiseman's first film provides a disturbing look at the treatment the state gives the criminally insane, and it became the subject of a complex legal battle that lasted over twenty years. After the film's screening at the New York Film Festival in the fall of 1967, the Supreme Court of Massachusetts ordered that it be banned and the negative destroyed. In 1969, the Superior Court allowed the film to be shown to professionals in the relevant social fields of law, medicine, and social services, but maintained the ban on public exhibition, a decision that was finally overturned in July 1991, when the Superior Court reversed the earlier ruling. The film shows a series of activities and procedures at Bridgewater, including psychiatric interviews and hearings, the force-feeding of an inmate who refuses to eat, daily routines such as bathing and shaving, a birthday party, and a funeral—all framed by scenes of the annual variety show organized by the staff with inmate participation. As an instructor of criminal law, Wiseman had taken his students to Bridgewater, and he says the idea for the film came from the shock of what he saw. *Titicut Follies* introduces many themes to which Wiseman would return, including institutional processing and the examination of a particular institution as social microcosm.

[*Title accompanied by sound bridge of group singing. The annual variety show at the Massachusetts Correctional Institute (MCI), Bridgewater State Prison for the Criminally Insane. The first shot begins with CU of one singer's face and quickly pulls back to reveal entire group of performers on the stage. The performers sing "Strike Up the Band" with pom-poms. In the course of the scene the camera moves in and pans all the individual faces in CU. Applause as the camera pulls back to reveal a wider view of the stage, then cut to CU of Eddie.*]

EDDIE (A GUARD): And it keeps getting better. Now we got to get the paper. The next one is a Western jamboree by Fred, Stan, Joe, and Steve, but it takes them a little while to get a guitar goin' or something. So, it reminds me of a little joke. I bet you people thought I had no talent at all. These two Beatles are walking down the street, and they saw Father Mulligan. And he had a broken arm. And they said, "Father, how did you break your arm?" He says, "I fell in a bathtub," and they said, "Gee, that's too bad, Father." So they continue to walk down the street, so one Beatle says to the other, "What's a bathtub?" And the other Beatle says, "The hell do I know, I'm not a Catholic." [*Laughter, applause. Cut to inmate taking off his clothes, other inmates in various states of undress, some guards visible, including Eddie.*]

GUARDS (*amid banging and chatter*): Come on, next. Where's Lindsay? Lindsay . . . take off your socks . . . Russell, stand here. Let's go . . . Next. Russell, come around. Next. Let's go. Lindsay, Harry, c'mon. Harold, over here, get your clothes. [*Cut to CU of an inmate being interviewed. Although we occasionally see the back of Dr. Ross's head, during this part of the interview we never see his face, the camera focusing instead on the inmate.*]

DR. ROSS: Was any actual sexual relation between you and the . . . this female child?

INMATE: Yes.

DR. ROSS (*overlapping*): How old, how old was the child?

INMATE: Only eleven.

DR. ROSS: Eleven? Eleven-year-old . . . And how did you feel about that you commit such crime?

INMATE: I didn't feel good about it.

DR. ROSS: Do you have any conscious experience or any recollection about the time, what did you have in your mind when you were involved to this crime? Remember? Have you been drunk, you been under drug? You been intoxicated?

INMATE: I was drinking.

DR. ROSS: You were drinking. What did you drink?

INMATE: Ah, whiskey.

DR. ROSS: Whiskey. Did you meet this child on the, this girl, on the street?

INMATE: Yes. She was on a bike.

DR. ROSS (*overlapping*): Is this girl is a very well-developed girl? Is a—looks a few years older than her age?

INMATE: No.

DR. ROSS: Eleven years? No? This could be a quite immature child, huh, a young girl?

INMATE: [*Nods yes.*]

DR. ROSS: You have this experiences or this practices before or this is just the first time?

INMATE: No, I had before.

DR. ROSS: You had that, this crime, you did commit this crime before? Or similar—you have been recorded for similar charges before?

INMATE: No, I never been caught before.

DR. ROSS: Never been caught but you have been in practice in this way that you abused a young girl, child?

INMATE: Even my own daughter.

DR. ROSS: Even your own daughter. Now, how you feel about it—you do things like that? How did your wife felt, how did your wife feel about it?

INMATE: My wife said something wrong.

DR. ROSS: There must have been.

INMATE: Myself, I'd just as soon, my law—the way I am right now, if I'm going—have to stay like this, I'd as soon go to jail and stay there. [*Cut to shot of a nude inmate, camera panning left to show guards continuing their strip search.*]

FIRST GUARD: McCready, take your clothes off . . . Come on this side now . . . Good, okay, let's go.

SECOND GUARD: Somersault, colored.

GUARD (*offscreen*): Somersault, c'mere. Richard, c'mere, Richard. Over here.

FIRST GUARD (*to Somersault as he undresses*): Take 'em off, c'mon. Put your hands out. Turn around. Turn around! Put your hands out again. Okay . . . Take your stuff and get over here. Take your stuff and get over here! Now get dressed. Here. [*Cut to CU of Dr. Ross. Now the camera focuses on Dr.*

Ross, smoking a cigarette, and there is only an occasional glimpse of the inmate.]

DR. ROSS: You know what the masturbation? How often you masturbate a day, or a week?

INMATE: Sometimes three, three times a day.

DR. ROSS: It's too much. Why you do this when you have a good wife and she's attractive lady?

INMATE: There's no reason for it.

DR. ROSS (*overlapping*): She must to have not been, she must to have not been giving you too much sex satisfaction, huh?

INMATE: No—

DR. ROSS: You tired about your wife, are you interested in other woman?

INMATE: I'm interested in other women, I, I don't know, I just, I can't, I—

DR. ROSS: Have you ever get your conscience about—to have mature women, a big tall, or husky, luscious-looking female?

INMATE: Uh-huh.

DR. ROSS: What you are interested in, big breast or small breast . . . in a woman?

INMATE (*overlapping*): I never thought of it.

DR. ROSS: Never thought of it. You have any homosexual experiences? I guess you have. What was it?

INMATE: You mean, uh, with someone else?

DR. ROSS: With men, with other boys.

INMATE: Yeah.

DR. ROSS (*overlapping*): You have. What was—?

INMATE (*overlapping*): When I was young.

DR. ROSS: What was it?

INMATE: Ah, just masturbating and stuff like that.

DR. ROSS: You try to masturbate other men, huh? Other boys?

INMATE (*overlapping*): They used to do it to me, and I used to do it to them.

DR. ROSS (*overlapping*): Masturbate. The public masturbation or common masturbation. You engage in a common masturbation with other men, other young men. How oft—, long you did this, how long you have these practices?

INMATE: Well, it started when I was in the Boy Scouts. We went on a hiking trip, went camping. And I started with this guy, who used to live near the house. He was quite old.

DR. ROSS (*overlapping*): You had, you've never had a guilt feeling when you masturbate? [*Cut to CU of another inmate in the common room.*]

OTHER INMATE: They, they, they was gonna take my balls outta me. I told the doctor I—before I come here—I told the doctor before I come here—I didn't want my balls taken outta me, so they took the cords out instead. Right there. [*Cut back to CU of inmate being interviewed by Dr. Ross.*]

DR. ROSS: Then actually you don't understand that you are a sick man?

INMATE: I know there's something wrong, otherwise I wouldn't do things like that. But that's the way I am, right, I—

DR. ROSS: You have been in jail, you've been in House of Correction, you've been in reformatory, you've been in Lyman's School and so forth, and you have been involved in criminal offenses, breaking and entering, assault and battery, driving without authority, and so forth. And then, additionally, you have moral charges. You are with your own daughter, with other young, immature children, female children, and then you have been trying to hang yourself, you've been assaulting other people, and you've been setting fire. And you've been . . . quite intolerant and, and apprehensive and—

INMATE: Restless.

DR. ROSS: —depressed and—do you think you are a normal man? What you think? And do you still believe that you don't need help? At some time ago, you told that *you* need the help.

INMATE: Well, I need help but I don't know where I can get it.

DR. ROSS: Well, you get it here, I guess. [*Cut to CU of the other inmate in common room looking into the camera. Camera pans right to show other inmates standing about in the room where they were strip-searched. One inmate's voice begins to rise above the general din. As the inmates file out of the room, he comes into view.*]

GUARD: Stowe, Curtis Stowe. Arthur Herald.

INMATE: . . . Biddledegah biddledegah Charles Goodman, biddeldegay Benjamin Kaplan, biddledegah biddledegaw biddledegah Volpe, biddledegah biddledegah Lieutenant Governor Richardson, biddledegah biddledegah parole

1. An inmate spouts nonsense.

board member, biddeldegah McCormack, biddledegale biddledegah and the all members on the parole board. Biddlegaw. Oh oh oh oh. Bid-dele-de-gay. I want all those men arrested. Biddledegah. Immediately. Biddledegah. From 168 pounds down now to 96 pounds, and all those known. Biddledegah. The Deputy Brewer and all those known, John F. Powers, biddeldegay Volpe, Charles Gorn, biddledegah Deputy Brewer and Brewer all out. Go back to von Braun. Biddledegah, and go all over the world, Biddledegah. Contribute to Nazi party. Biddledegah and tell Israel biddledegah, Palestine, Ben Gurian government biddeldgah biddledegee, give money, sheckle. Biddlegaw [*nonsense*] President Johnson [*nonsense*], biddlegah all my efforts, Chinese, Japanese [*nonsense*]. Biddledegah. We now know the truth, biddledegah twenty billion dollars [*nonsense*], Charles Gorman, biddlegah Volpe [*nonsense*], and now death. [*nonsense*] Biddledegah. [*nonsense*] I point 'em out [*nonsense*], for I am called Christ Jesus [*nonsense*], and I am called a Borgia [*nonsense*]. And John Kennedy walking the earth biddledegah, was now biddledegah in truth Christ, Jesus [*nonsense*]. They send from Mississippi niggers over this fuckin' part of the country biddledegah. John Kennedy, I say you sick boy. You listen to the wrong fuckin' people. Biddledegah. And they say people. Biddeldegah Black Muslims [*nonsense*]. No good, we send back to England to my sister there. Biddledpuh Biddledegah. And back to Mississippi, we put 'em in prison and we put a sign up there: "Niggers, don't let me see you fucking here by sun-up." [*Nonsense.*] Finished. Ooo. Cha.

Chee. [*Cut to guards motioning to inmate who had been interviewed, as they escort him out of Dr. Ross's office.*]

GUARD: King. King. Let's go. [*Cut to back of inmate in common room.*]

INMATE: Finished. In the name of the father, the son, the holy spirit, amen, amen, amen, amen. Amen, amen. Thy will is done again. Whatsoever sayeth, the marriage contract is already written, and I shall go to Pittsfield General Hospital and I shall wait. John F. Kennedy biddledegah, thy will is done and also Lucy Baines Johnson, biddledegah President Johnson, biddledegah, and all come over, stay at Kurdistan Holiday Inn, and Jacqueline, bring the children with you also. For all that thou sayest is done. For I say unto thee biddledegah oh biddledegah and the right side of my son disappeared on my side. I have honored thee and loved thee always. Therefore, I have completed my mission in life. I have spoke the truth of Jesus forever and ever, amen. Come in, Mr. President Johnson, and now order my release. [*Cut from the inmate along with others filing out of the room to guards escorting the interviewed inmate down a hallway, through doors, up a stairway, and into another room.*]

FIRST GUARD: You from King? Huh? [*The inmate nods yes. Once inside room, he undresses.*]

GUARD: Suicide . . . suicide, isn't he?

GUARD (*offscreen*): There an empty one?

GUARD (*offscreen*): Number 8 is empty. [*The first guard leads the inmate to cell 8.*]

GUARD: Is he a transfer from King?

FIRST GUARD: Yeah.

GUARD: Okay. [*First guard locks inmate in. The camera moves up to a small window in cell door and holds briefly on the inmate, his back to the camera, looking out the window. Snatches of a radio broadcast may be heard. A trombone is heard on the sound track playing a hesitant chorus of "My Blue Heaven," providing a sound bridge to the next scene.*]

RADIO: The news in Vietnam today is you can't walk down the street. Were you ever afraid? [*Camera pans the yard in LS. Inmates milling about and sitting on benches. Inmate playing "My Blue Heaven" on the trombone. Cut to interior CU of another inmate singing snatches of "Chinatown, My Chinatown," a television screen behind his left shoulder in the upper right of the frame. On the TV a female entertainer also is singing.*]

INMATE (*changing to another song*): When I lost the sunshine in roses / When I lost you, dear old gal / You break my heart, to say goodbye mother / When I lost you, now dear.

TV SINGER (*overlapping*): . . . Oh, how I love Johnny / My heart, I love Johnny / Oh, how I love Johnny / But he never knew/ But he— [*Singing inmate ascends stairway. Cut to guard walking down a corridor toward the camera.*]

EDDIE: Hello, John. What time do they open up these poor unfortunates?

JOHN: In about another minute or two.

EDDIE: A minute or two. They're not vicious, I hope.

JOHN: Huh?

EDDIE: A man could get hurt.

GUARD: You get this and I'll get the others.

EDDIE: Okay.

GUARD (*overlapping*): He starts here and I'll start there . . . You do what you want.

EDDIE: Very interesting work.

GUARD: Open all the doors, by the way.

EDDIE: Tuesday, got to open all the doors . . . [*To inmate passing by with bucket*] Hi, John. [*To man out of view in cell*] You going home in ten days?

INMATE (*offscreen*): You better believe it.

EDDIE: Hah? You going home or some other jail?

INMATE (*offscreen*): No, I'm going home.

EDDIE: Oh. You think your stay here has helped you? [*Laughs and mumbles.*] What doctor? Ross? Ross? Oh, so long.

GUARD: He'll be here shortly.

EDDIE: He'll be in Budapest. Hello, Arthur. [*In the corridor, more cell doors are opened, inmates coming out. One carries his bedpan. Cut to shot of inmate emptying his pan in the sink and returning along corridor. Cut to outside another inmate's cell.*]

FIRST GUARD: How come you got such a messy room?

INMATE: Hmm?

GUARD: How come your room's all messed up?

INMATE: Oh, I mind my business.

FIRST GUARD: You mind your business?

INMATE: Sure. I mind my business, yes.

FIRST GUARD: Oh, yeah? Is that why you've got a dirty room?

INMATE: Yeah.

ANOTHER INMATE (*offscreen*): Who's got the dust pan here?

ANOTHER INMATE (*offscreen*): Right here.

INMATE: That's right. [*Camera pans left to show the two other inmates cleaning up the room.*]

FIRST GUARD: You going to keep it a little cleaner tomorrow?

INMATE: Yes, I will.

FIRST GUARD: Huh?

INMATE: [*Inaudible.*]

SECOND GUARD: Okay, see you later, kid. Well, bye-bye now. Right.

FIRST GUARD (*as they lock inmate back in his cell*): This one's a good one.

SECOND GUARD (*moving to another cell*): Arnie, come on, Arnie. Hello, Arnie.

INMATE (ARNIE): Good evening.

SECOND GUARD: What's the matter?

FIRST GUARD: What you got in your mouth there?

ARNIE: I have something in my mouth, and—

SECOND GUARD: Take it out of your mouth. Drop it on the floor there.

ARNIE: Why you keeping a man from work? [*Inaudible.*]

SECOND GUARD: You want to go to work?

ARNIE: Yes, sir.

SECOND GUARD: Where?

ARNIE: Any old thing helpin' out.

SECOND GUARD: Wanna sell watermelons?

ARNIE: [*Inaudible*] for a sugar plant.

SECOND GUARD: Okay. How about singing us that watermelon song?

ARNIE: Where can I work? I'd like to know, *where* can I work?

SECOND GUARD: Where?

ARNIE: Where?

SECOND GUARD: Where? Well, whatever you feel like doing. What do you feel like doing? What *can* you do?

INMATE: Excuse me.

SECOND GUARD: What can you do? [*To another inmate being put in his cell*] Okay. Okay. Alright. Go ahead, then. Alright. [*To another inmate*] Hey, Stan. Hey, Stan [*inaudible*]. [*Stan is locked in his cell. Cut to another inmate, Jim, being led down the hallway. Camera follows guards and Jim through corridors and stairways to barbershop.*]

SECOND GUARD: How come your room's so dirty, Jim? How come you're—

JIM (*shouting*): Hey! The goddamn thing isn't dirty, is it?

FIRST GUARD: What?

SECOND GUARD: Louder.

FIRST GUARD: What'd you say? [*Guard slaps Jim.*] What'd you say, Jim? Huh?

JIM: I didn't say anything.

FIRST GUARD: What? I didn't hear you. Speak up, man, I can't hear you. What'd you say?

SECOND GUARD: Come on, Jim.

FIRST GUARD: Come on, Jim, let's go wash up.

SECOND GUARD: You'll get shaved.

THIRD GUARD (*in room*): Sit in that chair.

FIRST GUARD: How's that room, Jim?

JIM (*sitting in barber's chair*): Very fine.

FIRST GUARD: What?

JIM: Very clean.

SECOND GUARD: How come you put—

FIRST GUARD: What'd you say? How's that room? Huh? How's that room, Jim? . . . Answer me.

THIRD GUARD (*brushing shaving cream on Jim's face as the camera moves in for CU*): You gonna keep that room clean, Jim?

JIM: Yes, sir.

THIRD GUARD (*while shaving Jim*): How come you got it all dirty last night? Hmm?

JIM: Colder last—colder than it was yesterday, now, wasn't it?

FIRST GUARD: What did you say, Jim?

JIM (*voice rising*): A little cooler.

FIRST GUARD: Huh? What?

THIRD GUARD: What did you say, Jim?

FIRST GUARD: How's that room gonna to be tomorrow, Jim? How's that room gonna be tomorrow, Jim?

THIRD GUARD (*stops shaving Jim momentarily until he answers*): Hey, how's that room going to be?

JIM: Very neat, very clean.

SECOND GUARD: How come it's not clean today? You told me that yesterday. What happened? . . . Hmm? . . . How come you ripped all your clothes up?

FIRST GUARD: How's that room, Jim?

JIM: Very clean—

FIRST GUARD: Huh?

JIM (*overlapping*): —clean as I can keep it.

FIRST GUARD: What'd you say? Answer me, Jim. [*Camera moves to CU as Jim is shaved in silence. His lip is cut and bleeds from the left side of his mouth. The guards daub some of the blood with towels.*]

THIRD GUARD: Okay, Jim.

JIM: Thank you very much indeed. Thank you ever so much.

THIRD GUARD: Have a drink of water, Jim, before you go back.

JIM: Alright. On the house, isn't it?

THIRD GUARD: Yeah, on the house. [*Laughs.*] Go ahead, have a drink.

JIM: Thank you very much.

FIRST GUARD: You can have some more if you want, Jim. What did you say, Jim? [*Camera follows guards and Jim into the hallway.*] How's that room going to be tomorrow?

JIM: Very clean.

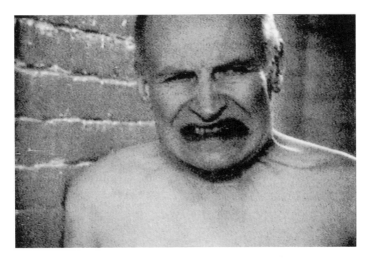

2. An inmate shouts that his room will be clean.

FIRST GUARD: Huh?

JIM: Spick-and-span, very clean.

FIRST GUARD: What? What? Real clean, Jim?

JIM (*shouting*): Yessirree.

FIRST GUARD: Huh? What are you doing, Jim? Good morning, Jim.

JIM: Morning.

FIRST GUARD: How's that room going to be tomorrow?

JIM: The very best of mornings.

FIRST GUARD: Huh? What? What did you say?

JIM (*shouting*): I said very, very clean!

FIRST GUARD: Louder, Jim!

JIM (*shouting*): Didn't I?!

FIRST GUARD: What?

JIM (*shouting*): Didn't I?!

FIRST GUARD: What'd you say? Can't hear you, Jim.

SECOND GUARD: What are you hiding, Jim?

FOURTH GUARD: Alright, c'mon, let's go. Right down here.

FIRST GUARD: Everything's gonna be clean? Huh? How's that room going to be? How's that room going to be, Jim?

FOURTH GUARD: Hold him up here, when you get there. Hold it.

JIM (*going into cell*): Thank you very much. Thank you very, very—very clean. [*Jim stamps around in his cell naked. The camera zooms in to CU of Jim covering his mouth, and then reverse zooms to a full shot as Jim continues stamping his feet and banging on the window. Again there is a forward zoom to CU of Jim, hand over his mouth.*]

GUARD (*offscreen*): Keep that room clean, Jim. [*Camera moves back to FS, holding briefly on Jim as he continues stamping. The camera begins zooming in again, and there is a cut to CU as Jim salutes the guards.*]

GUARD (*offscreen*): How about keeping that clean, Jim?

GUARD (*offscreen*): You play the piano, Jim?

JIM: Yes.

FIRST GUARD (*offscreen*): What'd you say, Jim? Huh?

GUARD (*offscreen*): What do you play?

JIM: I play the Umana.

GUARD: What?

JIM (*mumbling*): I play Umana at my home in Fitchburg.

GUARD (*offscreen*): Fitchburg?

JIM: Yeah. 84 Arlington Street.

GUARD (*offscreen*): Was you a schoolteacher, Jim? [*Camera moves in for another CU.*]

JIM: Short while. Bachelor of Arts. Junior High School. Teacher of arithmetic and mathematics.

GUARD (*offscreen*): Which college did you go to?

JIM: Fitchburg State Teacher's College. Fitchburg Normal School . . . Fitchburg Business College. Fitchburg High School.

GUARD (*offscreen*): Did you graduate with honors, Jim? [*Cut to CU of another guard in conversation elsewhere.*]

GUARD: —so I took it home. I didn't think about it, and I hung it in the closet. Jeez, about a week later my wife opened the door to this closet under the stairs and I'm telling you, the gas that got on my—on the clothes in the closet, you know? Her eyes were starting to water—oh, jeez. That gas hangs

3. A guard talks about tear gas clinging to his clothes.

around for months sometimes, you know? Gets in all the cracks. It's a bastard. The only thing that dissipates it is heat. Give it plenty of heat.

EDDIE: Is that how they get rid of it?

GUARD: That's how they get rid of it. Heat. Downstairs, he was in that cage. Downstairs. We had a couple of big fans in there, we had the heat blasting. We had those fans in there for about, steady for about a week, all the time goin', before we could get the gas out of it. What a mess. [*A string arrangement of "Misty" (?) plays on a radio offscreen for a few moments.*] One time they gassed a guy down there, I forget who the hell it was. Eddie Mitchell. He was in the bullpen. And they gassed him one day. I was on my days off, so when I came back I didn't know they'd gassed him. And I went downstairs. And jeez, the piss is really starting to spoil—my eyes are watering. They really were—I didn't know, ya know. I said, jeez, my eyes are watering. I couldn't figure out. I go upstairs, I start checking the book and, sure enough, they gassed Eddie Mitchell a couple of days before, you know. That gas, you know, it was right in the corridor . . . I don't like it, it seems to affect the shit out of me fast. I just get one whiff of it and whew. [*Cut to Eddie and Willie in CU, singing parts of "Chicago Town" in the variety show, followed by applause.*]

EDDIE: Thank you very much. Willie . . . and me! [*Cut to two-shot of Dr. Ross and inmate Vladimir talking in the exercise yard.*]

4. Guard and inmate sing at the Follies.

DR. ROSS: . . . get you out of this place, and you take a little bit some time, a medication, and then—

VLADIMIR: But that's what I'm thinking. See what I mean?

DR. ROSS: Don't worry.

VLADIMIR: Now you've given me the same story again: "We are going to help you." It's just that—may I ask just why I need this help that, that you are literally forcing on me?

DR. ROSS (*overlapping*): I'm not forcing anything—look, look, I tell you, I tell you something—

VLADIMIR (*overlapping*): Obviously I talk well, I think well. I am well, and you are ruining me just—

DR. ROSS (*overlapping*): May I say something? We not enforcing you, if you say I don't want to take—

VLADIMIR (*overlapping*): No, no, no. I don't want to stay here. I am a prisoner.

DR. ROSS: If you say I not want to take the medication, we agree. We not enforce you to take medicine.

VLADIMIR (*overlapping*): That's not the principle, doctor. That's not the principle. The principle is that I am here obviously well and healthy, and I am getting ruined. If we send me back to the prison where I might be able to get the—on the street as I should have been—

5. Psychiatrist and inmate in the exercise yard.

DR. ROSS: If I send you back to prison today, you might be able to get back in the same day to Bridgewater.

VLADIMIR: No, no, Doctor, not unless—

DR. ROSS: If you don't believe that, I let my—spit on my face, you know. For sure.

VLADIMIR: Now why should I, why should I do that?

DR. ROSS: Because that, if I say untrue, you know, unreliable things, that I should be punished. We send you back to Walpole today, you coming back tomorrow or maybe even tonight. Honest to God.

VLADIMIR: But Doctor—why—

DR. ROSS (*overlapping*): You wanna make, want to take a chance?

VLADIMIR: Yes, I certainly do—

DR. ROSS: We will do it.

VLADIMIR: Since you say that how—just why are you so certain that I should be back tonight or tomorrow?

DR. ROSS: Because they look at you, then they know that you, something's wrong.

VLADIMIR: No, no, but Doctor, Doctor, I mean, just—you are saying that I would be back here tonight or tomorrow. Obviously, I am, I am, I have been weakened since I have been here—

DR. ROSS: I tell you something—

VLADIMIR: —I figure that I have been done harm here since I have been here.

DR. ROSS (*overlapping*): I tell you something—

VLADIMIR: Now you tell me that if I should go back I will be back here.

DR. ROSS: Right.

VLADIMIR: Now obviously, then you must know something that I do not know.

DR. ROSS: Right. I tell you something—

VLADIMIR: Since obviously you have observed merely of schizo—

DR. ROSS (*overlapping*): I have to leave you. I have to leave you now—

VLADIMIR (*overlapping*): Doctor, merely of schizophrenia paranoia—

DR. ROSS: —but I have to tell you something. If you don't—

VLADIMIR (*overlapping*): Which is, excuse me, which is nothing—

DR. ROSS: Nothing?

VLADIMIR: —which is nothing really dangerous—

DR. ROSS (*overlapping*): Nothing dangerous?

VLADIMIR: —that's right. In some cases schizophrenia paranoia is dangerous, as the dictionary would, would say.

DR. ROSS: But practically is not dangerous?

VLADIMIR: Huh? Schizophrenia paranoia is merely the love of your mother and father. Or unless you are to, unless you just happen to get somebody else's schizophrenia paranoia, like, which does happen, which is, which is not agreeable to the body. My case, it happens to be the love of my mother and father, if, if it is schizophrenia, and in that case it is not, then obviously—

DR. ROSS: You mean that's why the man diagnosed a schizophrenic paranoid—

VLADIMIR (*overlapping*): Doctor, you merely look—

DR. ROSS: —because he loved his mother and father? Then I am schizophrenic too, because I love my mother and father. But I never been in a mental institution. Nobody thought I should be.

VLADIMIR (*overlapping*): That's right. I am using your words. You looked at me and you tell me I'm a schizophrenic paranoia. Just how do you know? Because I speak well? Because I, because I stand up for what I think?

DR. ROSS: Because you got, because you got the psychological testings. You got—

VLADIMIR: I did?

DR. ROSS (*overlapping*): Oh yeah, [*inaudible*].

VLADIMIR: Such as? A test which asks me how many times I go—wait a minute, Doctor—a test which asks me how many times do I go to the toilet? Do I believe in God? [*Brief blast of a prison siren.*] I mean, how ridiculous can you get? If I, I may never go to the toilet or I may go to the toilet, right? Or I may go to the toilet, or I may believe in God or I may not, it is really not the business of a doctor—

DR. ROSS: You quite closely associate the God with the toilet. [*Laughs.*]

VLADIMIR: No, this is the test! This—no, you see what I mean? Now, what does that have to do with my sanity? Obviously you pick out this on *your* test, and you know, this is *your* test, asking me—

DR. ROSS: (*overlapping*): Right, let's put the blame on me [*inaudible*]—

VLADIMIR (*overlapping*): No, no, wait a minute, Doctor. Your test asks me when I go to the toilet too—

DR. ROSS (*overlapping*): [*Inaudible.*]

VLADIMIR: —or even how often my friends go to the toilet, the test asks. It says, how often do your friends go to the toilet, right? Then it says, do you believe in God? Do you love your mother? Do you love your father? It is really, I should say, none, not the business of any kind of doctor or physiologist.

DR. ROSS: Physician?

VLADIMIR: No, physiologist. Ah, a physician might, might go for that too. And now you're keeping me here a year and a half and I keep saying the same story, I am being harmed.

DR. ROSS: Let's walk a little bit.

VLADIMIR: Now, after a year and a half of being harmed, you turn around and say if I should go back to the prison—

DR. ROSS: To the toilet?

VLADIMIR: No, no, to the prison, to the prison, you say that I might be back tonight or tomorrow. Then obviously you must consider that those, the surroundings have had something to do with it. With keeping me, keeping me well or— [*Cut to man exercising in yard. Camera follows him with voiceover of antiwar inmate speaking.*]

ANTIWAR INMATE: . . . How did they want, what do you call it, the first great war. How did the first great war start? Because of a demand by the Austria-Hungary dynasty for execution of the culprits who're already sentenced [*cut to CU of antiwar inmate*] to life imprisonment in Serbia, yet they demanded a prosecution and execution by Austria-Hungary laws. What does that mean? They wanted execution. The war was fought over execution, the same execution that is going on in Vietnam, Vietnam over American execution of these natives of Vietnam. They're not Viet Cong, they're not communists. Anyone that the American government doesn't like, they use, they foist on this term of *communist*. Because I speak the way I do, you gonna call me communist? I'm not a communist! Even though I have communist affiliations. Communist really means community-ist, that's what we are, community-ist, if you want to call us communistic, communist, because we're for a community, we like the world standards. We're for the people, and that's what they call these, what do you call it, people that talk about any matter, agitators. We agitate, do we start these troubles? I'm a communist because I expound my views about the world conditions. It's the duty of every citizen to expound his views or her views of what goes on in the world. If more of them expounded their views about conditions in the world, less chaotic conditions would exist, and a nuclear war is in the offing, because not what I say, not what all these warmongers or peacemongers blab about, because all through the ages, you'll find every time a new weapon was put out, they say these dreadnoughts, is the end of war. They said the submarine would end the war, what happened? The gas mask put an end to war. What happened? They got gas masks. What about these submarines that's supposed to control the seas? What happened? They got airplanes that drop depth charges. You look through the ages and you find out that for every new weapon put out, somebody else puts out a counterweapon. But, but the nuclear weapon doesn't stop because people are stockpiling. Anybody, anybody that starts stockpiling weapons eventually uses them. They get tired of stockpiling. And then they're just like a bunch of little kids, they figure they got toys to play with, they're gonna play with those toys, but at the first chance you get. You wait to 1967, you wait, in 1970s, you're going to see the greatest nuclear war of all time. In 1967, you're going to see what happened . . . I can tell you how the Vietnam situation got started.

PROWAR INMATE: Wait a minute. Vietnam, okay? Those people, the communists, are going to offer them something and they'll be fooled. The communists will give them nothing but regimented government. Strictly regimented government.

ANTIWAR INMATE (*overlapping*): But why did the war in Southeast Asia start?

PROWAR INMATE (*overlapping*): They're trying to plan people's futures and they cannot do it—

ANTIWAR INMATE (*overlapping*): No, no. The original navigators that flew recommending the missions in Southeast Asia used the abbreviation called S-O-Vietnam. It means to the nagivator who doesn't see anybody it means *Soviet*nam. Name. Soviet-name. And they hated—

PROWAR INMATE: Like I was saying, what those people like is what they're going to accept no matter who tries to fight it out of them. Nobody can stop them.

ANTIWAR INMATE (*overlapping*): There are forces that are beyond your mental abilities to realize, what do you call it, what happens. You are not qualified to judge the planetary system, universe system.

PROWAR INMATE: How about this, the communists are terrorizing those people—

ANTIWAR INMATE (*overlapping*): Oh, the communists, they're just plain natives, that's all. There's other factors, mitigating factors, that you don't understand about, that do take place in Southeast Asia.

PROWAR INMATE: Give me an answer. Why is terrorization of those people supposed to, supposed to—

ANTIWAR INMATE (*overlapping*): Show me who? Who?

PROWAR INMATE: —be able to take over their country and hold it in such a secure reign?

ANTIWAR INMATE: Look, look, they've had terrorism there in Southeast Asia for about three hundred years.

PROWAR INMATE: Strictly by the communists lately, oh yeah—

ANTIWAR INMATE (*overlapping*): Wait a minute. If want to stop the—

PROWAR INMATE: And Buddhists.

ANTIWAR INMATE: Oh, no, it isn't.

PROWAR INMATE: Oh, yes.

ANTIWAR INMATE: You want to stop that war in Southeast Asia—

PROWAR INMATE (*overlapping*): The Buddhists—

ANTIWAR INMATE (*overlapping*): Bullshit!

PROWAR INMATE: —by suicide are trying to kick out the government of Ky because they think he is collaborating with communists.

ANTIWAR INMATE (*overlapping*): It's their country, that's their, that's their natural prerogative, that's a natural right to try to kick out anybody that tries to influence their nation, influence their governments.

PROWAR INMATE (*overlapping*): Well, they have no proof, they have no proof about the collaboration with the communists. They're guessing.

ANTIWAR INMATE (*overlapping*): What's the American government doing there? Who, who puts the American flag—doing, hoisted over South Vietnam?

PROWAR INMATE (*overlapping*): Let John, let John tell you—

ANTIWAR INMATE: Alright. No, no, you tell 'em, what-d'ya-call-it. And what else? The main fact about South Vietnam people don't realize: there are French influences, there are still French, you could say drawbacks, from the French revolt. They're still trying to monopolize the American military there. You throw out the French from Southeast Asia, you have no war in Asia. In fact, Ky and some of the others are one of the, you could say, puppets of the French regime and they're just trying to promote, fill in the gaps that the French weren't able to do and there isn't a nation in the world that can do more than the French have started and America will reach the same rut as they are because there is one great factor that influences the war in Southeast Asia, this is this: America's the female part of the earth world and she's sex crazy. Her sexiness brings on wars, like the sperm that is injected, injected by man into a woman, and by a woman in her own body. It has the same effect [*Cut to panning CU of four inmates. On the sound track an inmate begins to sing the topical hit "Ballad of the Green Berets"*], same influence, only this is on a gijantic pattern, a gijantic pattern is finally—you mean to tell me that after you have a sex intercourse you feel fine, or you feel healthy? You don't. [*Cut to exercising inmate, camera following from behind. After the line "Men who mean just what they say," there is a cut to the inmate singing it, with the inmate with the trombone behind him, screen left. As the song ends, there are three shots of other inmates in the yard, followed by a cut to CU of Dr. Ross.*]

DR. ROSS: Mr. Malinowski, come here a moment. How you feeling? Hmm, good?

INMATE (MALINOWSKI) (*through window in cell door*): Not too bad.

DR. ROSS: Not bad? Alright. Did you eat, Mr. Malinowski, did you eat your food? No? Why, if you don't eat food, then we going to feed you, with tube through your nose. [*On telephone*] This is Dr. Ross, I like you prepare for two patients for tube feeding . . . two patients in F Ward . . . They doesn't eat for three days, yeah, yeah, one is Malinowski and the other one is Chicory, Joseph Chicory or Chicarky . . . Yeah, that's right, tube feeding, when you are, when you get ready, when you get ready? . . . [*Inaudible*] Well, I will advise the officer. Mr. LaPointe . . . [*Cut to guards leading Malinowski down corridor.*]

GUARD: Do you want him here or do you wanna—?

DR. ROSS: Now, Mr. Malinowski, do you realize that you're not eating too long and we should give you some food. Then, this is a question, whether you agree to drink this food or are going to put through a tube through your nose, into your stomach? Do you want to drink it, or we get the tube and put you in your nose? Whether you drink it or not? Do you want to drink it? . . . Let him sit down, maybe he drink it.

GUARD: You want to drink it or you want to have it dumped through your nose?

GUARD: Either drink it or he'll dump it down the tube through your nose. [*Malinowski is restrained on a table. Dr. Ross prepares for tube feeding.*]

DR. ROSS: Get some drinking water. Put the towel in there. Give me the towel. [*Dr. Ross covers Malinowski's genitals with a towel.*]

GUARD (*offscreen*): Water?

GUARD: This is vasoline. There ain't much of anything left.

DR. ROSS: Got any mineral oil?

GUARD: No. We don't usually use this, you know.

DR. ROSS: Do you have any other grease or oil or anything? . . . Any one of you gentlemen, write down on a little piece of paper whatever you need in F Ward. Mineral oil, jelly, bacitracin, ointment, what you need?

GUARD (*offscreen*): We needed thorazine or dexadrine. You were gonna get us a box of this [*inaudible*].

DR. ROSS: Got any grease, butter?

GUARD (*offscreen*): Butter. We've got plenty of butter.

DR. ROSS: Plenty butter. [*Camera moves in to CU as Dr. Ross inserts tube into Malinowski's nose.*]

GUARD: Boy, this guy's a veteran, he's been tube-fed before, he's a veteran. Swallow, just swallow, swallow, swallow, that's-a-boy. [*Cut to brief shot of Malinowski's corpse being shaved, then back to CU of Malinowski being tube-fed. The insert shot, like the others that follow, is completely silent.*] The marker's down there, way down there.

DR. ROSS: Here?

GUARD: Yeah, right there.

DR. ROSS: That's some water, yeah?

GUARD (*offscreen, on telephone*): Yeah, what d'ya want? Sam Virgil? [*To other guard*] Francis, Sam Virgil work Friday?

GUARD (FRANCIS): No, he didn't work all last week. He'll be in tomorrow.

GUARD (*offscreen, overlapping on telephone*): He says no. Okay.

DR. ROSS (*climbing onto chair with tube and funnel*): Got any clamp here? Any clamp, clamp? For thermostat?

GUARD: Clamp? [*Cut from MS of Dr. Ross holding tube and funnel to CU of mortician, then to CU of Malinowski's corpse being shaved by a guard/mortician, and then back to Dr. Ross pouring the food mixture into the funnel.*]

DR. ROSS: Got more food?

GUARD: Food? More food. [*Cut from CU of Malinowski with the tube in his nose to another CU of Malinowski's corpse being shaved, followed by a cut back to Malinowksi with the tube inserted.*]

GUARD: Save some for the other guy.

GUARD: It says it's broke. [*Inaudible.*]

GUARD: Ain't nothing to worry about.

GUARD (*offscreen*): Chew it. Chew your food.

DR. ROSS: You have him get me a jug. [*Cut from CU of two of the guards restraining Malinowski to CU of Malinowski's dead eyes being stuffed with cotton. Cut to fuller view of mortician working on the corpse, followed by a cut back to one of the guards.*]

GUARD: Fresh?

DR. ROSS: In a jug. Yeah, in a stainless steel jug. You have some more?

GUARD: Yeah.

DR. ROSS: Please get this jug of water into his [*inaudible*].

GUARD: Did you save some for the other guy?

DR. ROSS: Yeah, I'll need a whiskey. [*Laughter.*]

GUARD: Thanks.

DR. ROSS: Very good patient, very nice.

GUARD: Okay, good, Doctor. Here it is, kid, take it off. Hey, that wasn't bad. He's a veteran.

GUARD: He's a good one. [*Cut from MS of Dr. Ross removing tube from a prone Malinowski and wiping his face with a towel to MS of Malinowksi's corpse being fanned by mortician. Cut back to Dr. Ross cleaning Malinowski.*] I think he's been tube-fed before.

GUARD: I guess so.

DR. ROSS: Alright. That's it. You're clean. [*Cut to insert shot of Malinowski in his casket, then to Malinowski being helped up from the table after the tube feeding.*]

GUARD: Okay, you've had your dinner.

GUARD: He is an experienced kid at that. Oh, watch the tube, will ya, kid. [*Malinowski is led back to his cell, camera following. After he goes into his cell and the door is closed, there is a cut to a shot of Malinowski's casket being put in storage drawer in morgue. Cut to CU of sign saying "Happy Birthday."*]

VOLUNTEER 1: There's going to be a big blow, I can see it coming. [*Cut to LS of table. An inmate blows out candles on birthday cake.*] Whee-ee! [*A trio of inmates in costume sing part of "Have You Ever Been Lonely?" as cake is being served.*] [*Singing along with the song while cutting cake*] Alright, here's one whoozit of cake . . . oop, that one better wait.

VOLUNTEER 2: Do you think you're able to stand trial now?

INMATE: Oh, sure.

VOLUNTEER 2: Well, good, good.

INMATE: I feel good. I'm on medication. I wasn't—they just found the medication, you know. January, last January.

VOLUNTEER 2: What does the medication do for you?

INMATE: Everything. It relaxes my muscles. When I'm tense and nervous, I get—my muscles get tense and I feel like, you know, you get upset.

VOLUNTEER 2: Now you just wanna feel like—

INMATE: Yeah, it feels relaxed.

VOLUNTEER 2 (*overlapping*): —go to sleep.

INMATE: Not sleepy, but—I don't get angry, or nothing just, you know, bothers me anymore.

EDDIE (*singing*): 'Twas, let me see: 'Twas at the bar, at the bar, where I smoked my first cigar, and the nickels, nickels, nickels, roll away / It was there by chance that I stole a pair of pants and now I am serving thirty days.

NURSE: You know that fellow who's master of ceremonies?

VOLUNTEER 1: Yes.

NURSE: —they tell me he's the worst paranoid.

VOLUNTEER 1: Is that so?

NURSE: Eddie, how did you make him go through with it?

EDDIE: Who, Willie Willliams?

NURSE: Willie Williams—you would think—he was just so relaxed, and you'd think he'd been doing it for years. [*Eddie mumbles something.*] And he's a paranoid, they can't reach him.

EDDIE: You reached him, Alice.

NURSE: This is a letter from an inmate of mine. Imagine, they sent me this letter. I wish you could read it, really. An inmate from the other side, in the alcoholic. Look at the nice letter he wrote me, here it is, right here. Well, yeah, Wilhelm.

VOLUNTEER 1: Well, isn't that nice?

NURSE: Isn't it? And he sent this medal to me.

VOLUNTEER 1: He sent that?

NURSE: He sent that. Isn't that nice? I hope we cured him.

VOLUNTEER 1 (*overlapping*): But it really is a lovely letter.

VOLUNTEER 1: That's lovely.

NURSE: It is, it really is.

VOLUNTEER 1: It makes you feel good—

NURSE (*overlapping*): Well, it makes you feel good that you're doing a lit-

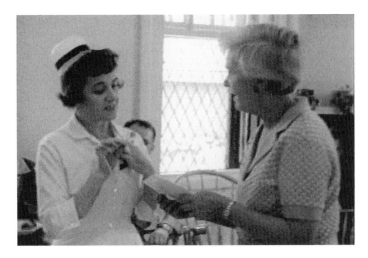

6. A nurse shows a volunteer her gift from a former inmate.

tle something for 'em, even at the time you don't think you're helping them, because they have such a problem. But when you get a letter like this, and then it makes you feel as though, well, you at least tried.

VOLUNTEER 1: . . . accustomed to this sort of thing.

VOICE (*offscreen*): Something new to me too.

VOLUNTEER 1: Come on, boys. Oh, look, you fellows standing back there. C'mon up here and show us how good your aim is. Oh, come on. What's so bashful? Come on now. [*Camera pulls back to reveal she is holding a makeshift bull's-eye for a game of Pin-the-Tail-on-the-Donkey.*] Alright, move over fellows. We got a, we got a fellow who's going to aim right in the middle. That's it, right up to it and stick it right—alright, put it on. That's the way . . . Good. Oh, I think you got licked, young man, I think you got licked that time. Yes, you got licked that time. Alright, come on, somebody else we need here. Come on, now, we need somebody else to get a really good—

INMATE: I'm off now—

VOLUNTEER 1: Well, nobody else has hit the spot yet.

INMATE: I'm off, I'm off. I'm gone.

VOLUNTEER 1: We have to know your numbers. Here we are, that's it, now here's the fellow that's going to put it right on the bull's-eye . . . right on the bull's-eye . . . Now line it right up with this. This is where you're com-

7. A psychiatrist on the telephone before the staff meeting.

ing, bang on. When you hear my voice, you know you're here. C'mon. Shoot. Shut your eyes. Come right at it, that-a-boy. Straight ahead, you're coming right for it, come on, little further, little further, c'mon some more, that's the way, now right on that bull's-eye. Right on that bull's-eye. Oh, that's perfect. Very good, you're inside the ring at least. Now hold the number. Come on now, who else? Come on now, who else? Come on over and try it. Well, is that everybody? Has everybody tried it? You know, this is the first time we've played this game, and I want you all to try it.

EDDIE (*singing part of "Chicago Town," then segueing into his own lyrics, in the process putting on his cap and dancing out the door*): It's do or die for MCI / And that is our gay philosophy / Us poor slobs will lose our jobs . . . [*Cut to a psychiatrist talking on the telephone.*]

PSYCHIATRIST (*on telephone*): Wait just a second.

SECRETARY (*on intercom*): Yes?

PSYCHIATRIST: Mary, do I have anything listed for court tomorrow? Or anything else?

SECRETARY (*on intercom*): No, you don't.

PSYCHIATRIST (*on intercom*): Thank you. [*Back to telephone*] I have nothing for court tomorrow. Tomorrow's fine . . . Oh good God, no, I'm usually here, unless I'm dead by then and I've got a cold and I may be . . . I usually get here by 8:15 or 8:00. So at your convenience . . . Okay, well, the earlier the better. Okay. Why don't you do me favor, give me a call—what time do you get up in the morning? . . . Alright, why don't you give me a call as soon as you roll out of bed, at home. Just to make sure I'm alive enough to get down here . . . Oh God, no! Well, let's put it this way, if I'm sick, with four children in the house I'll be awake, and usually I get up at 5:30 otherwise . . . Don't make it much later than that because I'm out the door to get down here . . . Okay, bye-bye. Okay, now—[*Cut to CU of Vladimir, who is now in the room.*] Vladimir, as I promised you before, if I see enough improvement in you—

INMATE (VLADIMIR): But how can I improve if I'm getting worse? I'm trying to tell you—day by day *I* am getting worse because of the circumstances, because of the situation. Now you tell me until you see an improvement, and each time I get worse . . . so obviously it's the treatment that I'm getting or the situation or the place or the patients or the inmates . . . Or I do not know which. All I want is to go back to prison where I belong. I was supposed to only come down here for observation. What observation did I get? You call me up a couple of times, you say, "Well, take some medication," medication for the mind? I'm supposed to take medication for—if I have some bodily injury, not for my mind, my mind is perfect. 'Cause I'm obviously logical, I know what I'm talking about. There's nothing—and I am excited, yes, that's the only fault you, you might find with me. And I have a perfect right to be excited, I've been here for a year and a half. And this place is doing me harm. I come in here, every time I come in here, you tell me I *look* crazy. [*Camera begins pulling back to reveal that Vladimir and the doctor are at a staff meeting.*] Now what's—if some, if you don't like my face that's, I mean, that's another story, but that has nothing to do with my mental stability. I have an emotional problem, now, yes, which I did *not* have.

PSYCHIATRIST: What got you down here?

VLADIMIR: They sent me down here for observation.

PSYCHIATRIST: Why?

VLADIMIR: They thought maybe—I went to see a social worker and I saw a psychiatrist and they said that, why don't you go down there, because I had a little problem.

PSYCHIATRIST: You felt the coffee was poisoned, you felt people were mixing you up in your thinking, you were shaking—

VLADIMIR: Not so. The only part that's true is coffee. Now what sort of treatment do I get down here? There are a hundred patients who are walking back and forth who are obviously doing me harm.

PSYCHIATRIST: Are you working here, Vladimir?

VLADIMIR: No, there was a, there was no suitable work for me here. All I've got is, all I've got is the kitchen. And all they do is throw cups around. In fact, it's noisy, they got two television sets, which are blaring. Machines which are going. Everything which is against the mind. There's one thing that a patient does need—and this is what I do know, absolutely, is quiet, if I have a mental problem or even emotional problem. Yet here I'm thrown in with over a hundred of them and all they do is yell, walk around, televisions are blaring, so that's doing my mind harm.

PSYCHIATRIST: Are you involved in any sports here?

VLADIMIR: There are no sports here. All they've got is a baseball, and a glove, and that's it. There's nothing else. Back at the other place I have all the other facilities to improve myself. I have the gym, I have the school, I have all kinds of—anything I want.

PSYCHIATRIST: Are you in any group therapy here?

VLADIMIR: No, there is no group—obviously, I do not need group therapy, I need peace and quiet. See what I mean? This place is disturbing me, it's harming me. I'm losing weight. Everything that's happening to me is bad. And all I get, all I get, is why don't you wait, why don't you take medication? Medication is disagreeable to me. There are people who, to whom you may not give medication. Obviously. And the medication I got is hurting me, it's harming me.

PSYCHIATRIST: Well, Vladimir, you say—

VLADIMIR: In fact, to be specific, it harmed my thorax. I do know that much, what it's harming.

PSYCHIATRIST (*overlapping*): Your thorax?

VLADIMIR (*overlapping*): Yes, right here. Yes, it has harmed me, it has harmed me in every way possible. Obviously. If you leave me here, that means that you want me to get, get harmed. Which is an absolute fact. It's plain logic, that proves that I am sane. Obviously.

PSYCHIATRIST: Well, that's interesting logic—

VLADIMIR (*overlapping*): Yes, it's absolutely perfect because if I am in a place, as if I were in some kind of a hole or something, right? And if you keep me there, obviously you intend to do me harm. Isn't that perfect logic?

PSYCHIATRIST: No, it isn't, Vladimir—

VLADIMIR: It's absolute perfect. I am getting harmed. I say I'm getting

8. An imate explains his situation at a staff meeting.

harmed. You tell me that until I show some improvement, yet each time you said until I show some improvement, I have been getting worse, medication has harmed me—

PSYCHIATRIST: Thank you, Vladimir.

VLADIMIR: No, no, I'm— [*Vladimir is led out of the room, away from the camera, saying something inaudible as he goes. Cut to CU of psychiatrist.*]

PSYCHIATRIST: He's been much better than this. And he's now, he's now falling apart. Now whether this is some reaction to his medication is certainly something we'll have to look at. However, he was looking a lot more catatonic and depressed before. Sometimes we find that on the antidepressants, you remove the depression and you uncover the paranoid stuff, and we may have to give him larger quantities of tranquilizers just to tone this down. So, not looking ready to be able to make it back in prison.

SOCIAL WORKER: He argues in a perfect paranoic pattern. If you accept his basic premise, then the rest of it *is* logical, but the basic premise is not true.

PSYCHIATRIST: That's right. He was very much more closed off and mute before. He'd open up in a one-to-one relationship but never at a staff meeting, and he's opened up over in medical rounds, some, and yet, this is why we had him brought up to staff, to see what would happen. And I think he's certainly shown that he doesn't—

STAFF MEMBER 1: At one time they sought executive clemency for him.

PSYCHIATRIST: Yes.

STAFF MEMBER 1: And it is true that he did learn English.

PSYCHIATRIST: Yes.

STAFF MEMBER 1: Well, now, he was building up with a great deal of hope to get out. And he did get to the Parole Board at one time. And he was—

SOCIAL WORKER (*offscreen*): It was shortly before he came here that he was due to go—

STAFF MEMBER 1: Yeah, he's now talking about the same thing, about his rehabilitation from his incarceration up to a given point . . . so he's reverting in a way to that kind of thinking.

SOCIAL WORKER: But I think he's terrified of leaving—

PSYCHIATRIST: And the louder he shouts about going back, the more frightened he indicates that he probably is.

STAFF MEMBER 2 (*offscreen*): This is known as Ganser Syndrome.

PSYCHIATRIST: Well, not quite, but—

STAFF MEMBER 2 (*offscreen*): Close.

PSYCHIATRIST: Well, I think what we have to do with him is put him on a higher dose of tranquilizers and see if we can bring the paranoid elements under a little better control, then see if we can get him back on medication— if he's taking it now, and I'm not even sure he is.

STAFF MEMBER 2: The psychological testing always showed there was paranoid—it was, was the thing that was going through it all the way.

PSYCHIATRIST: Right. [*Speaking into tape recorder*] Diagnosis: schizophrenic reaction, chronic undifferentiated type with prominent paranoid features. [*Cut to inmate bending over in a bathtub washing himself. Two guards, mostly offscreen, speak to him.*]

GUARDS: How's that, Al. That's good, huh? Take some of that chocolate pudding out . . . How's that feel? Al, why don't you lay right down in the water so you can get your back washed? Yeah, now soak your piles . . . How's that feel, eh? Lay right down there, Al. [*Laughter.*] . . . Don't drown, Al . . . Sit down, now, that's-a-boy. Back a little. Backwards, Al. Albert, sit down and face me. No, face me. How's that feel? Don't swallow that water. Water's [*inaudible*]. Watch your head. Right back, Al, here. Watch your head on that faucet. That-a-boy, Al. How's it feel?

INMATE (AL): Real good.

9. An inmate in the bathtub.

GUARD: Yeah? Warmed up well?

AL: Water's something special, something special, like champagne, eh?

GUARD: Like champagne?

AL: Very good, umm.

GUARDS: Why don't you drink a little cold water, Al? Yeah, we'll give you water. Al, don't be drinking that water. Al, take some water out of here if you want. Get it from the faucet here . . . Feels good . . . You feel nice and clean? Push right back, Al. You have four brothers?

AL: Gotta kiss the mirror in honor of them.

GUARDS: Wonderful. Nice kiss. Okay, Al? All set, Al?

AL: Yeah, had a good time.

GUARD: Okay, let's go. [*Al is led out of the room. Cut to a man put into his cell screaming in his underwear, followed by three shots of inmates milling about in common room and sitting on benches.*]

PRIEST (FATHER MULLIGAN): Peace be to this house [*cut from CU of handicapped inmate picking his nose to MS of priest giving last rites to an inmate in facility hospital bed*] and all who dwell herein. Sprinkle me with this salve, O Lord, and I shall be purified. Wash me and I shall be made blameless . . . May the Lord forgive you by this holy anointing, and his most loving mercy, whatever sins you have committed by the use of your sight,

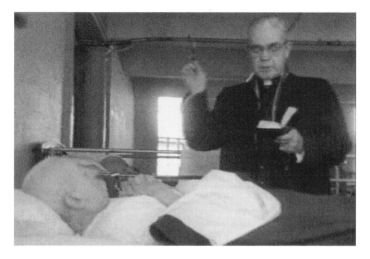

10. A priest administers last rites to a dying inmate.

amen . . . May the Lord forgive you by this holy anointing, and by his most loving mercy whatever sins you have committed by the use of your hearing, amen . . . May the Lord forgive you by this holy anointing, and by his most loving mercy whatever sins you have committed by the use of your sense of smell, amen . . . May the Lord forgive you by this holy anointing, and by his most loving mercy whatever sins you have committed by the use of your sense of taste and power of speech, amen. Now let me have your two hands, please. May the Lord forgive you by this holy anointing and his most loving mercy whatever sins you have committed by the use of your sense of touch, amen . . . May the Lord forgive you by this holy anointing, and by his most loving mercy whatever sins you have committed by your use of your power to walk, amen. May the Lord be with you and with your spirit, amen. Let us pray. Lord, Holy Father, almighty and eternal God, by pouring the grace of your blessing on the bodies of the sick you watch over with all interest and care, your creatures, be present in your kindness as we call upon your holy name. [*Cut from CU of inmate receiving last rites to earlier ranting inmate in the yard.*]

INMATE: What is intelligences? Intelligence is where? Even the blessed prisoner, Father Mulligan there with his confessional there, telling the truth. And he exposed it and calls it down to the warden Johnson and things like that. And they get around to it. Father, even the rabbi. Ah, not only the rabbi but the Christian Scientist and the minister. We know all about 'em. For I know everything because I'm psychic. I read their fucking minds. They're no good, they're money-changers, they're Judases. [*Singing begins to become audible in background*] And that's all. So, I'll tell you one thing, even Pope Paul is not without sin 'cause even him, and the cardinals, and the See of Trent, helped to mur—, crucify, the man named Pope Pius, and then he comes, and the minister too, and their fucking doctor and Pope John can tell you the same thing. It was never decreed that way. The vicar of the church is Jesus Christ [*inaudible*] and the blessed Virgin Mary, mother of—and I say he's unworthy of being the pope of this world, and I announce that the rightful pope now is Archbishop Fulton Sheen and the other one Cardinal Spellman, so help me God. I, Borgia, say so.

OTHER INMATE (*overlapping, singing while standing on his head*): For the glory of the glory of Father Mulligan, for the glory of his love and his holiness / For the glory of the glory of thy love / For the glory of the glory of the bishop / For the glory of the glory of the cardinal / For the glory of the pastor and the rabbi / For the glory of the glory of his love.

INMATE: She promised me she was going to send me cake and stuff. She's a liar, a liar, a defector of the truth, and so is Peabody. I say so. I, Borgia, say so.

OTHER INMATE (*singing*): For the glory of the glory of Father Mulligan. [*Singing carries over to shot of corpse in body bag in morgue drawer. The body is lifted and put into a casket.*]

GUARD: Wanna get the cover? [*The casket lid is screwed on. CU of a screw being turned in the lid. The casket is carried out to a hearse. One man mutters instructions to the others.*]

GUARD (*to casket*): I'm sorry, Jim. [*Cut to cemetery, where the casket is taken out of the hearse by inmates and carried over to a grave.*]

INMATES (*positioning the casket*): Don't be afraid. You've gone too far over. Joe, let me get up in the front. Let me get up in the front. That's it, take your time . . . Okay, that's alright . . . Now just stand right where you are.

FATHER MULLIGAN: I am the resurrection and the life, he who believes in me even if he dies shall live. And whoever lives and believes in me shall never die. Blessed be the Lord, the God of Israel, because he has visited and wrought the redemption of his people. He has raised up a horn of salvation for us in the house of David, his servant, as he promised through the mouths of his holy ones, the prophets from of old. Eternal rest grant to him O Lord—

INMATES: And let his perpetual light shine upon him.

FATHER MULLIGAN: May he rest in peace.

11. A guard hosts the Follies finale.

INMATES: Amen.

FATHER MULLIGAN: May his soul and the souls of all the faith departed through the mercy of God rest in peace, amen.

INMATES: Amen.

FATHER MULLIGAN: Remember, man, that thou are dust, and unto dust thou shalt return. That's all. [*Camera holds on the casket as all file away from the grave site, out of frame. Cut to performers at the annual show that opened the film. Applause. They sing "So Long for Now." The entire cast comes onto the stage.*]

CAST (*singing*): It's do or die / For MCI / And now that it's all over / We can tell you why / Us poor slobs will lose our jobs / Believe us, it could happen without half a try / The Department of Correction has a talent, you see / We'll never make the big time / But we've got our gay philosophy / Sing and dance and take a chance / Until another year, we're through / Until another year, we're through.

EDDIE: Aren't they terrific?

[*Camera zooms in and pans faces of performers on stage in CU, then zooms back out to full shot, and back into CU as music dies out. Cut to credits: Directed and Produced by Frederick Wiseman. Photography by John Marshall. Editor: Frederick Wiseman. Associate Editor: Alyne Model. Associate Pro-*

ducer: David Eames. Copyright 1967 Bridgewater Film Co., Inc. After the credits appears the following note: "The Supreme Judicial Court of Massachusetts has ordered that 'A brief explanation shall be included in the film that changes and improvements have taken place at Massachusetts Correctional Institution Bridgewater since 1966.'" This note is followed by another: "Changes and improvements have taken place at Massachusetts Correctional Institution Bridgewater since 1966." Copyright renewed 1995 Bridgewater Film Company, Inc.]

High School (1968)

High School was shot during five weeks in March and April 1968 in Northeast High School in Philadelphia and released later the same year. Northeast, a relatively good school in the public school system, is shown in the film to have many facilities and extracurricular activities for students, including discussion groups, sports teams, band and choir, and even sophisticated equipment for simulated space flights. The film also shows various classes, including language lessons, typing, history, home economics, physical and sex education, as well as teachers meeting with students regarding discipline and guidance counseling. Despite the school's middle-class affluence, the film questions the nature of its approach to education. Wiseman has said that his first impression upon seeing the school was that it looked like a factory, a perception that informs the structure of the entire film. From the opening sequence, with the camera approaching Northeast's fences and tall smokestack, to the ending, in which the school principal reads a letter from a former student about to be parachuted into Vietnam, the film suggests that the educational system is like an impersonal assembly line manufacturing consent, more concerned with socialization than knowledge.

[*Title:* High School: Osti, Inc., 1968. *Various shots through the windshield of a moving car: row houses, milk truck, storefronts. Through a fence, Northeast High School, Philadelphia, is seen at a distance. There is a cut to a closer view of the school with its smokestack prominent as the car takes the camera into the school parking lot. On the sound track is part of the pop song "(Sittin' on) The Dock of the Bay." The song fades out and there is a cut to a crowded hallway inside the school, followed by a cut to inside a classroom, homeroom teacher in MS.*]

HOMEROOM TEACHER: First thing we want to do is to give you the daily bulletin. You'd be surprised: a little notice somewhere that you might think doesn't concern you might change your whole life, might decide on what college you'll go to, or might decide on what activity. And then Joyce has a few things to say. Right, Joyce? Alright. The thought for the day: "Life is cause and effect. One creates his tomorrow at every moment by his motives, thoughts, and deeds of today." And this question of cause and effect, you know, as I say, I might read something that might change your life. [*Cut to CU of Spanish teacher.*]

SPANISH TEACHER: Anoche conocimos a un filósofo existencialista. [Last time we met an existential philosopher.]

STUDENT: Anoche conocimos a—

TEACHER: —a un—

STUDENT: —a un filósofo—

TEACHER: —existencialista.

STUDENT: existencialista.

TEACHER: ¿Quién puede pronunciar esta palabra? ¿Existencialista? ¿Carla? ¿El nombre del hombre? ¿Frances? ¿No? Si. [Who can pronounce this word? Existentialist? Carla? The man's name? Frances? No? Yes.]

STUDENT: Sartre.

TEACHER: Si, Sartre. Y el nombre de su apellido; pero el nombre? [And his first name; but the man's name?]

STUDENT: Jean-Paul.

TEACHER: Muy bien. Excelente, Roger. ¿Y ahora, hmm? Jean-Paul Sartre. [*Hisses*] S-s-s-s. Existencialista. [Very good. Excellent, Roger. And now, hmm? Jean-Paul Sartre. Existentialist.]

CLASS: Existencialista.

TEACHER: Este lado. Existencialista. [This side of the class. "Existentialist."]

HALF THE CLASS: Existencialista.

TEACHER: Este lado. [This side of the class.]

OTHER HALF OF CLASS: Existencialista.

TEACHER: A un filósofo— [A philosopher]

CLASS: —a un filósofo—

TEACHER: —a un filósofo existencialista. [An existentialist philosopher.] [*Cut to percussion students in rehearsal, camera then panning right to teacher conducting.*]

MUSIC TEACHER: 1–2–3–4, 1–2–3–4, up-down-3–4. [*Camera pans back left to students, one of whom strikes gong on cue, at which point there is a cut to CU of Dr. Allen in his office.*]

DR. ALLEN: What do you mean you can't take gym? You get dressed in the morning?

BOY: Yeah.

DR. ALLEN: Do you get undressed?

BOY: Yeah.

DR. ALLEN: Well, you can get into a gym outfit.

BOY: I can't take . . . Yeah, I know . . .

DR. ALLEN: Alright. Well, you get into a gym outfit!

BOY: I can't take gym, though . . .

DR. ALLEN: We'll decide that.

BOY: I have a doctor's thing—

DR. ALLEN: I am sick and tired of you talking. You just—

BOY: My mother was in, though—

DR. ALLEN: I spoke to your mother. Now look—

BOY: I'm going to the doctor today—

DR. ALLEN: Now look! You'd better be in a gym outfit. You'd better be in a gym outfit. We'll determine whether you take exercise or not.

BOY: I can't.

DR. ALLEN: We'll determine that.

BOY: I can't take gym! I can hardly . . . I'm not even allowed—

DR. ALLEN: Why don't you just—

BOY: I'm not even supposed to come to school!

DR. ALLEN: Hey, look! [*Rising from his chair and coming from behind his desk*] I'm going to tell you something. Don't you talk and you just listen! You come prepared in a gym outfit when you go to gym. Is that clear?

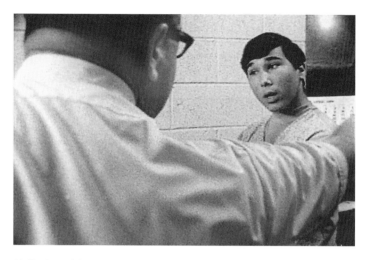

12. The dean of discipline suspends a student.

BOY: Yeah.

DR. ALLEN: Alright. Now don't tell us you won't do anything. No one's going to put you into an uncompromising position. But you'll come dressed in a gym outfit.

BOY: I said I would.

DR. ALLEN: You're suspended. Go wait outside.

BOY: But I said I *would!*

DR. ALLEN: Go outside.

BOY: Ahhh, man. I said I would.

ANOTHER VOICE (*offscreen*): You got a book out on the fifth of January— [*Boy walks out of the office. Cut to a brief shot of the school hallway, many students walking by the camera. Cut to CU of student in French class listening to teacher. The camera pans left across class to outstretched hand of the teacher. Cut to CU of a student, followed by CU of French teacher.*]

FRENCH TEACHER: Oui, mais avant de manger, il est nécessaire de— [Yes, but before eating, you have to—]

STUDENT: —préparer le dîner [prepare the dinner].

TEACHER: Préparer le dîner. Ou préparer le déjeuner? Ou préparer le petit— [Prepare the dinner. Or prepare lunch. Or prepare break—]

STUDENT: —déjeuner [—fast].

TEACHER: Oui. Mais en France c'est différent. En Amérique, on mange généralement dans la cuisine. Mais en France, où est-ce-qu'on mange le petit déjeuner? Le déjeuner? Le dîner? Où? Généralement, naturellement il y a des exceptions. Mais en France, où est-ce qu'on mange? [Yes. But in France it's different. In America, we usually eat in the kitchen. But in France, where does one eat breakfast? Lunch? Dinner? Where? Generally, naturally there are exceptions. But in France, where does one eat?]

STUDENT: Dans la salle à manger. [In the dining room.]

TEACHER: Exactement. Dans la salle à manger. Chez nous, en Amérique, c'est différent. On mange plutôt dans la cuisine; oh, il y a des exceptions, naturellement. [Exactly. In the dining room. In our homes, in America, it's different. Instead, we eat in the kitchen. Oh, naturally there are exceptions.]

STUDENT: Naturellement. [Naturally.]

TEACHER: Généralement, dans la cuisine. Oui? En France, non. On prépare dans la cuisine, on mange dans la salle à manger. [Usually in the kitchen. Right? In France, no. You prepare the meal in the kitchen, but you eat in the dining room.] [*Cut to MS of a student's father talking to guidance counselor.*]

FATHER: No, no, no, no. A flunking student—no, no—a flunking student couldn't receive such accolades as "Fabulous." "Fabulous." Now, that's all I'm saying! Sure, they're flunking—I could see maybe a C student have a "Fabulous" here. But a flunking student, "Fabulous"?—

COUNSELOR: —But, why don't—

FATHER: —"Fabulous!"

COUNSELOR (*overlapping*): Why don't you put it in reverse? Why didn't you say, why didn't you say that a student who can write fabulous papers shouldn't flunk? Shouldn't do things that would cause her to flunk? You see—no, it depends on the language!

FATHER (*overlapping*): You know, it's strange. I've always found that a man who uses the word *sympathy* is never sympathetic. Have you ever found that, Dr. Boodish? [*Mother giggles.*] Tell the truth . . . And I have no regrets. Alright, nothing.

COUNSELOR: No regrets?

FATHER: None.

COUNSELOR: What do you mean—?

FATHER: No. All I want you to say, that at least I'm right about these few papers. That's all.

COUNSELOR: What do you want me to tell you, that you are right about these papers?

FATHER: I want you to say that a girl who receives "Fabulous" and all these marks shouldn't flunk.

COUNSELOR: I can only say this: that the teacher in reading these papers thought they were fabulous, but that the total mark involves more than just those papers. That's all I can tell you.

FATHER: But I think this is a rather unique situation, wouldn't you say so? Rather unique?

COUNSELOR: Well, would you be happy if I say it's unique?

FATHER: I'd be happy.

COUNSELOR: Alright, I'll say it: I would say it's "somewhat unique."

FATHER: Is it compassionate for a teacher to write "Fabulous"? Let me get back to this again. And the girl figures she's doing well. "Very Good, Rhona!" And especially this "Fabulous," and then finally she gets her report card. And the girl is stunned: it's another E. Is it also fair for a girl—and I think Mr. Schuster will concur—this girl cause any trouble in her deportment? Is she wild? Talk a lot?

MR. SCHUSTER (*offscreen*): No. She did get a satisfactory mark in cooperation.

FATHER: Why did she get an E the first time? It's completely against her character.

MOTHER: In behavior!

FATHER: In behavior. Why did she get an E the first time?

MOTHER: Completely against her character.

FATHER: If you'd saw the girl you'd understand what I mean.

MR. SCHUSTER: An E!—

FATHER: Yes, an E.

MOTHER: Yes. In behavior.

FATHER: In behavior.

MR. SCHUSTER: What did she get in there—?

FATHER: An *E*.

MR. SCHUSTER: *E* is a grade; it's not a behavior mark.

FATHER: Did she tell—? What did she say?

MOTHER: Uh, 4, 3; the lowest you can get, I imagine.

COUNSELOR: We cannot judge Rhona's marks based purely on this teacher's remarks on these papers. This is all I'm saying.

FATHER: Rhona, limited in many ways, knew world events and the world around her. She knew the different forms of government, the different structures of types of government. And here Rhona failed—

COUNSELOR: Because she failed in all these tests! We can only judge on the basis of performance. You may have hidden talent in you, sir, but if you don't perform it, we don't know.

FATHER: True, true.

COUNSELOR: And the world will recognize you only by your performance.

FATHER: That's true, that's true.

COUNSELOR: But if you want your daughter to be basically a well-adjusted, ultimately, I'll use the word *happiness* in a very broad sense, and I know that happiness is not the ultimate thing in life, but it's important. You cannot impose preconceived values and dreams on an individual, including a child. You cannot do that. But again, I want *you* to understand that part of *your* job is to deal with Rhona as a sympathetic and understanding father but recognizing her limitations and the fact that she's a person in her own right and that if you impose too much your desires on her, even without pushing them or forcing her, she may react in a way which may be damaging to her too. [*Cut from CU of guidance counselor's gesturing fist to MS of student talking to Dr. Allen. Camera pans immediately to Dr. Allen at his desk.*]

DR. ALLEN: Michael, this had to do with your cutting, what is it? Physical Science?

MICHAEL: No sir. I never cut it. Mrs. Ganin was yelling at me after class and she starts going off. And you see, somehow I was making noise in the lunch line, and the truth is, Mr. Allen, I was behaving in the back of the room. I didn't open my mouth 'cause see the other kids were, and I didn't feel like goofing off. And she thought it was me. And she calls me up and she starts yelling at me and I say, "It wasn't me!" and she starts yelling, yelling, wah wah! So I figure, Mr. Allen, could you stand there and listen to a lady yell?

I figure I'd go out and talk to her later when she's calmed down. And she was pretty worked up. And I went to walk out and she goes, "You don't leave." And I go, "I'll speak to you later at a better time." And I walked out because—

DR. ALLEN: First of all, Michael, you showed poor judgment. When you're being addressed by someone older than you are or in a seat of authority, it's your job to respect and listen. She didn't ask you to jump from the Empire State Building; she's not asking you for your blood. She's asking for a little bit of time, to help you out. Now here's the thing: what you should have done is showed some character, by saying, "Okay. I will go to your detention, but may I speak with you and get this matter corrected?"

MICHAEL: She didn't assign a detention.

DR. ALLEN: Well, according to this—

MICHAEL: No, they sent me—

DR. ALLEN (*overlapping*): —"Given the choice of a detention at 7:30 or at 1:45 and you refused to take either." Now what is it?

MICHAEL: They sent me down to Mr. Walsh and I tried to explain it to him and he started yelling at me too.

DR. ALLEN: Well, no one is going to yell at you and—

MICHAEL: Well, I don't feel I have to take anybody's screaming at me for nothing—

DR. ALLEN: No, well, there's a point to that, but in the meantime it's time you showed a little character on your own, right?

MICHAEL: Yes, sir.

DR. ALLEN: I would take the detention and then you can come back and say, "Now, I took the detention, may I speak with you and get this—?"

MICHAEL (*overlapping*): I can't, I can't talk to that man—

DR. ALLEN: Well, you can try.

MICHAEL: Do you know, now another time in that class—this is another reason why, this is another reason why I won't take it.

DR. ALLEN: Why?

MICHAEL: I was given a—these kids took a book and they were going to throw it at me, right? And the teacher caught a kid with the book in his hand and he took it off the other kid's book. And the other kid stood up and says, "Give me my damn book back!" So Mrs. Ganin says, "You two get

13. A student takes detention under protest.

out! You know, I don't want language around here and no use to get up-roared." Do you know that they brought me into the detention room? They brought me into Mr. Walsh's room and they got me dragged in for nothing, and I tried to explain it to him and he says, "Will you take your detention?" Which was utterly ridiculous.

DR. ALLEN: Now, see, we are out to establish something, aren't we?

MICHAEL: Yes!

DR. ALLEN: We're out to establish that you can be a man and that you can take orders. We want to prove to them that you can take the orders.

MICHAEL: But, Mr. Allen, you see, it's all against my principles, you have to stand for something!

DR. ALLEN: Yes. But I think your principles aren't involved here. I think it's a question now of, of proving yourself to be a man. It's a question here of how, how do we follow rules and regulations. If there's a mistake made, there's an approach to it. I think you don't fight with a teacher; I think you ask permission to talk. And ask them to listen to you. Now, this is what you didn't do. Now if you take your detention—and after all, they didn't require much from you. The teacher felt you were out of order, and in her judgment you deserved a detention. I don't see anything wrong with assigning you a detention. Now I think you should prove yourself. You should show that you can take the detention when given it.

MICHAEL: I should prove that I'm a man and that's what I intend to do by doing what I feel, in my opinion, is what I am doing is right.

DR. ALLEN: Are you going to take your detention or aren't you? I feel that you should.

MICHAEL: I'll take it, but under protest.

DR. ALLEN: Alright, then. You take it under protest. That's good.

MICHAEL: Today?

DR. ALLEN: Yes, I'd like you to take it today.

MICHAEL: Will today after school be okay?

DR. ALLEN: Okay.

MICHAEL: What room? Room One-twenty?

DR. ALLEN: One-eighteen.

MICHAEL: Alright. [*Cut to hallway, camera following teacher on hall duty.*]

TEACHER: What are you doing here?

BOY: Going to the lunchroom.

TEACHER: Well, go the lunchroom. Goodbye . . . Where are you going? . . . [*To several students at pay phones*] You got a pass? You got a pass? Do you have a pass? How about you? Hang up! Let's go. It's for emergencies. Let's get on the ball . . . [*Cut to teacher coming back to students at pay phones later on*] I told you to get off of there. Let's go.

BOY: Excuse me, Mr. Murray, I'll see you tomorrow morning. A man's yelling at me.

TEACHER: You get a pass.

BOY: Alright, alright. Bye. I had to call my insurance company.

TEACHER: Well, you get a pass.

BOY: But I have lunch now, I have lunch. I was coming from my lunch.

TEACHER: Lunch means lunch, It doesn't mean make phone calls.

BOY: Alright.

TEACHER: You got a pass? Okay. [*Camera follows teacher on hall duty, the pop song "Simon Says" fading in on the soundtrack as he goes up to a door window and peeks inside. Cut to a record player in girls' gym, then the camera shows girls in the gym, all in identical one-piece uniforms, from the back. The girls do calisthenics to "Simon Says," the camera showing them from behind. Cut to CU of English teacher reading.*]

14. A teacher reads "Casey at the Bat."

TEACHER (*reading the Ernest Thayer poem "Casey at the Bat"*): "And when the dust had lifted / and men saw what had occurred, / there was Jimmy safe at second, and Flynn a-huggin' third. / And from five thousand throats or more there rose there a lusty yell; / it rumbled through the valley, it rattled in the dell; / it pounded on the mountain and recoiled upon the flat; / for Casey, mighty Casey, was advancing to the bat. / There was ease in Casey's manner as he stepped into his place, / there was pride in Casey's bearing and a smile on Casey's face. / And when responding to the cheers, he lightly doffed his hat, / no stranger in the crowd could doubt 'twas Casey at the bat./ Ten thousand eyes were on him as he rubbed his hands with dirt. / Five thousand tongues applauded when he wiped them on his shirt. / Then, while the writhing pitcher ground the ball into his hip, / defiance flashed in Casey's eye, a sneer curled Casey's lip. / And now the leather-covered sphere came hurtling through the air, / and Casey stood a-watching it in haughty grandeur there. / Close by the sturdy batsman the ball un-heeded sped— / "That ain't my style," said Casey. / "Strike one!" the umpire said. / From the benches black with people, there went up a muffled roar, / like the beating of the storm waves on a stern and distant shore. / "Kill him! Kill the umpire!" shouted someone on the stand, / and it's likely they'd have killed him had not Casey raised his hand. / With a smile of Christian charity, great Casey's visage shone, / he stilled the rising tumult, he bade the game go on. / He signaled to the pitcher, and once more the dun sphere flew, / but Casey still ignored it, and the umpire said, "Strike two!" / "Fraud!" cried the maddened thousands, and the echo answered "Fraud!" / But one scornful look from Casey and the audience was awed. / They saw his face grow stern and cold, they saw his muscles strain, / and they knew that Casey wouldn't let that ball go by again. / The sneer has fled from Casey's lips, his teeth are clenched in hate. / He pounds, with cruel violence, his bat upon the plate. / And now the pitcher holds the ball, and now he lets it go, / and now the air is shattered by the force of Casey's blow. / Oh, somewhere in this land of ours the sun is shining bright. / The band is playing somewhere, and somewhere hearts are light. / And, somewhere men are laughing, and little children shout, / but there is no joy in Mudville— / great Casey has struck out. [*Cut to MS of girls hitting softballs on T-ball stands in the gym, then to CU of same. Cut to CU of hands chopping walnuts.*]

HOME ECONOMICS TEACHER: What's the problem with the baking soda? . . . Did you use too much? You've got to taste the soda in it, right? An even more efficient way to use that knife is this. See here. If you pivot it from here you may cut yourself . . . [*Cut to two-shot of teacher and a student.*] One part granulated sugar and one part brown sugar, right? Now you need another measuring cup. You'll find one in the closet, right here.

BOY: Yes, ma'am.

TEACHER: Right . . . And Gary, what about this brown sugar? How is he going to measure it?

GARY: Packed.

TEACHER: Packed. Absolutely right . . . Okay. [*Cut from CU of boy's hand sifting sugar to CU of the same teacher in Fashion Class.*]

TEACHER: What's your number, doll?

GIRL: Eleven.

TEACHER: Eleven? Hurray! . . . She sure is, isn't she? And isn't she a beauty. Just look at that. She is a vision for sure. Let's have number 14, ahh . . . you may disappear. Now, wait a minute, girls. Wait a minute. I think this is a good time—hold it, it's a good time to talk about clothes. A girl came into my class today in a culotte costume, and it looked just about—you know, uh, it looked as sporty as this. If it were on someone with slimmer legs, I think it might look good. Could you find someone to model it Friday? With real thin legs, honey. And girls, look, don't wear culottes to school because you're almost just like that. Your legs are all too heavy for the stuff. Don't wear it too short, it looks miserable. I love you, goodbye. Okay, next, let's see. Now I think if this young lady—she's got a leg problem too. If she did something about those stockings she might well look better. Could you get

15. A teacher evaluates the girls' fashion designs.

a matching pink or flesh-colored stocking for Friday? Yeah, something that fits in. Salmon color—

VOICE (*offscreen*): Pink.

TEACHER: Or white. Or white. Alright. Would like to see you again on Friday. What's your number, honey? Number 14, and you will take care of that? We're not even asking about it because I think she's got a pretty nice color here. Looks good. And it's the leg thing that makes it difficult. Alright. And let's see our last one, and I think that this young lady has done a lovely job of really putting some style into this particular garment. Let's see how she looks. She's done a nice job. And this, this is a sample, girls, of what you can do. This gal, she's got a weight problem; she knows it, and she's done everything she can to cut it down. I mean, she designed this garment herself with the idea of making it gracious and graceful and she handles it well. She handles herself beautifully, see that? Okay. And that's what you can do with fashion and design. But these are the important things, girls: to walk with your shoulders high and proud. And this is all the time. Around Northeast High School this is the favorite walk. And you've got, you just got to do something to conquer it. You really must. Handle yourself beautifully. When you stop for a pause, as here, for a turn . . . [*teacher demonstrates as she speaks*], put your foot back and pull your shoulders back. In other words, "I'm not in a hurry. I'm not trying to hide in a corner. I'm beautiful. I have everything in control." Alright?

STUDENT: Mrs. C, are you going to have music playing?

TEACHER: Yes, there will be music on Friday. It's very short time on Friday. And when you turn, this is the favorite, this is the favorite turn, kids. Now watch it. Watch it. This is the way they go here. You come along, see . . . Now you're not here to show your derrière. Therefore, if you are showing your backside on the stage at all, it's merely a quick turn in this fashion, and Miss Fisher did it, a kind of swing turn. Alright? And watch these feet. Don't ever end up with the feet like this. If you want to test this, girls, if you want to test this, look down a long corridor. Right across here some- times from one end to another and watch the kids come up the hall. And this is the way they come. All you girls. You see. Whereas if you get your feet, you get your weight, right straight over your feet and walk, one al- most in front of the other, you are doing something for yourself. Okay? 'Course, I look like a fat lady. But the point is that you look much more grace- ful, much more beautiful, if you don't do this. Are there any questions? [*Cut to CU of typing teacher.*]

TYPING TEACHER: Any questions? Everyone ready? Anyone not ready? Begin. [*Clatter of students typing as the teacher sets timer. Shots of rows of typewriter carriages, typing chart, hands on keyboards.*] . . . Stop typing, please. Alright. As I read the paragraph from the book, let's follow on what we typed. "The two men went down with me, down the long road, comma, space, and in no time at all we had reached the lake and found the path up to the spring. Period, double space, capital W. We had made the hike in less than two hours. Semicolon, space. The day was fine for it, comma, space, mild and cool, comma, space, and the three of us felt fine. Period. New para- graph, indent five, capital We. We had a snack at the spring and then picked up our guns and went on down the path. Period, double space, Capital W. We looked high and low for signs of game, comma, space, but the birds had seen us and screamed at us all the while, comma, space, so that what game there might have been near the lake hid from us or took to its heels. Period, double space. We called it a day and turned back home. Period, double space. Capital W. We had not fired one shot." [*Cut to FS of teacher in Social Studies class.*]

TEACHER: Now there are various types of families. We have the family, for instance, in which the dominant individual is the mother. Now this is a nat- ural sort of thing. You can see in many of the natural habits of, let's say, the lower animals, the mother is designed with an eye first of all of taking care of the youngster before, before it is able to function on the outside. And af-

16. A teacher discusses the matriarchal system.

ter the child or the offspring is born, she takes care of it. Now in some cases, birds, some of the animals mate for life. But frequently it's a sort of a seasonal thing, the father is finished his obligations maybe after he protects the female, and they may never see each other. They don't talk much about women in the Bible, in the Old Testament. Moses was the big shot, and the various other people that I'm not too well acquainted with. Once in a while a woman gets in just by accident. Now, that's not true in the modern Jewish family. You know who runs your household pretty well. Your mother collects the money; she takes care of the bills, pays them, she does the shopping, she handles all the economical sort of things. Once in a while she is nice and asks your father if he would like to look at the new car they are going to buy, or if she is in difficulty with you she will have your father speak to you, but ordinarily it tends to be that way in a great many of our families. So that we go back to that matriarchal system. [*Cut to CU of woman doctor speaking at a podium in auditorium to girls' assembly.*]

DOCTOR: . . . She says why if a man and a woman live together does society then say they're married? I think that's great! Because society does have a way to take care of regular, responsible, stable unions. I think promiscuity is what any society cannot tolerate . . . That's a good point. Why do you have your menstruation period? You know, there's *not* an awfully good reason for it. One of the inventors of the birth control pill up in Boston, a very eminent gynecologist, has said that he doesn't, he can't think of any good reason why women have to continue to menstruate if they don't want to.

That with the use of the pill, which really regulates your cycle—this is what the pill does: you take it for, say, twenty days, and then you don't take it for a few days. You take it, you see, according to doctor's orders. You don't just pop these things in your mouth an hour before a date. It's a medicine. [*Laughter.*] It's a medicine that you take according to a prescription. You must obtain it from a doctor and you take them just as you do any other medicine, regularly and continuously. You have had practice in controlling your feelings and impulses ever since you have been a baby. By the time you get to be a high school senior, you don't eat all the chocolate cake you want to because you don't want to get fat. You do your homework whether you want to or not. You take your college boards even if you don't feel like it that day. You don't walk into Strawbridge's and steal dresses off the rack. [*Murmur of laughter from students.*] There is no better answer. You have learned by now, as part of being human, that you can't have what you want when you want it. The girls that haven't learned that and the boys are impulsive, and they never connect what they are doing today with what happens tomorrow. [*Cut from MS of woman doctor speaking to CU of class counselor.*]

CLASS COUNSELOR: Now if this becomes style five years from now, that's something else. But right now for formal wear it is not style. It's style for a very small percentage of people. And we are going to do in this school what the majority wants. Until this kind of rule changes, this is what we're going to do, the majority wants a formal affair, which means a long gown—

BOY: The majority of students?

COUNSELOR: —or cocktail length of gown.

BOY: The majority of students?

COUNSELOR: That's right.

GIRL: Excuse me. What's the cocktail length?

COUNSELOR: Knee length.

GIRL: Here?

GIRLS' GYM TEACHER: The knee is not above the knee. That's what you want.

GIRL: But that's my knee.

GIRLS' GYM TEACHER: No, it isn't. If you fell on that part of your anatomy you would not injure your upper thigh.

COUNSELOR: Not in a dress, anyway.

GIRLS' GYM TEACHER: [*Laughs.*]

COUNSELOR: No, I think that it's nice to be individualistic, but there are certain places to be individualistic.

GIRL: I didn't mean to be individualistic.

COUNSELOR: No, I'm not criticizing. I say it's nice to be that way, but there are certain times to be that way. Uh, I think you can be individualistic in your dress, but it doesn't have to be . . .

GIRL: I happen to enjoy a short gown. I didn't know it wouldn't be accepted to the prom. I didn't do it purposely, this is what I enjoy.

COUNSELOR: What does formal mean?

SECOND GIRL (*overlapping*): You can wear that to the breakfast.

GIRL: Well, formal means dressy. I didn't think of it as a gown.

COUNSELOR: Ohhh.

GIRLS' GYM TEACHER: Formal means more than dressy.

COUNSELOR: Formal is—when you get an invitation for a formal affair it says white tie or black tie; it doesn't say that the girls or women wear any length they want. It means a floor-length gown. You get an invitation to a cocktail party, it doesn't mean a floor-length gown, it means a knee-length gown or a floor-length. But formal means a long gown for a young lady, middle-aged lady, elderly lady. See what I mean? And for a man it means a tux, and it's determined by the time of day whether it's white tie or black tie. There's no question.

GIRL: I don't know the other, really the whole story. I didn't know they weren't permitted. This is what I felt like wearing.

COUNSELOR: It isn't that they are not permitted. It's a matter of what you are going to do in a situation like this. This is offensive to the whole class.

GIRL: I didn't really mean it to be—

COUNSELOR: Well, I know you probably didn't mean it to be this, but this is what it is.

GIRLS' GYM TEACHER: We bought an atmosphere by renting the Sheraton ballroom, which is very formal—

COUNSELOR (*overlapping*): We could have had the dance in the gym—

GIRLS' GYM TEACHER: We could have had the dance in the gym and then—

GIRL: (*overlapping*): No, my, no, my—but, bu—

GIRLS' GYM TEACHER: It would have been a little different.

17. A discussion of what constitutes acceptable prom attire.

COUNSELOR: Maybe a couple of go-go girls up on the stage with a fifty-dollar orchestra and we would have had a nice dance. But this is not just a dance, this is the Senior Prom. This is formal. It's the one time in your life that your class looks so different that you don't recognize each other. It's the first chance you have to be young ladies and young gentlemen.

GIRLS' GYM TEACHER: I've had a boy ask and I've had a girl come up and say, "Can my boyfriend wear a dark suit because he cannot afford the money for the rental of a tux?" I said, "No, he can't." Because then my husband has the right to wear the beautiful suit he just bought; but we have to pay—what is it?—ten or fifteen dollars to rent a tux. Now, my husband has nothing to do with the school, but he is honoring the youngsters by coming dressed properly.

COUNSELOR: And I wouldn't think of coming without wearing a tux; I rent one every year.

GIRLS' GYM TEACHER (*overlapping*): I have to wear a long gown. I'd love to—and I can't walk in it! I can't get into the car comfortably! [*Cut from CU of teacher to girls hanging on rings in gym, being timed by the teacher.*]

GIRLS' GYM TEACHER (*checking stopwatch*): —5–6–7–8–9–40. Oh, boy! We're feminine. 4–5–6–7–8–9–Tarzan! 1–2–3–4–5–6–7–8–9–Super Tarzan! 1–2–3–4–5–6–7–8— [*Cut to brief shot of school hallway, janitor sweeping*

18. An English teacher discusses the poetry of pop music.

floor. Cut to MS of teacher, camera quickly zooming in to the cover of the LP Parsley, Sage, Rosemary and Thyme, *which she is holding.*]

ENGLISH TEACHER: The dark fellow here is Paul Simon and the blonde is Art Garfunkel. The poet is Simon. And if you felt that he's a poet now, wait till you hear some of his poetry. And you'll notice on the board that I have some things that you are familiar with: images, setting, figurative language, thematic words. And we'll be finding how, how he says what he does say. What do they want to say about our lives, and how? And I think the best way to start is by looking at one of the best of the poems, "The Dangling Conversation." That's the first one on your sheet. The process we'll use: first, we will read the poem, then listen to it. Then we'll talk about it and see how all the various poetic devices reinforce the theme, and see what you think about it, and then we'll listen to it once again, and I bet it means some- thing a little bit more to you. [*The teacher then reads the lyrics of the song.*] And notice how not only the devices reinforce the theme but also the very rhythms, the melodies, and how they use their timing. Now, when I taped these, they were from monaural and stereo records and the tape is a little fast; it's the Drama Club's tape recorder, so you have to be a little patient at the very beginning. [*Teacher turns on tape recorder. CU of reel-to-reel tape recorder as Simon and Garfunkel sing, followed by various shots of the teacher's and students' faces. As the duo sing the phrase "borders of our lives," there is a cut to a girl alone in the hallway, the camera reverse zoom-*

19. A student explains to the dean of discipline why he hit a classmate.

ing from her. With the line "Can analysis be worthwhile," there is a cut to a shot of a cleaning lady looking into cardboard boxes. The song fades out on the line "And now the room is softly faded. . . ." Cut to back of Dr. Allen's head in his office.]

DR. ALLEN: Hey, you! Turn around, pal.

BOY: Sir—

DR. ALLEN: Don't "sir" me. Don't feed me that "sir" business. You punched this guy in the mouth. On what basis?

BOY: Sir, sir, he started mouthing off, and then he started laughing, so I—

DR. ALLEN: Yeah, that doesn't give you a right to hit him. If he was a six-foot-two, two-hundred-and-fifteen-pound fullback, you wouldn't be so quick to punch him in the mouth . . . P-E-R-G—

BOY: —O-L-I-N-O.

DR. ALLEN: Where do you come in to hit this guy? . . . He has a right to erase the board—

BOY (*overlapping*): That's not what it was over.

DR. ALLEN: —Just as much as you have the right to write on it. You didn't have permission to write those names on the board, did you?

BOY: Pardon me, sir, but that wasn't what it was over.

DR. ALLEN: What was it over?

BOY: Sir, just before class started, you know, we had an argument and I didn't do nothing—

DR. ALLEN: Well, you're not supposed to do anything. You don't strike or hit anybody! [*Cut to CU of Pergolino in profile, revealing a scar along his nose.*] Levine wears glasses on top of it, yet you still hit him.

BOY: Sir, I wear glasses, too.

DR. ALLEN: That's why you're going to be suspended, for throwing the first punch, and not—

BOY: Yes, sir.

DR. ALLEN: Don't give me that "yes, sir" business! I don't like the "sir" business. You know why? Because there's no sincereness behind it. [*Cut from CU of Pergolino to CU of Eileen's mother.*]

TEACHER: And, how about the poor, poor teacher. Whoever it was?

EILEEN: I don't know . . . I don't know what it is she said that we did but—

TEACHER: —being inhuman to another human being. That's what it amounts to.

EILEEN: But all I know is that she got Sue in a lot of trouble and—

TEACHER: Sue who?

EILEEN: The other girl. And, and I don't think Sue had any—she told, she said that we locked her in the closet. I mean—

TEACHER: You mean Sue and you?

EILEEN: I mean the class. Nobody locked her in the closet as far as I know. Look, I would've— If she had been locked in the closet I sure would've heard that and turned around and looked.

TEACHER: She may have had a little more control than that. That much noise, it's a little embarrassing to her. She wasn't going to call everybody's attention to it.

EILEEN: It wasn't fair! Like, Sue was just messing around, just as much as us. The rest of the classroom—and now Sue's in so much trouble just because of that one teacher; and because Sue got in trouble I blame a lot on that teacher 'cause Sue—

TEACHER (*overlapping*): Now, let's keep looking at that because again this is my concern, Eileen. Sue got in trouble because of the teacher. Sue did nothing to help? Whoever Sue is, I don't know. I'm glad you didn't answer me when I asked her name because it's easier to talk.

EILEEN: Just messing around like everybody else.

MOTHER: Look, can you tell me what messing around means? This is what I've been trying to find out for months. Every time you would say "messing around," what does it actually consist of?

EILEEN: I don't know. Everyone talking, laughing—

MOTHER: But just plain talking and laughing isn't offensive.

EILEEN: Oh, we were catching a book or something.

MOTHER: Oh, you threw a book around—

EILEEN: Not just me!

MOTHER: But whoever was involved.

EILEEN: I know I did a lot. I did a lot. I talked back a lot.

MOTHER: Did you talk back to the teacher?

EILEEN: Yeah.

MOTHER: And this is what you call "messing around."

EILEEN: Well—

MOTHER: Isn't it more disrespectful—?

EILEEN (*overlapping*): What I did, what I did was disrespectful. What the rest, what everybody else did was messing around . . . I don't know.

TEACHER: You see what Mother is saying, at least what I'm saying, I think what your mother is saying is that we hope, Eileen, that you don't set your standards by the so-called everybody else, but you set your own standards by what you know is the thing to do. I repeat, there's no doubt the teacher was not holding the class, was not doing the job that you, you think she should have done, from what you say. I'll accept that. But, you know, who breaks the circle when things go around and around and around? Someone has to be mature enough to move out of the circle and into the straight, right? Someone has got to break away from it. You're intelligent, you're mature, you have the background. You can be the one who can do it. Why don't you offer the positive kind of leadership that you can. That you know you have, that I know you have, that Mother knows you have. You can be a real force in any group, Eileen. Can't you? The kids rally around you a bit—

EILEEN: Well, not really.

TEACHER: I've seen you in the lunchroom.

MOTHER: Oh, Eileen can. Yes, Eileen can—

TEACHER (*overlapping*): Your daughter is a potential leader. It shows wherever she is. I've seen her once in a while in a group. You can see who the leader is in a group. And she has it.

MOTHER: Eileen has a very set mind and if she—

TEACHER (*overlapping*): Good!

MOTHER: —decides that something should be done, this is what she pursues. This I know about her.

TEACHER: I think that's good.

MOTHER: I think it's excellent in many ways. But I've often said to her, "Eileen, use your determination for right. And as long as you do, you will be all right." And one thing, this is the one thing that bothers me so much, the main thing in our home has always been respect for an adult. I was brought up that way; my husband was. And we've been trying to teach our children the same thing. To me, I think one of the worst offenses is being disrespectful to an older person. Irregardless of what the condition may be. You can say the same thing in a pleasant manner that you can in an offensive way. And this is one thing that's disturbed me recently about Eileen. That even at home, now, she—I don't say that the language that she uses is wrong, but it's the manner that a sentence is brought forth. And I told her, "Eventually, Eileen, this is going to hurt you outside." And finally it has. [*Cut to MS of guidance counselor talking with student and her parents.*]

GUIDANCE COUNSELOR: And I think that you would kind of have to decide, Arlene, how you would feel about where you stood in your college class. Whether you would rather be in an easier school and toward the top of the class or in a harder school and toward the bottom of the class.

ARLENE: I think I would gain more by being like in the middle or the top than at the very bottom, not being able, you know, to keep up with everybody else.

GUIDANCE COUNSELOR: Do you want a college course, then, dear, where at the end of four years you would be finished with your education and able to go out and make a living, or do you want the kind of course where at the end of four years it is likely that you would be going on with your education?

ARLENE: I'm not sure right now. I think I want to go on to four years of col-

20. A guidance counselor discusses college plans with a student and her parents.

lege and, maybe if I become a teacher, stop and then I can always take courses again. Go higher. Get a higher degree.

GUIDANCE COUNSELOR: Uh-huh.

ARLENE: Or, I think, uh, a social worker or psychologist has to go five years—

GUIDANCE COUNSELOR: Or six years, or seven years. It would depend on what you chose after that.

ARLENE: I don't think I want to go for more than maybe five or six years, or more than five.

GUIDANCE COUNSELOR: Well, I think you've given me kind of a pretty comprehensive idea of what you're looking for. [*Turning to the father*] And then I would have to ask you, sir, the hard, hard question of how much you could contribute to your daughter's education?

FATHER: Well, uh, that's a hard question to say because if she lives away from home, then it's a different story altogether. And if she's at home, it's another story. But the way she's talking, she doesn't want to stay home. So I would say, about maybe about a thousand dollars, fifteen hundred is about the best I could give her a year to go away to college.

GUIDANCE COUNSELOR: Uh-huh. Then it would seem to me that, Arlene, that the most realistic way to plan it would be to think about where you could go if your father could give you a thousand dollars to fifteen hundred dollars, and then to try for scholarships at some other places that might be somewhat more expensive. But I think you kind of have to plan for where you would go if you didn't get any financial aid from someone. I mean, you always have to—you can look at the brighter side about where you would like to go. You can have all your dream schools, but then at the bottom you ought to have some college of last resort where you could be sure that you would go if none of your dreams came true. [*Cut from CU of guidance counselor to CU of Rhona's mother.*]

MOTHER: Rhona is the recipient of a ten-thousand-dollar Hero Scholarship to any college anywhere in the country she wants to go.

FATHER: I guess, I'm not saying she is college material, but at least she can have some type of education following—

MOTHER: She can go to any college and do whatever she wanted to.

COUNSELOR (*to Rhona*): Tell me again. Do you think you want to go to college? Do you think, what courses—

RHONA: Yes.

FATHER (*overlapping*): You see, Dr. Boodish? You're lying to the man, now! Now, talk, you don't want to go to college!

RHONA: Well, I do! But not the kind of college that you want me to.

COUNSELOR: What kind of college do you want to go to?

RHONA: I want to be a cosmetician.

COUNSELOR: Cosmetician? Well, that's not a college, is it?

RHONA: Well, it's a beauty culture school.

COUNSELOR: It's a beauty culture school. It's not a college. The requirements for that are different than for college.

RHONA: Yes.

COUNSELOR: You don't have any foreign language.

RHONA: No.

COUNSELOR: You don't have any algebra; you don't have geometry. So that actually, as far as going to college, you're not even prepared to go to college. Do you feel that you are disappointing your parents by not going to college? Now, tell me the truth.

RHONA: Yes.

COUNSELOR: You feel your parents are disappointed?

RHONA: My father.

COUNSELOR: Your father is. Tell me, would you feel better if you knew your father really accepted the fact that you didn't go to college? Do you feel a bit guilty for not, for not going to college?

FATHER: You say—

RHONA: Well—

COUNSELOR: That you are disappointing your parents?

RHONA: I'm disappointing my father, but I don't think I feel guilty about not going.

COUNSELOR: You don't feel guilty at all.

RHONA: Not guilty.

COUNSELOR: I see.

RHONA: It's my life.

COUNSELOR: It's your life.

RHONA: I feel that what I want to be is more important than what he desires me to be.

COUNSELOR: I see. But you know your parents are disappointed? Your father in particular. You can't undo the past. Even if somebody has made a mistake and been wrong and unfair, you can't undo the past. The only thing that you can do is try to do better in the present so that the future will be better. So what I'm suggesting to you: work as hard as you can, do the best you can, and confer with Mr. Schuster about this and let's see what happens by the end of the semester. Okay? You go back to class now, or are you through?

RHONA: I'm through.

FATHER: Thanks again, Dr. Boodish.

COUNSELOR: You're welcome.

RHONA: Thank you very much.

COUNSELOR: You're welcome and goodbye. Oh, incidentally, how about gym?

FATHER: This is the strongest girl in the school.

COUNSELOR: What are you going to do to pass gym?

RHONA: Well, I have to do my makeups.

21. A counselor talks with a student's family about her performance.

COUNSELOR: And that's necessary for graduation, you know.

FATHER: It is?

COUNSELOR: It is. She has to pass—

FATHER: I just wish, Dr. Boodish, she was as smart as she is strong . . . Alright, thank you, Doctor.

MOTHER: Very strong girl.

COUNSELOR: Tell me. I'm going to ask your daughter a question. How did you feel about that remark that your father just made?

RHONA: I liked it.

COUNSELOR: You liked it?

RHONA: Yeah.

COUNSELOR: Good. Okay. [*Family files out the door. Cut to a school hallway, a janitor walking down the corridor with a mop over his shoulder.*]

VOICE OVER PUBLIC ADDRESS SYSTEM: There is a car in the students' driveway, blocking the exit of two other cars. [*Cut to MS of four teachers eating lunch in the school cafeteria.*]

TEACHER 1 (*offscreen*): I don't believe in giving—

TEACHER WITH DARK FRAME GLASSES: Give them jobs.

TEACHER (*offscreen*): —I don't believe in giving; let them earn it. I think people have got—there's too much relief going on, that's all. We are too much to a point where they are giving all the time.

TEACHER WITH SILVER FRAME GLASSES (*overlapping*): You're all hung up, you're all hung up on the Protestant ethic.

TEACHER (*offscreen*): There are so many facets to this. I don't believe in what Bill says. I don't believe 100 percent in what Bill says—

TEACHER WITH DARK FRAME GLASSES (*overlapping*): No, I can't think—

TEACHER 1 (*offscreen*): —about giving things away. I don't think anybody appreciates anything. Look at your own children. When you give 'em, do they really appreciate it? Sometimes if they work for it a little bit, Bill, they appreciate these things more.

TEACHER IN GRAY SUIT (*back to camera*): Look at this money that we are giving away to the world—foreign aid. They're laughing at us.

TEACHER (*offscreen*): They're cramming it right down your throat.

TEACHER IN GRAY SUIT: Actually, that foreign aid business—we're really giving money to the guys that are buying from the rich people and from the manufacturers over here. That's where the money's going. It's not just being given to them; it's going the other way. But the thing is, there is so much money being wasted. [*Cut to shot of chart showing evolution. Camera pans left across room to Dr. Allen in front of a class at his desk.*]

DR. ALLEN: Yes. W. H. Silvers. Now what was he trying to do? What was his purpose? Yes, Adele?

ADELE: He was trying to establish an eight-hour workday [*inaudible*].

DR. ALLEN: Yes, he wanted higher wages; he wanted an eight-hour workday, but he tried to unite—this is the important thing about him—he tried to unite *all* labor unions of the country into a federation membership. What on the horizon or what existed that forced labor to turn to collective bargaining? What was there a lack of?

GIRL (*offscreen*): Communication—

MR. ALLEN: Yes, communication. Lack of security, concern for the job. The important thing is this: let's get to the beginnings—first of all, there was the lack of security . . . Second of all, there was a lack of communication— the attitude of the employ*ees* or of the employ*ers* toward the employ*ees*, with regard to working conditions, with regard to living conditions, with regard to wages—very little communication. [*Cut to students in a class-*

22. A teacher surveys student attitudes regarding class and race.

*room listening to another teacher. As the teacher, one of those at the lunch-
room table, talks, the camera pans to him in CU.*]

TEACHER: Alright, we have evidently a great imbalance in American society. We have, on the one hand, we have an affluent society—and that's one
America—and on the other hand we have another America—and by the
way, that's the name of a good book by Michael Harrington, called *The Other
America.* And what is this other America? Another America that's not—
America of poverty. America that's not sharing in the affluence of American society. And King was there to try to uplift this other America. You
know what the Department of Labor says should be the comfort level of a
family of four—a man, a wife, and two children? What they should earn to
be comfortable. Not moderately comfortable, not, you know, affluent, but
just moderately comfortable in our society. Know what the figure is, any
idea what it is? Christine? How much?

CHRISTINE: Nine thousand.

TEACHER: Yes, a little over nine thousand dollars. So you can imagine. Do
you know what percent of the American population earns over nine thousand dollars? It's not the majority. Let's determine some of the attitudes in
this class and see how we come out. Alright, how many of you would be a
member of a club where a minority of the members of the club were Negro? How many would accept that situation? You would be a member of a

club if the minority of the members were Negro? Alright. . . . Okay, fine, put your hands down. How many would not be a member of a club? . . . Alright. How many would be a member of the club where half the members were Negro members, the other half were white? . . . Alright. Put your hands down. And how many would not be a member of that, that club? . . . Alright. Don't—remember, there's no right or wrong answer; it just, I'm just trying to determine what attitudes are. [*Cut to FS of school choir.*]

CHORAL STUDENTS (*singing scales*): Do Mi So Do—

TEACHER: You forgot so soon? Go—

STUDENTS: Do Mi So Do So Mi Do Mi So Mi Do So Mi Do So Mi So Do— [*Cut to CU of teacher listening to student's comments. Cut to student discussion group, one boy speaking.*]

MARK: —'cause Northeast is such a cloistered and secluded place. [*Inaudible comment offscreen.*] It is! The policy at Northeast is to avoid conflict— [*Teacher and students talk simultaneously.*]

TEACHER: Oh, there are good points, Mark, but can't you find anything good about this school?

MARK: It's got lots of room, except not for as many kids as are in it. It's very nice, well ventilated. [*Laughter.*] I can't say anything about the people who go to it, though, really. With very few exceptions. And most of the people I have, I can make those exceptions about are right in this room, with maybe five or six exceptions. And the rest of the school stinks, in my estimation. You know, I'm not qualified to make, you know, gigantic judgments about the school, but I think in its attitude toward education and its relations with the world today this school is miserable. It's cloistered, it's secluded, it's completely sheltered from everything that's going on in the world. And I think it's wrong and has to be changed and I think that's our purpose here. And not to talk about films.

TEACHER: A lot of you are so negative that I can see someday somebody coming up and saying, "You know, you kids just don't belong. You spoil Northeast; Northeast High would be nice—"

MARK: That's just what happened! Mr. Simon pulled me in to his office and said, "You don't look like a Northeaster, son." [*Several students talk simultaneously.*]

SECOND BOY: I think one thing that has to be changed around is the fact that you have these, see like, you have these variables existing within the school system in Northeast. And the thing about it that makes it so alien

23. A student describes the moral vacuity of the school.

or, or fails toward us is the fact that you have to, like, conform to these ideas which people like Mr. Simon, Dr. Allen—

TEACHER (*overlapping*): Why do you pick on him? Alright, he's got problems— [*Laughter.*]

SECOND BOY: I would also like to say that—

TEACHER: I would like to say that he is in a position where maybe you'll find others who are not of the same opinion. The only difference is that he has a job as vice principal that is in contact with the students. He handles student activities. Now, I'm not saying that Mr. Simon is the only one that says these things. The rule, the rule is, is very—I think you'll agree—consistent among many members of the faculty. And don't just pinpoint Mr. Simon. He may be right, he may be wrong, but he's the one voicing it all the time. But he's voicing it, a quite common feeling.

SECOND BOY: Well, I'll say something good about the school. I'll say that scientifically and technologically Northeast is an advanced school apart from other high schools in the country.

TEACHER: A compliment! I'm going to faint.

SECOND BOY: Apart from other high schools in the country, possibly, possibly in the world also. This school in those, in that particular field, is the leader. As Mark has said, morally, socially, this school is a garbage can. Let's face the facts.

TEACHER: Morally? Completely?

SECOND BOY: Yes.

TEACHER: Well, I venture to say that the moral problems you have here in general are in existence in most schools.

SECOND BOY: You see, the trouble is—

TEACHER: Perhaps more so. I don't think it's that bad. [*Cut to CU of teacher who had read "Casey at the Bat" earlier.*]

TEACHER: Now, boys and girls, we have a very new plaque out in the hall, if you've noticed, outside the main office, framed, which has a special thought for the day, written to attract your attention. Now I think it's very fine. But, as always, we have on our bulletin another thought for the day, and this one, especially in my field, is very important, but in any kind of research to have the right words for what you have to say in these days, to express things so that people do not misunderstand you. "The dictionary is the only place where 'success' comes before 'work.'" . . . For the tenth- and eleventh-grade boys who signed up for Food Experiences for Boys, you must go to room 130 this week to verify your registration. The Spectator Club will discuss Martin Luther King's assassination today at 3:15 in Room Two-twenty-eight. [*Cut to shot of school hallway crowded with students. A policeman keeps watch, holding his nightstick. Another shot of the crowded hallway. Cut to LS of school auditorium filled with students, several boys in drag as cheerleaders skipping down an aisle and onto the stage. Girls dressed as football players ascend stage from the other side.*]

CHORUS: Northeast Mambo! Olé! Olé! Northeast Mambo! Olé! Olé! Northeast Mambo! Olé! Olé! [*Cut to MS of gynecologist at microphone in front of auditorium filled with boys.*]

GYNECOLOGIST: —And in general, the more a fellow gets into bed with more different girls, the more insecure he is. And this shows up actually later, in all the divorce statistics and in the marriage statistics. The more intercourse either a boy or a girl has had prior to marriage, the less likely they are to make successful marriage partners, husbands, wives, and the greater—in other words, you can graph it right on a graph, the more girls a fellow's gotten into bed with or vice versa, the higher the divorce rate, the greater the sexual inadequacy, and the failure of compatibility. As with anything else, the real pros in the field keep it to themselves and aren't profligate. [*Taking a written question*] "Is it possible to impregnate a girl by rubbing the surface of the vagina?" With what? Your nose? No. [*Laughter and applause*

24. The gynecologist cracks a joke in the boys' assembly.

from boys.] And I might add, this brings up one other good point. This brings up one other darn good point. Virginity is a state of mind. By that, I have seen several girls who have been physiologically, or by physical examination, virgins; the hymen, the mucous membrane covering the so-called, the cherry—it's called the cherry because it produces red fluid when it's busted—is intact. I have seen girls whose hymens were so small that I couldn't pass a finger through them. [*Laughter.*] In fact, I once saw a girl— I happen to be a gynecologist and get paid to do it. [*Laughter and applause from boys.*] I once saw a girl who had rickets when she was a baby, whose bony structure was so deformed that I could get my finger in this way but not broad ways—her bony structure down there—who had succeeded in becoming pregnant. Sperm happen to be very actively motile. They have a good ability to move on their own. And many a girl has become pregnant through spray. If you are not prepared to handle the responsibility of that girl's becoming pregnant or having a baby, you've got two choices: one, make sure there's adequate protection to prevent having a baby; two, if there isn't, don't. Because you are just as much responsible, if not a little bit more, than the girl if a pregnancy ensues. Nature sets us up that the male is the aggressor and the female is the passive in this set of circumstances. It takes a girl longer to get sexually aroused than it does a boy. This is the nature of the beast. [*Cut to images from sex education film of animated diagrams of the female reproductive system.*]

SEX EDUCATION FILM NARRATOR (MALE): We can get a better idea of the relationship of the fallopian tubes and ovaries if we view them from the front. Under normal conditions an ovum matures in the ovary, then passes down the fallopian tube on its way to the uterus. When gonorrhea spreads upward, the infection can cause damage, which blocks the fallopian tubes, sometimes causing severe complications. As in a boy, untreated gonorrhea can make a girl sterile, unable to become a mother . . . However, a girl with gonorrhea can become a mother; but this creates another problem. When the baby is ready to be born, there is danger that she may transmit the disease to the child when it passes out of her body. [*Cut to schoolyard, a two-shot of the gym teacher talking to a former student now in military uniform, while boys in gym uniforms play volleyball and basketball in the background.*]

GYM TEACHER: You didn't get hit, eh? Good. Glad to see you. You have to go back? When do you get out?

BOY IN UNIFORM: First of September.

TEACHER: That's terrific. September? Oh! September '69.

BOY: You remember Halsie?

TEACHER: Is Halsie back?

BOY: He came back. He was wounded.

TEACHER: I heard that. I didn't see him.

BOY: Pepe was wounded also. Saw a lot of guys—Pepe got hurt, he was really—

TEACHER: Pepe was shot up pretty bad. Uh, Pepe was a guy—I guess about five yards from one of them mines in one of those little holes they dig, and they popped up with an automatic rifle on him, opened up. Really got him in the foot, pretty bad. And he turned around and he killed the guy, but he's done for soccer or anything like that forever. He can never play that again.

BOY (*overlapping*): He was good.

TEACHER: Yeah. He was a good soccer player. He's through with that. And first they thought they might have to amputate. But he was down the naval hospital for quite a long time, and then he came up with a cast and crutches, and then he came up with a cane, and the next time I saw him, this last time I saw him, he was walking pretty well, but he'll never be able to hit with that foot or anything 'cause they're rebuilding it. Yeah. He was pretty—when he first came back, he was pretty melancholy-like, you know? And natu-

25. The gym teacher talks with a former student returning from Vietnam.

rally so. But I think he's got himself adjusted now. He seems to be alright, I'm glad to say. I'm glad you didn't get hit. [*Cut to LS of boys' gym, boys in gym volleying with large ball.*]

BOYS (*as they pile on the ball*): I've got it! I've got it! [*Cut to student mission controller in space flight simulation.*]

STUDENT: You're almost there! Jan, you have nineteen seconds, Jan. 18–17–16–15–14–13–12–11–10–9-8-7-6-5-4-3-2-1. That's it. You've landed. Hurrah!! Yay! [*Applause.*]

STUDENT: Cherry, disconnect audio, please.

TEACHER (MR. MONTGOMERY): Is the hatch clear?

STUDENT: The hatch is clear, yeah.

STUDENT: Here we go.

MR. MONTGOMERY: Alright.

STUDENT: Okay. [*Applause as hatch opens and student astronauts emerge.*]

STUDENT: How're you doin'?

STUDENT ASTRONAUT: I've got something for you, man.

STUDENT: Thanks.

STUDENT: Good going.

STUDENT ASTRONAUT: Hello, Dr. Haller!

DR. HALLER: Hi! How do you feel?

STUDENT ASTRONAUT: Great!

DR. HALLER: Do you? Oh.

STUDENT ASTRONAUT: Terrific.

DR. HALLER: You made it! We're so proud of you.

STUDENT: The beard—

VOICE: He's got the strength of a bull.

STUDENT ASTRONAUT: Mr. Gordon. Good seeing you again.

STUDENT: Jan, you look really good.

VOICE: You look grizzly, Jan, real grizzly. Congratulations, Jan.

STUDENT: Mr. Montgomery, hug all three of them now.

MR. MONTGOMERY: I'm going to help get, I'm gonna just start getting this thing off him, okay? [*Teacher helps remove the helmets from their spacesuits.*]

STUDENT: Look at that beard, man! Whoa! The beard . . . Hey, the beard.

VOICES (*simultaneously*): Hey! Fabulous. I'll talk to you later. Thanks a lot. Hold on! Hold on. Scott! . . . Scott! Good job. Scott, man, Scott, how're you doing? Scott! [*Cheers.*]

MR. MONTGOMERY: We received a telegram this morning and I want to read it at this time. "Students and faculty of Northeast High School, Attention Robert Montgomery. I should like to take this opportunity to extend my best wishes to each of you for your continued success with Project SPARC. Specifically, my heartiest congratulations to astronauts Jan Gabin, Harvey Rubin, and Scott Cherry, upon completion of 193 hours of simulated flight." The telegram comes from L. Gordon Cooper, NASA, Astronaut. [*Applause.*] This is man Number One, Number Two, Number Three. Okay— [*Various voices as the astronauts move through the crowd. Cut to drum major and school marching band rehearsal.*]

DRUM MAJOR (*marching out onto stage*): Drums! Roll 'em. [*The band plays two ragged choruses of "Hey, Look Me Over." Cut to Dr. Haller at podium at teacher's meeting in the auditorium.*]

PRINCIPAL HALLER: Now, let me read you this one, if I'm able to get through it. This is written from, and I might say that the letter that I'm about to read is from Bob Walters. Bob Walters, as Fran could tell you, she could write his biography, was a boy without parents who might have been a nobody. He

26. The principal reads the letter from a former student now in Vietnam.

certainly was not a high academic student; he was most average or sub-average in many ways. But a few teachers who cared [*insert two-shot of the teacher who taught the lesson on "The Dangling Conversation" and the teacher who led the film discussion group, followed by another of the girls' gym teacher*] made a great difference in this boy's life. His letter comes on stationery marked USS Okinawa. I hope I can get through it, if I don't, Hy, you'll have to go on. "Dear Dr. Haller, I have only a few hours before I go. Today I will take a plane trip from this ship. I pray that I'll make it back. But it is all in God's hands now. You see, I am going with three other men. We are going to be dropped behind the DMZ, the Demilitarized Zone. The reason for telling you this is that all my insurance money will be given for that scholarship I once started but never finished, if I don't make it back. I am only insured for $10,000. Maybe it could help someone. I have been trying to become a Big Brother in Vietnam, but it is very hard to do. I have to write back and forth to San Diego, California, and that takes time. I only hope that I am good enough to become one. God only knows. I really pray that the young men in your cooking classes will use this change of learning very well. Thank you, Dr. Haller, for helping these men become good, very fine cooks"—he should have said "Thank you, Mrs. C." "My personal family usually doesn't understand me. They don't see, they don't understand why I have to do what I do do. They say that I'm a real nut to do such work, but [*turning page*] . . . thus they say: 'Don't you value life? Are you crazy?' My answer is 'Yes. But I value all the lives of South Vietnam and the free world so that they and all of us can live in peace.' Am I wrong, Dr. Haller? If I do my best all the time and believe in what I do, believe that what I do is right, that is all I can do. Dr. Haller, if anything happens to me, James C. Heckwicker," I think it is, "will send you a telegram and in time he will send you the money. Please don't say anything to Mrs. C"—but I did—"she would only worry over me. I am not worth it. I am only a body doing a job. In closing, I thank everyone for what they all have done for me. Yours truly, Bob Walters. Thank you all again very much. Please forgive my handwriting. I am a little jumpy. Please understand." Now when you get a letter like this, to me it means that we are very successful at Northeast High School. I think you will agree with me.

[*Brief fade to black followed by end credits: Produced and Directed by Frederick Wiseman. Photographed by Richard Leiterman. Editor: Frederick Wiseman. Associate Editor: Carter Howard. Assistant Cameraman: David Eames. This film is dedicated to Katherine Taylor and The New World Foundation whose interest, encouragement, and support made it possible. © 1968 Frederick Wiseman. Copyright renewed 1996 Frederick Wiseman.*]

Welfare (1975)

Welfare was filmed at New York City's obviously overburdened Waverly Welfare Center in lower Manhattan. Shot over a four-week period in February and March of 1973 and released in 1975, the ironically titled *Welfare* presents a series of encounters between welfare workers and applicants and clients. The film views the welfare system as an overloaded bureaucratic nightmare in which genuine need is sometimes indistinguishable from freeloading. This was Wiseman's lengthiest film to date, and its running time of 167 minutes is itself an expression of the Kafkaesque bureaucracy through which welfare applicants must navigate. Significantly, after we enter the Center at the beginning of the film, Wiseman includes no further exterior shots in his trademark transitional montages; instead, the camera remains indoors, emphasizing the engulfing nature of the welfare process. It is not coincidental that, chronologically, *Welfare* comes between *Primate* (1974) and *Meat* (1976), Wiseman's darkest films, both of which depict a determinist worldview that is consistent with the treatment of some of the welfare clients. The film is careful to show clients from a variety of racial and ethnic backgrounds, and racial tensions and class difference, two aspects of American society explored in varying degree throughout Wiseman's oeuvre, emerge here as consistent themes.

[*Title.*]

PHOTOGRAPHERS (*several voices*): Okay. Okay, that's it. Just have a seat. [*Montage of faces of welfare clients having their photographs taken.*] Okay. Okay, just have a seat. Okay, Mr. Hamilton, just have a seat. Hold your head straight, dear . . . Okay, have a seat . . . Okay, sir, just have a seat. Sientese. Have a seat. Have a seat. Okay, just have a seat, please. Okay, have a seat.

27. A Native American client looks for some help.

Mr. Wells, would you mind removing your hat, please? Okay, fine. Okay, have a seat, please. [*Exterior of Waverly Welfare Center, New York City. Cut to a closer view showing clients waiting in line for doors to open. Inside the building, clients in waiting room, some sitting, others standing about. Several shots of individual clients and workers calling out cases.*]

WORKERS (*several voices*): Three-A . . . Alexander Carswell . . . Four-C.

NATIVE AMERICAN CLIENT: Indian people here, you don't like here, you know. I'm a, I'm Apache from Oklahoma, you know. [*Cut to CU of Native American client.*] They don't want to give you nothin' because I'm a Indian. What's happened to the Indian people? You know, what's happened? He no good? No good? I'm a human being like anybody. Like a white or black or something [*three insert shots of other clients*] like that.

ANOTHER CLIENT (*offscreen*): —Get outta here, outta here. You Indian—

NATIVE AMERICAN: You understand? They don't want to help him, you know, they don't want me helping, 'cause I'm an Indian people, you know. And I don't see too many Indian people in this country, you know, in New York. He go—I escaped from this reservation you got in Washington, you know. I takin' off from there [*cut back to CU of Native American*], because in there like a, like a camp, a concentration camp. He take all my land, you know, and puts me in a reservation like a jail, you know, and now he don't dig it too much. He don't dig it. The government, he don't like any Indian people. You understand? He preyed into Indian people, you know. And so now, every time I go, he say, you Indian, get outta here. I don't want see Indian in this place. That's no good. You know, you know, that it's no good. Because, you know, if he supposed—I'm a human being, you know, like anyone, like you, like anyone, like any people, you know.

WORKER: Call Social Security.

NATIVE AMERICAN: Yes, ma'am.

WORKER: Now call 39 Broadway.

NATIVE AMERICAN: Okay, ma'am.

WORKER: So far as we know, they have made no provisions to issue ID cards to their claimants.

NATIVE AMERICAN: Right. That's what I tell you.

WORKER: But, on the other hand, welfare cannot give you one, either, because you're not on our rolls. The best thing for you to do when you get your check is to go to a check cashing place, or maybe your landlord will cash it.

NATIVE AMERICAN: Yes, ma'am.

WORKER: Keep going to SSI until they come up with some ID so that you'll be able to cash your check.

NATIVE AMERICAN: Young lady, if they don't give you the pictures, you don't get—

WORKER: Sir, sir. We cannot give it to you because your checks don't come from us.

NATIVE AMERICAN: Wait a minute.

WORKER: Your check does not come from us so we cannot give you an ID card. You go in with an ID card from one department, and you're getting your check from another department, it's not going to help you.

NATIVE AMERICAN: I know, but I need the picture for change my check.

WORKER: Sorry, we can't give it to you. You'll have to get it from them. And in the meantime—

NATIVE AMERICAN: She, she told me yesterday—

WORKER: —and in the meantime, try the check cashing place.

NATIVE AMERICAN: Ma'am, no. Listen, ma'am, you know. I just go in yesterday, in there, you know, walking, because I ain't got no money. I walking all the way up from Broadway, 39, and I explain my situation. He say he don't give you a Medicaid card in there, and he don't give you ID card there, you know. He say go to Fourteenth Street and maybe he can solution your case, you know, and maybe help.

WORKER (*overlapping*): Nevertheless, this is a problem that you will have to take up with them. Waverly is no longer responsible.

NATIVE AMERICAN: But what can I do now for change my check?

WORKER: You'll have to go back where you got your check. You have your check in your pocket?

NATIVE AMERICAN: You know, I just, I just tried, you know, to get the, this picture because—

WORKER: I've explained to you several times that we cannot give it to you. Sorry.

NATIVE AMERICAN: Right. I know. I know so my check coming and the check coming—

WORKER: Take it to the check cashing place.

NATIVE AMERICAN: Yes, but—

WORKER: And in the meantime—

NATIVE AMERICAN: If don't have ID, they don't give it to me, young lady.

WORKER: Keep going to 39 Broadway and tell them you're having difficulty cashing your check and you need some kind of ID.

NATIVE AMERICAN: Are you said I telling, yesterday, I telling I suppose to get a picture here—

WORKER: We can't give it to you here.

NATIVE AMERICAN: —because, you know, you know, he don't, he don't, he don't give it to me. He don't want to give it to me. How I going change the check?

WORKER: I'm sorry. Waverly can't either. Waverly is not responsible.

NATIVE AMERICAN: So I suppose to—you loose around the ear.

WORKER: Thank you.

NATIVE AMERICAN: Yeah. So, you know, what I can do now?

WORKER: Go back to 39 Broadway and when you get your check, go to the check cashing place.

NATIVE AMERICAN (*overlapping*): And explain to him the situation again? Okay. Thank you very much, young lady. [*Cut to CU of another worker interviewing couple.*]

WORKER: So you were out of the apartment in November?

FEMALE CLIENT: That's right.

MALE CLIENT (LARRY): November twenty-eighth, to be exact.

WORKER: November twenty-eighth, and then you went . . . But over here it says you went to the halfway house December twenty-seventh. That's a month later.

LARRY: Yes.

FEMALE CLIENT: Okay. We were staying—

LARRY: What, what she's saying is, what did we do from November twenty-eighth to—

WORKER: To December twenty-seventh. Where were you?

LARRY: I was in and out of, uh, jail. It was, like, one day at a time. Like, they would, you know, they would, uh—

WORKER: But, but—it says you were only in jail for one day.

LARRY: I know that, but previous to that, too, uh, you know, like, they just would—we went into restaurants and we were just eating and not paying our bill because we didn't have any money. So they picked us up, you know, like on that and we would spend the night in jail or something and then they would release us out in the street again.

FEMALE CLIENT: And we were staying in a, and, we were staying with some, a friend of mine.

WORKER: When you worked for the, the department—

LARRY: Yeah.

WORKER: You know, you were making good money.

LARRY: That's right. It was like I stayed in each position for about a year or a year and a half. I kept taking the civil service exams. That's how I got promoted. I started as a union clerk grade 3, then I went to supervising clerk, and then I became, uh, each case, uh—

WORKER: See, we haven't—

LARRY: So, in each case, a year, two years, you know, in each job there, I think, you know—

WORKER: Yeah. We haven't got your accounts. Right? We've just got the letter from the bank saying that your accounts are closed.

FEMALE CLIENT: He lost the passbook.

LARRY: I can't, can't we just—

WORKER: No. No, wait a minute. And then you're telling me you only had these amounts in each account. But you were making relatively good money. I can't understand how—

LARRY: One hundred and ninety-eight dollars in rent was one item.

WORKER: I know. I know.

FEMALE CLIENT: And what about for food? We had to spend on food.

LARRY: That's right. We spent money on entertainment.

WORKER: What kind of entertainment?

LARRY: Movies.

FEMALE CLIENT: Movies.

LARRY: Drinking, now and then.

WORKER: How come you've never worked?

FEMALE CLIENT: I'm an epileptic and I can't work.

WORKER: Okay.

LARRY: We had, we had to pay electric there, and so on.

WORKER: Have you got a medical—

FEMALE CLIENT: I don't have any medical because my doctor, uh—

LARRY: We have Medicaid. That's the only thing.

FEMALE CLIENT: Medicaid is the only thing I have.

WORKER: Are you under any medication?

FEMALE CLIENT: No, I don't take any medication because the doctor told me I don't need it. It's just that I got to take it easy and relax and I'm not allowed to work. I wish I could. I would work.

LARRY: They gave us the Medicaid because we, you know, we're in this situation.

FEMALE CLIENT: That's right.

WORKER: Well, the reason I'm asking you all these questions—

LARRY: Yeah.

WORKER: It's true you're an emergency. So we are giving you the emergency interview. But every aspect of, you know, of your application has to be gone into. Okay? Okay. I'm surprised you asked that being that you were a supervisor in social services. You should know.

LARRY: Well, you know, uh, sure, but, yeah, at the, at the moment I'm thinking in terms of, uh, answering your questions and of, uh, you know—.

WORKER: Did you ever get Social Security under your father's—

FEMALE CLIENT: My father I don't know because my father was in the army and I haven't seen him since I'm six years old.

WORKER: I see. Where's your mother?

FEMALE CLIENT: My mother's on Pelham Parkway. She gave me a little money and then she told me go hang myself or commit suicide and every time I contact her she hangs up the phone. The counselor at the rehabilitation center tried and she claims she doesn't know me. He tried. My sister tried. I got money from my sister, a little bit, and then forget it. She didn't help me and neither did my mother, and my mother doesn't want any part of me. I tried calling her, and every single time she hangs up the phone, or go hang yourself or sleep in a jail. That's why, that's why I can't get any response. My sister's out in Stony Point. I asked if I could stay up with her. I can't because she works. Her husband—

LARRY: If we could stay with relatives, we'd be glad to do so.

FEMALE CLIENT: We sure would. I've tried my aunt who lives on Fourteenth Street, and my grandfather's got cataracts and he needs to stay in the house, so I can't ask her for help.

WORKER: Did you both apply for the SSI?

LARRY: Yes, we have.

WORKER: You both went down there?

LARRY: Yes.

WORKER: You're just living together. You're not married?

FEMALE CLIENT: No.

WORKER: Right.

FEMALE CLIENT: No . . . If I knew where my husband was, I wouldn't even be around here. I don't know where he is. I haven't seen him.

WORKER: Did you—

FEMALE CLIENT: I have a partial disability on my hand. I have cerebral palsy.

28. A couple explain their emergency situation.

I used to wear a brace . . . I'm epileptic, too. I used to take Dilantin, but the doctor took me off of it.

WORKER: You're legally married?

FEMALE CLIENT: Yes, I am. I don't know where my husband is.

WORKER: Well, did you ever go to court?

FEMALE CLIENT: No.

WORKER: Are you divorced?

FEMALE CLIENT: No, I'm not.

LARRY: That's Family Court I think she's talking about.

WORKER: You know, your husband might be working, making a *very* good salary. Now, he's legally responsible for you.

FEMALE CLIENT: Oh, I know that. Don't you think if I knew where he was I'd be going to him? I don't know where he is. The last time I seen him was in the summertime.

WORKER: This summer?

FEMALE CLIENT: That's right. And it was late at night. I usually would see him at night and it was very quick. He was always with me. Right, Larry? You know, when you were with your wife? . . . Right?

WORKER: Well, that's—

LARRY: Do you have any cigarettes, ma'am? May I ? [*Worker gives Larry a cigarette, which he lights.*]

FEMALE CLIENT: No, he, 'cause sometimes his wife was working in the Welfare and we've been looking—

WORKER: You're married also?

FEMALE CLIENT: That's right.

LARRY: Yes.

FEMALE CLIENT: I know it sounds complex.

WORKER: Did you put down that you're married? Is your wife working?

LARRY: Is she working? I don't know where she is. I don't have a wife. What'd you tell her I have a wife for?

WORKER: Didn't you say that he has a wife?

FEMALE CLIENT: I thought he had a wife.

LARRY: She's my wife.

FEMALE CLIENT: I don't know what I'm saying. I don't know. Forgive me, I don't know. I'm sorry, Larry, okay? I don't know. I really don't know.

WORKER: Are you married or aren't you?

LARRY: To her? No.

WORKER: Not to her. Are you married to someone else?

LARRY: No.

WORKER: So what gave her the impression that you were?

LARRY: Maybe it's a wish that she had that—

FEMALE CLIENT: Maybe it could be a wish, I don't know . . . I haven't eaten in a couple of days and I'm hungry and I'm, you know, I get a little excited. So I'm sorry, Larry, okay?

LARRY: I don't feel too hot either. My system is all—

FEMALE CLIENT: I need some food; I need some sleep.

LARRY: Aches in every part of me.

WORKER: Alright, this is for the housing.

FEMALE CLIENT: Where do we bring that?

WORKER: This is on the fifth floor. Now you have to go—after that you have to go to employment. Okay?

LARRY: Yes.

WORKER: Okay. So—

FEMALE CLIENT: Have we been accepted?

LARRY: If she said she's going to house us—

WORKER: If we're going to house you that means—

FEMALE CLIENT: Okay. Thank you, miss. I just want to be reassured. Thank you. And then we gotta eat because we're starving.

WORKER: So could you please go up to the housing first?

FEMALE CLIENT: Miss, where's that? What floor is that?

WORKER: On the fifth floor. And this is on the fourth floor. The employment is on the fourth.

FEMALE CLIENT: Go up there now and then we come back to you?

WORKER: Yes.

FEMALE CLIENT: Thanks.

WORKER: You're welcome. [*Shots of clients gathered around applications desk. MS of one client holding a baby.*]

RECEPTIONIST (*offscreen*): You go to the third floor to the replacement group . . . the third floor. Anna, tell her to go up to the third floor of the replacement group.

WORKER: Señora, que vayas al tercer piso, al groupo donde dan los cheques, el groupo E. El primero, en el tercer piso. [Go to the third floor, to the group where they give out the checks. Group E. The first group on the third floor.]

POLICEMAN: Okay, next. [*A woman comes into frame and up to the desk.*]

RECEPTIONIST: Who's next? . . . Why are you here, dear?

CLIENT: I wanted to [*inaudible*]—

RECEPTIONIST: Did you get part of the check? . . . How much of the check did you get?

CLIENT: I received sixty-six. Sixty-six.

RECEPTIONIST: How much you supposed to get, dear?

CLIENT: One hundred fifteen, fifteen.

RECEPTIONIST: What do you get, one or two checks?

CLIENT: I don't know; I think one.

RECEPTIONIST: One? . . . Who's next? Come on, peoples, move down . . . Drop that in the box. Have a seat, wait for them to call you name. Who's next? Come on, people. Move down, please.

FEMALE CLIENT: I'm going to drop over dead. And they do it while I'm sleeping. They're dope addicts. They took everything. They took all my Medicaid, my Social Security. They took it all.

RECEPTIONIST: Quick service group on the third floor.

WORKER (*offscreen throughout*): Okay. In here it tell you about the supplemental security income for the aged, blind, and disabled. And now if you already, you already—wait a second, you already received Social Security disability payments?

FIRST ELDERLY MALE CLIENT: Yes, uh, well—

WORKER: Okay.

FIRST ELDERLY MALE CLIENT: I don't know. Supplemental payments. You know, the increase was something like that? Whatever it's supposed to be.

WORKER: Do you get money from Social Security?

FIRST ELDERLY MALE CLIENT: That's what I'm told. See, my stuff comes to the Holy Name Society, 8 East Bleeker Street.

WORKER: Oh.

FIRST ELDERLY MALE CLIENT: And I get so much a day to get a room or whatever I can.

WORKER: But you get that money from Social Security?

FIRST ELDERLY MALE CLIENT: They told me eighty-four fifty. Now whatever this is, I been going to see off and on.

WORKER: What, I'm asking you, do the people at the Holy Name, that's where you live?

FIRST ELDERLY MALE CLIENT: No, I don't live there. I just, I have to live wherever I can.

WORKER: Okay. So you have to go to 39 Broadway. I want you to go back to wherever it is you stay or wherever it is they get your papers, and tell them, and show them this, and tell them that we, we say you have to go through 39 Broadway. Right. That's your Social Security office. Okay? Because you apply, you qualify for Social Security, not for here.

SECOND ELDERLY MALE CLIENT: You have to go to the Holy Name and talk to them?

FIRST ELDERLY MALE CLIENT: That's right.

WORKER: And show them this and see that they understand what we said.

FIRST ELDERLY MALE CLIENT: Yes.

WORKER: And, uh, and then they'll direct you to 39 Broadway. Okay?

FIRST ELDERLY MALE CLIENT: And that's before I can get on the welfare, or whatever it is?

WORKER: They'll take care of you there.

FIRST ELDERLY MALE CLIENT: At this address, here?

WORKER: At 39 Broadway. At 39 Broadway. That's where you got to go now. No, 39 Broadway, downtown.

SECOND ELDERLY MALE CLIENT: 39 Broadway.

WORKER: Yes. Okay?

FIRST ELDERLY MALE CLIENT: Yes. [*The two men slowly walk away from camera. Cut to insert shot of woman and policeman in waiting area.*]

RECEPTIONIST: Who's next? Is there a next? [*Cut to three-shot of couple with baby being interviewed in Spanish, but their conversation, which carries over five shots of clients and their families in the waiting area, is inaudible. Cut to CU of client, Mr. Love.*]

WORKER (ELAINE): That check from Social Security for a hundred dollars on Friday.

CLIENT (MR. LOVE): For food.

ELAINE: And today is three days later. Why are you—

LOVE: They sent me back here.

ELAINE: Who sent you back?

LOVE: Social Security.

ELAINE: You got a hundred dollars from Social Security Administration on Friday.

LOVE: They, they sent me back here.

ELAINE: Wait, Mr. Love. Did you get a check for a hundred dollars on Friday from Social Security?

LOVE: No, uh, forty dollars—

ELAINE: And you'll be getting a hun—

LOVE: —Two weeks and then, and then, I had sixty dollars Friday for food.

29. A client tries to account for his expenditures.

ELAINE: And what happened to the sixty dollars?

LOVE: For food and—

ELAINE: What happened to the sixty dollars you got on Friday? You're covered by the Federal Social Security Program now.

LOVE: Well, those checks—

ELAINE: You're not covered by the local Welfare Center. You've got sixty dollars from—

LOVE: Social Security and Welfare were having an argument.

ELAINE: Mr. Love, if you got sixty dollars for food money on Friday, you're expected, it's to last for a little while. The twenty-eight hundred dollars you blew in two months, you can't—

LOVE: I had to pay my doctor bill. I had to pay my doctor bill.

ELAINE: You should have talked to Medicaid.

LOVE: I had to pay my doctor bill.

ELAINE: Mr. Love, if you got sixty dollars—

LOVE: I didn't have no—

ELAINE: —from Social Security on Friday, you're not going to get any money today.

LOVE: Yes, I paid my—

ELAINE: The money was for food and—

LOVE: Then gimme that and I'll go back to Social Security and I'll tell Social Security—. [*Mr. Love snatches his papers back and leaves. Cut to an old woman who takes pills at a drinking fountain, then walks down hallway. Cut to her emptying trash from her bag into the wastebasket. Shot of more people waiting and in line at the applications desk. One comes toward camera up to the receptionist.*]

CLIENT (RIVERA): Where's this for? Over here, I guess. [*He drops a form in a box.*]

RECEPTIONIST: Who's next? Come on, people, please move down. [*Cut to CU of pregnant client being interviewed.*]

WORKER: Miss Sloppo, you must bring us—how many months pregnant are you?

CLIENT (MISS SLOPPO): Five.

WORKER: You must bring us a letter from the hospital. The doctor can write anything that he wants to. In order to qualify for public assistance, you must bring a verification letter from a hospital. Are you attending any clinic?

SLOPPO: No.

WORKER: Why not?

SLOPPO: I have no money.

WORKER: That is not a requirement. That's not a requisite for you to go to a public clinic. You go there and you tell them that you don't have money and then they will fill out this form for you. Elaine.

SLOPPO: All this says is verification of pregnancy.

WORKER: This is not what we want. We want it from a doctor. There's a certain form. If you go to a city hospital, they'll give it to you. Now, you realize that a doctor can write anything that he wishes. Sometimes—

SLOPPO: Oh, yeah, but five people have seen this letter.

WORKER: Elaine, Elaine, are you taking this for verification of pregnancy?

ELAINE: Yeah, there's an EDC date on it. It's signed by a doctor and—

WORKER: So that, that, well, you'll take that instead of the, the form from the hospital, right?

ELAINE: Yeah, sure. It's just from a private doctor.

WORKER: Okay, it's accepted. [*Cut to shot of clients exiting an elevator and walking down a corridor. Among them are the couple from the emergency interview looking for the housing office.*]

WORKER (TOM): It indicates to me that she may be using a loose term, but broadly. Very broadly. [*Cut to a two-shot of the two workers looking over a form.*] It may not be detrimental to her. The hospital note tends—the letter from the hospital indicates that there were apparently extenuating social circumstances. It may be a question of lousy conditions. Now the, the format is first the home visit, according to Kaye, within forty-eight hours. Second, the phone calls to both central agency and SSC. And then the—on the first sheet you'll see a nine, I think it's a four-ninety-two. These forms, I have them there, I'll give them to you. They have to be processed within forty-eight hours of the, uh, phone calls.

WORKER: You haven't answered my question.

TOM: What's that?

WORKER: BCW already knows about it. Why do we have to notify BCW?

TOM: Just to get a clarification on it. Just to see exactly; her description of it leaves a lot open. She describes it broadly as a child neglect or abuse. A woman is accusing herself. I'm sure that, I'm pretty sure you'll find that she's using the term without quite understanding what it means. [*Worker returns to her desk to meet with client.*]

WORKER: Miss Zimmerman, we're going to take the child off the budget because it's not with you at the moment, and if you get the child back, you let us know about it. Okay?

CLIENT (MISS ZIMMERMAN): Okay. She'll be back as soon as I get another apartment. See, that's the problem right now.

WORKER: How long have you lived in this apartment?

ZIMMERMAN: About nine months. But like there's, there's rats and gas leak and the whole bit.

WORKER: The, the Central Registry, they're the ones who took the complaint. Now, I don't know who made the complaint. I think it was the hospital. Women's Infirmary. Said that you have some diseased pets in the house?

ZIMMERMAN: Yes, one dog is diseased. It's not my dog, though, and it doesn't live there.

WORKER: Yes, but you can't let the child near the dog. It doesn't matter that

30. A client discusses her case with a worker.

it's not your dog. The dog is in the apartment, and that has nothing to do with—even though the conditions of your apartment are bad, and probably you'll be able to move, it's still a diseased dog and they're not going to let the child back as long as you've got a diseased pet in there. Some diseases the child can catch.

ZIMMERMAN: It's, it's not there all the time. It's there once in a while. It's my boyfriend's dog, and he doesn't live there.

WORKER: But it only has to be there for a little while for the child to catch something. And that's why the doctors I don't think are going to let you have it back until you get rid of the dog for good. So, why don't you tell your boyfriend to come pick it up?

ZIMMERMAN: Okay.

WORKER: But, anyway, somebody will be visiting your house in the future, so clean it up.

ZIMMERMAN: Okay. Do you know about when? See now, I put in a complaint about three weeks ago with the building inspector and no one ever came, and they, the housing got a real runaround. And nobody knew nothing about it . . . So, like they say, there's no record of violations.

WORKER: No. Somebody will help you. You need a lawyer to help you with that. You can't do it yourself. So I'll give you the phone number of this lawyer that works for the Mobilization for Youth, because—

ZIMMERMAN: Okay.

WORKER: Here's the number, or else you can go in person and tell him that—

ZIMMERMAN: See, I don't know why the building inspector won't come, he [*inaudible*]—

WORKER: They take a couple of months to come because they're understaffed, etcetera, etcetera. They won't come. When I had to wait for a building inspector for myself, it took a year and a half.

ZIMMERMAN: That's ridiculous.

WORKER: So don't count on that. That's why you have to go to somebody who's legal. See, that way they can help you do it a lot faster.

ZIMMERMAN: The caseworker says that they don't want to move me because there's no record of any violations and I can't move there—

WORKER: That's why you have to put in the violations and then you will be able to move. See, you have to say, yes, there are violations.

ZIMMERMAN: I have to go to a lawyer? Okay.

WORKER: Okay? So, you have her number. So that's okay, you can go home now.

ZIMMERMAN: Okay. Thank you very much. [*Client walks away from camera down corridor to an elevator. Cut to CU of another worker talking with another client.*]

WORKER (SAM): You had a fire and the emergency occurred in August. You settled the emergency because you resolved it because you lived with your friend.

CLIENT: Right.

SAM: Now there are new circumstances. Now you, if you want to, uh . . . uh, if you want to correct the situation by, by having a new apartment, you must make a fair hearing. This is your only course.

CLIENT: I, I don't think this is fair.

SAM (*overlapping*): We can't solve it in the Cen—

CLIENT: I don't think this is fair. I don't think this is fair.

SAM: We can't solve it in the Center. They, we won't give you this money.

CLIENT: I don't, I don't think this is fair at all. There's something's that's gotta be done somewhere because it will continue—

SAM: Why, why are you so reluctant about asking for a fair hearing?

CLIENT: I'm not reluctant about asking for a fair hearing. I am reluctant to a certain extent. The reason why is because it's going to take a longer period of time.

SAM: How do you know it's going to take a longer period of time?

CLIENT: It takes at least three weeks for a fair hearing, doesn't it? Does it not?

SAM: Yeah, but . . . but how long—?

CLIENT: Yeah. Meanwhile, my friend has moved out and where am I?

SAM: Your friend hasn't moved out yet, has he?

CLIENT: He's moving his things.

SAM: When is he moving?

CLIENT: He's in the process of moving his things.

SAM: When is he moving?

CLIENT: He's—all his things will be out within the next two days. And I have responsibilities also.

SAM: By the way, are you enrolled in a WREP Program or any of the programs of D-E-R?—

CLIENT: Yes. Yeah. Uh-huh. I am.

SAM: You're enrolled right now in some—?

CLIENT: Yeah. In the WREP Program.

SAM: When do you start?

CLIENT: Well, the guy's been sending me out, they send me to the unemployment section. Now the guy's been sending me out to, to different jobs and told me to call him this week, so he could send me somewhere else.

SAM: Are you, are you, ever enrolled in a narcotic program?

CLIENT: Yes, I was. I was a drug addict at one time, but when I came out I started working and I've got my own apartment and from there I started building on my own two feet. And then I, I—from there I bought a dog, a Great Dane, that I had to—responsibilities toward her. Now, I'm, being with the fire, I only have the dog left. And it's me and the dog, and I've lost my job. And y'all said y'all would do, would give me some kind of help and it hasn't been done yet. And that's another reason why the hotel wouldn't be suitable. I would have to get my own apartment.

SAM: Because of the dog, you mean?

CLIENT: Right. Because I have a dog, too.

SAM: Well, I think there's only one course for you to do. And you can go to, to the state and make a fair hearing, and we'll, we'll be over there and—

CLIENT: What happens in the meanwhile?

SAM: With our records—what?

CLIENT: What happens . . . meanwhile, when the guy moves out?

SAM: He hasn't moved out yet, right? You're still living there.

CLIENT: Not, not completely. But within the next two days. It takes three weeks for a fair hearing. What happens, what do I do in that time?

SAM: There's nothing we can do, unless you come—you want to live in a hotel meanwhile?

CLIENT: You going to take my dog? I'll live there. Y'all give me furniture, clothes money, and—

SAM: We're not, we're not giving assistance for your dog.

CLIENT: I know, I know!

SAM: We're concerned about you, right?

CLIENT: Between the dog, me and my friend, work it out. We work it out between me and the dog.

SAM: In other words, the dog can stay with your friend.

CLIENT: It's my dog, but I don't know. I don't know if he wants the dog to stay. I'm not sure. I, that, I would have to work out with him. Like I said, I might be able to work out a furniture situation with him, or, and the dog. I don't know. But the fact that I came down here was because, that I was told that I would have a place to go, which is an apartment and that, and that is where I could take my dog and live, and, and, and work for a living.

SAM: Where's your friend moving to?

CLIENT: On, on, he's moving on the West Side.

SAM: And you mean to tell me you can't stay over with your friend?

CLIENT: He told me it's too small. The apartment is too small.

SAM: For a day or two?

CLIENT: He has, he has his woman. His woman is with him, too. Now, so all along I still been—

31. A client debates with the assistant director of the Welfare Center about applying for a fair hearing.

SAM: Let me, let me ask you. If this woman lives with him, too, he's still living in your apartment?

CLIENT: Not my apartment.

SAM: Well, he's living with *you*. If this woman lives with him, lives with him means present—

CLIENT: Right. And he's moving some of his things, he's in the midst of moving some of his things to the West Side. He hasn't moved everything yet.

SAM: But you just stated that a woman is living with him.

CLIENT: Right. His, his—

SAM: Then you're living with this man.

CLIENT: Uh-huh.

SAM: So the woman is living with him, and with you, also. You're living in the same apartment.

CLIENT: Right. There's three of us plus a dog.

SAM: Now there are three of you, plus a dog.

CLIENT: Right. But it's his apart—, it's his home. It's not mine. It's his home.

SAM: It, it gets more involved—

CLIENT: It's his home.

SAM: —As we go along.

CLIENT: It's the man's home.

SAM: Now you have a dog, and you have a woman, and you have—

CLIENT: I don't have no woman. No—

SAM: He has the woman.

CLIENT: Well, what goes on with him is not my concern. He just lets me— I rent part of the apartment to sleep there. I sleep there and, and do what I have to do.

SAM: Listen. Do me a favor. Make the fair hearing at 488–6550.

CLIENT: Still. I'm being rejected again. It's, it's still a runaround. Thank you for your help.

SAM: Okay.

CLIENT (*walking away, glaring*): Thank you for [*inaudible*]. [*Cut to two-shot of another worker interviewing a client.*]

WORKER: We're not allowed to pay back this much. You should come in on the time that you have—

CLIENT: Well, the fair hearing kept me there. I don't want to hear that. I don't want to hear that shit at all. You didn't feed me, he fed me. You're supposed to send those checks. I'm single issue. You never sent them. You never sent them.

WORKER: You're supposed to come in for single issue checks. We are not supposed to send them.

CLIENT: They were sent before, single issue, always without a fucking problem. But now there's a problem.

WORKER: Listen. You don't have to use that foul language because I don't have to listen to it.

CLIENT: Well, can I have today's food money, then?

WORKER: You can't have today's food money, but you can—

CLIENT: Why not?

WORKER: Your day is due tomorrow. You go according to this date—I told you that already. The best thing I can do is give you the rent money from before that you didn't pick up, and to give you your rent money from the first to the thirty-first. I'll give you an appointment for tomorrow to come in and get your food money.

CLIENT: And I'll still have to stand out there at six o'clock tomorrow morning.

WORKER: No, you won't have to because I'll give you an appointment today.

CLIENT: Will I still have you tomorrow? [*Cut to another client being interviewed.*]

WORKER: There's a little problem here. Did you apply after January 1 or before?

CLIENT: Before.

WORKER: You had no active case here before January 1?

CLIENT: No.

WORKER: If that is true, then we can accept you for thirty days, until the Social Security Department gets around to accepting you.

CLIENT: Alright. Well, the girl downst—

WORKER: Do you have a letter from them?

CLIENT: Yeah. I showed it to the girl. I don't have any of my papers with me now. But I showed, you know, the interviewer downstairs, like, you know, my psychiatric reports. I showed her the referral slips from SSI, and I been—

WORKER: Do you have that with you now?

CLIENT: No. I don't have it with me now.

WORKER (*telephone ringing*): Okay, alright.

CLIENT: But I been coming back here every day for two weeks. Like she said, get a notarized letter for this, a notarized letter for that.

WORKER: Get the application group. Applications.

CLIENT: Yes. Yes. Yes.

WORKER: And so now you're here in housing. So you must have had a referral from them to housing, right?

CLIENT: Yes. Because they say they only give out a hundred and sixty dollars—

WORKER: That's a lot of money for rent.

CLIENT: A hundred and sixty dollars.

WORKER: A hundred seventy.

CLIENT: Yeah, they say they only give out a hundred and sixty. My rent is a hundred and seventy. Right.

WORKER: It's difficult. Do you live alone?

CLIENT: Yes. I went to, I went to the landlord. Right? The landlord is out of town. He's in Aruba. But his attorney that's handling the case gave me a letter saying that they will deduct the ten dollars for some burglar alarm system. She rejected that. So she told me if I get a letter from my mother, a certified letter from my mother, saying that my mother would get me the ten dollars a month, I would be accepted. Alright? I got the certified letter from my mother saying—

WORKER: They can't tell you anything but—

CLIENT: —saying that she would give me ten dollars a month to make up the ten dollars difference, and she rejects that and sends me up here.

WORKER: So they're telling you you're not eligible.

CLIENT: She's told me she's giving me the food and money and all that other garbage, you know, but there are—she wants me to relocate instamatically . . . She just wants me to move somewhere.

WORKER: Your case is accepted, though?

CLIENT: Yes. [*Several shots of clients waiting, reading, walking about, including Miss Zimmerman, continuing until the two-shot of Mrs. Johnson and Matthews.*]

WORKERS (*offscreen*): Morillo. M-O-R-I-L-L-O. First name, America . . . I-L-L-O . . . America . . . You know, upstairs, there aren't two people that do it the same way . . . There aren't? . . . If you're going to need an interpreter, I'll have to go find someone . . . I don't speak Spanish.

HISPANIC CLIENT (NICOLASSA): ¿Eres una meuradora, y una investigadora social? [Are you an investigator? A case worker?]

MATTHEWS (*offscreen*): Don't cry, c'mon. Look. Look. Hold it. If I get my check today, which I think I will—they owe me two checks. You cool people with me now. Don't. Come on. Don't do that. Come on. Come on.

NICOLASSA (*continuing through Valerie Johnson and Ms. Matthews speaking*): ¡Mira! Como estoy ahora andando con baton, nunca no andando con baton. [Look how I am now. I'm walking with a cane. I never walk with a cane.] [*Cut to two-shot of Johnson and Matthews.*]

MATTHEWS: Do you want to go [*inaudible*]?

JOHNSON: I just got out of the hospital.

MATTHEWS: What were you in the hospital for?

JOHNSON: I got an operation.

NICOLASSA: Deme ese pajito que está por allí. Deme ése, ése. [Give me that walking stick that's over there. Give me that one, that one.]

MALE WORKER: Mrs. Johnson—?

JOHNSON: Yes.

NICOLASSA (*in Spanish*): Bueno, entonces haga todo más posible y cuando saben [*inaudible*]. Yo no puedo cancelarlo. Yo estoy que no puedo andar, y la malencia del gobierno, el gobierno, el gobierno no puede romper mi gobierno. [Well, then, do what you can, all that is possible, and when you know (*inaudible*). I can't cancel this. I'm not able to walk. And the maliciousness of the government. The government cannot break its rules.]

MALE WORKER: Mrs. Johnson, do you have your referral slip?

JOHNSON: I'm put in the Markwell Hotel for a week and my check was supposed to come there between the first and the third. It didn't come. The man gave me two days to put me out of the hotel—

MALE WORKER: Now, Mrs. Johnson, according to this, Social Security gave you a check on the sixth of January?

JOHNSON: For food money.

MALE WORKER: How much did they give you?

JOHNSON: On Jan—, a hundred dollars food money until—

MALE WORKER: Okay, now—

JOHNSON: They say my check will be there in ten days. It's been fourteen days. I meet the mailman every morning. No check come—

MALE WORKER: Well, Mrs.—

JOHNSON: I can't pay no rent and I'm supposed to be on hotel budget and I ain't even—ya ain't, ya ain't even had me listed. They told me that I wasn't even on the roll.

MALE WORKER: Were you receiving assistance here before, Mrs. Johnson?

JOHNSON: Yes, I was.

MALE WORKER: May I see your Medicaid card?

JOHNSON: This the new one they gave me and they done put the wrong date on that. I got to get that changed.

MALE WORKER: Excuse me. Excuse me. Now—

JOHNSON: They—I was supposed to be issued for a month.

MALE WORKER: Now, how long are you, were you on assistance in this office before you were sent to the Social Security?

JOHNSON: Since March.

MALE WORKER: Since March of, uh—

JOHNSON: This year, last year—

MALE WORKER: Of 1973, yes. And your case was transferred from this office to Security—

JOHNSON: Disabled, because I'm disabled. [*Cut to worker talking to another worker.*]

MALE WORKER: She claims she's been on assistance here since March. She was living, she was—she has a rent receipt from the Hotel Marquez dated one-two-seventy-four.

FEMALE WORKER: Uh-huh.

MALE WORKER: So apparently it's a conversion. But here they have her as— can you make this out here?

FEMALE WORKER: SSI beneficiary.

MALE WORKER: Which means that she was a conversion.

FEMALE WORKER: Which means that she was a conversion, yes.

MALE WORKER: For her to give, for them to give her—for them to give her one hundred dollars, she obviously is a conversion.

FEMALE WORKER: It's a conversion—

MALE WORKER: There's nothing we can do.

FEMALE WORKER: Either that or they would have assumed in error that she was, and it doesn't seem like it since she's been in receipt of assistance since March.

MALE WORKER: But I don't understand when they say "needs home relief."

FEMALE WORKER: Well, apparently, they just are hoping that she can get some help here or wanted to get rid of her, either one.

MALE WORKER: I, I was wondering if they were inferring that her eligibility had been denied for assistance, but—

FEMALE WORKER: Did she give us the phone numbers? No, they never give us phone numbers to call.

MALE WORKER: No, they don't. She says now she's at the Hotel Vasquez.

FEMALE WORKER: Oh, yeah, well, she'll have to register change of address with them, and we cannot help her here. It looks as if she's a conversion case.

MALE WORKER: Yes. She's a conversion case. Obviously. Yes. Well, I'll inform her. [*Worker walks away from camera. Cut to CU of Mrs. Johnson.*] . . . The point is, Mrs. Johnson, once a case has been transferred or converted to Social Security by this office, we are not able to make any address changes that occur in January. You must wait until they mail you a check, Mrs. Johnson, because Social Security already gave you one hundred dollars for your Janu—

JOHNSON: Food money, food money.

MALE WORKER: Until—

JOHNSON: For ten days.

MALE WORKER: Yes, until the other check arrives. They are responsible for any checks issued you in January, Mrs. Johnson.

JOHNSON: That's what they said.

MALE WORKER: That's true.

JOHNSON: But they said y'all, Welfare, have to make out my budget and I'll bring it over there to them and *then they* will take over from there.

MALE WORKER: How much rent were you paying here, Mrs. Johnson?

JOHNSON: I was paying a hundred and forty dollars a month.

MALE WORKER: One-forty a month?

JOHNSON: Yeah. And the hotel is going to cost, uh, uh—

MALE WORKER: Well, if you were getting—do you have cooking facilities at your—?

JOHNSON: Yeah. Forty-seven dollars for cooking facilities, but the hotel don't have no—

MALE WORKER (*overlapping*): And the rent was one-forty?

JOHNSON: One-forty a month.

MALE WORKER: That means it's seventy dollars semi-monthly. In other words, we were—your budget, the budget you were receiving from us, was a hundred and seventeen dollars.

JOHNSON (*overlapping*): Every two weeks.

MALE WORKER: Every two weeks. Correct. Now, the Social Security budget will be two hundred and fourteen dollars a month. Do you understand that?

32. A client pleads her case.

JOHNSON: Yes, but I ain't got no, no check from—

MALE WORKER: But they gave you one hundred dollars advance—

JOHNSON: Yeah.

MALE WORKER: —toward your food check.

JOHNSON: Food money.

MALE WORKER: Right. Now they will send you a check at your address here.

JOHNSON: They been supposed to send it. It wasn't even on the roll. But now they gonna have to put me in a hotel because I'm getting put out of this here place.

MALE WORKER: And they are responsible for the address change.

JOHNSON: And they want—

MALE WORKER: I'm going to give you a letter and I want you to go there right away so they can make an address change for you, Mrs. Johnson. I'm terribly sorry.

JOHNSON: I've been there, and the man said they don't make no change. You can call them. I don't have money to be rippin' and runnin' in that rain. And I just got out of the hospital from a operation. A serious operation.

MALE WORKER: Well, I tell you. With the new Social Security budget, there is no increase in rent. There are no provisions made for any increase in rent.

You are to live on a flat grant. Not to exceed no more than two-oh-six, eighty-five a month regardless of how much rent you pay. You will get one grant. Do you understand that, Mrs. Johnson? Whether you pay fifty dollars a month or a hundred and fifty dollars a month rent—

JOHNSON: One hundred sixty dollars a month rent.

MALE WORKER (*overlapping*): The fact is that Social Security does not increase or decrease your budget like we used to.

JOHNSON: No. They say *you* would, you will figure out how much my budget will be in the hotel and they will handle it from there.

MALE WORKER: But we cannot change any budgets after January first, Mrs. Johnson.

JOHNSON: Well, I was—

MALE WORKER: The person may have been mistaken.

JOHNSON: —being put in the hotel before January the first.

MALE WORKER (*dialing telephone*): Actually, your case is probably at 39 Broadway. They sent you to the other office because they were too crowded?

JOHNSON (*overlapping*): I called. I called 39 Broadway. She said, she said that I was just, I would just have to lay and wait and they might not be till the end of next month before I receive any kind of rent money or food money. I'll be put out by then . . . Now, I returned the rent money here, right? I didn't return it to the Social Service. I return my rent money here.

WORKER: I'm calling 39 Broadway now to see if they can find you listed, okay?

NICOLASSA (*simultaneously with Mrs. Johnson*): ¿El Señor Meléndez con este teléfono, eh? Que yo necesito para mejor aclarar porque yo no voy a poder a venir más aquí. ¿Sabe? Quiero si me mande, a ver, a un sitio donde me pueden hacer el cheque a cuidado de la persona. Ve si encuentro una tarjeta aquí. Right? . . . ¿Yo no voy a poder a venir aquí, right? ¡No me oye bien! Ese cheque mío a cuidado de ese señor. [Is Mr. Melendez at this telephone number? Because I need him in order to make things clear. Because I'm not going to be able to come back here, you know? I want to have a place where they can send my check in care of someone. See if I can find a card here. Right? I'm not going to be able to come back here, right? Are you listening? For my check to be sent care of this man.]

MALE WORKER: I'm calling 39 Broadway now to see if they could find your record, okay? [*On telephone*] This is Waverly. Can you find a Valerie Johnson for me, please? The Social Security number, 4-3-7-5-8-3-8-6-7. She was referred to us again for a change of address. I understand, effective January, that we are not responsible for any address changes, or budget changes rather. She is, actually is requesting a budget change . . . Yes, she wants to put in a change of address, right. It's 4-3-7-5-8-3-8-6-7 . . . Yes, would you please? . . . She's going to check her rolls, Mrs. Johnson, okay?

NICOLASSA (*overlapping*): ¿En mi apartamento, me lo dijo pero no la podía ver, hm? ¿Cuál es la dirección de ese señor? Hable entonces con él. Entonces me mande ese cheque a cuidado de ese señor [*inaudible*]. ¿Usted qué cree? [In my apartment, he told me, but I couldn't see it. What's this man's address? Then talk to him. Then I was sent this check in care of him. What do you think?]

WORKER: No se puede. Allá [*he points*]. [I cannot do it. Put it there.]

NICOLASSA: ¿No? ¿Pero el teléfono, el teléfono? Me hable con él que venga a buscarlo. ¿Tengo guagua? Yo no puedo. Yo le pago bien a él esa guagua. Why? [What about the telephone? You speak with him to come and get it. Do I have to take a bus? I'm not able to. I pay him well for that bus. Why?]

MALE WORKER: ¿Conoce al señor Meléndez? [Do you know Senor Melendez?]

NICOLASSA: [*Inaudible.*]

MALE WORKER: ¿Yo te llamo mañana por la mañana, okay? Yo hablo con él. [I'll call you tomorrow morning, okay? I'll speak with him.]

NICOLASSA: Okay. ¿El teléfono en projecto? [The number on the card?]

MALE WORKER: Lo tengo. [I have it.]

NICOLASSA: Sí, no puedo venir. [I cannot come back.]

MALE WORKER: Sí, okay, Nicolassa. Goodnight.

NICOLASSA: Goodnight. Bye-bye. So long. Bye. [*Inaudible.*] [*She leaves.*]

MALE WORKER (*on telephone*): Yes, hello . . . Do you have—is the address 31 East First Street? It's possible. See, she says she, she was serviced at 1657 Broadway. Now I don't know why they would service her up there if she's got this First Street address. Do you have a birth date on her? Yeah . . . [*To Mrs. Johnson*] She has a Valerie Johnson there, 31 East First, First Avenue.

JOHNSON: They got the address wrong. That's what it is. That's me. That's me. That's me.

MALE WORKER: No. But she has a different Social Security number.

JOHNSON: She got it wrong, then. My ID was lost. But I had to come get duplicate copies of everything. That's me. Valerie Johnson.

MALE WORKER: Well, here, your, your office is 125th Street. Did you go way up there, too, at 230 West 125th Street? Well, this is when you lived at East Twenty-ninth Street. You don't live there anymore, do you?

JOHNSON: No, that was, that was the old—when I first got my Social Security card.

MALE WORKER: Well, this is the correct number that we have here. Your account number, your Social Security number, seems to be correct. She's checking it out for me, okay? Hold on.

JOHNSON: She's got it wrong. I'm the only Valerie Johnson there. They told me my check would be returned to that center.

MALE WORKER: Now, you, you didn't pay rent at this address for January, did you?

JOHNSON: I ain't got no check for January to pay no rent with, and brought the two rent checks in here, and turn'd them in to y'all for December because you was, I was moving in the hotel.

MALE WORKER: But they eventually gave you the December checks. Is that correct?

JOHNSON: No, they didn't give them to me. Y'all still got 'em.

MALE WORKER: You got no checks for December here?

JOHNSON: No. I brought 'em in to y'all. One for the first and one for the—

MALE WORKER: I mean your welfare checks, your welfare checks.

JOHNSON: My welfare checks, I turn'd them back in to y'all. Both of them.

MALE WORKER: You had no money for December here?

JOHNSON: I had food money.

MALE WORKER: But no rent money?

JOHNSON: But the rent money I brought back here.

MALE WORKER: Because you were supposed to have moved?

JOHNSON: Because they was putting me in a hotel soon as the, the January first start.

MALE WORKER: What happened to the rent money they gave you for the new hotel? [*On telephone*] Yeah? Excuse me.

JOHNSON: They only paid it for one week. Here's the receipt. You got the receipt.

MALE WORKER (*on telephone*): Okay. Well, thank you.

JOHNSON: They only paid it for a week. I put down the seventh, and then Social Security was supposed to have my check mailed before this rent was due, and they didn't have it. The man was nice enough to let me stay there two days over and then he couldn't let me stay no more after no check was come and I couldn't pay.

MALE WORKER: Uh, you did not pay this hotel any rent. Is that correct?

JOHNSON: Yeah. I pay this here.

MALE WORKER: Just one week.

JOHNSON: One week and—

MALE WORKER: And you stayed a week and two days. Is that right?

JOHNSON: My check was supposed to come bef—, the third—between the third and the seventh, and it never did come.

MALE WORKER: Now, let me ask you a question, Mrs. Johnson. Why, why does Social Security have your old number, your old address? Did you ask them that?

JOHNSON: Because when I got put out of here, I didn't have nowhere else to go but to that old apartment. So I went back in that old apartment.

MALE WORKER: Is this—we—

JOHNSON: And I told the landlord—

MALE WORKER: This, you received from this office a week's rent to pay this, this hotel here?

JOHNSON: Right. And food money.

MALE WORKER: Do you know if they made a change of address when you did it? When we gave you a week's rent here at the Markwell Hotel.

JOHNSON: They put the check, the address, the Markwell Hotel then. After I had to move out of there, I went to Social Security, told them [*insert shots of various clients, including Miss Zimmerman*] how I had to move out of there and only place I had to go was the old apartment. She sent me with this letter for y'all to send me with a budget.

MALE WORKER: You spent the whole hundred dollars since the sixth of the month? In two weeks?

JOHNSON: I pay my light, my electric and gas bill out of it. Bought a few groceries and it was gone. Bought me two little sweaters—

MALE WORKER: Mrs. Johnson, can you wait till tomorrow morning? I think we should work on this properly.

JOHNSON: You know what I think.

MALE WORKER: This man apparently—

JOHNSON: The Valerie Johnson that they got at 39, uh, uh, uh, uh—

MALE WORKER: At 39 Broadway, yes.

JOHNSON: —Broadway. That's me. That they made the mistake in the number because I didn't see this lady in person. She took the information on the phone.

MALE WORKER: Don't you think that if you came in in the morning, Mrs. Johnson, we could clarify this better? Perhaps that is your case down at Broadway. There was a different [*cut back to CU of Mrs. Johnson*] Social Security number.

JOHNSON: They got the check down there. Right?

MALE WORKER: Well, she didn't say. She just gave me your name.

JOHNSON: Would you call and ask and I'll go down there and have her verify that there is no more Valerie Johnson on First Avenue? I'll even—

MALE WORKER: You say 31 First Avenue. Do you think it's a mistake?

JOHNSON: No. It ain't. There ain't no 31 First Avenue. It's 31 East First Avenue. They don't even have no address like that.

MALE WORKER: No. It's 31 East First Street. Yes.

JOHNSON: Street. Right. It ain't—

MALE WORKER: I asked her for your birth date to verify further whether you were the person, and she did not have your birth date listed there.

JOHNSON: Well, she didn't ask me my birthday when she was asking me on the phone.

MALE WORKER: Then you did see someone at 39 Broadway?

JOHNSON: I talked to her on the phone and I been talking to her—

MALE WORKER: Why don't you go there in person, then?

JOHNSON: —almost every day.

MALE WORKER: Why don't you go down to lower Broadway right now?

JOHNSON: Would you call her and ask her?

MALE WORKER: Well, the rent you owe is for December, is that correct?

JOHNSON: December and January. I ain't got no check for January. Not for emergency food money. And I'm still waitin' on my check.

MALE WORKER: See, this is very complicated, Mrs. Johnson—

JOHNSON: I've been waiting.

WORKER: —because if you owe December rent—

JOHNSON: I don't owe it. I brought it in and gave it here to y'all—

MALE WORKER: Yes, well, then we are—

JOHNSON: —and y'all got December rent.

MALE WORKER: Then we are probably responsible for that December check. Social Security would—

JOHNSON: That's what they say. Y'all responsible for it.

MALE WORKER: Yes. And Social Security—

JOHNSON: Now, they gone give me January, but y'all got my December, which puts me two months behind.

MALE WORKER: Then we're going to have to send you to reception so you get an appointment for Group 4, which is the group that gives out checks *here*, Mrs. Johnson. Do you understand? . . . You want me to call reception to see if we can get you an appointment now?

JOHNSON: Yes.

MALE WORKER: For the group here?

JOHNSON: For to see about my December check. Would you call 39 Broadway?

MALE WORKER: This comes from fifty, 57 Broadway. [*Cut to female worker standing over male worker's shoulder at his desk.*]

FEMALE WORKER: Yes.

MALE WORKER: Whatever this means, I don't know. She's—

FEMALE WORKER: Hold on a minute.

MALE WORKER: She's under the impression that the security worker wants a budget from us. But according to this, there's nothing they can do for her. They gave her a hundred dollars on one-six. Now, she was referred—she claims she was given a check by us to the Hotel Markwell on one-two and returned the December rent checks.

FEMALE WORKER: Alright. She was purposely given—

MALE WORKER: Now she's back at this address.

FEMALE WORKER: She was purposely given the check on one-two to replace the December checks that were lost. That's probably why they were able to give it to her here.

JOHNSON: No, they were mailed to me in the mail and they told me they was putting me in the hotel so I saved the checks and brought 'em in here. Now, when I went to Social Security, they said they didn't even have me on the roll to—no check had been sent out to me. No kind o' way. So they gave me emergency *food* money.

MALE WORKER: Obviously—

JOHNSON: At 39 Broadway office they got Valerie Johnson, but they got the wrong address.

FEMALE WORKER: I don't see any way that this office can help her here. I imagine that was some kind of a replacement check.

MALE WORKER: I would assume. But, according to this, there's nothing they can do for her and she needs home relief.

FEMALE WORKER: Yes. She was a grandfathered-in case, was she? We do know that.

MALE WORKER: She was, I'm sure she was, for them to give her a hundred dollars.

FEMALE WORKER: Did you check the roll?

MALE WORKER: I can't get, I can't get Security. I'll have to check the roll to see if she—I'm sure she—

FEMALE WORKER: To see if she was grandfathered in—

MALE WORKER: I'll check the roll. May I have your Medicaid card again, Mrs.—never mind. I have it here. [*Cut to Mrs. Johnson at female worker's desk.*]

FEMALE WORKER: What it appears to be is that the money you were given here early in January was to replace money that was given to you in December or that was owed to you from December or whatever. You are definitely on Social Security's rolls. You're on there to the amount of . . . two hundred and forty-one dollars and forty-six cents a month. They may give—

JOHNSON: But they—

FEMALE WORKER: Hold on a minute. Hold on. You hear me through and then I'll hear you through. That is the amount that we budgeted you for when we turned your case over to them.

JOHNSON: That was—

FEMALE WORKER: What? What?

JOHNSON: That was for 31 East—

FEMALE WORKER: Okay. Hold on a minute.

JOHNSON: But you made me a new budget when you put me in a hotel—

FEMALE WORKER: Hold on. For two hundred and forty-one dollars and forty-six cents a month. They may give you some extra to make up for the fact that you have lost your food stamps. I think they make some financial allowance for that. So you would be getting a little extra. Now, that is for your budget at 31 East First Street. You're not living there anymore.

JOHNSON: Right.

FEMALE WORKER (*overlapping*): But you moved after the first of January, if my understanding is correct. Therefore, I do not believe—

JOHNSON: You still made out . . . you still made out a new budget and told me my check would come to the hotel there.

FEMALE WORKER: In this office.

JOHNSON: You had, you had to make out a hotel budget in order to send my check to this hotel so I have enough money to pay.

FEMALE WORKER: Alright. We'll have to wait now till we hear from them downstairs. I understand somebody down there is looking up your record.

JOHNSON: Yeah.

FEMALE WORKER: We'll see what they did. I'm just telling you that my understanding is that if you moved, your case has been turned over to the Social Security Administration. Okay. Well, let's see what they come up with from the record downstairs. If something unusual has occurred and the change was put through, fine. [*Insert shots of various clients, including Miss Zimmerman.*]

JOHNSON: It seems like they ain't doing nothing but messin' me around because see, like, I'm gettin' put out of everywhere, you know, and, and I, I don't have, I don't have no more food money and things because they told me definitely that my check would be out in a few days.

MALE WORKER: Miss Matthews, can you get Mrs. Johnson [*camera returns to the conversation, a two-shot of Matthews and Johnson]* to come here in the morning? Explain to her that perhaps we would have more time to find her record, we would, more time to—

MATTHEWS: You can't find her record?

MALE WORKER: They looked downstairs. The lady, the woman in the group—

JOHNSON: No. Nobody . . . She didn't go, she didn't go to no—

MATTHEWS: —talking to Miss Perry.

JOHNSON: She couldn't give you any information without the records. That's what she said but she don't remember.

MATTHEWS: Look, mama.

JOHNSON: But she got it wrote in the record, she say. If you get the record—

MATTHEWS: Look, mama, if they don't have you record, if they don't have you record, they don't know nothin' about you. You could be Jane Doe. You understand where I'm coming from? They don't know nothin' about it so you can't—Come here, you got somethin' in your eye.

JOHNSON: They got us a mole. That man down there can go get the record, see—

MATTHEWS: Open your eye.

JOHNSON: That man down there could go get my record.

MATTHEWS: Let's go downstairs. I'll talk to Miss Perry.

MALE WORKER: Hey, hey, get your stuff.

JOHNSON: I will. Are you ready yet?

MATTHEWS: Yeah. I'm waitin' for my checks to be taken downstairs.

MALE WORKER: Mrs. Johnson, in the event that they don't find your record—

MATTHEWS: Here, this yours?

JOHNSON: Yeah.

MATTHEWS: Please don't forget nothin'.

MALE WORKER: Miss Matthews, rather, Mrs. Johnson—

MATTHEWS: She can stay with me until tomorrow if necessary.

WORKER (*overlapping*): That'll be fine. In the event they don't find your record tonight, please come here early in the morning. And go to the reception desk.

MATTHEWS: Does it—can she get a receipt? I mean, uh—

JOHNSON: They ain't even going to give me an appointment.

MATTHEWS: —uh, an appointment?

MALE WORKER: She will in the morning.

MATTHEWS: She can get an appointment downstairs for tomorrow?

JOHNSON: No.

MALE WORKER: I doubt if they will give it to her now, but she will get one in the morning.

JOHNSON (*overlapping*): No, no. Not now.

MATTHEWS: In the morning, she'll get an appointment to come back?

JOHNSON: No, you know they ain't goin' to give me—

MALE WORKER: On an emergency basis they can give her an appointment. [*Mrs. Johnson, Mrs. Matthews, another female client, and two workers talk at once. Mostly unintelligible.*]

JOHNSON (*overlapping*): You know that. You know they ain't gonna give me no appointment.

MALE WORKER (*overlapping*): Excuse me, excuse me. See Mr. Matthews tomorrow—

MATTHEWS (*overlapping*): —maybe he's my father.

WOMAN (*overlapping*): —call her number. And if they don't call her number, if they don't call her number till five o'clock in the afternoon, she will not get an appointment until the next day.

WORKER: —on an emergency basis we can get her an appointment tomorrow—

MATTHEWS: —they just gave me a appointment for Wednesday.

JOHNSON: Well, will you give me a letter saying it's a emergency basis? Will you give a letter to bring back to this man? . . . 'Cause I'm going to bring it back to him.

WOMAN: I got to have all these examinations—

MATTHEWS: Valerie, Valerie, Valerie, Valerie, Valerie, Valerie. You not going to get nowhere up here arguing with him. He's doin' his job. A man can't do no more than—

JOHNSON (*overlapping*): I've been here. I was here Friday. I was here last Wednesday, I was here on the second.

MATTHEWS (*overlapping*): Baby, he only got a certain amount of authority. You can't fight with him. Come off, come off with me.

WOMAN (*overlapping*): Is that the lady?

JOHNSON: Did you find my record?

MALE WORKER: I did get 39 Broadway. They have a Valerie Johnson there with a different Social Security number and they got her at 31 Avenue—

JOHNSON: First Avenue.

MALE WORKER: —uh, First Avenue.

FEMALE WORKER: 31 First Avenue.

WOMAN: I know. But they gets—listen, this is the, look, this is the third time that I've been here.

MATTHEWS: It makes me mad—

WOMAN: No, but they don't care nothin' about that. They gonna send her, she gonna have to go back to three places.

MALE WORKER: You know what's curious? You know what's curious? Look at the slip they give her to go here. 165 West Forty-sixth Street. I couldn't even get information to give me a number on it.

FEMALE WORKER: I cannot get them to give me an address on it. They transferred me from person to person. [*Everyone continues talking at once, most of the remaining dialogue in the scene overlapping.*]

WOMAN: You see, now, that's different. But did she tell them that she was eligible? But did she tell them that she was eligible?

MATTHEWS: But she's mentally retarded. If that ain't eligible, what the—

WOMAN: But does she have a doctor to, or psychiatrist or somethin' to, uh—

MATTHEWS: Don't you know they send everybody here to Jay Street before you can get—

WOMAN: I know, but you don't see no psychiatrist at 330 Jay Street. I been there.

MATTHEWS: I ain't no psychiatrist and I can tell—

WOMAN: Right, but I—

MATTHEWS: You ain't no psychiatrist and you can tell—right.

WOMAN: Right. Right, but I—

MATTHEWS: So you know he can tell.

WOMAN: But they don't give you the complete test, but they don't give everybody the complete medical over at 330 Jay Street.

MATTHEWS: Two and two ain't twenty-two, baby.

WOMAN: Right. But look—

MATTHEWS: I mean, but that's what I was telling her. Ain't no need in arguing with him.

JOHNSON: —get put out in the street.

MATTHEWS: No, you ain't goin' to get put out in the street. Come walk with me downstairs and I'll talk to Miss Perry and she'll try to find your record, okay?

WOMAN: Listen. They got they procedures down and you know—

MATTHEWS: —she gets upset, she gets upset, and I don't want any shit, you know, she almost has seizures—

WOMAN: I know, I know, I know.

MATTHEWS: Valerie, Valerie, Valerie, Valerie. Look. I'm gonna get my check. [*Three shots of clients and the interview area.*]

FEMALE WORKER: So, I think what she needs to do tomorrow is to go to the Social Security office. [*Cut to MS of two women in waiting room.*]

FEMALE CLIENT 1: . . . Because they said that you can't have your own apartment and all that baloney if you're under twenty-one.

ZIMMERMAN: Well, that's bullshit.

CLIENT 1: I know, and I went to court, so now—but I'm not going to see them unless the lawyer comes, because then they just hassle you around and, you know, run all that shit—

ZIMMERMAN: Well, they told me I had to get a lawyer to get a buildings inspector down in my house.

CLIENT 1: To get a what?

ZIMMERMAN: A buildings inspector. We got rats, and the wall's falling down.

CLIENT 1: And they let your baby live there? *They're* supposed to come, no building inspector.

ZIMMERMAN: I know.

CLIENT 1: [*inaudible*] building inspector.

ZIMMERMAN: I came here with about five apartments already and they refused them all.

CLIENT 1: Yeah? How much were the rents?

ZIMMERMAN: Uh, one was a hundred and thirty-five, one was a hundred and sixty. Now I got one for ninety dollars. They can't refuse me now.

CLIENT 1: No, like Eddie called. My son is only five months old and, you know, my mother's real sick, you know, asthmatic and stuff like that, and my father has had heart attacks. We don't get along anyway. You know, she's mad because I'm not married and I have the kid, and I, now I tell them I want my own apartment and they tell me I can't have it. When I was pregnant I came here. I was five months pregnant and they made me come here like six or seven times and they tell me, okay, we're going to give you, open your own budget, open your own budget and they told me no, you know. I didn't even have carfare to come here. This place gives you a big runaround. They're full of shit.

ZIMMERMAN: What you should do, get your parents to write you a letter.

CLIENT 1: I got, I got a notarized letter.

ZIMMERMAN: Saying they won't support you.

CLIENT 1: I know. I got a notarized letter from my mother's doctor saying that she's very sick and me and my son shouldn't be living in the house. I got a notarized letter from my father that he doesn't want me in the house. That's how they are. Usually they put the baby in your mother's custody or somethin' but they put him in my custody. You know, but I'm on Beth Israel methadone program and they're pretty good. Private programs aren't as good as city programs, you know. It's much better.

ZIMMERMAN: —if they try to take my kid. Now Welfare—I have the letter from my shrink saying that I'm mentally stable now. Because I got off for mental disability two years ago. They want to know whether I'm stable or not, enough to have the kid. So I talked to my shrink and he says, well, what do you want to tell them? [*Short laugh.*] So I said, tell them I'm not crazy no more.

CLIENT 1: Oh.

ZIMMERMAN: So, I got a together shrink, you know.

CLIENT 1: Yeah, because they do try, you know. That's less, less money for them to be giving you. You know, that takes the baby away.

ZIMMERMAN: Yeah. Right. They took her off my budget just because she was in the hospital, for a week. So now I have to get her—if I get this place, I have to get her back on before the seventh. So I'll have a little money left.

CLIENT 1 (*Leaving*): Excuse me.

ZIMMERMAN: Take it easy. [*Cut to MS of Zimmerman as she walks away, camera following.*]

WORKER: No way it can be reopened. [*Cut to CU of another client being interviewed.*] State law provides that if it's closed for more than—

CLIENT: You give me technicality. I'm telling you about a condition, man, that means I might be not eating, or have no place to stay, and you telling me about technicality. What you tellin' me? No, 'bout state law. What'd you give me a check for, when I came down here last time for?

WORKER: I didn't give you a check.

CLIENT: I'm talking about . . . Now, now, you that tech—, you're that technical, that you know, you understand what I'm saying, when I say "you," I'm not speaking about you.

WORKER: Your case was open the last time you came in the center, and that was three months ago.

CLIENT: How could it be open when I got a notification statin' that the case was closed? What are you tellin' me? You tellin' me something completely contrary to what—

WORKER: I'm telling you the last time you were here—wait a minute now.

CLIENT: What you mean, wait a minute? Don't tell me to wait a minute.

WORKER: I'm telling you the last time you were here, on the eighth of November, your case was open, which was why you got a check here.

CLIENT: Well, alright, then. I'm telling you that I got no official notice that even, would even indicate that I should come down here.

WORKER: Ask for a fair hearing.

CLIENT: Well, who do I ask for a fair hearing? [*Client rises and begins to leave, as dialogue following is heard on soundtrack.*]

MALE CLIENT: I need five operations. They have my records that say I need these operations, from my doctor, from their doctor. [*Cut to client speaking.*] I have the brace now, orthopedic brace. I can hardly walk. But then I have to come down here and fight for my check and the—some mornings

I can't get up, out of bed, and my doctor is mad, you know, that I should sign my way into a hospital. Where would I live when I come out?

FEMALE CLIENT: —the hotel is nowhere near here. You know—

MALE CLIENT: I have a tumor on my back. I need a left ear operation. I have hernias. They have it all down in my record.

FEMALE CLIENT: Yeah.

MALE CLIENT: I was at the Social Security office yesterday, on Forty-sixth Street, the annex, and they told me to come down here and I would get a check here. And now these people say I'm supposed to get a check back up there.

FEMALE CLIENT: That's exactly what happened to me. The Social Security sends you to the Welfare and they says the Welfare will give you a check and the Welfare says that the Social Security is supposed to give you a check and nobody gives you a check.

MALE CLIENT: I don't have no rent money or food money and I have no carfare money.

FEMALE CLIENT: And I don't have, I don't even have, and you have to sneak under the trains, to get in the trains to go see the offices.

MALE CLIENT: That's how I came here, by sneaking on the train.

FEMALE CLIENT: To get down to the offices and once you're in the office you wait around for hours and they don't care. They, they—people got lost and the man at the Social Security says that he's took care of two and a half million people, he had to take care of. So if a couple of thousand don't get their check, he's doing a very good job. [*Shot of policeman walking down aisle of waiting room. Cut to shot of Sam on telephone.*]

SAM (*on telephone*): They told her to bring in a letter from Social Security and they told her to bring—yeah, yes. [*To community worker*] Well, what did they tell you today?

COMMUNITY WORKER: They told us to come back tomorrow.

SAM (*on telephone*): They told her to come back tomorrow.

COMMUNITY WORKER: Fill out the application and come back tomorrow.

SAM (*on telephone*): To fill out the application and come back tomorrow. [*To community worker*] Well, you were given an appointment for tomorrow. Listen.

COMMUNITY WORKER: Right. But then she don't have no money for today.

SAM (*on telephone*): But she doesn't have no money for today. And the social worker is, you know, a real—he says that he can't help her out and is puzzled . . . [*To community worker*] You have some place to stay tonight?

COMMUNITY WORKER (*to client*): ¿Tienes un apartamento? [Do you have an apartment?]

CLIENT: Sí. [Yes.]

COMMUNITY WORKER: Yes, she has her own apartment.

SAM: The only thing they can do—we'll give you an appointment for tomorrow. If you can't, if they don't, refuse to help her tomorrow, then come up and I'll go downstairs with you, okay?

COMMUNITY WORKER: But I want some money for today so she—

SAM: They won't be able to give you money today. There's, there's no way they can give you—she got a place to live and it's not an emergency, they claim.

COMMUNITY WORKER: But she don't have nothing to eat.

SAM: Nothing we can do about it. [*On telephone*] She said, they claim, that there's no food money in the house, you know?

COMMUNITY WORKER: Okay. Dame la cartera. La cartera, tu, ya. [Give me your wallet.] [*To Sam*] Look, that's all she has.

SAM (*on telephone*): Okay. [*To client*] Make the appointment. Take the appointment and come back tomorrow morning as they requested. And if she runs into a snafu tomorrow, if she runs into some sort of a problem tomorrow, you and her come upstairs and see me, okay?

COMMUNITY WORKER: Well, what is she going to do for today? That's all I want to know. She's a sick person.

SAM (*overlapping*): Listen, there's nothing they—they won't give her any money today.

COMMUNITY WORKER: Not even, you know, a few dollars so she can eat?

SAM: Nothing. Nothing at all. Better come back tomorrow morning.

COMMUNITY WORKER (*to client*): No te pueden da nada. [They say they can't help you today.]

CLIENT: Ese señor me dijo que iban a darme un cheque hoy. [This man told me they were going to give me a check today.]

COMMUNITY WORKER: You see. I told her she was going to get a check.

33. A community worker argues for emergency help for his client.

SAM: I just spoke to the applications, the head supervisor there, and they won't be able to help you.

COMMUNITY WORKER: Well, what's she going to do—starve?

SAM: What, I didn't say you should starve. Did I say you should starve?

COMMUNITY WORKER: What she going to do? She don't have no money.

SAM: What are you—do you represent a poverty agency or what?

COMMUNITY WORKER: No, a community center . . . Aldrich Community Center.

SAM: She didn't live in a vacuum all these years. She knows the grocery man and she knows different people. She can get credit for a day. She didn't live in a vacuum. All these years she lived in New York. She worked. She knows people. She knows grocery men. She knows neighbors. She has some sort of relatives. She knows people—

COMMUNITY WORKER: She's never taken welfare before and now that she comes for help, you know, nobody wants to help her. If you're going to tell me if she won't be here every time for Welfare, they're not going to understand what you're saying.

SAM: Nobody said they're not going to help her. They can help her. She brought back the requirements as she was told to do.

COMMUNITY WORKER: And she doesn't get no help and she brought the requirements.

SAM: They, they say they won't be able to see her till tomorrow. That's it. There's nothing more I can do on that. I'd like to help you out but there's nothing I can do. Tomorrow, I'll personally go down with you. Tomorrow, if she runs into any problems, but not today.

COMMUNITY WORKER (*overlapping*): It's going to be the same thing today as tomorrow. Because she signs an application today, and then—

SAM: —they won't see her until tomorrow—I didn't see the appointment . . . originally, I had not seen the appointment. When you first came up, I had not seen the appointment for tomorrow.

COMMUNITY WORKER: So what's so big about an appointment when you could do it today? She's willing to stay here.

SAM: Did you see how many people were downstairs?

COMMUNITY WORKER: This is an emergency case, right?

SAM: Every case is an emergency case.

COMMUNITY WORKER: Do you eat?

SAM: Every case—

COMMUNITY WORKER: You eat, right?

SAM: Do you eat?

COMMUNITY WORKER: Yes.

SAM: Do you eat?

COMMUNITY WORKER: Yes.

SAM: Okay. I eat also. And I'm proud of it. I'm proud of it.

COMMUNITY WORKER (*overlapping*): I'm in good health, but she's not in good health. She had an operation, right? So what is she supposed to do?

SAM: It's all I can do. There's nothing more we can do about it. Nothing more we can do. [*Various shots of workers sitting at desks, talking on phones, going through files and records, secretaries typing. An empty desk stacked with files. A woman types into an IBM machine, activating computer cards and tickertape. Men in computer room program and load computers. Computerized lists and checks are printed. Various people enter Welfare Center. Clients sit in waiting area.*]

34. One client (r.) tells another of his forthcoming marriage to Governor Rockefeller's sister.

WORKER: Nineteen-C. [*Four shots of clients waiting. Cut to two-shot of two men sitting and talking.*]

CLIENT 1: I make a lot of phone calls trying to get a job. No one wants to give me a job. I'll get a job, though.

CLIENT 2: Can you cook?

CLIENT 1: Yeah. I can cook.

CLIENT 2: Were you ever on a ship?

CLIENT 1: Yeah. Small ships, small boats. As a matter fact, I was on, last ship I was on was a French aircraft carrier.

CLIENT 2: Oh, yeah?

CLIENT 1: Yeah.

CLIENT 2: What were you doin' there? Cooking?

CLIENT 1: I was wandering around. Visiting. Going south.

CLIENT 2: Been Europe and Asia?

CLIENT 1: Never been in Europe and Asia.

CLIENT 2: Been out of the country?

CLIENT 1: Yeah.

CLIENT 2: Where?

CLIENT 1: Canada.

CLIENT 2: It's the only place I've been.

CLIENT 1: Montreal. Toronto. London.

CLIENT 2: I'm marrying Governor Rockefeller's sister.

CLIENT 1: You are? That's good.

CLIENT 2: Well, I'm worth a fortune, myself, this year when I get my money. So, she's giving me three thousand dollars.

CLIENT 1: Three thousand dollars?

CLIENT 2: Yeah. Two thousand five hundred for a month, five hundred a month or so—

CLIENT 1: Doing pretty good. I haven't worked for, since October.

CLIENT 2: I'm going to sing and dance on television.

CLIENT 1: You're kidding.

CLIENT 2: My brother-in-law, my future brother-in-law, Nelson and John Rockefeller, are going to set it up.

CLIENT 1: What are you doing here, then?

CLIENT 2: Broke. You know.

CLIENT 1: Broke. I know how you feel. I'm not a success.

CLIENT 2: Ah, you know how—you'll get your money.

CLIENT 1: I don't even have a credit card. Here. I got twenty-three cents in my pocket. Don't even have a credit card. No, I gave up all my credit cards four or five years ago. No good. Pay cash. On the barrelhead.

CLIENT 2: I'm going to the Bronx.

CLIENT 1: Cash on the barrelhead.

CLIENT 2: Did you ever do any fighting?

CLIENT 1: Fighting? No. I'm a peaceful man.

CLIENT 2: Never had any fights?

CLIENT 1: Nah. Not in a long time. My wife hit me on the head, I think.

CLIENT 2: You still married?

CLIENT 1: Yeah. She'll never get rid of me. [*Cut to two-shot of two other clients speaking.*]

CLIENT 1: I'm going down to find out if I can get shelter, a Catholic Worker, and possibly I can . . . see if I can call state employment.

CLIENT 2: What did you say that she said? You had to have a physical and then after that a psychiatric exam?

CLIENT 1: No, no, no, no, no, no, no. You have a physical on like the first. Then, on the second, you wait a day, and then you go back on the third. Apparently they do blood tests and things like that.

CLIENT 2: You come back here, two days later?

CLIENT 1: Come back here on the fourth. It's the soonest you can get back here, assuming the fourth is a day that they're open.

CLIENT 2: Not on the weekend or something.

CLIENT 1: It's probably another weekend. By then I'll be very hungry, and I—

CLIENT 2: I don't know if I'm going to take all that.

CLIENT 1: Oh, I'm sure you will have to. It's procedure. She told me. [*Cut to FS of a man standing by a post in waiting area.*]

CLIENT WITH FORMS (*pulling papers from his pockets*): I fill out all these papers. I could show you VA, this, that . . . Wherever the blacks dominate, it's a, it's a catastrophe for any poor slob seeking assistance. And I got stuff here . . . I could show you . . . so much stuff here . . . this, that, that . . . all these are different things, all these are places I've been . . . show you names . . . written numbers here, names, all these centers, every one of them. I'm a veteran. They say I'm not a Korean veteran because I went in nineteen-seventeen-fifty-three, and officially according to the VA, it ain't over till one-fifty-five. That I'm positive of, because I would have had a wartime disability only it was before—

OTHER CLIENT: Well, I was in fifty-two, fifty-two.

CLIENT WITH FORMS: I was in the navy before that.

OTHER CLIENT: It was in the army and at that time and it don't make a *damn* difference—

CLIENT WITH FORMS: You couldn't get VA assistance?

OTHER CLIENT: No, they give you shit.

CLIENT WITH FORMS: You can get VA assistance. Did you go up to that place, 529 Eighth Avenue? Somethin's awful funny here. Somethin' doesn't meet the eye. Look, all these places I've been at. No carfare. None. I don't eat.

35. A client complains about the bureaucracy of the welfare system.

Walk the streets. I got medical proof of my sickness. I'll have it tomorrow, if these—I'll have it Monday or Tuesday, rather. I didn't get to mail these letters out. I ain't got stamps. I've been here four times this week. Four times. And they keep sending me out, and every place I go keeps sending me back here. Now, you figure that one out. Here I was all day one day. Look at these forms they fill out. A whole rigamarole of forms. Papers, papers, papers. I got more [*digging in his pockets again*] . . . Here's one . . . Here's another one. Here's another one and another one . . . Here's my hospital card from the VA, I'm a veteran. [*Cut to another man with papers walking unsteadily out of the Center.*] I got a driver's permit. I been at twenty, thirty places. I— [*Another shot of unsteady man leaving Center, followed by a shot of the reception area.*]

WOMAN (*on telephone*): Hello, David. You're not going to believe what's happening here. Tuesday morning I came over to the Waverly Center. [*Cut to CU of woman speaking.*] Waverly says bring back a passport. Bring your notarization from your father that he's not willing to support you anymore. So you fill out this application, bring back letters from your doctors that when you were dismissed, when you entered, all this crap. And, and they gave me an appointment, so Thursday morning, want also a notarized letter from my roommate that she was no longer going to put up with me after Friday. Well, I have a letter from her, but the poor kid does not have the time to notarize it. So, I came back. I was really—forgot the appointment on Thursday because I've been depressed and kind of upset. I come back today. I went to talk to the worker. She would not read the letter from the department of—oh, yesterday I went down to the World Trade Center, Department of Social whatever-it-is from the city. Yeah. Well, she would not read that letter, nor would she read the letters from the two doctors. She said, I'll give you an appointment for Monday. I said, I'm sorry, I have one dollar to my name and I have not got a place to stay this weekend. She said, sorry, all I can do is give you an appointment for Monday. I said, you've got to be kidding. I am out of an institute. Out for manic depression and I am depressed, lady. What do I do? "Come back for your appointment on Monday." Do you believe that? . . . This coming Monday! Uh, she really doesn't care. None of them care. I told her I have no friends. I told her I have no place to go. I told her that I have a dollar, that I walked up from Bleeker Street. I have a notarized letter from the hospital. I have a notarized letter from everybody. I have every goddamned thing they asked for. And they said all we can do—I spoke to the office manager—is you can come back Monday morning for an appointment. I said, Lady, what do I do for the weekend? I am sick. I was discharged Monday from a psychiatric institute for manic depression. This is friendly New York for you and the New York Welfare Department. Maybe she thinks I should sleep in Port Authority for the weekend. Yeah, that's what they—oh, first they, even down at the State Department or whatever it is, she said women's shelter. She said, but you really couldn't go there. There's a lot of sickies there. A lot of dykes, a lot of really, you know, bad news people. I said, really, lady, I would freak out. There's no way I could handle that. And she said, well, I'm sorry. It takes at least maximum forty-five days to get approved for welfare. I said—they wouldn't touch me in the hospital. What the hell do they expect me to do? . . . What? . . . Yeah. That's not a bad idea . . . Well, I'm writing a letter to the *Village Voice*. Maybe I'll call Hillary, too. Geraldo Rivera? Okay . . . Yeah . . . I think he might be very interested in it. [*Cut to two-shot of white man and black policeman.*]

MAN: You're going to see more hanging than you ever saw in your life.

POLICEMAN: I've seen a lot of hanging.

MAN: Hanging.

POLICEMAN: Oh, yes. I lost my brother at five years old. Hung.

MAN: They'll hang.

POLICEMAN: Yeah.

MAN: They'll hang like crazy.

POLICEMAN: What can I tell you?

MAN: Like crazy.

POLICEMAN: What can I tell you?

MAN: You can't tell me anything.

POLICEMAN: There it is.

MAN: There's no way to control it, man.

POLICEMAN: There's no way to control *anything*.

MAN: Then what are we talking about?

POLICEMAN: We all act like savages.

MAN: That's right.

POLICEMAN: That's the way this country was founded.

MAN: Savages.

POLICEMAN: Yeah. It is.

MAN: We're all savages.

POLICEMAN: All of us. Black, white, blue, green, purple, all of us are savages.

MAN: There's no way we can conduct ourselves as gentlemen amongst ourselves?

POLICEMAN: Yeah, there is. That can be done. But nobody wants to take time out to sit down and find it.

MAN: I do.

POLICEMAN: You do? By calling me nigger? Telling me you goin' to shoot me with a three-five-seven magnum? How am I supposed to take that?

MAN: The next time, the next time three guys do this up against my head, I'm going to shoot them.

POLICEMAN: Well, you got a right against those three guys.

MAN: You better believe it, baby.

POLICEMAN: Those three, *only* those three. You don't come here and threaten me. I ain't never seen you before.

MAN: That's right.

POLICEMAN: I ain't put my hands on you. And you come here and you threatening me.

MAN: You black are about ten percent of the population—

POLICEMAN: Yeah.

MAN: —and you account for sixty-three percent of the crime.

POLICEMAN: Well, what can we tell you?

MAN: Statistically, you don't have to tell me anything.

POLICEMAN: What you want me to say? What do you want me to say?

MAN (*overlapping*): How come ten percent are worth sixty-three percent of the crime?

POLICEMAN: So now what you trying to say is all of us are bad.

MAN: No.

POLICEMAN: Um?

MAN: No. *No* one is all bad.

POLICEMAN: So, so this is what the whole thing is about. You're trying to judge the whole by one.

MAN (*overlapping*): I've never met a completely all—no, I'm not.

POLICEMAN: You cannot do that.

MAN: I've given you a statistic.

POLICEMAN: You cannot do that.

MAN: What do you mean?

POLICEMAN: Statistics don't mean anything to me. Really. 'Cause there ain't a man out there in the street that I'm afraid of. Nobody gonna take anything from me.

MAN: Cain slew Abel.

POLICEMAN: Yeah, but Abel wasn't looking.

MAN: His brother . . . That's right.

POLICEMAN: I don't trust anyone.

MAN: I assume they were white.

POLICEMAN: Oh, you can assume what you want to.

MAN: Whatever.

POLICEMAN: You can assume what you want to.

MAN: [*Inaudible*]—necessary. It's not a, it's not a hang-up about the black.

POLICEMAN: I know this. This I know.

MAN: Why are the blacks, uh—

POLICEMAN: Well, uh, the bl—

MAN: Get whitey, get whitey—

POLICEMAN: So why was it before get nigger?

MAN: —get whitey. Get nigger?

POLICEMAN: What goes round comes round.

MAN: They didn't have to get nigger. They could hang a nigger. They didn't have to get him. They could hang him.

POLICEMAN (*overlapping*): They could hang a nigger. Just like, you know, that's your race. That's your race. Put that away. Hang a nigger anytime you want to.

MAN: Any time.

POLICEMAN: Right after lunch. Hang a nigger.

MAN: Mississippi.

POLICEMAN: Yeah.

MAN: Get out of town by sunset.

POLICEMAN: Uh-huh. Uh-huh.

MAN: Your ass is black, get out of town.

POLICEMAN: Yeah, it is.

MAN: Don't be here when the sun sets.

POLICEMAN: Right.

MAN: That's Mississippi.

POLICEMAN: No, that's all over.

MAN: Well, what about my town?

POLICEMAN: What is your town?

MAN: New York.

POLICEMAN: New York? New York is my town, too.

MAN: We never did that.

POLICEMAN: You never did what?

MAN: We never talked.

POLICEMAN: Huh?

MAN: We never talked, get your ass out of here, get your ass out of New York . . . because you're colored.

POLICEMAN: Really?

MAN: Really.

POLICEMAN: You sure of this?

MAN: Absolutely.

POLICEMAN: You're positive?

MAN: Can't be positive. Only a fool is positive.

POLICEMAN: Alright, then. Alright, then.

MAN: A fool is positive.

POLICEMAN: So don't come here and tell me . . .

MAN: But I never heard it—

POLICEMAN (*overlapping*): You can't tell me something you—

MAN: I never heard it—

POLICEMAN: —positive about, I don't even want to hear it.

MAN (*overlapping*): But I never heard it. I never heard it. I never heard it.

POLICEMAN: Oh, there's a lot I never heard of.

MAN: But I was really amazed when I saw these three goddamned blacks beating my head, and kicking my head in.

POLICEMAN: You keep bringing that up.

MAN: Kicking my head in.

POLICEMAN: You keep bringing that up.

MAN: Well, it's a fact, man.

POLICEMAN: Well, I've got nothing to do with that.

MAN: Well, certainly—

POLICEMAN: I've got nothing to do with that.

MAN: But they got a particularly sadistic delight in beating whitey's head in.

WORKER'S VOICE IN BACKGROUND (*calling client*): Roberto Cabilla.

MAN: That covered all the hangings and all the, uh, you know. That covered everything. They didn't even know.

POLICEMAN: That made up for all of it.

36. A white racist needles a black policeman.

MAN: That made up for all of it.

POLICEMAN: Just once, that one little incident with you has made up for everything? Well, then, everything should be straight now.

MAN: They're so hateful, so hateful.

POLICEMAN: Everything should be straight now.

MAN: No, the only thing straight is that I'm going to get a gun. And when I see a black man coming up to me, I'm gonna blow his belly out.

POLICEMAN: Uh-huh.

MAN: I'm not gonna blow his belly out. I'm going to hit him in the balls.

POLICEMAN: Uh-huh.

MAN: So that he'll not progenerate.

POLICEMAN: You think they make only one gun?

MAN: One gun to blow his balls completely off.

POLICEMAN: That's all they make. That's all they make is one gun?

MAN: I'm gonna—I'm a gunner sergeant.

POLICEMAN: What's that mean?

MAN: I was a marine sergeant.

POLICEMAN: What's that mean?

MAN: I killed about five hundred men in the war. I never saw them. But now I'm—

POLICEMAN (*overlapping*): How you know you killed them?

MAN: —gonna see that black when he comes up to me and a Puerto Rican—

POLICEMAN: Oh, now it's a Puerto Rican.

MAN (*overlapping*): And I'm gonna blow him right—yeah.

POLICEMAN: And if I talked to you in half an hour, there would be an Irishman and a Chinaman.

MAN: Sure.

POLICEMAN: Yeah. Okay.

MAN: Sure. But at the moment, it's Puerto Rican and a—

POLICEMAN: Yeah, what was it? Two blacks and one Puerto Rican? Or two Puerto Ricans and one black?

MAN (*overlapping*): It happened to be three blacks.

POLICEMAN: It happened to be three blacks and one Puerto Rican.

MAN: When this, when this happened, yeah.

POLICEMAN: Oh, when that happened. The Puerto Rican wasn't there when this happened.

MAN: Kicking my brains out. Now, don't tell me, man.

POLICEMAN: I'm not. I can't tell you anything.

MAN: They got a real delight, kicking my brains out and I'm trying to fight 'em.

POLICEMAN (*overlapping*): I didn't see it. I can't tell you anything. I'm just going—

MAN (*overlapping*): —Get that whitey, get whitey, you, whitey—punks.

POLICEMAN: Did you do anything to them?

MAN: Yeah.

POLICEMAN: What?

MAN: If I'd got a hold of him, I'd strangle him.

POLICEMAN: I, I didn't say, I said, did you do anything *before* they started hitting you?

MAN: Of course not.

POLICEMAN: Hmm? You just walking down the street—

MAN: One guy got me on the back of the neck. I'm down. There it is. I'm down. I'm out.

POLICEMAN: I feel for you.

MAN: I got up to fight 'em. They ripped me off.

POLICEMAN: I feel for you, myself.

MAN: Yeah, you feel.

POLICEMAN: I feel for you. I'm serious.

MAN: You would have protected me?

POLICEMAN: Probably. Probably.

MAN: With the badge and everything.

POLICEMAN: Probably.

MAN: You would have pro—

POLICEMAN: I've put my life on the line for less than that. For a country I don't have.

MAN: For a *country* you don't have?

POLICEMAN: For a country I do not have.

MAN: I don't have a country, man.

POLICEMAN: Oh, well.

MAN: You people have got it.

POLICEMAN: Oh, we got it now? Oh, so now it's our country and you're just living here?

MAN: I won't fight anymore for this one.

POLICEMAN: Yeah?

MAN: Thirty years ago I fought for this one. Not any more. Not to bring up the swine that's coming up on the streets.

POLICEMAN: What swine are you talking about now?

MAN: Hah.

POLICEMAN: What swine are you talking about now?

MAN: What do you want, baby?

POLICEMAN: I don't want anything.

MAN: What do you really want?

POLICEMAN: Actually, I don't even feel like talking to you, but since you're here, to tell you the truth—

MAN: What? You'd rather ignore the whole thing, eh?

POLICEMAN: That's—isn't that what you're doing?

MAN: No.

POLICEMAN: No?

MAN: I'm bitching like crazy.

POLICEMAN: Hmm.

MAN: I come in here and they can't even give me a room to sleep tonight.

POLICEMAN: Why?

MAN: Why?

POLICEMAN: Why?

MAN: Well, ask them, don't ask me.

POLICEMAN: They should have told you.

MAN: Why?

POLICEMAN: Didn't you talk to the lady? So you tell me what she told you.

MAN: I got a fractured skull. I been two months in the hospital and out. I got a letter from the hospital and I'm persona non grata . . . What should I add? For my country.

POLICEMAN: Yeah.

MAN: Two Puerto Rican paramours, three colored concubines—

POLICEMAN: Oh, now it's five of 'em, now it's five of 'em.

MAN (*overlapping*): Six children, six children. Well, it's only a story.

POLICEMAN: Hmm?

MAN: What should I do? I've already . . . I paid more taxes than my president.

POLICEMAN: We all paid more taxes than your president. You ain't said nothing.

MAN: Is there anybody here to talk to me, or what are you going to do with me?

POLICEMAN: The lady's been talking to you already. I don't know what she told you.

MAN (*overlapping*): They haven't talked to me yet.

POLICEMAN (*overlapping*): Yes, she has.

MAN: It's getting late.

POLICEMAN: So, what are you doing? You going to the hospital now?

MAN: Yeah. You gotta call the hospital. I want to go back. May I use your phone?

POLICEMAN: Ask the sergeant in there. He'll let you use any phone you want to.

MAN: Never the twain shall meet, eh?

POLICEMAN: If that's the way you feel. If that's the way you feel.

MAN: That's the way I know, baby. We're never gonna make it, never gonna make it.

POLICEMAN: Anyway, I'm not gonna try, stop trying, till I'm dead.

MAN: Now, this is not my country. You don't even comb your hair. You gonna be—

POLICEMAN: Who don't comb what hair?

MAN: Black is beautiful.

POLICEMAN: I got the right to wear my hair *any* way I please.

MAN: Black is beautiful, man.

POLICEMAN: I know it is. I know it is.

MAN: Black is . . . blood.

POLICEMAN: To you.

MAN: I'm getting a three-five-seven magnum and blowing every black that I can right out of the business.

POLICEMAN: So now, two wrongs goin' make a right, now?

MAN: Right. And when we finally get rid of the ten percent of black—

POLICEMAN: Just get rid of all of us.

MAN: Get rid of all of you.

POLICEMAN: Never. Never.

MAN: Not the way you progenerate.

POLICEMAN: No way. No way. No way.

MAN (*overlapping*): Oh, man. You're like rabbits. You're like rabbits.

POLICEMAN (*overlapping*): No way.

MAN (*overlapping*): You're like rabbits. But where we're gonna beat you is because you don't have any home. [*Insert shots of clients waiting.*] When it gets so goddamn bad, these streets are gonna run with blood.

POLICEMAN: Yeah, well. One thing I can tell you is—

MAN: And you're only ten percent.

POLICEMAN: —it won't be all black [*cut back to man in CU*] blood.

MAN: Oh, they'll be, you'll get some whiteys. They're getting some whiteys. They're getting a few cops.

POLICEMAN: Uh-huh.

MAN: They're dedicated to get cops.

POLICEMAN: Uh-huh.

MAN: There's, you know, the blacks are dedicated to get cops.

POLICEMAN: Oh, we all are?

MAN: They killed, they killed many, many cops.

POLICEMAN: I'm dedicated to get a cop?

MAN: Oh, you got to get him.

POLICEMAN: Oh, I got to get him?

MAN: Badge or no badge. You got to get him. Oh yeah.

POLICEMAN: That sounds a little far-fetched.

MAN: Now, that's not even the Muslim. They're even taking them out—the far-fetched Muslim. But it's not even far-fetched Muslim. They're out to get the cops. But we're not gonna allow it. And because the fact that you're in a minority, you're gonna die. You're gonna be worse off than you ever were.

POLICEMAN: I see. You have to remember—

MAN: Back to Africa, and that's it.

POLICEMAN (*overlapping*): You have to remember a minority started this country.

MAN: Not a minority.

POLICEMAN: Oh yes it was.

MAN: Oh no.

POLICEMAN: When the British ruled this country, how many people were in America, man?

MAN: Oh no. That was a political and a religious minority, but they were white. They were white. They were white.

POLICEMAN: Oh. And this is different. This is different.

MAN: Like the man says, biologically, and nomalogically, and pharmanology, everything, the black, pharmasominally—

POLICEMAN: Is what?

MAN: Different.

POLICEMAN: Different than who?

MAN: The white.

POLICEMAN: Hmm?

MAN: The white.

POLICEMAN: In what respect? . . . In what respect am I different from you? . . . Hmm?

MAN: You figure it out. Take your whole people.

POLICEMAN: I'm no different from you . . . except maybe a little prouder.

MAN: Don't put it—prouder?

POLICEMAN: Maybe a little prouder. That's right.

MAN: Man, you got nothing going.

POLICEMAN: Who got nothing going? I got *everything* going.

MAN: Nothin'. You got nothing going.

POLICEMAN: Really? Bet you I got more going *now*—and I'm only twenty-two—than you had in your whole life.

MAN: I'm fifty-one, man, and I fought wars.

POLICEMAN: [*Inaudible.*]

MAN: And I've, I've fought wars. Twice as old—

POLICEMAN: I've fought 'em, too. Ain't no big thing. Ain't no big thing. And I fought in a war that was worse than yours. 'Cause I saw who I was killing.

MAN: Never seen him.

POLICEMAN: Oh, I saw who I was killing. Every man I shot down I saw.

MAN: I never saw the men that I killed.

POLICEMAN: That's the difference between your war and mine.

MAN: I had an order.

POLICEMAN: We all had orders.

MAN: You're prejudiced, and that means that—

POLICEMAN (*overlapping*): At whom?

MAN (*overlapping*): You had a particular reason to kill a man.

POLICEMAN (*overlapping*): At whom? At whom am I prejudiced?

MAN (*overlapping*): I never killed a man I ever—

POLICEMAN (*overlapping*): Tell me, whom am I prejudiced—

MAN (*overlapping*): I never killed a man—I never killed a man that I, I, I never had anything against a man that I killed.

POLICEMAN: Then what were you doing in the war, then?

MAN: Surviving.

POLICEMAN: Isn't that what we're doing?

MAN: Simply surviving.

POLICEMAN: Isn't that what we're doing?

MAN: Oh no. Not the way the blacks coming up now. Black is beautiful. Black is powerful. Black is—

POLICEMAN (*overlapping*): —still survival.

MAN (*overlapping*): Power.

POLICEMAN (*overlapping*): Still survival.

MAN (*overlapping*): Power. Power.

POLICEMAN (*overlapping*): It's all survival.

MAN: You got nothing going, man.

POLICEMAN: I got everything going.

MAN: Man, you say black is power. You gonna eighty-six out.

POLICEMAN: Eighty-six out. I might as well get all my business together. Say goodbye to everybody.

MAN: Say goodbye to everybody.

POLICEMAN: Well, see, I didn't know, you know. Now that I know—

MAN: Well, you don't think you're gonna make too goddamned much—

POLICEMAN: Hmm?

MAN: You don't think you're gonna make too goddamned much.

POLICEMAN: No, man, I'm gonna make everything I want.

MAN: Oh. Take a look at TV right now. We're in the greatest goddamned spot.

POLICEMAN: I got everything I want. Everything I want.

MAN: What have you got?

POLICEMAN: What do we have?

MAN: What have you got? Not even expression.

POLICEMAN: Tell me.

MAN: Not even leadership.

POLICEMAN: Oh, I—at what? At what?

MAN: At any level.

POLICEMAN: At any level?

MAN: You blacks can't even lead, each other. You can't even lead each other.

WORKER (*offscreen, overlapping*): Why do you waste your time with him?

POLICEMAN: I got nothing better to do. I haven't got anything better to do.

WORKER (*offscreen*): It gets on my nerves. I can't work over here.

POLICEMAN: Alright. I'll finish in a minute.

WORKER (*offscreen*): Okay. Thank you.

POLICEMAN: Okay. [*To man*] It was nice talking to you. I learned a lot from you.

MAN: It wasn't—you haven't, you haven't learned a goddamned thing.

POLICEMAN: Yes, I did. I learned that I don't have long to live. That's good to know.

MAN: You're killing yourself.

POLICEMAN: I don't want to die just like that. If I know what's coming, I can prepare for it.

MAN: It all depends on who shoots you, who hangs you— [*Two insert shots of white clients and one of another black policeman.*]

POLICEMAN: Really.

MAN: I got no respect.

POLICEMAN: Well, that's you.

MAN: No respect.

POLICEMAN: I got enough for both of us.

MAN: Oh?

POLICEMAN: I got enough for both of us. [*Cut back to man.*]

MAN: I hope it will keep us alive.

POLICEMAN: It's going to keep me alive. [*Cut to two-shot of another police-man talking with a client.*]

OTHER POLICEMAN: Your name is MacDonald, right?

CLIENT (MRS. MACDONALD): Yes.

POLICEMAN: Mrs. MacDonald, I'm—

MACDONALD: They say I'm not going to get no—

POLICEMAN: Sweetheart, listen—

MACDONALD: No more white tickets. I done got 'bout four of 'em already.

POLICEMAN: You listening to me?

MACDONALD: Yeah.

POLICEMAN: I asked you to be patient, and when the lady comes back from lunch, I told you that I would come over and let you know. Right? I would check it out for you, right?

MACDONALD: Yeah. But is she back?

POLICEMAN: No, she's not back. She's not back.

MACDONALD: Well, there ain't but three chairs in there.

POLICEMAN: Be patient, alright? Have a seat over there and I take care of it for you. Okay?

MACDONALD: Please, 'cause I got to go to my program.

POLICEMAN: Alright . . . [*To other policeman coming through the door at the same time*] Excuse me. [*Cut back to white racist from previous scene with policemen, one in the shot and the other out of frame, near exit doors.*]

POLICEMAN 1: Listen, mister, go on, go to any place you want. I don't really care. Just get out of the Center, huh?

MAN: This is warfare.

POLICEMAN 1: Oh, boy. Mister, just get out of the Center.

MAN: You know, the interesting thing is that I see that every cop is black. What is this? If I were, if I were a white man with any particular thing I would probably think there was prejudice. What the hell is everybody in social welfare and everything black?

POLICEMAN 1: 'Cause we want to help.

MAN: No. I think I'll get a—what the hell is it, a N-double-A-W-P—?

POLICEMAN 2: C-P.

MAN: —C-P for white people.

POLICEMAN 2: That's good.

MAN: For white people. They gotta protect themselves. You see, the reason I didn't break your head, the reason I didn't break your head was because I knew that I knew goddamn well I could do it. But you hit me like a tiger. You were actually, wanted to do it. I knew I could have busted your back and if it weren't for these guys—

POLICEMAN 1: Mister, why don't you go on out, huh? Mister, would you please—

MAN: You couldn't put, you couldn't put him in a ten-pound bag when I get through with him.

POLICEMAN 1: Yeah. Okay, fine, yeah.

MAN: Do you believe it?

POLICEMAN 1: Right. So go on out of here.

MAN: —with the bands right on top of it. You're that great, man. But if you think you can take me, take my hand right now, put one foot to me, and show these black men how great you are.

POLICEMAN 1: Mister, would you please go on to the hospital or wherever you're goin'. We're going to have to—

MAN: No, I want to get another thing—

POLICEMAN 2: C'mon, the day is over, man. [*Cut to shot of the others outside glass door looking at this conversation inside. Some words are exchanged between the man and a worker, but we do not hear them.*] Let's put the man out.

POLICEMAN 1: Alright, everybody, let's push him right out, that's all. [*The worker and Policeman 2 shove the man out the glass doors of the lobby and the metal exit doors.*]

MAN (*as he is being shoved out*): Oh, Jesus Christ. You're all, you're all going to get it—

WORKER: [*Inaudible.*]

MAN: Hold it—

POLICEMAN 2: —I don't know why you always make me get stuck doing this. [*Laughs*].

MAN: Let me in. [*Cut from CU of policeman's nightstick wedged between the two exterior doors so they are unable to open to LS of blind man in lobby.*]

BLIND MAN: Will somebody show me to the elevator?

MAN: Is it [*inaudible*]?

BLIND MAN: Yeah.

MAN: Here, [*inaudible*].

BLIND MAN: Well, I don't know . . . I need a new Medicaid card— [*He takes his papers and hands them to worker at desk.*]

MAN: Just sit down here. They'll take care of you. They'll take care of you.

BLIND MAN: Thank you.

MAN: Okay. [*The blind man takes a seat. Cut to LS of a woman sitting alone in a waiting area. Cut to CU of client listening to worker Noel.*]

WORKER (NOEL): The reason why they want to close your case is because they have tried to verify your husband's income for several months and nobody has cooperated.

CLIENT (*overlapping*): He brought the income in. It's right here. It's right here in the record. We brought it in—

NOEL: When was that?

CLIENT: —and they took a photostatic copy. Would you look in the record and find it? Every check that I have to go through all this bullshit? Then one time he didn't bring it in—it's in there in the photostatic copy. That's it right there. You gonna keep telling me he didn't bring this, the card, the pay stub, in? He don't get paid off a check. He get paid off an envelope.

NOEL: What did they tell you at the conference that was held on this case? When you received the notice that your case was going to be closed?

CLIENT: They did not send me a notice telling me my case was going to be closed.

NOEL: Well, you had a conference. Didn't you go to the conference?

CLIENT: Yes, and they did not tell—

NOEL: Well, you wouldn't have known about the conference unless you'd known your case was going to be closed.

CLIENT: I asked for this.

NOEL: Yes, but I mean you asked for it because they sent you this here.

CLIENT: They didn't sent nothing out to me because when I came into the office I asked them for a fair hearing. So they advised me to go upstairs to this lady. And she sent me a notice of appointment when to come in.

NOEL: And that's Miss Horowitz you saw, right?

CLIENT: And they did not discuss nothing about no case closing or nothing. You think if they told me my case was going to be closed I'd be sitting up here?

NOEL: Well, the conference was held according to all of this. I want to ask my supervisor about this. Wait here. [*Cut to two-shot of Tom and Noel.*] No, Tom, you're misunderstanding me. [*Noel leaves, camera holding on client.*]

TOM: Yes, I know what you're, uh—

NOEL: She got this. [*Cut to two-shot of Tom and Noel.*]

TOM: Right. Right.

NOEL: She called the number.

TOM: And she got the fair hearing.

NOEL: She got this conference. The conference said her case would be closed. So they're sending her this notice saying, yes, your case is going to be closed.

TOM (*overlapping*): Yes, but she didn't intend to have a fair hearing with the conference, right?

NOEL: Well, my question is this. She says that she gave them the information they wanted.

TOM: But, I mean—

NOEL: *And* if you look in the record—

TOM: Yeah, but I'm asking you, did she have—

NOEL: You will see that in fact she did.

TOM: Yeah, but I'm not—

NOEL: So I wonder why they're closing the case.

TOM: Oh, that, okay. Ah, this is from, from George Drew's office.

NOEL: Horowitz worked on it.

TOM: Alright.

NOEL: Should I go up and give Horowitz a run for her money?

37. One worker challenges another on a case determination.

TOM: Alright, alright. Go up and ask her, yeah, go up and ask Horowitz why they're closing her case.

NOEL: Fabulous. Let's go.

TOM: Right, that's what the whole— [*Noel picks up file and walks out of the office.*]. Thanks, Noel. Thanks, Noel. [*Cut to camera following Noel from corridor into another large office.*]

NOEL: Excuse me, is this Miss Horowitz's office? [*Cut to Noel talking to Miss Horowitz.*] . . . And you agree that the case should be closed. Is that what this means?

HOROWITZ (*reading from file*): "Client working for five years" . . . Yes, that's what it means, whatever action is necessary. Because I have no proof that this man is, has left the home. In fact, I don't believe he has.

NOEL: Well, no, but she was asked to bring in the pay stubs. Right? That is what the closing is for. She says she brought them and there is a copy of them in here . . . Did she show you that?

HOROWITZ: Well, she asked me—what she took—she asked me to change the budget and put it back in her name, that he's not living with her [*inaudible*].

NOEL: I mean, is this what she brought me? Is that sufficient? Does that answer the closing notice?

HOROWITZ: It's more involved than just what the man is making.

NOEL: Yes, I know, there is more involved, I agree with you. But we have to go by what is on *this* paper here. And it says, "We are closing it because for the last five years you have never brought your pay stubs." He's bringing them now.

HOROWITZ: Yeah . . .

NOEL: So you have to leave it open.

HOROWITZ: He's bringing them now and he's saying he's living with his wife and—

NOEL: Well, we'll get into that later.

HOROWITZ: That's the thing you have to go into now.

NOEL: Yes, of course.

HOROWITZ: —because that's the case decision.

NOEL: So, finally they find out how much money he's making and now—

HOROWITZ: That's right.

NOEL: She says he's no longer in the home. But my point is you cannot go ahead and close it, because she brought the stubs.

HOROWITZ: If she has complied. You know, I'm not the fair hearing section, uh—

NOEL: Yes, but you had the conference on her.

HOROWITZ: Yes. At the time I had the conference I didn't have proof of current income. He showed me something from a year or two before or something. I didn't see that one from her, the current pay slip.

NOEL: But is that sufficient, what I showed you here?

HOROWITZ: Yes, I would say it is.

NOEL: Okay, so it can't be closed. Are you going to void this nine-thirteen then? . . . 'Cause her case is going to be closed unless someone calls up and says stop it. Or however you do that.

HOROWITZ: I have to change the [*inaudible*].

NOEL: So her case will remain open?

HOROWITZ: Yeah.

NOEL: Okay, thanks. [*Cut to Noel returning to Tom's office.*] . . . Tom!

TOM: Yeah. What did she say?

NOEL: I pointed out to Miss Horowitz the error of her ways.

TOM: Yeah.

NOEL: She's upset because she does not believe the woman's story that conveniently her husband has disappeared as soon as this is taken care of, rather, that he's out of the home. She wants the case transferred to her name because the checks are going out in his name. I think we just don't do that on her say. We'll have to find out where he is.

TOM: Yeah, right—

NOEL: Meaning write to his employer. See what address is there.

TOM: Right, yes.

NOEL: Check housing—

TOM: Right.

NOEL: —'cause they live in separate housing.

TOM: Yes, right, you have to be—

NOEL: See if he's listed on that.

TOM: —to send a letter, a registered certified letter by—

NOEL: Now, you should also know that she says her children are starving.

TOM: Her what?

NOEL: She wants some money. Do you want to give her any?

TOM: Well, I can't—

NOEL: Okay.

TOM: They can't close it on that, they have to—

NOEL: No, the closing, yes, they will not close. But she wants the money today. Of course, they can't give her any unless the case is reclassified into her name.

TOM: So they have to reclassify it then because—

NOEL: Well, they can't do that until we've checked it out.

TOM: No. Well, I don't know how they . . . Now, let me think. They have to reclassify it to her name before they can give it, right, under the checks?

NOEL: Right.

TOM: However, she has a perfect right to ask for a fair hearing despite the hearing she had upstairs.

NOEL: No. She doesn't need a fair hearing.

TOM: Well.

NOEL: We've already decided her case is not to be closed—

TOM (*overlapping*): Okay. Fine. Okay.

NOEL: —because she did at the last minute bring the pay stubs.

TOM: What I say, then, they would have—I would suggest—

NOEL: But now she's saying don't count the pay stubs because the guy does not live there any longer.

TOM: If they, if she's without funds they have to, they have to service her financially, they'll have to make the switch on the basis of our ongoing investigation—

NOEL: Well, you really shouldn't say that because that's the group they don't have to decide that.

TOM: That's their decision, but that's—

NOEL: So I'll just work on our investigation.

TOM: Right. They'll have to make whatever change is necessary to service her and, on the basis of our investigation, we'll either— [*Tom's voice fades out as camera follows Noel walking away and back to his own desk.*]

NOEL: Miss Horowitz has made a mistake. You did bring the pay stubs or your husband did, whoever did. We have to verify where your husband is now. Did you tell Lillian Waldhouse that he had moved out?

CLIENT: Yes.

NOEL: So he's off their records?

CLIENT: Yes, because I had the new lease they sent in the mail yesterday for me to fill out for that.

NOEL: Are you married to him?

CLIENT: Yes, I'm legally married to him. I have my papers here.

NOEL: Do any other children live in the home besides these listed here: Patricia, Leroy, Priscilla, Denise, and there's another Patricia?

CLIENT: No, they have—Gwendolyn it's supposed to be. There's Gwendolyn, Patricia, Denise, and Leroy. Michael and Irvin have left.

NOEL: Well, we'll have to refer this to family court.

CLIENT: So why can't they give me just an emergency check? For, for some food.

NOEL: Well, it's not that simple because they have to take your husband off the case . . . and they can't do that, they can't make any changes in the welfare budget without sending a notice to you and giving you fifteen days to say go ahead and do it, or I don't care, or say nothing, or protest it or whatever you want to do. Even if this move is in your favor. In this case it would be in your favor to take your husband off the budget. Today. They can't do that for fifteen days. So I think you're in a bind. But I'll take the record up to the group. It's not my responsibility, money matters. And I'll explain to them that we're referring it to court. And . . . since welfare is really based upon what clients say, they really have to believe what you tell them . . . until it's proved otherwise. How long have you been on welfare?

CLIENT: Let's see . . . 'bout eight or nine years, maybe ten.

NOEL: Well, I can take this up to the group. [*Noel gets up to leave. Cut to client slowly walking away.*] Do you want to sign this carbon? [*Some inaudible chatter. Cut to Noel and Tom.*]

TOM: And that's all we have. Do you have an entry in the—

NOEL: No, no, I have—

TOM: Okay, right.

NOEL: I'm still working on that.

TOM: We have to process it until our investigation is through. Whatever manipulations they have to make. [*Camera follows Noel and client walking. Shot of worker checking employee time cards. Shot of large office space with many desks and people working.*]

WORKER: To start with, the reason that we send people to Jay Street [*cut to two-shot of client and worker*], the reason that we send everybody to Jay Street is because we want to see if you're able to work or not, because that's the most important factor in determining what type of assistance is appropriate. See, we have different types of assistance, based on whether or not you're more able to work, and the Jay Street report says that you are employable. How much school have you had?

CLIENT: Well, I went to the ninth grade.

WORKER: In New York?

CLIENT: Yes, in New York.

WORKER: And what do you have in the way of an employment background?

CLIENT: Well, I don't have too much of a, an employment experience due to the fact that, you know, I just been released out of prison after eleven years.

WORKER: Where were you?

CLIENT: You know, I was in Clayton, Comstock, what have you. Nevertheless, I was released out of prison.

WORKER: Oh, so you've been in jail several times?

CLIENT: No, this is my first time in prison, but I did eleven years in prison, so I don't have too much of a backing, you know, background.

WORKER: What was the charge?

CLIENT: Homicide.

WORKER: Are you now—you served the complete sentence, are you on parole or probation?

CLIENT: I'm still on parole. For four years.

WORKER: Did you manage to pick up any special training or anything like that?

CLIENT: Well, yes, tailoring. My first few years in prison, I took, I picked up tailoring, but I'm not that, well, you know, skilled in tailoring due to the fact that I dropped it, you know. I have to brush up on it.

WORKER: So what happens is, we send you over today to the WREP office. That will be this morning, right from here. And first you're seen by somebody from the New York State employment service, because they would have full-time jobs, and certainly if you can get a full-time job that would beat anything that WREP would offer. If they don't have a full-time job or it looks as though they're not going to have one very soon, then they forward you to the WREP and you'll have another person, like another caseworker, who will, again, ask about your employment background and see if they've got anything that looks good. It's very important to get the phone number of that person because, just in case, let's say, you're unable to keep an appointment or something, they right away start telling me to close the case, you know, and this is, this is one of the problems you might have, so in general, I'm also going to give you my phone number because I'm going to have your case here so that, I mean, if some complication comes up, right away call, so that you won't, you know, there won't be any misunderstanding, because it's much easier, you know, to settle things out before they happen. [*Cut to LS of office, worker at desk. A man comes into frame and hands files to worker.*]

WORKER (*on telephone*): Hold on. (*To man*) This is not it. (*On telephone*) Hold on. (*To man*) C-A—these (*she hands the man other files*). (*On telephone*) You know, this is what he's telling me— [*Cut to the man looking though files, not finding the one he's looking for. Cut to shot of another man walking down corridor away from camera.*]

WORKER (MISS HIGHTOWER): I've been a supervisor since 1966 and I've seen people who've been supervisors since 1969 who are getting all the [*cut to MS of Miss Hightower*] very best jobs, and I don't like it.

WORKER (SAM): Uh, who got, who has the best jobs?

HIGHTOWER: Why, you take Miss Anonie, she's frozen in. Nothing, no one can touch her. You take this woman here, she's, she's pleading hardship. You take Mr. Morris, he's pleading union delegate. He can't be moved.

SAM (*overlapping*): He is a union delegate.

HIGHTOWER: Right. It's what I'm saying, and they pull super seniority, so that by the time they finish I have no seniority at all. Because everybody else—well, you take Suskie, who have been out of here and she's pleading hardship. Well, it's more hardship for me.

SAM: Well, . . . she's a sick woman, she has to—

HIGHTOWER: I have to come from New Jersey. What are you talking about? I get up at five, five-thirty every morning—

SAM (*overlapping*): Well, she had a heart attack—

HIGHTOWER: —and spend a lot of money. I spend more money to get to this job than anybody else on staff. You wouldn't believe it, the money I spend to get to this job. That's right. Whether I come by train, whether I come by my personal car, or what. It's very expensive to come from New Jersey.

SAM: You know, at one time the department didn't have anybody on the staff who lived out of state. You know that?

HIGHTOWER: Don't give me about out-of-state. I've been on this—when I first came to the department I lived in New York. Not only did I live in New York—

SAM: Yeah, I know that.

HIGHTOWER: I was a homeowner in New York, having a house sixty by one hundred at one-fourteen-forty-five 179th Street, St. Albans, very wealth—

SAM: I know that.

38. A welfare worker's complaint.

HIGHTOWER: A very wealthy section. Right?

SAM: I know that, well—

HIGHTOWER: Now, I own property in New York. I'm entitled to work in New York, and lived there for many, many years.

SAM: I know that!

HIGHTOWER: The reason I went to New York, to Newark, was because my stepfather died and left my mother all alone in the house. So I went to live with her. When she died, she gave, the house came to me, by inheritance. What was I going to do, throw the house in the street? Right?

SAM: Well, if you have any grievance, why don't you discuss it with Stanley? Mr. Seligman.

HIGHTOWER: You can't discuss it with Stanley, he has his favorites. Like I said before, I should have gotten the, I should have been the supervisor of General Service, because I had the seniority, I had the training, I've had the courses, I've been to Fordham. I've had Casework 1, Casework 2, Personality Behavior 1, Personality Behavior 2, Administration and Juvenile Delinquency. Now that fits me for something. I haven't been just sitting on my rear. Not keeping abreast of the times. I've always kept up, and I think I deserve better than the kind of fast shuffle I've been getting here in this welfare department. Because this man is a czar and he's going to put in who he wants to put in. That's all.

SAM: So why don't you discuss it with him, if you have—

HIGHTOWER: What's the use in discussing it?

SAM: Why do you take it out on me?

HIGHTOWER: Because you called me in. And that's why I have resorted to C.O. because I figured they must have some kind of job down there even if it's no more than interviewing people for, maybe, jobs in the department or whatnot, because I can do interviewing and whatnot.

SAM: Are you forgetting about this memo?

HIGHTOWER: If Mr. Seligman wants to speak to me, you know, you can tell him that this came through and that Miss Hightower would like to see him in reference to this memo.

SAM: Okay.

HIGHTOWER: Before I have to resort to grievance machinery. [*Miss Hightower leaves Sam's office. Cut to Sam writing at his desk. Cut to another worker coming into Sam's office.*]

WORKER (*in doorway*): Listen, I didn't hear anything further on our friend Curtis Rosser because he was going to Legal Aid or M-F-Y, one or the other. So, if they, if you should get a call, the big question is, who is he?

SAM: He gets assistance under how many names?

WORKER: Three different names. We don't know, and each, each one used the other as a, a, the landlord in the particular case, so if he's being evicted, who is evicting who?

SAM: I spoke to the arresting officer.

WORKER: He's evicting himself.

SAM: You had him arrested the other day.

WORKER: Yeah.

SAM: He, he had a, a record a mile long.

WORKER: Yeah. He had a big record.

SAM: Big record. Well, he doesn't fear getting busted. He doesn't fear getting busted.

WORKER: No. All these guys. It's the normal routine of things. Uh, they're not excited about it.

SAM: He wasn't excited about it.

WORKER: Nah, it doesn't bother them. They're accustomed to it. Anyway,

I'm only letting you know this, in case they, you should get a call. But the big problem is, who is who? We don't know who the man is. We don't know that he—

SAM: Well, I called out Jack Williams, and he answered to Jack Williams.

WORKER: Alright, now it's Curtis Rosser. There's another guy, Jack Kiger. [*Laughs.*]

SAM: You better warn the—

WORKER: Well, this is why I put in each record. Besides, we don't have the record—

SAM: Yeah. I called out Jack Wil—, Jack. He answered. You know, and he came, he came over.

WORKER: Anyway, the district attorney has all the records anyway, so we take no action until this is disposed of by the court.

SAM: How stupid can he be to come in today? Over here he knows that—

WORKER: They have chutzpah to the end.

SAM: Oh, so they locked him up and he still came in again to this office.

WORKER: It doesn't faze him. What's he got to lose?

SAM: Unbelievable.

WORKER: Okay, Sam.

SAM: I'll see ya. [*Worker walks out of office. Cut to shot of a client walking around waiting area, clients lined up in front of application desk. Cut to one of them at the desk.*]

CLIENT (MR. HARRINGTON): I just want to see if it's too late to put this in. She told me to come back, maybe [*inaudible*], to get an appointment for tomorrow, maybe. It was too late for it to go from downstairs. They're all closed.

WORKER: They're closed Thursday?

HARRINGTON: Uh, Friday.

WORKER: No, you're supposed to get it in the mail.

WORKER 2: You were supposed to bring this in this morning, Mr. Harrington.

HARRINGTON: But you said, today you said you'd give me an appointment for tomorrow, I mean I talked with someone.

WORKER: Alright. I'll give you one for tomorrow.

HARRINGTON: That's what you said. They asked if Friday— [*Shot of a man walking through waiting area. Cut to woman complaining.*]

NICOLASSA: Si pues yo estuve ayer allá y para acá me llevaron allá y me dijo que no podía y me planté . . . y cuando me caí yo me planté un billetico de cinco pesos y me dijo que no podía y me iban con el carro hacer compras y una niña y a ella no tenía para repagarle eso . . . y lo puso de mi padre pa'que ella coma bistec y . . . ni en nombre de mi papá . . . no . . . y después se le pierde. [Yes, I was here yesterday and they said they couldn't and I stood my ground . . . and with the help of a little five-dollar bill . . . and then when I fell he said he couldn't and then he went shopping with the child so that she could eat steak . . . Not even in the name of her father . . . and it's lost.] [*Cut to worker in previous discussion with Sam walking away from the camera through waiting area. Shot of more people at applications desk.*]

CLIENT: That was my food allotment, right?

WORKER: That is correct. [*Cut to CU of another client talking with worker.*]

CLIENT: I get forty-two dollars for food, okay. Now, if—is that all the money I'm going to get?

WORKER: That's correct.

CLIENT: That's it.

WORKER: It will not pay the rent.

CLIENT: Okay. That's what I thought. Now, will, when it goes to getting my—

WORKER: Unemployment.

CLIENT: —the unemployment.

WORKER: They take that into account.

WORKER'S VOICE IN BACKGROUND: 25A.

CLIENT: Are they going to deduct that?

WORKER'S VOICE IN BACKGROUND: 25A.

WORKER: Yes, yes. In other words, if you get twenty-five dollars a week unemployment, which is the minimum minimum, that's fifty dollars every two weeks, which is in excess of our budget. Which means they would close your case immediately.

CLIENT: So the maximum allotment I can get approximately right now from you coupled with unemployment is about fifty dollars a week. As you see it?

WORKER: Even less. No, no, no, no, no, no, no.

CLIENT: Alright, give me, I'm trying to find out the figure I can get—

WORKER: They won't pay this rent. See, in the event that you were to find an apartment for a hundred and fifty dollars—

CLIENT: Wait a minute. Okay, now, all I care about is, if I had a hundred and fifty instead of a hundred and seventy-five, you're telling me they wouldn't pay it.

WORKER (*overlapping*): Yeah. Right. Okay, let's assume it was a hundred and fifty.

CLIENT: Alright, now, because they won't consider, they won't put a maximum limit on that and say, ah, this is, you know, we will treat this as a hundred and fifty and the rest she has to make up.

WORKER: They cannot do that. That's correct.

CLIENT: Well then, um, what am I—I'm supposed to relocate somewhere?

WORKER: That's correct. This isn't my, uh—

CLIENT: That's insane . . . Alright.

WORKER: Be that as it may, that's, uh, okay, let—

CLIENT: I want to find out how I can get that maximum allotment of a hundred and fifty dollars.

WORKER: You would have to live in an apartment for a hundred and fifty dollars. They will not allow you to live in an apartment for more, and only pay partial. That's not legal. That's, you know. This is the city, well, actually, state law. That they allow only a certain amount per person.

CLIENT: How do you contest it?

WORKER: You file for a fair hearing.

CLIENT: Okay. That's insane.

WORKER: Your beef is not with me. Your beef is with the law. Now the law that I am citing you, that I am telling you, is that the fair hear—the rent allotment for one person may not exceed one hundred and fifty dollars. That's a state law and this is what your beef is. You wish to either question my—

CLIENT: No, I wish to get that one hundred and fifty, period.

WORKER: Then you would have to go and—

CLIENT: Okay.

WORKER: Now, that's what it is. Now, one hundred and seventy-five, your contention is that you are entitled to that, and that you're willing to make up the difference, and what I'm contending is that it's not, you know, they're not going to go for that, and you can ask them. That's what they're there for, okay?

CLIENT: Well, it just seems that if you've worked, if your rent is over a certain amount, you have problems.

WOMAN: This is the Taft-Hartley Law established in 1937, ain't a thing but old charity.

WORKER: What?

WOMAN: The Taft-Hartley Law was imposed on the welfare system.

CLIENT: Thank you. Thanks a lot. [*Client leaves, and another client comes up to the desk.*]

CLIENT 2: They told me to come here and fill this out.

WORKER: Well, it has to be the sixth—

CLIENT 2: Right.

WORKER: Okay?

CLIENT 2: Thank you.

WORKER: Okay. You're welcome. Bye.

CLIENT 2: What am I going to do for today?

WORKER: I don't know. [*Cut to LS of waiting area. Several shots of clients, including Larry and his partner.*] . . . Twenty-C. [*Several more CUs of clients.*]

ANOTHER WORKER (*offscreen, calling another client*): Edwin Acevedo. [*Cut to CU of client, Jerry.*]

MAN: You don't have no place to live now?

JERRY: No, I have no place to live. That's why I'm here by the Welfare now to see that I get me a place to live so I can live like a decent human being, you know. Because, not that I feel like I have a right to, but I think when you be in this country, I think you have a right to, if you are an American, or not. *Und* I believe in it. You know. I think this country is still a good country who really would like to help, you know. But right now they don't know about me, so I have to go there and find out. Because when you got hit on the brain, they're not declare you for crazy, but, uh, you never can tell if the doctors, what they might find, you know. I mean, I don't run around with a machine gun *und* a knife *und* an axe, you know. I'm not that crazy yet. But I'm a nice guy, you know. I just want to be in fairly good condition like any, any person has the right to, you know, so, *oder* if they don't like me anymore, I guess they have to send me back to Germany, but I don't think they will do that because I am too long in this country. So, if they don't want me to send me to Germany when they won't give me any here, gee. I think I better look for a nice tree to hang. It must be a nice good hanging place. You know? But it get a little short down in here when you're getting any air. Oh-oh, that will be no fun.

MAN: But that will only last for a few moments if you choose that way.

JERRY: Umm, well, that will only last for a few moments. But takes a long time to be down there in the, in the dirt.

MAN: Oh, sure, a long time—

JERRY: You never come up then. You never come back again. You just be, uh, down there forever. And that's the way that goes. And I guess everybody has that luck too. I think so. I'm positively sure of it, that everybody has to die, you know. That nothing you or me can do about it. It just comes around. You see, God is not a man like, uh, Social Service, you know. He doesn't come around and say, well, this man is poor, let's give him a couple of hundred bucks. No, he only helps you when he feels like it. And sometimes, he—

MAN: Sometimes he does.

JERRY: He wants you to die, too. Oh, yeah. There's nothing you can do about it because he is that. He is God. He make the human being. Right? But he can do what he feels like. You know. And there's nothing that anybody can do about it. Even Jesus Christ. You know. You ask him. He would say, well, you not in order *mit* God, you have to die because you cannot fool around *mit* God that much. You have to be all the time good. Well, once in a time, once in a while you can be bad, *und* he forgive you.

MAN: Once in a while?

JERRY: Oh, yeah, he forgive you. You know, but, uh, you better not do something real bad, then he says, alright, Jerry, uh, down in Hell you go. *Und* you never come back.

MAN: But you've been a pretty good man, haven't you?

JERRY: Well, what, right now when you ask me—

MAN: How you wonder—

JERRY: —how do you feel in your head? I said, well, I don't feel like going

39. A client listens to another client's metaphysical musings.

to a nuthouse. But I wish I could see a doctor. Maybe I could go into a hospital. Maybe—

MAN: Maybe Welfare could help you see a doctor.

JERRY: Yeah, maybe they send me to a hospital, you know, and I get straightened out by the, by a doctor. You know. Maybe it is something wrong from an accident I had, you know. I don't know. I just walk around. Hah! One time I went downtown. I blacked out.

MAN: And then walked all the way downtown and—

JERRY: They stole from me fifty dollars, two packs of cigarettes, my driver's license. Everything is gone. The only, the only proof I have is my passport from Germany. That is all what they could really get. And I got an American license in there, too.

MAN: And how old is your passport? I imagine it's—

JERRY: Oh, it's still good until '76. [*Cut to crowded waiting area.*]

MAN: Until '76?

JERRY: Yeah. [*Several shots of waiting clients.*]

WORKER (*calling client*): Antonia Sanchez. [*More shots of clients. Kids dueling with umbrellas in waiting area.*]

WORKER (*calling client*): Constance Jacks—, Constance Jacks—, Jackson.

WORKER (*calling client*): Francisco Sepulvia. [*Cut to workers at desk. One walks up to window and calls out a client's name.*]

WORKER (*calling client*): Mary Corman. Mary Corman . . . [*Client with baby comes up to the window and shows her identification. Worker hands her paperwork.*] Check this, Miss Corman, to see if it's correct. [*Cut to shot of another worker listening to Elaine.*]

ELAINE: 'Cause she's pregnant doesn't mean she automatically gets welfare. She has to answer a few questions. And that's what was happening when she got up and left.

WORKER: But she's been pregnant since, let's see, since October, of, uh—

ELAINE: And what does that mean?

WORKER: That means, somewhere along the line, either Waverly or Lower Manhattan, are not understanding the problem. But the immediate, the immediate problem here is food for her baby, right?

ELAINE: She has to be eligible. She has to be eligible. And we want a few questions answered. Now, in the middle of the interview, she got up and left. Now what do you want me to do?

WORKER: I want you, I want you to give her food for her baby, right?

ELAINE: She has to be eligible before she gets food for the baby.

WORKER: But she is eligible. She showed you a prenatal form that she—

ELAINE: If someone is pregnant, they just come into welfare and get money? Is that in the rule book now? I must be missing something because I've never seen it.

WORKER: Would you show me in writing that, that—you show me in writing why she's, that she's not eligible. Why isn't she eligible?

ELAINE: Who told you in writing that she's not eligible?

WORKER: What?

ELAINE: What are you talking about? What do you mean she's not eligible?

WORKER: You said that she's ineligible.

ELAINE (*overlapping*): I didn't say that.

WORKER (*overlapping*): You show me in writing that she's not eligible.

ELAINE: I said she was being asked a few questions, and in the middle of the interview—

WORKER: What, about her husband? That's secondary, about her husband.

ELAINE: Do you have a complaint?

WORKER: I have a complaint, yes.

ELAINE: Well, what do you want me to do about it?

WORKER: Well, I want you to—if you can't answer it for me, I want some-body that can answer it for me. Why you can't—

ELAINE: When the interviewer is willing to come back, she'll be interviewed again.

WORKER: Then why wasn't the interview finished?

ELAINE: She got up and left in the middle of the interview.

WORKER: Because you were asking her about her husband. She wants food for her baby, right?

ANOTHER WORKER (*at desk*): The baby's not even born. How's the baby gonna eat?

WORKER: She needs food, she needs a layette and so forth. Accor—, according to the rules and regulations that I know of, the first thing that's primary is getting food for her baby, right? Secondary is finding out about the hus-band, as far as I'm concerned.

ELAINE: Why—?

WORKER: Now, if you can't answer it, direct me to somebody that can help me.

ELAINE: Does the client want to be interviewed again?

WORKER: Right now, yes.

ELAINE: Well, she'll have to wait until the clerk is able to call her again.

WORKER: Oh, by the way. Another thing happened on Friday: she was told to come in on Friday, by the, by the—I came down here personally and get an interview for her. And when she came in on Friday, she was turned away. She was turned away.

ELAINE: You personally got an interview for her?

WORKER: I came down here, and she says, and I talked to, to people at the desk and they said that they would interview her on Friday. She came in on Friday. They said, we can't interview you because we're working on checks.

ELAINE: Well, this is the first time—

WORKER: I don't think my, I don't put clients through a, through a hoop.

ELAINE: Well, are you assuming that we are?

WORKER: What?

ELAINE: Are you assuming that we are?

WORKER: I assume that you are. If you're, if you're, if you're interviewing her and torturing her by asking her about her, about her husband and so forth, when the primary thing—

ELAINE: And that's torture?

WORKER: I think it is.

ELAINE: Ah, ho. Well, I don't think it's torture to ask somebody—

WORKER: Well, close to it, anyway.

ELAINE: Okay, look—

WORKER: But, anyways, will you see her today?

ELAINE: Tell the client to have a seat in the waiting area, and when she's finished whatever she's doing, and when she has nobody else to call, she'll call her again. She's got to go through all these slips, because she left in the middle of her interview. When she's finished with all these slips, she'll then call the client back. Okay? [*Cut to worker writing something on a slip of paper and giving it to the client.*]

CLIENT (*taking slip of paper*): Okay.

WORKER: Look, you know, keep as calm as, you know. And, uh, I'll try to find out. I'm gonna try to get a social worker to call downtown to find out what's happening. Because yours is a special case. You're, you're the first case that I know of in which you're in the federal system, and you're pregnant and you're going to have a baby, you know, and that. Somewhere along the line, you'll have to receive money for that unborn child. And in the past, ADC mothers were given allowances four months after they're pregnant. Now you're being denied this. And I want to find out the reason why. So just be a little calm, as I say—if they, if they come up to you and say that they can't do anything for you today, come up and see me. And meanwhile, I'll, I'll try calling the prenatal clinic. If that doesn't work—

CLIENT: I'll check with you later because they went to lunch, and like, she's taking a long time, and she's got about six or eight people before she's, you know, call me again, you know, and that'll be around four o'clock.

WORKER: Well, I'm going to call Mr. Inge again and find out what he can get you, you know, a little ahead of time. Try to be patient, okay?

CLIENT: Okay.

WORKER: And I'll do my best.

CLIENT: Alright, thank you very much.

WORKER: You're welcome. [*Cut to CU of worker on telephone.*]

WORKER (*on telephone*): Hello. Could Mr. Shupolski be seen there by our client, uh, to change a lease? The client is Sondra Oppenheimer. Alright. This is the problem. Mrs. Rivera is the tenant that, that you have. But Mrs. Rivera moved out October. And our client is saying that her husband, from whom she's separated, got the apartment from his sister. The landlord has not been informed of this. I'm calling to inform him and ask him if he'll put the lease in the name of Oppenheimer . . . I know this, but I'm asking you, if I send her there, can these arrangements be made? [*Cut to MS of supervisor, worker, and Mr. Rivera.*]

SUPERVISOR: But when is your appointment for Manpower to get a physical examination?

CLIENT (MR. RIVERA): On the twentieth.

SUPERVISOR: On the twentieth.

RIVERA: Of next month. From here, from here to then—

SUPERVISOR: When did you lose your job?

RIVERA: About three days, two days ago. She told me she didn't want to use me anymore. She told me she was tired of—

SUPERVISOR: Well, then, your situation is changed since the last time you came here.

RIVERA: Oh, God, yes. It changed.

SUPERVISOR: Well, then. What do you, you, what do you think we're, we're magic, that we guess at what your problems are?

RIVERA: No, you, no idea of you guessing, just the idea that you, you verbally promised my wife, you told my wife, don't worry, go home with your husband, we gonna give, we're gonna send you a check by the month so you can be able to eat, and this, until you go to Manpower. Now I turn around—

WORKER: Does the wife have an active case here?

SUPERVISOR: I, I don't know whether we accepted her or not. You're gonna have to—

WORKER: Alright, check it out.

SUPERVISOR: We'll have to, we'll have to, we'll have to give you an appointment for the interview group today. [*Turning to another worker*] Give this fellow an appointment for the interview, interview group today.

RECEPTIONIST: He can come over here, yes.

SUPERVISOR: No, no. Alright. Alright. Give him one, give him one now because he's supposed to, he's supposed to see the interview group. Then, she'll give you an appointment. Let me go over, let me go over and talk to Elaine about it.

WORKER: Okay. [*Cut to shot of people in line at applications desk.*]

RECEPTIONIST: Okay, hold onto this, dear. Drop this in the box. Wait for them to call you name. [*To next client*] Did you get any part of your check? None? No pro-ration check? [*First client drops form in the designated box and walks into waiting room, camera watching her as she walks away across reception area.*]

ELAINE: When did he last get paid?

SUPERVISOR: I don't know, but you'd better call up the landlord [*cut to supervisor talking with Elaine*] and find out whether this is actually so. He said he lost it two or three days ago.

WORKER: Well, he's not supposed to get paid until the tenth. That's what she said.

SUPERVISOR: Well, you better call up the landlord and find out what it is because if he doesn't have anything, we'll have to give him something.

WORKER: And a Miss Robinson had called on Friday about that case and I was going up to the home—

ELAINE: Did she mention he was laid off?

WORKER: No, she didn't mention it at all.

ELAINE: Well, that's very strange. The social worker didn't mention on the phone he was laid off.

SUPERVISOR: Well, you better check it out, anyway, because, uh—

ELAINE: Well, he has to be seen by me meanwhile. I only have two, three workers in. I need some workers.

WORKER: I worked at the desk this morning.

ELAINE: And also, she's leaving half a day. She's got to go to disaster training or something.

SUPERVISOR: Who has to go to disaster training?

ELAINE: Um, Roz.

SUPERVISOR: What kind of disaster training?

ELAINE: You know the thing where you go every six months or something in case there's a fire, flood, or something?

SUPERVISOR: Well, we'll keep her here today. She can find out some other time. Who does she have to go to disaster—?

ELAINE: Roz. Excuse me. What's the thing with disaster training? Can you take another day or is it definitely today?

ROZ: It's definitely today.

ELAINE: [*Inaudible.*]

SUPERVISOR: Well, we can't release her today.

ELAINE: Boy, look at this book.

ROZ: It's, uh, I'm telling you, it's a whole thing.

SUPERVISOR: Disaster training?

ROZ: Yeah. Here. I got notes. I got—in case of disaster, I man the telephones. We have, we have artificial telephone calls coming in from central office. I swear, we answer it, and we have to, go back and—

SUPERVISOR: How long do you have to be there?

ELAINE: Preparation for the atomic bomb.

ROZ: All afternoon. I go twice a year. Last year I went, I went December 14, '72. And today is February fourth. And the last time I went was February '72. That's twice a year.

ELAINE: Look, if he accepts this, uh— Is Arcadie Rivera here? Or just the wife?

SUPERVISOR: He's here.

ELAINE: If he keeps this Manpower appointment, he gets no money until—

SUPERVISOR: No. He's not going out there. He's not going there until the twentieth. But you'd better check him out anyway, just to make sure.

ELAINE: Well, let him get a slip from the desk.

SUPERVISOR: He got a slip from the desk.

ROZ: Alright. What do I do with this?

ELAINE: We need some more workers. Frank Farkis hasn't called in.

SUPERVISOR: Frank Farkis hasn't called. Alright, we'll try to get, we'll try to get Peter Barry . . . We'll try to get Peter Barry and, let's see, who else?

ELAINE: How about Larry Janice?

SUPERVISOR: How about Larry Janice. Alright. I'll see if I can get him.

ELAINE (*calling another client*): Soonavin Ali . . . Miss Ali, you're going to have to go back to Waverly Welfare Center. We're very sorry. There's some mistake. Take this message back.

WORKER (*offscreen*): He's legally responsible to take care of the children.

CLIENT'S DAUGHTER: We know that. [*Cut to CU of woman speaking.*]

WORKER: And her.

DAUGHTER: Yes.

WORKER: As long as she's married.

DAUGHTER: Yes.

WORKER: But she went to court yesterday.

DAUGHTER: That's why she got down to court.

MRS. GASKIN: —been down to court twice.

DAUGHTER: She's got another time to go. But he didn't show up.

WORKER: But he didn't show up. It has to be in the court's hands so long as he's getting income. And then he's not using it while he's in the hospital. It's for the children. It's for the use of the children.

DAUGHTER: So what, what are you trying . . . ? What she going to do, take the checks from him if he don't want to give them to her?

GASKIN: I been to court.

DAUGHTER: What's the alternative? She's been to court.

WORKER: When did she go to court?

DAUGHTER: Yesterday.

GASKIN: Yesterday. And I went last week.

WORKER: What do the courts say?

DAUGHTER: He didn't show up. They sent out a warrant for him.

WORKER: Well, he's in the hospital. He couldn't show up if he's in the hospital.

DAUGHTER: Well, what do you want her to do if he don't show up and he's got the checks and don't give 'em to her?

WORKER: The, the only thing I can suggest is that—I talked to the application supervisor, and she said if you feel you've been treated unfairly, she'll—

DAUGHTER: Of course we feel—why you think we back here now?

WORKER: —You'll have to apply for a fair hearing.

DAUGHTER: Oh, in the meantime, what they going to do with the fair hearing? What they going to do? Starve to death? He's in the hospital. She's sick. She's got diabetes. She's got arthritis. She's got heart trouble. What is she supposed to do while she waiting for a fair hearing?

WORKER: Wait a minute.

DAUGHTER: Since November I been walking around, running 'round with this woman.

WORKER: You know, you're makin' it sound like my fault. I'm tellin'—

DAUGHTER: Well, it's not my fault either.

WORKER: I'm tellin'—

DAUGHTER: It's not his fault. He's in the hospital. It's not her fault. She's sick. Whose fault is it?

WORKER: I'm tellin' you what they tellin' me. They have, they have—

DAUGHTER: Who's responsible for her?

WORKER: Who's responsible—

DAUGHTER: If her husband is sick, he's in the hospital. And she's sick.

WORKER: He's getting disability payments from the union.

DAUGHTER: Can she take the—can she take the check from him?

WORKER: He's legally responsible for her support.

DAUGHTER: That's why she's taking him to court, 'cause he doesn't take care of his legal responsibility.

WORKER: The responsibility is in the hands of the court.

DAUGHTER: The court sent her here. I have a letter from the court telling her to come here.

WORKER: This was given—now, this was before the case was rejected, the case was rejected on the twenty-fourth, and this was given to her—

GASKIN: The same day I came here.

DAUGHTER: When you rejected her, she had this letter.

GASKIN: They told me to go here, Social Security, and that's where I went.

DAUGHTER: She went to Social Security and Social Security sent her back here. They ain't goin' to take care of her.

WORKER: Well, Social Security is evaluating your application. That's a different thing altogether.

DAUGHTER (*overlapping*): Okay. But the new—well, who's responsible for her?

WORKER: Mr. Gaskin.

DAUGHTER: But he's in the hospital, as you very well know.

WORKER: I, I understand he's in the hospital.

DAUGHTER: Now what is she supposed to do?

WORKER: Check's upcoming—

DAUGHTER (*voice rising*): Go down there and take checks that don't belong to her? They belong to him.

WORKER: Well, he has a responsibility.

DAUGHTER: He don't want to give them to her . . . We're goin' into a vicious cycle again. And I'm getting tired of it.

WORKER: Well, as I said before, you'd have to apply for a fair hearing.

DAUGHTER: Oh, how long's a fair hearing going to take and what she goin' to do in the meanwhile, while she's waiting for the fair hearing? She's been here since, she's been coming here since, since November.

WORKER: It's her responsibility to try to get Mr.—

DAUGHTER: What do you think she's trying to do?

WORKER: Well—

DAUGHTER: Why you think she's goin' to court?

WORKER: You keep shouting at me and you don't—

DAUGHTER: You sending me 'round into a vicious cycle. I'm tryin' to tell you, honey, I'm tired—

WORKER: I'm not sendin' you—

DAUGHTER: She is sick. He is sick. Who is going to take care of them?

WORKER: I am not sending you anywhere.

DAUGHTER: You told me now to wait for a fair hearing. What she goin' to do in the meanwhile?

WORKER: Well, you'll have to ask the applications supervisor to re-entertain the application.

DAUGHTER: What do you think I'm here for now? Why, why I'm here talking to you now for this?

WORKER: You're shouting at me.

DAUGHTER: Well, I'm goin' to do a bit more than shouting if you don't stop this. Ever since November, you talkin' about shouting, I've been trying to take care of this woman. What do you want from me? . . . Sending us around all over these different places and they sending us back around in circles.

GASKIN: Where you supposed to go?

DAUGHTER: That's what I want to know. She said go to court. She went to court. Go to Social Security. They send her back here . . . They're up there sittin' on they behinds upstairs, that's why they can't do nothing for nobody and sittin' here all damn day, and they sendin' you all around the court. And the court sendin' you here . . . She, she refused you. [*Cut to workers talking among themselves.*]

WORKER: It doesn't, it doesn't mean she's getting any. She's not getting any. She did go to court. She's got proof in her hand. She went to court . . . So that's why I'm suggesting you re-entertain the application.

ELAINE: Okay. However, we want to know—we don't even know where she's even living at the present time.

WORKER: Well, that you'll evaluate.

ELAINE: I think she's living uptown.

WORKER: She may very well be living uptown, but you don't know till you interview her and ascertain her whereabouts.

ELAINE: Well, she's paying rent—is she paying rent now?

WORKER: You can check through the court what address she applied from.

ELAINE: Yeah. Um, what—it's eighty-seven dollars she's getting a week?

WORKER: No. It's in his name as a union benefit.

ELAINE: Right.

WORKER: In his name. But she claims—

ELAINE (*overlapping*): If he's hospitalized, then why isn't she getting that money?

WORKER: See, it's not, we cannot tell him. The court's telling him to give—

ELAINE: Yeah, but we want to call social— [*To Mrs. Gaskin*] You have a seat outside, please?

WORKER: We're discussing it, Miss Gaskin. Just wait outside over there.

DAUGHTER: That's not the first time we've been sent—

ELAINE: Excuse me?

WORKER 2: I told you that wasn't the same daughter.

DAUGHTER: Send her back home to what?

ELAINE: Alright, do we have to call the hospital and find out if he is actually hospitalized or retired or something?

WORKER 2: No, the only place I called was the union.

ELAINE: Alright.

WORKER: But see, the check's in his name.

ELAINE: Yeah. However, if he's hospitalized all the time, what—where are those checks going and who's cashing those checks?

WORKER: He's coming home on weekends. He may be—

ELAINE: Can we verify that he's coming home on weekends?

WORKER (*overlapping*): We don't know. This is what she said now. I didn't verify a thing. I just got to her this morning, she—

ELAINE: Alright.

WORKER: —stormed in on me upstairs.

ELAINE: On the fourth floor? The daughter?

WORKER: Yeah, the daughter.

ELAINE: I'll tell them I said it's okay to give them—then we'll see.

WORKER: Alright, if the money is in his name. If it were in her name, it would be different.

ELAINE: Okay, hold it. [*All three speak at once, mostly unintelligible.*] He is responsible for his wife and his children.

WORKER: He is, but that's why she went to the court, because he's not giving her a penny.

ELAINE: Oh, alright.

WORKER: She has to be in court on the twenty-first.

40. Three clients talk at once.

ELAINE: Alright; give her—tell her to get a slip at the desk.

RIVERA: Now they telling me to go work, when I got a letter from the doctor saying I'm not [*cut to CU of Mr. Rivera*] supposed to be working.

DAUGHTER: —and she went and tore your letter up?

RIVERA: And she went and tore the letter yesterday up. Ask the supervisor.

DAUGHTER: Get another letter and let her tear that one up.

RIVERA: Yeah. I'm going to get another one. The doctor told me to pick one up today. [*Client, Mrs. Gaskin, Rivera and an onlooker all talk at once.*]

DAUGHTER: My father is sick . . . He's been, he's in the hospital since November. I been running back and forth with this woman for months. They send us back in a circle. We go to court, from the court to the hospital, from the hospital to Social Security, to Welfare, back to Social Security, to the hospital, to the court. She got, what do, she ain't got one dime and we're all suffering trying to take care of her. Then when you try to help yourself, they don't help you at all.

RIVERA: —over there, and what they do is give me a runaround, too. They did that—

DAUGHTER: That's . . . that's, how it is that, that—that's how it is with the whole damn system.

RIVERA: Not only that—

DAUGHTER: When you try and help yourself, nobody helps you.

RIVERA: Not only that, but then if I come around and then she comes and tears the letter in, I beat the brains out of her. Then I go to jail.

DAUGHTER: Then you got to go to jail, and then where's your wife, right back in the circle again.

RIVERA: They—no—then they got to help her whether they like it or not.

DAUGHTER: Well, I guess that's what you got to do.

RIVERA: That's right.

DAUGHTER: —gotta do, gotta do—

RIVERA: That's what I'm going to have to do. That's what I'm going to have to do.

DAUGHTER: I got to come here with my mother. I got, I got to, I got children. I got to take care of all my family, got children. My mother is a woman that have fifteen children. She took care every one of them. My father work like a slave. He's sick. He's got to go through this? I've got to go through this? No. Somebody goin' to do something for her, and I'm not going to leave here and I'm not going not one more day because I am tired and she's tired. If we got, we got the kids out of school. They don't even have no shoes. What do they want from us?

MAN: See, they—

DAUGHTER: I know you're tired, because I am. And I'm not—

MAN: —the Welfare Department is actually the New York runaround.

DAUGHTER: You better believe it, 'cause all you goin' get is a runaround.

MAN: The New York runaround.

DAUGHTER: Did you go upstairs?

MAN: No, I don't go upstairs.

DAUGHTER: You go up there and—

RIVERA: Sometimes they don't allow you to—beyond certain points.

DAUGHTER: They get angry with you because you interrupting their coffee break. I made the mistake of interrupting their coffee break one day when I went there. I followed them over and I sat down. You know what they tell me? Come back tomorrow morning.

RIVERA: So then they give you the runaround. [*Several shots of people in waiting area, including pregnant client.*]

WOMAN (*changing baby's diaper*): Stop kicking. You stop kicking. You stop kicking. You stop kicking. [*Cut back to Mrs. Gaskin, her mother, and worker.*]

DAUGHTER: See here, she lives in North Carolina. She's here on a temporary basis, because her husband works here in New York. But she lives in North Carolina. Her husband lives in New York. That's what—

WORKER 2: Excuse me, please. Miss Silver . . . [*Elaine comes over.*] I asked Mrs. Gaskin for proof that she's living at eighty—

ELAINE: Nine.

THIRD WORKER: Nine Columbus. She has nothing—

ELAINE: Is this a housing project? What address did you give the court as your home address?

GASKIN: Uh, the [*inaudible*] address.

ELAINE: How long were you in North Carolina?

GASKIN: I'm not here to stay. I'm only here temporarily basis.

ELAINE: Then why are you even in New York?

GASKIN: Because I'm sick. I been, because I been—

ELAINE: —in a hospital in North Carolina.

GASKIN: Wait a minute, wait a minute. When I was living here. Let me explain it to you. And I—

THIRD WORKER: How long did you go to North Carolina for, Mrs. Gaskin?

GASKIN: Three years ago. Yes.

ELAINE: Uh-huh. So for the last three years you've been living in North Carolina?

GASKIN: Yes, but I've been coming back, to this doctor. She can verify it.

WORKER 2: When did you come to New York, the last time?

DAUGHTER: In Novem—

GASKIN: In the first part of November.

ELAINE: You came back the first part of November? Why did you come back to New York?

GASKIN: I had to come to the doctor, and when I came here—

ELAINE: This is the only doctor that can take care of you—?

GASKIN: That's only—

ELAINE: And what do you suffer from?

GASKIN: I have—don't you see it on there?

ELAINE: Diabetes. You mean no other doctor in North Carolina can take care of you?

GASKIN: Well, it was too expensive.

DAUGHTER: Do you mind, do you mind, if I explain it to you because she—

ELAINE: I do mind. You mean you came all the way back to New York to go to NINA Health Clinics because there's no other doctor—

DAUGHTER: You tell her, you tell her about how you came about moving to North Carolina.

GASKIN: I've been trying to tell her now.

ELAINE: Alright.

GASKIN: The reason why I went to North Caroline to live. We were, we were living in the house—, hou—, housing project.

ELAINE: In New York?

GASKIN: Yes. My husband was working. Every time he got a raise, they wanted a raise. So he decided he wanted me to move. So he—

ELAINE: He wanted what?

THIRD WORKER: He wanted her to move.

ELAINE: Oh.

GASKIN: So in order to move down there, he had to go to the VA. The VA gave him—lent him money to buy his house.

ELAINE: Is the VA welfare?

GASKIN: I don't know. I didn't take care of that business.

ELAINE: Then he might have been on welfare in the Veteran's Administration.

GASKIN: I don't know.

ELAINE: It is a form of welfare. Alright.

GASKIN: He got money from the VA. The VA lent him money to buy his house. So it's not paid for yet.

ELAINE: Oh, to buy his house? If you get accepted on welfare in New York, which I don't know, you'll have to sign over that whole entire house to the Department of Welfare in New York.

GASKIN: It's not my house.

ELAINE: You're co-owner of it, aren't you?

GASKIN: My husband is the one that—

ELAINE: Well, you'll have to, *you* will have to sign over that house. You'll have to bring the deed to welfare. That—

GASKIN: I don't have the deed. This is what I'm trying to tell you. I don't have anything.

ELAINE: You'll have to go to your husband who is hospitalized and get the deed.

GASKIN: Didn't I tell you that every time I went to the hospital they tells me I'm not to bother with him. Well, how can I get in if they don't let me in to him?

ELAINE: When anybody has the resource such as a house or co-op or anything like that, they must sign it over to the department before they can get assistance. That is considered a resource. You have money invested in that house.

DAUGHTER: She don't have no—

ELAINE: Look. I don't know too much about resource. We got a resource consultant. Excuse me.

DAUGHTER (*overlapping*): You, you goin' to tell her that she can sign over a house that belongs to her husband?

ELAINE: Her husband is responsible for her and—

DAUGHTER: —[*inaudible*] going to court now. She is very much aware of that. She can't make him give her anything.

ELAINE: I would like to see the deed and see whose name is on the deed.

DAUGHTER: You can get it from him yourself. He won't give her anything.

GASKIN: He didn't even meet me in court. That's why I'm back here.

DAUGHTER: She was in court yesterday with it and he did not show up. What do you expect from her, to take the deed from him? If he maintains that he's not going to give her anything—

GASKIN: She told me I should go in and take—

DAUGHTER: You the one who told her to take it, to take his checks out of the mailbox, right? What do you want her to do?

ELAINE: The interview cannot continue.

DAUGHTER: What do you want her to do?

ELAINE: I am just telling you—

DAUGHTER: To take money from him?

ELAINE (*overlapping*): I'm not yelling and there's no reason for you to continue yelling.

DAUGHTER: Why should you yell?

ELAINE: As long as you're yelling, the interview will not continue.

DAUGHTER: Why should you yell? You going to tell her she must go? You are telling her, you are telling her—she don't want to talk about it. You see, my voice is down.

ELAINE: Come back tomorrow morning.

DAUGHTER (*overlapping*): No, I'm not coming back tomorrow. You are telling, you are telling her to go and, to go and break into a mailbox and to take the man's checks. How can you tell my mother to take his checks? [*Elaine walks away, back to her desk.*] You see how she's walking away from me? How you going to tell her to take his check out of his mailbox when his name is on them? He says he's not going to take care of her and she's taking him to court.

GASKIN (*overlapping*): Miss, will you give me my papers? Miss, will you give me my papers back? My letter. Give it back to me, please.

DAUGHTER: It's easy for her. She's not going to use this as no cop-out. After she going to tell her to break in a mailbox and take some, and take some checks that don't even belong to her.

GASKIN: Tell her to tell the lawyer— [*Client and her daughter talk at once.*]

DAUGHTER: And if, and if the checks, if the house—

GASKIN: She told me, she told me.

DAUGHTER: —if the man, if the man has got the deed to the house and he maintains that he's not going to her, then what is she supposed to do? Take it from him?

RIVERA: Welfare—to give it to them, but those who needs it, they're not going to give it to them. But I got news for her, man.

DAUGHTER: Huh?

RIVERA: Go home, man.

DAUGHTER: I'll go up to see, to see the what-d'ya-call-him again.

RIVERA: I want her to give me a letter saying why I'm not accepted. [*Inaudible.*]

DAUGHTER: She just wanted some excuse to walk out of here. After she going to tell you to break in some mailbox and take something that's not even yours.

GASKIN: That's what she want me to do.

DAUGHTER: And tell—how you going to make him sign over the house?

GASKIN: I don't know.

DAUGHTER: Let her go over and tell him to sign the house over.

POLICEMAN: Your problem has been taken care by the other lady that went upstairs.

RIVERA: Yeah, but I want to know what's the problem with me, why I can't get Medicare to my wife.

POLICEMAN: You gonna have to wait till that lady comes back.

ELAINE (*overlapping*): Excuse me, one minute. Let me just speak. His wife's case is being accepted through the mail, and he should leave the Center. He'll be getting a check in the mail. So as far as I'm concerned, this case is over with.

POLICEMAN: Well, anyway, the worker's been talking to him.

ELAINE (*overlapping*): No, the worker walked away. No, the worker's not seeing him anymore.

RIVERA: No, she didn't walk away from me, because I was quiet . . . I was quiet.

ELAINE: I know what my worker, where my worker went.

POLICEMAN: Well, listen. You see—

ELAINE: My worker is not going to see him anymore.

POLICEMAN: Why don't you talk to—who's you director? Who's you supervisor down here? Who, who's your supervisor down here?

ELAINE: Wait. Wait a minute.

RIVERA (*overlapping*): You told me and, to go home, and I don't—and any minute, any moment now, and I ain't got Medicaid and—

ELAINE: Wait a minute, wait a minute. Let me just talk.

POLICEMAN: Look. Go over there and sit and be cool. Alright?

ELAINE: Look. I am the supervisor and I know where my worker went. The worker told the clients to leave the area. He's walking away! The worker asked the clients to leave the area. The determination on the case was made. They will get a check in the mail. Now he was carrying on and disrupting and I would like him removed.

POLICEMAN: Let's take care of these problems we're dealing with now.

ELAINE: Well, which problem you want to take care of first?

POLICEMAN: The one you having right now.

ELAINE: I'm having two problems right now. It's quite obvious.

DAUGHTER (*overlapping*): What she want to do, she wants to cop out.

POLICEMAN: Which one you want to deal with now?

ELAINE: Alright. You want to deal with this pers—, people—

POLICEMAN: Me? You asking me?

DAUGHTER: She wanna cop out . . . She's ashamed to walk away.

ELAINE: You're disrupting the area.

DAUGHTER (*overlapping*): I'm not disrupting anything.

ELAINE: The worker cannot work and there's a whole commotion around here.

POLICEMAN: Let's take care of the problem that you're dealing with now.

ELAINE: Which problem is that? These people?

POLICEMAN: Whichever one you taking now.

ELAINE: Okay. These people will be interviewed any time they want to lower their voices and conduct the interview in a low voice.

DAUGHTER: Well, I lowered my voice, and she still insists on walking away. She's just using this as a cop-out. She's going to tell my mother to go and break in a mailbox and take some checks that don't even belong to her, that belong to my father. She's going to say she wants the house. Okay, my mother don't own the house. How can she give her the house?

POLICEMAN: You keep quiet now. Are you finished now?

RIVERA (*overlapping*): Alright. I keep—

POLICEMAN: Just, just go over there and sit down and wait for your worker to come down. Alright?

RIVERA (*overlapping*): I'll keep quiet.

POLICEMAN: Do you, do you have a supervisor?

SUPERVISOR: Yeah. I'm the supervisor.

POLICEMAN: Alright. Well, why don't you deal with this? I'm a patrolman here, that's the only—if there is an arrest to be made, I'm here. Otherwise, social work is social work.

ELAINE: Excuse me, Mr.—Sergeant, whatever you are.

SUPERVISOR: Alright. Can he sit here till five o'clock and at five o'clock you put them out?

ELAINE: Wait. An inter—, yeah. Now, my worker will not work if this man sits there without an interview. The interviewer is not coming back.

SUPERVISOR: Is he, is he—

ELAINE (*overlapping*): The interview is over. Miss Bell walked away.

POLICEMAN: Listen, let's deal with what you have here. This man is, is— [*to Mr. Rivera*] you go, you go away, man, go away, and stay over there. [*To Elaine*] Let's deal with what you have now.

ELAINE: Okay. This interview will continue any time they lower their voice and conduct the interview in a low voice.

DAUGHTER: I lowered my voice and she still persisted.

SUPERVISOR: Alright. Alright.

POLICEMAN: I don't even have to be there, to just—

SUPERVISOR: Alright. We're going to take care of you. Let's all calm down.

ELAINE: Okay.

SUPERVISOR: Who's taking care of this woman?

ELAINE: Miss Bates is talking to them—

SUPERVISOR: Miss Bates—

ELAINE: —but they continue to cause a scene and have a very loud voice and that disrupts—

DAUGHTER: That—I told you that you told me to—

SUPERVISOR (*overlapping*): Alright. Can we try it again?

ELAINE: I did not. I asked you—

SUPERVISOR: Can we try it again? Without any, without any problems?

DAUGHTER: I would like you at least to sit in on it because she's asking for some, she wants my mother to sign over something that don't belong to her—

ELAINE: Oh, excuse me. What it is, is they own a house in North Carolina and I told them the resource policy concerning—

SUPERVISOR: If you want something—

DAUGHTER: Alright.

SUPERVISOR: If you want something you've got—

DAUGHTER: Alright, just a, just a moment. We understand that. It's not that my mother is not cooperating. My mother never signed anything. My mother don't—why don't she get it from my father? She don't have the right to give her anything. She's asking—

SUPERVISOR: Where is your father?

DAUGHTER: In the hospital. She knows where he's at. She knows this. She told him.

SUPERVISOR: What the problem on the whole case?

ELAINE and DAUGHTER (*at once*): The problem is—

GASKIN: The problem is, I asked, I went to the hospital. My husband is in the hospital. I asked the people at the hospital, that—told them about my health and they told me to go to welfare, so I didn't go to welfare, I went to court first. They gave me a referral to come here. When I came here Monday, they told me to go back to Social Security. Social Security told me, give me a referral to come back here and said get for the children, not to me. They'll give me—

DAUGHTER: Because she's in need, she can get from the Social Security.

SUPERVISOR: Okay. It's an ADC case for the two children or—

GASKIN: Yes. I have two children.

SUPERVISOR: Two children?

GASKIN: Yes, sir.

SUPERVISOR: What's the story?

ELAINE: All I know is her legal residence is North Carolina and wants welfare in New York 'cause she's here on a visit. Seems to me that's the story.

GASKIN: After, after my husband was sick—

DAUGHTER: No, my father works here and he was sending her money to North Carolina and after he took sick—

ELAINE: And she—to North Carolina and there are no doctors in North Carolina. And the only doctors that can take care of her—

DAUGHTER: She never told her that.

ELAINE: Her diabetic—

SUPERVISOR: Now, wait a minute.

ELAINE: —condition is a New York doctor. So she came up here.

DAUGHTER: She never told her that.

GASKIN: —no doctor there. The doctor there was too expensive.

DAUGHTER (*overlapping*): She's dramatizing things.

GASKIN: I been to a doctor there before but I have a doctor here and I—

SUPERVISOR: Is your legal residence, is in North Carolina?

GASKIN: But my husband is here.

SUPERVISOR: But is, is yours?

GASKIN: I don't know how it is.

ELAINE: They own a house in North Carolina, so I would assume the source of her legal residence—

SUPERVISOR: Were they on welfare in—

ELAINE: She claims no.

GASKIN: No.

SUPERVISOR: No? Did we, did we check it out?

ELAINE: No. We haven't done so as yet. She claims that her husband was sending her checks.

DAUGHTER: He was.

ELAINE: Now the husband is hospitalized and can no longer send her checks.

DAUGHTER: He's in the hospital. I mean—

SUPERVISOR: Did they write us a letter?

GASKIN: I don't know. See, when I went to the hospital—

ELAINE: We'll have someone visit him in the hospital.

GASKIN: To see his social worker.

ELAINE: If they will lower their voices, we will continue the interview.

SUPERVISOR: Alright. Alright.

41. A welfare worker talks with her supervisor as tensions mount.

GASKIN: When I went to see his social worker—

SUPERVISOR (*overlapping*): Alright. Let's all be, let's all be quiet. Let's sit down. Let's see if we can get this, this show on the road, alright?

DAUGHTER: And, and, and you, you request that we lower our voice. I request that you stop being so dramatic, and putting words into my mother's mouth saying things she did not say. She never told you there's no other doctor in North Carolina.

SUPERVISOR: We're never going to get anyplace this way. Let's, let's, let's continue. Let's continue with the interview.

ELAINE: Alright. Now, let's solve the other problem. Miss Bell is not continuing that interview over there. The determination on the case was made and I want the patrolman removing those clients in that area over there.

SUPERVISOR: He can't remove them till five o'clock.

ELAINE: That's, this, the waiting area is over there—

SUPERVISOR: Alright, we'll, I'll put them in the waiting room.

ELAINE: Well, you—

DAUGHTER: Incredible.

SUPERVISOR: Now let's sit down and let's sit down and interview this client.

ELAINE: Well, Faith is doing it. They can go back there. [*Cut to CU of Mr. Rivera.*]

RIVERA: Since I came here, she's been giving me a hard time because she must don't not like me, I guess.

SUPERVISOR: She's just been giving you as hard a time as we've been getting from you, I think.

RIVERA: This is the first time I come here and even yelling. We've been here three—since October I been going back and forth and they been giving me the same rap. Bring another letter, so I bring another letter.

ELAINE: Did you bring a letter?

RIVERA: That's not the one. Bring this one. Or bring that one.

ELAINE: Well, wait a minute. If you've got grounds since October. We've only seen you this month, right? So, obviously, other people are giving you runarounds.

RIVERA: Yes. True.

ELAINE: It's a very strange thing, 'cause everybody's giving you runarounds. You were in another center. You were in Waverly.

RIVERA (*overlapping*): I was over here and they—

ELAINE: Alright.

RIVERA: —and they closed my case.

ELAINE: Alright. I'll tell you something. See, all centers work the same and all centers want proof. They just don't hand out money.

RIVERA: What proof?

ELAINE: And we're not the only center doesn't.

RIVERA: I've got all the proof you want here.

ELAINE: We—every center works by certain rules and regulations and procedures.

RIVERA (*overlapping*): I understand.

ELAINE: And when you come into us, we all work the same way. The other center that gave you the runaround since September or October, and now you think we're giving you a runaround, but we're only working the same way that they're working. Okay.

SUPERVISOR: You're just using the wrong language.

ELAINE: This is it. Okay. I am—

SUPERVISOR: Because you're not, because you're not bringing the information we need.

ELAINE: Everyone is giving them a runaround.

SUPERVISOR: That doesn't mean—

MRS. RIVERA: May I ask you something? You say that my sponsor is legally responsible for me.

RIVERA: Yes. He did.

ELAINE: No. I didn't say that.

MRS. RIVERA: Well, he's my guardian, right?

ELAINE: Well, he's more responsible for you than welfare. And we'd like to have a contact with him before we give you money.

MRS. RIVERA: Now, what is it with my sponsor? I could not get permission to marry, with my sponsor?

RIVERA: Yeah. You tell us that.

MRS. RIVERA: If he's responsible for me, why couldn't he—

ELAINE: I'm not a marriage counselor. I don't know anything about marriages or anything like that. I know about welfare.

RIVERA: How long you think it will take us to get help? At least, man, this is the—

SUPERVISOR: We're accepting your case now. I mean, you're just killing a dead horse.

RIVERA: No, I'm just asking you, 'cause I'm uptight, man. I'm really uptight for money. I show you what I got in my pocket and what I have ate all day today since I been here. You see? That's what I got to my name. You understand? That's all. I pull out my wallet and I show you the same thing. I don't have a dime to my name, practically.

ELAINE: Get a job.

RIVERA: Yeah. You want to help me get a job?

MRS. RIVERA: He does. That's all you say. That's the only vocabulary. Get a job, to everybody that comes in here.

RIVERA: What about the letter my doctor send you that said I was unable to go to work because I have to be rehabilitated?

ELAINE: It's inconclusive, the doctor's statement. That's why we're giving you a medical examination.

RIVERA: Everything's inconclusive. All I want to do is to get help until I get on my feet and, believe me, I wouldn't be here after you, you. Man, I wish I was by myself. God!

MRS. RIVERA: And if you were here by yourself, she would gladly help you.

RIVERA: Of course. If I were by myself she just might do that, help me then. I'm a man, aren't I? Now—I'm sorry. What do you suggest? I go home, of course.

SUPERVISOR: We're accepting her case.

RIVERA: Okay.

SUPERVISOR: Let's leave it at that.

RIVERA: Alright.

SUPERVISOR: Let's, let's not, let's not bring it any further. Let's not quarrel about it. The fact is her case is being accepted. We're not refusing her. But there are certain other items like the, the letter from her, her uncle that we need. That's all there is to it.

RIVERA: Okay, then. For the bills that I got of the doctor bills, what I do, I just hold onto them? I got, I got plenty of bills for her.

SUPERVISOR: Right now, right now, there's nothing much we can do about your bills until we find out whether you're eligible or not. She's eligible.

RIVERA: But, the meantime is that since October I been—you know what I been doing? I have to sell my medication, my methadone. You understand? And I'm not about to go to jail for nobody anymore, you understand?

SUPERVISOR: It's tough. Tough.

RIVERA: If that's what you going to have to make, they going to make me do here—

SUPERVISOR: Well, that's up to you. I mean, the path you take is up to you. We've accepted, we've accepted her. Now if, if the situation changes and we accept you, that's a different story, but right now—

RIVERA: All I really, all I want right now is concern that I get something to help her. You understand?

SUPERVISOR: If we're not accepting your case, we can't give you a Medic-aid card.

RIVERA: But you're accepting her. You can give her a Medicaid card. Not me.

SUPERVISOR: She's getting, she's getting a Medicaid card. She'll get one.

42. A client explains his desperation to the assistant director.

RIVERA: Okay. Okay. That's settled. Then I'll go home.

SUPERVISOR: Okay then.

RIVERA: Thank you.

SUPERVISOR: Alright. [*Mr. and Mrs. Rivera walk out of the interview area. Shots of reception desk, policeman taking notes, waiting room, WREP worker sweeping corridor.*]

CLIENT (MR. HIRSCH): "No, we can't give an appointment; it's too late. [*Cut to CU of Mr. Hirsch*] You have to come back tomorrow." Right? I said I don't have any money. I got ten cents. My rent is due tomorrow. I have nothing to live on.

SAM: You just told me, you just told me—

HIRSCH: I haven't eaten for three days.

SAM: You just told me you ripped off Kor—, you ripped off Korvette.

HIRSCH: I got caught ripping off Korvette's for a hundred and ten dollars worth of stuff.

SAM: And they let you go. Right?

HIRSCH: That's right. After I spent two hours explaining how I ripped off the other four stores over the last six months.

SAM: And you just ripped off, you said you ripped off—

HIRSCH: Woolworth's.

SAM: Woolworth's last night.

HIRSCH: Today. For seven bars of chocolate.

SAM: Seven bars of chocolate. And you believe that it's—

HIRSCH: I ate three and I gave four away.

SAM: And you believe it right to steal, right?

HIRSCH: No.

SAM: Then why—

HIRSCH: It's absolutely wrong. It's absolutely—

SAM: You just told me—

HIRSCH: —wrong to steal.

SAM: Before—

HIRSCH: Did I say it was right?

SAM: You told me it was right.

HIRSCH: I said it was necessary. There's a difference between right and necessary.

SAM: Why's it necessary?

HIRSCH: Because I don't have the money to buy what I have to steal because the Social Service Department doesn't see fit or the Social Security Administration doesn't see fit to give me enough money to live on.

SAM: Excuse me. You're a Social Security case now?

HIRSCH: Yeah.

SAM: So why do you come to Welfare?

HIRSCH: They sent me, with a referral slip that I got that was stolen last night along with a billion dollars worth of original research that I've been working on for three years. Psychic research. Mind control research. In a red folder. Stuff that—it was handwritten.

SAM: Why don't you go downstairs? Make an appointment. Do it right. Make an appointment with the income maintenance people.

HIRSCH: For tomorrow?

SAM: Fifth floor. Yeah. Do it right.

HIRSCH: What do I do for tonight? What do I do for rent money? What do

I do for food money? I haven't eaten in three, three days now, except what, except what I steal, except what—I can't steal a chicken. I can't steal a steak. It doesn't fit in my pocket. I can only steal Hershey bars and chee—, packages of cheese and, you know, little cans of fruit.

SAM: Mr. Hirsch, there's nothing we can do for you.

HIRSCH: I know.

SAM: There's nothing we can do. I'm sorry.

HIRSCH: I know you can't. Social Security can't because I'm over the maximum. You can't because it's too late.

SAM: You received a check from us recently.

HIRSCH: No, I didn't. It was sent back. A hundred and thirty-seven—a hundred forty-seven dollars and thirty-five cents. I never got it. It was sent to the hotel I was at, but I had to check out because I didn't, I didn't get it on the sixteenth. It came on the eighteenth and I wasn't there anymore because I didn't have the money for the rent. So the manager sent it back on the nineteenth, and then Mr. Fagin for some reason sent me to Social Security. I don't know why. Without any money. Without ever seeing that check.

SAM: Mr. Fagin says you received that check.

HIRSCH: I never received *any* check.

SAM: Well, discuss it with Mr. Fagin. Don't discuss it with me.

HIRSCH: Where's Mr. Fagin?

SAM: He'll be here shortly. Have a, wait outside.

HIRSCH: Sure. Why not? I'll wait. I've been waiting for the last hundred and twenty-four days since I got out of the hospital, waiting for something— Godot. But you know what happens, you know what happens in the story of Godot. He never came. And that's what I'm waiting for. Something that'll never come. Equity. Justice. Justice, under, under this great democratic society of ours where everybody is equal under the law, you know. Lincoln said that, didn't he? All men are created equal? Lincoln never took an army physical, you know. He should have known better. What's equality? Equality is when somebody has and somebody hasn't and the one that hasn't tries to rip off the one that has, and the one that has tries to keep what he's got and there's nothing in the middle anymore. It's you either have it or you don't have it.

SAM: Yeah.

HIRSCH: It's not a matter of, you know. There's no middle class any more. There's just the rich and the poor. And I'm one of the poor. In fact, destitute, not poor. And I don't like the feeling. Not with twenty-two years of education behind me. Not with seventeen years of service to this state. Not with a twenty-two-thousand-dollar-plus income when I was working. Plus my private practice was worth another three or four thousand. No, but after being in the hospital for seven months and eight days, up until September—

SAM: Do me a favor. Sit outside.

HIRSCH: —and not being considered fit to go back to work, and having to resign rather than being fired—

SAM: Sit outside.

HIRSCH: —because I've only got another eleven days to go before they fire me from that seventeen-year job.

SAM: Sit outside. I want you—go sit down, huh?

HIRSCH (*going to sit down*): Sure. I'll sit down. Shut up. Why not? You're the law, man, you're the *man*. Everybody's the man when you don't have anything. Everybody's the boss when you're broke. It's got to change mighty fast because if it doesn't change in the next fifteen years, by 1988, there will be no United States of America. There will be nobody here worth saving. Everybody who is worth saving will be someplace else. And I'll be the first to leave. Because for forty years and seven months I've tried. God knows I've tried to help . . . Now I can't even help myself, let alone anybody else. How can you help anybody on eleven cents? Five days . . . [*Sighs heavily, looks upward.*] Lord, I don't know why, but you still won't, you still don't want me to live. You still don't want me to do anything that I want to do. You still want me to do your thing, and suffer. I guess suffer for everybody else who's gone before . . . Okay, if that's what you want, that's what it's gonna be. We've had this agreement for a while now. I'm not backing down. If you want to, that's your business. I'll stay with it till it's over, whenever that is. And if you don't want me to eat, if you don't want me to sleep, if you don't want me to work, I won't. [*Insert shot of WREP cleaner.*] And if you want me to keep wandering the way we've been wandering for 5,735 years, I'll keep wandering. [*Cut back to Mr. Hirsch.*] You know that doesn't bother me. Even if there's no one, no one in this whole world that will listen to me, I'll wander, until you're, you're ready to decide where I belong. A place, a home, people, friends, whenever that'll be. I got all the time in the world. And thank God, all the patience and the strength and the understanding. Thank you. [*Bows his head.*]

[*Clients walking down corridor and into a waiting room. Shots of various clients waiting, including Larry, his partner, Mr. Harrington, and the ex-convict. Final shot is of a crowded waiting room, ambient sound carrying over the final credits. Final credits: Directed and Produced by Frederick Wiseman. Photographed by William Brayne. Editor: Frederick Wiseman. Camera assistant/assistant editor: Oliver Kool, Sync: Ken Sommer, Mix: Richard Vorisek. A Zipporah Films Release ©1975 Welfare Films, Inc. All Rights Reserved. Copyright renewed 2003 Zipporah Films, Inc.*]

High School II (1994)

High School II was filmed in New York for eight weeks, during April and May 1992, at the Central Park East High School on Manhattan's upper East Side, and released in 1994. Over twenty years after *High School*, Wiseman returns to the topic of public education and draws many fascinating parallels between the world of high school then and now. Where the earlier film looked at a predominantly white school, the student body of Central Park East is racially more diverse. Classes and individual lessons in literature, writing, science, history, and sex education are shown, as well as teachers' staff meetings and meetings between teachers, parents, and students. Unlike the earlier *High School*, scenes of students talking among themselves are also shown. While Wiseman was shooting *High School II*, the trial of the four white Los Angeles policemen accused of assault with a deadly weapon and use of excessive force in the beating of a black man, Rodney King, a year earlier, concluded on April 29 with an acquittal, despite the apparently incontrovertible evidence of a videotape showing the beating. (A subsequent federal prosecution resulted in the conviction of two of the officers.) Anger at the verdict erupted into widespread violence in South Central Los Angeles, and the ensuing tensions inform many of the scenes in the film.

[*Title. Two exterior LSs of New York City streets by Central Park East Secondary School (CPESS). Shots of street signs indicating the school's location as East 106th Street and Madison Avenue. Cut to shot of street corner as a school bus goes by, with Central Park visible in the background. Cut to shot of front entrance as students enter school. Inaudible background conversation.*]

BOY (*offscreen*): Shawn, wanna go with me? Why? (*Cut to a meeting inside a room, beginning with shot of three teachers at desks meeting with student, out of frame left.*)

FEMALE TEACHER (SHIRLEY): From your perspective, now, as you look at our society, right at this moment, we have lot of unemployed people—

BOY (*offscreen*): Uh-huh.

SHIRLEY: —We have great—

BOY (*offscreen*): Lot of homeless.

SHIRLEY: —alright, a lot of homeless people, a great deal of inequity as far as the wealth is concerned. How can democracy use the experience of what's gone on in the labor movement from the socialist point of view, perhaps, to effect change or . . . (*Camera pans left to boy.*)

BOY: Well, I think what it is is that, for instance, I mean, this is the best time to talk about it, but this thing that happened Rodney King. The decision that was made is probably not made because the people were racist, that they, the jurors, didn't make the decision because they, well, "I don't like a black guy." I think it was more the fact that they were more middle class. They moved into a middle-class neighborhood and the middle class are the people that want the protection from the police and want the police to be believed. And if you—and the—and that's one way to get it, by, you know, voting for—well, you have to give them the benefit of the doubt. They need to get this person, he was drunk, and he did, they need him off the road. And they, you have to give them that. Things like that are going to continue to happen. When things like that continue—you see what's happening in L.A. right now. The reason it's total chaos there is because there's no guidance, there's nobody to hold them, and that's why people are just getting killed. I mean, it's terrible what's happening, and it's not right.

SHIRLEY: So how does socialism impinge on that?

BOY (*overlapping*): Well, the way socialism, socialism explains it.

SHIRLEY: Okay.

BOY: And it tries to make a unity between groups, because they're saying, they're saying it's not black on white thing, it's a social, it's poor and rich thing. They're saying that, as you see, there was an Asian and there was a, and two Latin, and two Mexicans or Latinos on the, on the jury. And they decided the same way. It's not because they, it's not because all the groups just had a conspiracy against the, Rodney King, but it was because middle, there was, they're all middle class. They moved into a middle-class neighborhood. And that's a big problem. There's, there's, they say there's political reasons they don't want to do it in L.A. County, but that's a huge, that's a huge thing to, when you have—it seemed like the most problems are really between the social classes and not really, even though the—it just hides itself under racism.

SHIRLEY: So you think that socialism might give democracy a—

BOY: Well, it might give unity to groups to—

SHIRLEY (*overlapping*): —a better chance—

BOY: —make democracy.

SHIRLEY: —to work. That's an interesting thought.

BOY: Well, because you see, I mean, people, for instance, they say, you know, get Jerry Brown because he'll get Jesse Jackson, and Jesse Jackson will get black votes. But it's not really, it's not, it's—you need to find somebody who's going—Bill Clinton got a lot of middle-class black votes. It's not because he had Jesse—he said he was going to get Jesse Jackson. He said it was because he had middle-class ideas that these middle-class blacks believed in. And that's—so it's not a racial thing, it's socially what people want. And that's how, if you can unite a certain, a peoples under, say, the lower class or the lower middle class or the middle class then—the lower class is usually the largest—then you would get democracy because those, then if they're united under ideas and they, with no racism they're all split up because everybody believes that this white person's going to take my job, this Jew's going to take my job, this Mexican's going to take my job. And if you have everybody united then there would be democracy, because then the majority would get their idea what they want across and to the government. [*Cut to shot of students in school hallway. Shot of three male students walking by looking at a brochure.*]

FIRST BOY (*to another boy who is looking at a brochure as they walk past the camera*): Like it?

SECOND BOY: [*Inaudible*]. [*Cut to CU of teacher asking a question of a student intern.*]

FEMALE TEACHER: I want to ask you, before you start, when you first started your internship—now I know you're excited about it—what, if anything, did you feel intimidated by, or what was fearful, if anything?

GIRL: Well, I had no idea what the stock market really was. All I knew was that there was a New York Stock Exchange and I was downtown by Wall Street and, you know, they would buy and sell stocks for their clients. I didn't know, like, how much money was involved or how much you can get into it mentally. And, I don't know, I just—like when you watch like movies like *Wall Street* it's like a whole different aspect of it. They really never show like the life of a sales assistant or the life of a secretary, which is like kind of equivalent to a sales assistant, and I think that when I went to this office I was like, wow, you know, I never knew all this and was like just rushing into my head all at once and I think that's why I kind of motivated myself to learn this as quick as I could because if I wanted to continue working there, then I would need to pick everything up. And I think that, when, like when I tell people that I work at Lehman Brothers, it's like Lehman Brothers! So I, I kind of, it kind of pushed me to really like get a stable position in the firm, therefore, you know, because, like when I want to go to college or if I want to go and work on another firm or something, when they look at my resume they can see Lehman Brothers and they can call and I won't have like a bad report on myself. They'll be like, you know, she's a wonderful worker and, you know, she really goes and when you need to tell her what to do she just jumps and does it by herself, so, I don't know, I think that I've grown a lot mentally and physically within the firm. [*Cut to CU of African-American boy listening to the codirector of the school.*]

CODIRECTOR (PAUL): It's a high school that works best for those people who really want to be here. You have mixed feelings about being here on a lot of levels . . . Let me take a chance and ask you a question, Ayou. Do you think of this as a white school, as a school run by white people, and that it would be different if you were in a school that was—and is part of your anger at the school anger that is racial, that, because Debbie and I, the codirectors of the school [*camera reverse zooms and pans right to show Paul and Richard*], are white, Richard's white, and more of the staff is white than African-American or Latino, do you think of it that way sometimes? Even though—

BOY: A lot of times.

MOTHER: Now what school isn't?

FEMALE TEACHER: This school.

MOTHER (*overlapping*): Well, that's a private school. I'm talking about a public school.

PAUL: Other than your school. I think that that's—I think that your mother's right.

TEACHER (RICHARD): Can I, what, I'm curious, from your point of view in terms as a student, what would be different for you if more of the teachers were Latino or African-American? How do you think it would be different for you learning?

BOY: I don't want to sound prejudiced, but if I had a black teacher I think I would give him more respect than I would give you, 'cause he's black.

RICHARD: Okay.

MOTHER: I totally disagree with that.

PAUL: That's a real feeling. I mean, that's a real feeling of a young man and it's—I disagree with it, I don't know if I disagree with it. I think it's a real concern.

RICHARD: Let's just explore a little more, though. Bridget, do you respect her?

BOY: No.

RICHARD: Okay, more than you do me or Angelo? Dave Smith, do you interact with him?

BOY: Yeah!

RICHARD: You do?

BOY: A lot of times.

RICHARD: But you would give him the same amount of respect?

BOY: Not some of the time.

RICHARD: Some of the time, okay. I mean, I think it's a real feeling, but I think you've got to also be—it's this issue: you got to take some responsibility and control for your actions. But, I mean, I think it's, I mean, it's, that's your feeling.

MOTHER: Yeah, but I—

BOY: I don't feel that all the time, though, but if, I don't feel that all the time, 'cause you have to respect all people no matter what race they are, but, it just flashes through my mind some time. I think that's the feeling that every kid gets.

PAUL: I think that a lot of kids get that feeling. I do, especially at times like this, and I think that you have it more often than other kids, I suspect.

RICHARD: What does that feeling lead to, Ayou? Does it make it impossible for you to learn in my classroom, you think?

BOY: I can learn in your class 'cause I like you. I like you more than I like Bridget but, it just flashes through my mind some time.

MOTHER: And coming from a person's point of view plus a student in school also myself, I've told my son over and over he's going to find that it doesn't matter what color skin a person is. When he walks in a class, he might have a, a black professor that can't stand him, and he will feel it. So right now he has to learn to relate to people just because they're people. I'm talking from a old point of view. Sometime your worst professors are the same color you. Because somewhere in their heads there's a problem going on too. And it can't be—you have to be responsible for your actions. I mean, all of us have a little prejudice in us, and I tell my son that, but it's how we use it. That's the most important thing, I keep telling him. I'm not saying he shouldn't have feelings, but it's how he uses his feelings. That's what's important. All of us have some bias towards something. I'm sitting in the chair, I have them also and I'm not going to lie. But, it's the way I use it. [*Cut to MS of physics teacher talking to students.*]

TEACHER: Eight seconds, so how, what time is it will be the highest point?

BOY: Eight.

TEACHER: Well, hold on, if you, if I'm here and we're going to throw a catch, we're going to play catch, just imagine, we'll shrink your thing—and it takes eight seconds for me—

BOY: Four, four, four.

TEACHER: Good! Where is four? The highest point, right here, good.

BOY (*overlapping*): —the highest point.

TEACHER: So wait, hold on, now we're talking, at one second where would the ball be? If you're going to throw it to me, where would it be, just think of it in the air roughly.

BOY: Around here [*points at an imaginary spot in the air*].

TEACHER: Two seconds?

BOY: Right there.

TEACHER: Three seconds [*changing position of the point*]? Four [*again changing the position of where she is pointing*]? What is this, what's particular about this four?

BOY: It's the highest point.

TEACHER: Good! Now five, it'll start coming down lower and lower. You

43. Making a point in the physics lesson.

need to graph that. But table it. What I'm saying is now, D-Y, do we know the D-Y formula? Do we know how to find D-Y?

BOY: Yes.

TEACHER: How?

BOY: Yes. How many seconds times T squared plus—

TEACHER: —plus or—you have to be careful with the positive and nega-tives. [*Cut to CU of girl studying math problem with two other students.*]

GIRL WITH PONYTAIL: Blue, that's the other guy. He swings and misses and the ball hits the ground right before the boundary line.

GIRL WITH DREADLOCKS: Doesn't have to be in the blue. Doesn't have to be in the blue. He just hits it over the thingy at whatever distance and you already have the angle.

GIRL WITH PONYTAIL: He hits it over the net at a distance of fifteen meters and the ball lands right before the boundary line.

GIRL WITH DREADLOCKS: Yeah.

GIRL WITH PONYTAIL: Okay. And then I can just, like, explain how I got the— oh wait, no, so the ball lands in front of the boundary line in five seconds.

BOY: On the other side.

GIRL WITH PONYTAIL: Where's it gonna go? In front of him? Wait, okay, so, red hits the ball from inside the boundary line with a nice serve. The ball flies over the net—you heard that, right?—it flies over the net—

GIRL WITH DREADLOCKS: You have to say what kind of serve, you say it was a backhand serve or something.

GIRL WITH PONYTAIL: That's what I had. Okay, red hits the ball from inside the boundaries with a nice backhand—

FEMALE VOICE (*offscreen*): What was your problem. You have to find, what?

GIRL WITH PONYTAIL: —no, I don't like that.

GIRL WITH DREADLOCKS: You don't want a nice backhand, just a backhand serve.

GIRL WITH PONYTAIL: So with a backhand serve, and the ball flies over the net at a distance of fifteen meters. The ball hits, hits the ground right before the boundary line five, after five seconds.

GIRL WITH DREADLOCKS: On the other side.

GIRL WITH PONYTAIL: Over the net, with, over the net. [*Cut to two-shot of teacher and boy.*]

TEACHER: Yeah, why don't you say it to me as if I, you know, we're doing it in the committee.

BOY: Alright. I just have to look at this country here, I guess. Okay, this map shows from 1938 to 1939 all the countries that Germany had taken over, the ones that are shaded in. See?

TEACHER: Okay. And that's—

BOY: Okay, yes, and notice these are the closest ones.

TEACHER: Right.

BOY: So he tried to start off, he tried to start off—

TEACHER: Those surrounding countries.

BOY: —surrounding countries. Expanding.

TEACHER: Did he, is this the point at which you're starting then, in '38, in other words, this is after it's already happened, 'cause you have some over here where you're showing Germany attacking, so maybe, oh, this is '42, '45. Okay, I understand, I understand now. I understand now, okay.

BOY: Okay, this shows how many countries he had to take over in a period of time. This is when he was just beginning to take over countries, so he started off, I guess, these were like the weak ones, because he, they just, he

44. A student explains his work on European history.

just probably overpowered them quick 'cause you see Poland's a big country, Czechoslovakia and Austria. Now—

TEACHER: So wait a minute, is there anything else you want to say about them in terms of explanation? I mean, do you, are you going to talk about the order in which, or do you know the order in which Germany attacked those countries?

BOY: Well, no, they don't really say that. They just say—

TEACHER: 'Cause it might be—

BOY: I went to a lot of books—

TEACHER: —it might be a good idea to find out the progression, how he changed.

BOY: Like which one he took over first. [*Cut to CU of student, Gilbert, talking with his teacher.*]

TEACHER: Did you speak with Joe about the situation that you're in in this class?

STUDENT (GILBERT): What situation?

TEACHER: You know, that things do not look good. It looks like you're not going to get a passing grade unless you—

GILBERT: What?!

TEACHER: That's what he told me!

GILBERT: Joe is . . . [*motions at his forehead to suggest craziness*].

TEACHER: You need to speak with him before the end of class today.

GILBERT: Class is ridiculous.

TEACHER: You want to be an engineer. Whether or not you think it's ridiculous, you have to be successful in it. I want you to talk with him before the end of class today, find out exactly what it is you have to do to get a passing grade. Because supposing we get this thing, this mess with Morris, Phil straightened out, right? They're going to ask us for a transcript, right? And on the transcript they're going to look to see that you passed every single class that you were registered for this year, right? And if you didn't, your acceptance—

GILBERT: I did!

TEACHER: Well, you haven't yet!

GILBERT: I know I'm passing Electronics, I'm passing Great Books, I'm taking this class. My internship is great.

TEACHER: How about—what's your status in this—I know your internship is great, what's your status in this class, that's what I'm talking about.

GILBERT: Personally, you want to know what my opinion?

TEACHER: I want to know an accurate assessment of what—

GILBERT (*overlapping*): Oh, that's not what we learn here in this class, no accuracy, estimate, just—

TEACHER: Gilbert, stop bullshitting me—

GILBERT: That's true!

TEACHER: Just tell me what your grade is going to be in this class in June. What is it going to be, *S*?

GILBERT: *S* plus.

TEACHER: *S* plus?

GILBERT: Yeah.

TEACHER: Okay, now when I talk to Joe today at lunchtime, what's he going to tell me that your grade is going to be in this class?

GILBERT: I don't know. I don't read minds, so I don't know.

TEACHER: He's going to be wrong about the grade he's going to give you in this class?

GILBERT: Yes.

TEACHER: Gilbert!

GILBERT: He's going to be wrong, 'cause he probably might give me low grade but I'm going to prove to him that I'm not.

TEACHER: When?

GILBERT: I'm doing it now, I'm working.

TEACHER: Okay, how?

GILBERT: My work.

TEACHER: I'm going to talk to him at the end of today and I want to hear that he had a conversation with you—

GILBERT: What are we going to talk about?

TEACHER: About what you have to do to get a passing grade in this class.

GILBERT: . . . Okay.

TEACHER: Okay. I'll see you in advisory. [*Teacher leaves. Three shots of students working at computers. Cut to shot of hallway, relatively uncrowded, student drinking from fountain. Cut to CU of student Lev.*]

PAUL: With this joke, who did you think was going to laugh, who did you think the joke, who was the joke for?

BOY (LEV): It was for Nathan!

PAUL: It was for Nathan. So you thought Nathan would enjoy you saying or think it was funny that you were saying that somebody was going to beat you up after school?

LEV: Yeah. He doesn't, he doesn't, and I just say I just—

PAUL (*overlapping*): I don't get it, I just really don't understand how you could think a teacher would think it's funny that you shout across the room that you're going to get beat up after school. That doesn't make sense to me.

LEV: I was just playing around and he—

PAUL: But you said it was a joke.

LEV: Uh-huh, I was just playing around.

PAUL: And you thought that he would—

LEV: It wasn't like, it wasn't like a ha-ha joke, it was just like, and I'd just be like, I'm just kidding, Nathan.

45. The coprincipal tries to understand a student's practical joke.

PAUL: Now when you say playing around, what does that mean to you, Lev? I'm not sure what you mean by playing around?

LEV: I'm just kidding, I'm just joking around, it wasn't a ha-ha funny, it was like—I was just kidding—

PAUL: Jokes and kidding and playing around all, to me, sound like somebody should be having fun. And is that what you, is that what you meant to happen, that Nathan would have fun with this? Don't, when you say kidding around, playing, jokes, all of those things, in my mind, make me think of somebody having a good time or having fun or laughing. And you thought by telling Nathan that Tom was threatening you and he was going to get you after school, that that would be fun for Nathan?

LEV: I was just, I was just kidding, I wasn't, it wasn't for real.

PAUL: So, why were you saying it if it wasn't for real?

LEV: 'Cause it was, it was, it was, I was just playing around!

PAUL: Well, I'm, I don't understand it. I mean, I really don't. And I think it's very inappropriate, Lev. It certainly changes the way things are in his class. His class is supposed to be, and as far as I'm concerned, is a serious place for learning. That's where you're getting your math and science instruction. And I think if you're tearing that apart by having these kind of jokes and joking about physical violence, do you know, do you know—Tom, did you ever read the rules of the school about violence and hitting and hitting back and that kind of stuff?

BOY (TOM): Yes.

PAUL: How about you, Lev, do you know them all? You've read them?

LEV: Hmm.

PAUL: And what about jokes, what about fooling around?

LEV: It says you're not allowed to do it.

PAUL: Why, do you think?

LEV: 'Cause maybe someone might take it seriously and they—

PAUL: That's part of it. Did you take it seriously a little bit, Tom? I mean, you've been involved in a lot of these things before, and you've been involved in fights and threatening people after school, right? Did you think in any way that he wanted to fight? Did a little piece of you think he wanted to fight? [*Tom shakes his head no.*] Do you think anybody else in the class could have thought you wanted to fight?

TOM: No.

LEV: See, I don't like fighting people.

PAUL: Then why did you joke about it, Lev?

TOM: He likes to annoy people.

PAUL: He what?

TOM: He likes to annoy people, okay?

PAUL: He likes to annoy people?

TOM: Yes.

PAUL: Susan, you want to join us? I would love for you to join us. I hear you kind of—he likes to annoy people?

TOM: Yes.

PAUL: Did he get you?

TOM: You can even ask Nathan.

PAUL: What?

TOM: You could even ask Nathan.

PAUL: I could ask Nathan about that—well, I can. Does he like to annoy you?

TOM: What?

PAUL: You?

TOM: Yes. Sometimes, though.

PAUL: Sometimes? Did he annoy you today?

TOM: Yeah.

PAUL: You know, Lev, I have that feeling that that's true. What do you think? You do like to annoy people . . . Jokes about violence lead to not so serious things, not so funny things about violence, and pretty soon you got a fight. Somebody thinks you're waiting for 'em outside after school, they're going to get some friends to go with them to make it safe, and that's the way we have bad fights here. [*Cut to teacher looking over a student's notebook with him.*]

TEACHER: Okay, wing, the vestigial wings, right?

BOY: Right, and it's female.

TEACHER: Male, okay, and then you're going to do—alright, the other way that it's called a reciprocal cross.

BOY: Right.

TEACHER: Okay, do you have some sort of assumption about how many offspring, you know, like how many eggs she's likely to lay and what the hatch rate is supposed to be?

BOY: Do I have it?

TEACHER: Yeah.

BOY: Not yet.

TEACHER: Why don't you just throw out a number.

BOY: How many eggs she'd lay?

TEACHER: You know, based on what you've seen in the vials that you've had, like how many pupae cases?

BOY: Maybe one female, like fifty maybe?

TEACHER: Okay, say fifty, I think it's high, but say fifty. Alright, she has fifty eggs, right? Now suppose that this characteristic is dominant—and you can actually look it up and see if it is or not, but let's just do the theoretical—suppose it's dominant.

BOY: Right.

TEACHER: How many of those fifty offspring are going to have vestigial wings?

BOY: In the F-1?

TEACHER: Yeah.

BOY: All of them.

TEACHER: Right, fifty of the total, so if you were going to do like data, you know, project the data, if dominant, fifty offspring, and assuming fifty offspring, all fifty would have vestigial wings.

BOY (*overlapping*): —vestigial wings.

TEACHER: Suppose it's recessive.

BOY: Then, then none of the them would have the vestigial wing characteristic.

TEACHER: So you have—

BOY: Have two—

TEACHER: A hundred percent of them, okay.

BOY: A hundred percent.

TEACHER: Okay, right, and then you do an F-2 and you have to do if dominant, if recessive, and remember that you're mating, you know, the brothers and sisters essentially.

BOY: Oh, I understand.

TEACHER: Okay. And you might want to do a reciprocal cross there too. You have to figure it out on paper, see if that makes sense.

BOY: Alright.

TEACHER: Okay? Now do you know how the sex-linked heredity pattern works?

BOY: Not too well, but not really.

TEACHER: Let's just review it. [*Camera pans to another boy who has just arrived.*]

BOY WITH BLUE CAP: I was at Mt. Sinai trying to print my paper. And that's why I'm late. But it didn't work. Because they don't have the program I have.

TEACHER: You were at Mt. Sinai before nine o'clock in the morning?

BOY WITH BLUE CAP: What? Yeah.

TEACHER: I'm impressed.

BOY: Hey, I was up at six o'clock this morning.

TEACHER: Well, that's very good! That's very good. There's hope for us yet. Be nice if you were here by nine o'clock.

BOY WITH BLUE CAP: The whole—I don't have, I could have came, I could come here first, but then I would have had to go there anyway, so I figured—

TEACHER: It's alright. A reasonable judgment. You know, in the future, if you ever have to do that one thing that really makes you be, would make you be beyond criticism, is to make a phone call and leave a message.

BOY WITH BLUE CAP (*overlapping*): Alright.

TEACHER: Very good thing, communication. [*Turning back to first student*] Okay, suppose that you have a female, right, and you're going to look at the chromosomes, and this situation, two Xs.

BOY: Alright.

TEACHER: Okay? And for male, what would the chromosome—?

BOY: X and Y.

TEACHER: Right. Now if you have a sex-linked characteristic, what that means is—you tell me what it means: where is the gene?

BOY: The gene is found in the X?

TEACHER: Yeah, it's going to be on the X chromosome, so let's just make a little circle there to mark it, alright? That's sex-linked. Now, most of these genes are recessive.

BOY: Sex-linked?

TEACHER: Yeah, most, most mutations are recessive.

BOY: Right.

TEACHER: You know, there are some exceptions to that, but . . .

BOY: The wing. I think the wingless fruit fly is domination.

TEACHER: You think it is? I thought it was recessive.

BOY: Actually, it's in the book.

TEACHER: That's exciting if it's dominant. Is it sex-linked, do you know?

BOY: No, I'm not sure.

TEACHER: Okay, we'll find out, you'll find out in July. But okay, what percent are going to be vestigial-winged?

BOY: What percent are going to be vestigial? Seventy-five percent?

TEACHER: Right, okay, and what's the ratio of the sexes?—

BOY (*overlapping*): But this is confusing me because both the X chromosomes are, have—

TEACHER: The gene, right?

BOY: Right.

TEACHER: So what you're figuring out here is really what kind of crosses do you have to make to tell you whether or not the characteristic is sex-linked . . . You have to play around with this with different parts of possible combinations, then come to some conclusion about which crosses you would have to do to give you the information, if it were dominant and sex-linked, if it were recessive and sex-linked, okay? So—and by the time you finish fiddling around with these different possibilities, you will truly understand, you know, this whole concept of Mendelian genetics and how you can tell, just by counting numbers of fruit flies with different characteristics, something about the genotype. [*Cut to shot of boy arranging small genetic models.*]

BOY: Uh-huh.

TEACHER: So sit with it a little bit, wrestle with it a little bit, and we'll speak in another half hour. Okay? [*Two shots of students working at desks and computers. Cut to the same teacher now going over a girl's work with her.*]

TEACHER: Okay. And now you want—let's see what else you've dealt with in this. You see, essentially, you've got a lot of good information here. It just needs to be structured so that it makes more . . . did you find any information about how Down syndrome, you know, what it is about Down syndrome that causes mental retardation? An explanation of that? . . . [*Examining student's work and writing on it*] Okay, you talked about amniocentesis, right? So, maybe the last section is how amniocentesis can be used to detect Down syndrome . . . The conclusion is most satisfying if it relates somehow to ss—, right, okay? So it's a terrific beginning, now you have to type and you have to just reorganize it a little. [*Student leaves, and another sits down with the teacher.*]

BOY IN RED CAP: I wouldn't have known what time it was anyway because the clock in my room went, the batteries went dead, so [*inaudible*] or something.

TEACHER: You're behind. I mean, you've had a lot of work today, it's a double period . . .

BOY IN RED CAP: I know!

TEACHER: So get to work. And go and look at what Enrique has done in terms of—

BOY IN RED CAP: That's what I was going, that's what I was, that's what I was thinking about when I, when I was walking to school, I should read Enrique's paper to see what he got.

TEACHER: Did he have live vestigial, live vestigial-wing flies? Do they have—

BOY IN RED CAP: I have to go check the data.

TEACHER: Yeah, you have to get some more of those. Get another culture started, alright? That's really critical.

BOY IN RED CAP: Another culture?

TEACHER: Uh-huh. You know what I mean by culture? Another group of flies breeding. [*Student leaves. Cut to shot of two students listening to Paul.*]

PAUL: One of the ways that we've thought about the school is that if kids have developed five habits of mind—and we're going to suggest a sixth very soon—if they've developed five habits of mind, five ways of thinking about things, they will, they should be able to graduate from here because, if they can do these things, think of perspective, from whose perspective is something being presented? Like when you read history it's always from someone's perspective. What's your evidence, how do you show your evidence for something that you're presenting? If you're going to present your point of view about something, that's fine, but show me your evidence. Where did you get those ideas from? How is the thing that's being presented connected to other things? What if things were different? It's a supposition. And who cares? I mean, why does it matter, why are we looking at this anyway? If people can think in those three ways, in those five ways, we think that they'll be in pretty good shape to be able to graduate. The five—I'll tell you an interesting thing about the five habits of mind. We have in the last year had visitors. One was a lawyer, and he said, those are interesting habits of mind, that's exactly what I learned in law school, and if you learn a way of thinking like that, then you'll be a good lawyer. Another was a journalist who was a, wrote a column in a newspaper in Maryland, I believe, and he said, that's what I learned when I was at journalism, a journalism major. And the third was a physics teacher, and he said, that's the scientific method. If you really think about it, that's the scientific method. Habits of mind are what thoughtful people do all the time. And there are other ways of looking at them, and you all could come up with five different habits of mind. But they are, you know, a respect for evidence and a respect for perspective and a way of seeing things in their complexity, not simplistically. [*Cut to shot of students wheeling computers out of a room into hallway, followed by a cut to MS of Debbie at a table talking with a family.*]

46. The coprincipal welcomes a returning student who has had a baby.

CODIRECTOR (DEBBIE): You know, the reason we had, wanted a meeting is to try to increase the, you know, the possibility that this is going to work well this spring, and that we're all going to have a happy time together. Alright? The other purpose is to say congratulations, it's nice to see you back, welcome back. So has it been a nice five weeks for the new baby?

PAUL: How old is the baby?

GIRL: It has.

DEBBIE: Six weeks?

PAUL: Six weeks?

DEBBIE: What about for you?

STUDENT'S MOTHER: Okay. Back to normal.

DEBBIE: Does the baby sleep, how often, long does she sleep at night?

GIRL: He.

DEBBIE: He! I just had a granddaughter, too.

GIRL: I was just so happy.

DEBBIE: How often does he sleep at night?

GIRL: He sleeps every three hours but sometimes . . .

FEMALE TEACHER: You have to get up a lot in the night?

DEBBIE: Are you getting up or [*to mother*] are *you* getting up?

MOTHER: She was getting up—

GIRL: But now she's—

MOTHER: But now I'm going to start getting up.

DEBBIE: He's being bottlefed?

GIRL: [*Nods yes.*] Well, I guess yesterday he was being, he was crying like, he probably knew I was coming to school. [*Some overlapping dialogue.*]

PAUL: He probably overheard some conversations or something?

DEBBIE: What about you, what role do you play in it?

BROTHER (JOHN): Just spoil him, that's all.

GIRL: He babysits too.

PAUL: Start to teach him about cars yet?

JOHN: Hmm?

PAUL: Start to teach him about cars yet, John? [*More overlapping dialogue.*]

JOHN: I just play with him.

DEBBIE: Are you glad it was a boy?

JOHN: Umm [*nods yes*].

DEBBIE: How about you?

GIRL: I wanted a girl.

DEBBIE: Which did you have first, a boy or a girl? [*Mother points at John.*]

DEBBIE: Was he cute?

MOTHER (*nodding yes*): I wanted a boy.

DEBBIE: You wanted one?

MOTHER: That's [*inaudible, pointing at John*].

DEBBIE (*to other teachers*): What did you want first?

MALE TEACHER (DAVID): Don't ask me.

FEMALE TEACHER: I don't, I don't—let's see.

PAUL: We'll skip you here.

FEMALE TEACHER: I don't remember, I guess maybe a boy, I don't remember. I guess maybe a boy, I don't know.

DEBBIE: I wanted a girl, and when I got in the hospital and had a baby girl they said oh well, don't feel badly, it's only a girl, and I said, what do you mean, I'm delighted.

MOTHER: With John I wanted to have a girl, I had a boy. But with the grand-baby I wanted a boy.

DEBBIE: You turned out alright, okay, John? Okay, so now the dilemma is there's a lot of issues. It's very hard to go back to school when you have a little baby, right? I mean, there are a lot of complications in your life, you know, how much sleep you're going to get, how you're going to do study-ing on the side, your own friends, and, and all your—

MOTHER: On the part of the baby, he's going to stay with me in the room in the bassinet so she could sleep.

DEBBIE: So she could sleep—

MOTHER: Right. This way when she comes out of school she'll go home, do her homework, then she'll be with the baby.

DEBBIE: But she is kind of, lived two lives, right, to be—how old are you?

GIRL: Fifteen.

DEBBIE: To be a fifteen-year-old and to be a mother, so that's complicated.

PAUL: And a student.

DEBBIE: And a student. So she's going to be a fifteen-year-old, with friend-ships, and she's a daughter, and she's a sister, and she's a mother—there's a lot of—and you want to graduate, you're determined to do that?

GIRL: Yes.

DEBBIE: At the moment you're hoping to do it here?

GIRL: Yes.

DEBBIE: Are you—the reason I say that at all is that I would love it to work out that way, I really would.

GIRL: Yeah, I want it too.

DEBBIE: Some schools where it's also possible to bring your child with you to school have some advantages, so just keep that in mind, I mean, there's not a defeat if you decide at some point that you want to be somewhere where the baby can come to school with you.

MOTHER: 'Cause I'll take care of him. I don't work, so—

DEBBIE: Alright. It's important to know that that option exists. There are some nice schools that we know of where that's possible, and if at any point you feel like it or she just feels like she appreciates your doing it but she would like to have it with her, that's possible, you need to know that's possible. Alright, so there's that one issue. Then the second issue is the complicated social dilemma in school between you and . . . [*turns to Paul*].

FEMALE TEACHER: Frankie.

DEBBIE: Frankie! . . . So, and then that's for you too. How is it for you? If you, would it be helpful if, I mean, is it impossible—I—do you ever have a conversation with him about, do you two just avoid the subject, what do you do?

JOHN: Really, we never talk about it.

DAVID: You guys are still hanging out, though, right?

JOHN: Once in a while—

DAVID: Yeah, yeah.

JOHN: —'cause we work together, so. For the St. John's Ambulance.

DEBBIE: And you were once very close friends. What is it, what do you think you are now?

JOHN: Well, you can't only blame it on him.

DEBBIE: You could, but you don't.

JOHN: I can't really blame it on him.

DEBBIE: But you still feel angry at him?

GIRL: Not as before.

MOTHER: It's all over.

GIRL: Things are, you know, slowing down, everything is, you know, he's being good, he's doing his part, you know.

MOTHER: He's coming over to see the baby.

DEBBIE: This is new?

GIRL: Yeah, this is new, this is recent.

MOTHER: Now he's . . . they working it a little better, since he's been coming over they—

DEBBIE: And you have a way of thinking about it which, you can see it as something that you and Frankie, you both made a mistake about, I mean both did, both chose? [*Girl nods yes. To mother*] Do you feel that way about it?

47. A student mother talks about her situation as her mother listens.

MOTHER: Not really. Okay, it was a mistake in both of their part, but it's here, what can we do about it, you know, we've got to keep—

DEBBIE: Sometimes you're just mad at one and you feel like it's all his fault.

MOTHER: No, no, I cannot blame him. I blame, mostly I blame her, 'cause she should have taken care of herself. And I feel she should have, the type of mother I am she should have come up to me and talked to me and if worse would have come I would have taken her for birth control and the baby wouldn't be here. See?

DEBBIE: In the future that's what we're going to do?

MOTHER: You know, it was something you don't want to think about, but when you have girls you have to.

DEBBIE: Okay, so, that, and you still have to.

MOTHER: Yeah, I have a little one, a twelve-year-old.

DEBBIE: No, but even for her, you know, it's one thing taking care of one child.

MOTHER: Oh, yeah.

DEBBIE: It's not necessary to have five children while you're trying to get out of school.

MOTHER: Well, he's been coming over to see the baby and he's been—they've been talking and not much of arguing now.

DEBBIE: So that, if you run into each other in school, what will it be like?

GIRL: We did it today.

FEMALE TEACHER: What happened?

GIRL: I walked into the bathroom and he kept walking. And he just said "Hi," and went, and that's it.

DEBBIE: Well, what about the other friends, other kids around the school, you know there are people who are going to try and make trouble now, do you think, some of your girlfriends— [*Girl begins to cough.*] Are you all right?

JOHN: No.

DEBBIE: What do you think, David?

DAVID: I just turn it around.

DEBBIE: What do you think, are there kids who are going to try to make trouble?

DAVID: From what I have seen today, no, I, everybody's really glad to see you, you know, in class and in advisory. Yeah, I can't tell, there's no way of telling.

GIRL: The person that I had problems with before and all the trouble was with his girlfriend, that's it, but so far today I had a nice—

DEBBIE: She's not in school but she's in the neighborhood.

GIRL: [*Inaudible*] Tuesdays.

DEBBIE: Now if you see trouble coming, one of you sees trouble coming, what would you do about it? Like you see yourself getting very angry?

JOHN: Best you can do is try avoid it, but if they keep on looking for trouble and there's nobody around, you got to solve it your own way. We don't, we don't know how that's going to be until it happens.

DEBBIE: Let's think in this school. Inside this school.

JOHN: Inside the school?

DEBBIE: Or right out front of the school.

GIRL: We're always supposed to come inside and inform somebody, that we don't find any of you, the teacher—

JOHN (*overlapping*): After school it's mostly like PJ or Santiago or Tom or Mark Letsky's around, just tell them.

DEBBIE: If you do it even though it seems at the moment like you're so mad, that's what I'm worrying about, like sometimes you can get so mad that you decide—

JOHN: Just control your temper, that's all.

MOTHER: No, we had a talk about that. We sat and we talked, and I had explained it to her and I explained it to him, and that's what we said, you know, to get one of the teachers or you get Debbie or you get Suzanne and let— they have to do something about it, and the fact that she's not attending school and you are.

FEMALE TEACHER: Would there ever be a time when there wasn't someone around then? Doesn't sound like there ever would be.

JOHN: No, 'cause, there was a couple of times there's nobody around, but really there's never problems during the time. We can't tell now.

PAUL: In front of school?

JOHN: Yeah, in front of school.

PAUL: Three-thirty, four o'clock. [*Several voices speak simultaneously.*]

MOTHER: —when I spoke to her, she hasn't—

DEBBIE: You go home, is that an issue? Does she go home before you go home?

JOHN: Well, I got to go to work—she did, she does go home before I do, yeah.

MOTHER: Before there was a problem. I was mostly with her, so I spoke to Frankie's mother, so Frankie's mother got her and spoke to her and told her, you know, this got to stop, you better leave her alone. So she's been going through where we live but she hasn't bothered, she doesn't stop, she keeps walking, you know, so—

DEBBIE: The first time, I mean, if you hear there's any trouble, would you promise to call me right away?

MOTHER: Oh yeah. Or Paul or any one of yous.

FEMALE TEACHER: Paul or Suzanne. I think that's what's really critical, that there are quite a number of us around that you can get in touch with. And even if you have a worry about, that's something happening—

MOTHER (*overlapping*): I told her if Frankie starts bothering her, come up to Suzanne, come up to somebody, you know.

GIRL: What I don't like about is right from the school she has to take it all the way to where I live and around here.

FEMALE TEACHER: This isn't anything we have control—

DEBBIE: I know, unfortunately we don't have much control.

GIRL: I know, but why start it in the school then? That's what I don't understand.

DEBBIE: I just want to make sure that you get, have no reason not to come every day, that you feel comfortable when you're here, and nothing happens that makes you feel that you're not safe. [*Cut to shot of students at lockers in school hallway, followed by shot of two students and teacher talking in the hallway.*]

FEMALE TEACHER: I know, I walked by, I couldn't believe it.

GIRL: He drew the brain on the computer.

TEACHER: You did that on the computer?

GIRL: He drew a neurotransmitter, a nerve impulse [*cut to shot of girl walking past camera in a school hallway, right to left*], the synapse between two neurotransmitters. [*Cut to shot of a boy walking past the camera in hallway in the opposite direction. Cut to teacher talking to student, Matt, with his head down on his desk.*]

TEACHER: Usually when you have a false start, don't throw it away, keep it and say, right on the top, abandoned, but—

BOY (*sitting next to Matt*): Can I go to the bathroom? Look what I wrote [*turning pages of his notebook*]. This, this, this, this.

TEACHER: Good, that's good, you can go to the bathroom and come back, take a little break and write again. Matt?

MATT (*head remains down on desk, face hidden throughout*): Yeah?

TEACHER: There may be a couple of sentences, even though you don't like the whole thing, that you wrote in your abandoned piece that you can use when you start it again. So that's—where'd you throw it? Unscramble it up and smooth it out and just leave it as an abandoned part of your writing, 'cause people use that.

MATT: I don't think that's possible.

TEACHER: No, okay, so next time don't do that. It's your work, don't throw it away. So what you need to think of is another way to start.

MATT: That's what I'm doing now.

TEACHER: Alright. Is that why your head's down?

MATT: Yeah.

TEACHER: Alright, I'll be back in a minute and see how you're doing. [*Moving to another student*] How'd yours start?

BOY WITH WHITE CAP: I'm just writing a little poem now. I think I'm going to finish this one anyway.

TEACHER: I like that one. If we could think of what happened.

BOY WITH WHITE CAP: I am going to finish it.

TEACHER: I love it.

BOY WITH WHITE CAP: Figured out something.

TEACHER: Did you?

BOY WITH WHITE CAP: Mmm.

TEACHER: What's going to happen?

BOY WITH WHITE CAP: He was asleep in his car having a dream about—

TEACHER: Alright. William, let me see yours . . . [*Montage of five shots of various students in the class.*] Oh dear, okay. [*Cut to shot of teacher at a desk with another student.*] Okay, a thesis statement is like the main point or the main idea that you want to direct the reader to think about. So, let me see what your thesis is that—

GIRL: I ain't started yet.

TEACHER: Okay, looking at the question, how and why do law and morality affect changes in each other? What, what are the main points that you know you want to talk about?

GIRL: About morality.

TEACHER: Hmm-mmm, and what else? Good.

GIRL: And how it changes things, makes laws.

TEACHER: So you mentioned the word *morality*, you mentioned the word *laws*, and you mentioned that they change each other. Okay? So you want to make an opening sentence that discusses the point of what you're gonna talk about. That's called the thesis. When you write your thesis sentence, why don't you call me over and show me and I'll see how it is.

GIRL: Okay.

TEACHER: Okay? [*Cut to shot of a girl walking down school hallway away from the camera, followed by a shot of a boy walking past the camera left to right. Cut to shot of two teachers talking in hallway to a student.*]

TEACHER (LORRAINE): Tell us the change. I want to hear the good news. What's the change? What happened?

GIRL (AMIRE): It all worked out.

LORRAINE: When?

AMIRE: I got my work done last week!

LORRAINE: Last week? Did you get her to work, then, last week?

TEACHER (DAVID): Is it, you just say, you get your work done, but there's the amount of the work that you get done, there's a percentage of the time that you spent avoiding work, doing something else.

AMIRE: But I got my work done—

DAVID: That's greater than the percentage of the time that you get work done.

LORRAINE: Okay, well, let's deal with the good news. Did Amire get some work done last week?

DAVID: I think she's getting more work done, yes.

LORRAINE: Okay, so—

DAVID: I suppose, yeah, alright, I'm not going to qualify it any more. You understand the fact that I want you to get more work done.

AMIRE: Yes, I understand that. [*Cut to LS of class with desks pushed together for seminar discussion, followed by CU of teacher.*]

TEACHER (SHIRLEY): We talk about fiction, right? Plays and tragedy are part of fiction. Why do we read this? Why do we bother with it?

GIRL IN WHITE SWEATER: Sometimes fiction does have bearing on real life. It may not be all real, but it, some of it can be associated to real life.

SHIRLEY: Alright. What seems to be the common recurring themes over time?

GIRL IN MULTICOLORED JACKET: That someone is setting someone up, you know—

GIRL IN WHITE SWEATER: Deception.

GIRL IN MULTICOLORED JACKET: Yeah, right, deception, basically that's what it is.

VOICE (*offscreen*): Murder.

SHIRLEY: Deception and murder.

GIRL IN MULTICOLORED JACKET: And also revenge, in a sense.

SHIRLEY: All those nice human characteristics. Yeah. Well, what about, anything else, I mean, you've told me—

GIRL (*offscreen*): [*Inaudible.*]

SHIRLEY: Bad things, what about the other things, is there any good in it?

GIRL: It's love, I mean.

SHIRLEY: Why do you say it with that face? What do you think, Maurice, is love? . . . What do you think about—is love exemplified in this play?

BOY (MAURICE): [*Inaudible*] with Edgar and Gloucester.

SHIRLEY: That's true, with Edgar and Gloucester, it's shown there. Where else?

GIRL IN WHITE SWEATER: With, uh, at the end with Cordelia.

GIRL IN BLUE SWEATER: Cordelia and Lear.

SHIRLEY: Cordelia and Lear. A different kind of love. It's very interesting how many kinds of it. Where else did we see a very nice instance of love between man and woman, I mean [*inaudible*].

GIRL IN MULTICOLORED JACKET: France and Cordelia.

SHIRLEY: France and Cordelia, that was a nice kind of love. The one between Edgar and Gloucester, despite everything. Another one between Lear and Cordelia, that's three different kinds. Anything else?

GIRL IN BLUE SWEATER: What about Goneril's love for Edmund?

GIRL IN DENIM JACKET: That was a selfish love.

GIRL IN BLUE SWEATER: That, yeah.

SHIRLEY: How would you describe, I mean, Goneril loved Edmund, it's not only a selfish love, there's something troubling about that love because Goneril was already—

GIRL (*offscreen*): Married.

GIRL (*offscreen, simultaneously*): She was already married.

SHIRLEY: Taken, so to speak, you know, and in a sense it was an illicit kind of love. What else, how, well then, how do you describe Regan's love for Edmund?

GIRL (*offscreen*): That was like—

GIRL IN WHITE SWEATER: Probably like jealous. She didn't want her sister to have him.

48. Students consider the nature of love in *King Lear.*

GIRL IN BLUE SWEATER (*overlapping*): She just wanted him 'cause her sister wanted him.

SHIRLEY: So you have the examples of three very nice kinds of love. And it's very interesting, I hadn't thought of it before today, that Shakespeare really does show the whole range. You have love between a father and a child, love between a man and a woman, and love between, what was the other one?

GIRL (*offscreen*): Kent and Lear.

SHIRLEY: Kent and Lear as friends! People who depend on each other. So that's three to two, right, we can do without the two, Regan and Edmund and Goneril and Edmund.

GIRL IN DENIM JACKET: Then you could say there was a lack of love between—not even—I don't even know if it was a lack of love, but just being that Edmund was the illegitimate son, he felt he had to do something in order to get attention. That's kind of like what we see today in society.

SHIRLEY: And you talk about, if we, we have to mention the not-so-good things, we talk about blindness. Who failed to act when they could have acted and maybe—

GIRL (*offscreen*): Gloucester.

SHIRLEY: Gloucester. And poor Gloucester paid for it, you know, well why?

BOY (EDDIE): I'm laughing at the way you said it.

SHIRLEY: Why? Why?

EDDIE: It was funny the way you said it.

SHIRLEY: You don't think he paid for it?

EDDIE: It's just funny the way you said it.

SHIRLEY: Alright, okay. Well, tell me, Eddie, what do you think about [*laughter*], what do you think about Shakespeare and this man? Why would he, and, you know, what did you think of the play? You had least to say because of your—

EDDIE: It's alright. It's alright.

SHIRLEY: It's what?

EDDIE: It was alright.

SHIRLEY: It was alright?

EDDIE: Yeah.

SHIRLEY: In what way?

EDDIE: It was interesting. It was this, this is just funny, I found it to be funny.

SHIRLEY: You found it funny? In what way? Give me a, when you say funny—

EDDIE: Well, just the way—

SHIRLEY (*overlapping*): It's funny ha-ha?

EDDIE: The way all the people, that's the way that all the characters acted, was—it's almost like real life.

TEACHER: Well then, is that funny?

EDDIE: It's funny 'cause it ain't happening to me!

SHIRLEY: But this great—

EDDIE: But, seriously, it's like almost like real life and it's like amazing that he could write stuff like that all the way back then.

SHIRLEY: Yeah, which is way back in the—how many—you, you did your research, sixteenth century.

GIRL (*offscreen*): Sixteenth century.

SHIRLEY: And he was writing about an earlier time. So it suggests to us that people perhaps don't change so readily? Maybe people are not, you know we—

EDDIE: People still act like that now.

SHIRLEY: Yeah!

GIRL (*offscreen*): Like they say, time repeats itself.

EDDIE: It's almost like, it's like, almost like a Mafia type thing, that's what it seemed like, everybody's killing each other, taking over power—

SHIRLEY: Well, I guess.

EDDIE: [*Inaudible*] greedy.

SHIRLEY: And I guess if you read *Macbeth*, it's even a better, you had, some of you read *Macbeth*—

EDDIE: Yeah, we did, I did.

SHIRLEY: —in Division 2, and now certainly the Mafia holds up very well there, yeah.

EDDIE: I like that one better, though.

SHIRLEY: You like *Macbeth* better?

EDDIE: Yes.

SHIRLEY: Why?

EDDIE: I guess cause we did it, part of it, as a play.

GIRL (*offscreen*): And we did *Romeo and Juliet*.

GIRL IN DENIM JACKET: For some reason, I keep getting *Romeo and Juliet* mixed up with this, like at the beginning of the book, when they had the fight at the beginning, Romeo and Juliet, I keep thinking that was the beginning of this book, I don't know.

SHIRLEY: But why is that so? I mean, is that a fair—why is that so?

GIRL IN DENIM JACKET: Because this one joins sort of at the beginning of the book.

SHIRLEY: Well, it's the same writer, right?

GIRL IN DENIM JACKET: Yeah, I know, that's why I'm—

SHIRLEY: So you would find similarities.

GIRL IN BLUE SWEATER: And they're both a tragedy, right?

SHIRLEY: Yes. Alright. Okay, so the end of the play then, we have, we hope, there's—it's sort of like, oh, remnants of things left and these people have to build again. It's like the whole cycle of life.

GIRL IN WHITE SWEATER: The only part that I found confusing is when they started with the letters, who is writing letters to who and about what, is the only part of the play that got confusing, until we got towards the end when all the letters, you start finding out who wrote all the letters.

SHIRLEY: But if you come back to what Eddie said earlier on about it being like real life, is real life confusing?

TWO GIRLS (*offscreen*): Yes.

SHIRLEY: Well, that's, you know, I think we have to keep that in mind, because really we don't have very simple lines—lives—where we sort of have one thing happening just so and another thing happening, so we can all get it really very nice and straight. We have complicated lives, and lines cross all the time, and this is what literature is about. [*Cut to two teachers talking with Franz and his father.*]

TEACHER (BRIDGET): We expect—we, meaning the teachers—expect, and I'm sure your father does, for you to have a sense of how you're doing in your classes, but it was also the timing. You asked me a week before the evaluations were due, how am I doing? It's not like in the middle of the term or something. So that made me nervous because I thought, you mean, all this time you weren't worried about it until now, or—

BOY (FRANZ): No, I was kind of worried but just let it out. More important also, the evaluations are coming up, so most of the times a lot of kids will ask their teachers, how am I doing, how am I doing?

TEACHER: Were you, were you asking Bridget, "Bridget, how do you think I'm doing?"

FRANZ: Right.

TEACHER: Or were asking really—

FRANZ: First I asked, how am I doing?

TEACHER: Right.

FRANZ: And then I kind of rephrased it after she explain, you should know how you're doing and then you say, how do you think I'm doing. And then, she said, how do you think you're doing?

TEACHER: But your first question really was, you wanted Bridget to tell you how you were doing.

FRANZ: How I'm doing.

TEACHER: And you did, did you have an idea of how you were doing?

FRANZ: Well, kind of.

TEACHER (*overlapping*): What was your idea of how you were doing?

FRANZ: Well, kind of bad, kind of good.

TEACHER: What was the—

FRANZ: In-between.

TEACHER: What was the kind of good?

FRANZ: The kind of good was getting my work in and being able to understand it, and the kind of bad was either not completing it, being incomplete, or turning it in late.

TEACHER: Okay. What—do you have any sort of thoughts about these—?

FATHER: It, I mean, as you might expect, every evening I, there's, how's it going, Franz, what did you do? What are you working on? And you try not to press it too much. It's "I finished it at school," it's "Can I go to the gym?" it's, you know, baseball practice, all the things you expect. Franz has been good about saying things that he's done well. He's absolutely silent about things he hasn't done. You know, I kind of want to turn this into a different tack because Franz and I have had a lot of conversations recently about honesty. First of all, first of all, his responsibility to be honest to me, 'cause I'm his father and his custodian. And even more importantly, to be honest with himself. And what's troubling me in all this is, well, two questions: number one, does Franz want to do well, fundamentally. I, I think he does. I think he does, I mean, we've had a couple of conversations about it. He's left me with the general impression he has been in that sort of satisfactory zone, maybe what we would normally call a B, B-minus zone, which I told him is unsatisfactory. He's much too smart. You much too talented for that. But you need to determine for yourself that you want to be better than that. So that's one piece. But the other piece is, really been, I mean, at, I'm not sure that Franz has decided that he wants to do well. I think Franz, I know Franz doesn't want to be, doesn't want to get in trouble, know Franz wants to get through school and be able to do all the things he wants to do. But Pat Reilly talks about fire in the belly. It's a nervous energy. It's when you sit down to a test and you're prepared for it, but you're jumpy, you're edgy, it's like when a performer, you know, he's read his lines, he's worked his lines, and he's nervous. But it's a very different feeling from being unprepared. It's, it's basically it's a will to win. It's a will to achieve. It's a desire to get that result. It's been, it's been self-motivated. Well, what do you think about that?

FRANZ: Well, I understand what you're saying. Also it does happen. I also think that I need to improve most of the, mostly in, or really I need to really speak to you guys, like Bridget, Dave, and you also, to see what I can do to have a very consistent plan that will work consistently.

FATHER: I think you, we need to go back to what do you want, 'cause certain things are going to happen no matter what.

TEACHER: Can you answer your dad's question? What is, what is your goal?

FRANZ: Well, for my job career or—

FATHER: No, for you.

TEACHER: For your, for you as a student.

FRANZ: Well, I need to be successful in life.

TEACHER: And what would that be?

FRANZ: Well, my real, my dream is to be a architect.

TEACHER: Okay, but as a student here, at this school.

FRANZ (*overlapping*): To pass the grade.

TEACHER: To pass.

FRANZ: To get through and also be able to not just pass by a hair, but be able to, teacher say, well, I'm very, very proud of you 'cause I know you gonna pass since day one or whatever because I can tell you smart! I know I'm smart, my father tells me, my teachers tell me, but I know that as did come from myself and that's really my goal, to say to somebody to come up to me and say I'm happy for you, I think, glad you didn't pass, just pass by a hair, pass by maybe—

TEACHER (*overlapping*): Right, sounds like your dad, your dad's expectations are somewhat higher than what you have for yourself, and what—that your dad's are that you could do very, very well, that B and passing—B is better than passing, and so better than passing is not what your dad wants for you. He wants something very—he wants you to really use your mind and do very good work here.

FRANZ: I also do but—

TEACHER: You want that too?

FRANZ: Yeah, and then also I want to do better than passing, like better better, and also I want to really do very good. I want to do, as the highest I can go. I have to do it myself. I can't have people say, got to do this right now. Got to try and encourage yourself. [*Cut to CU of Paul on the telephone.*]

PAUL (*on telephone*): —be happy to meet with you, have you fill out an application. When you come for your tour, for your visit, you want to bring report cards, standardized test scores, recommendations from teachers . . . Good, send it with the application, great. If you have report cards, that kind of stuff, bring it with you, and we'll do the best we can. [*Cut to shot of female teacher on telephone.*]

TEACHER (*on the telephone*): Nori didn't come home last night and her mother's very, very worried, she doesn't, you know, know where she is, so we're just trying to talk to anybody who might have some idea of where she might be, might be able to help. Do you have any ideas? Have you seen her? You haven't talked to her in awhile? Do you, are you still pretty good friends? I know you were very close friends when you were here. Do you, do you, can you think of any place that, you know, that she might be that . . . She didn't talk to you about, she didn't talk to you, I guess, about leaving home? . . . Do you, do you know any other friends that you think she might be at? [*Cut to shot of Paul talking with Dave.*]

TEACHER (DAVE): I mean, I think this, that meeting that we had was a clear example of a dysfunctional person trying to, trying to deny reality with their child. I'm not sure that a meeting is gonna, is gonna—

PAUL: Well, that's another perspective. That's an interesting perspective.

DAVE: Because, I don't know, it's almost as if—

PAUL: Well, then, maybe, I mean, what would we do with an alcoholic or a dysfunctional parent? We would, we certainly have dealt with that before, we've dealt with it with Susan Boss.

DAVE: Yeah, we ignore the parent and focus on the child.

PAUL: So it's, no, not always, we haven't ignored the parent. I think we've been rather successful with parents.

DAVE: Yeah, but what we do is, what we'd say is try to come to common agreement. We wouldn't deal with her issue of, of dysfunctionalism. We deal with the fact that we have some common issues that we, that the parent and school can connect on. We both want the same for the child.

PAUL: Well, the other thing is that it's not only rattling our cages and it's not only pushing our buttons. It's also . . . is it a real threat to the school?

DAVE: Potentially. I mean, let me put it like this: an accident can happen, and she can take it and move it into a political arena that could have potential ramifications, as we well know . . . And the idea of people out in the front, you know, chanting and picketing, it's nothing that we want to live with again. [*Cut to shot of five students sitting around a table talking.*]

BOY IN WINDBREAKER: That's weird. Had a gun pointed at your face. You didn't even know—you didn't know they were going to shoot you or nothing?

GIRL: That happened to you?

BOY IN WINDBREAKER: Last week.

BOY IN WHITE CAP: What, what happened?

GIRL (*overlapping*): Last week? Oh, my God.

BOY IN WHITE CAP: What?

BOY IN WINDBREAKER: Last week.

BOY IN WHITE CAP: You had a gun pointed in your face like this [*points finger at other boy's temple*]?

BOY IN WINDBREAKER: Not like that, but like this is—

JOSÉ: Cops?

BOY IN WINDBREAKER: No, this car. Also, I was talking to my friend on the corner.

BOY IN RED CAP: Gee.

BOY IN WINDBREAKER: 119? And then I realized it's a little hot. 'Cause it's like—

JOSÉ: It's always hot down there. [*General laughter.*]

BOY IN WINDBREAKER: —No, but I am saying, it's—

BOY IN RED CAP: There's always shots in the middle of the night, man.

BOY IN WINDBREAKER: Right at the corner, [*inaudible*] right there?

JOSÉ (*overlapping*): This guy is dangerous, man.

BOY IN WINDBREAKER: I was looking at my friend right there, and this car just pulled out on the corner, but like the windows are dark, and he just pulled it down a little, halfway, and I looked at the car, and it was like this [*points as if his hand were a gun*].

JOSÉ: Alright.

BOY IN WHITE CAP: With his hand out like that [*makes similar gesture*]?

GIRL (*overlapping*): What he was aiming at?

BOY IN WINDBREAKER: I don't know. I think he probably confused me with somebody. My friend and I just looked at him like this.

GIRL: What'd you do?

JOSÉ: Remember *Boyz N the Hood?*

BOY IN WINDBREAKER: I just looked at him like—

BOY IN WHITE CAP: I would have ducked.

GIRL: I would've been running down the block.

BOY IN WINDBREAKER: If you'd run, they would have said, that's him, shoot his ass. If they see you close face up they'll be like, no, it's not him.

BOY IN WHITE CAP: Can't outrun a bullet.

BOY IN WINDBREAKER: I know. So I just, like, I just looked at him. I thought about—

BOY IN WHITE CAP: "Don't shoot me. Would you shoot me? Make sure I'm dead. Don't make me suffer." [*Overlapping chatter.*]

JOSÉ: That's the most dangerous thing.

BOY IN WHITE CAP: But imagine being that guy that was in—that got pulled out his truck?

GIRL: Oh, man—

BOY IN WHITE CAP: Can you just imagine? You got all these people, crazy, pissed off, and not even at you. It wasn't even your fault, man. Just because you got long, blond hair—

BOY IN WINDBREAKER (*overlapping*): He probably didn't even know what was going on when they pulled him out of the truck.

GIRL (*overlapping*): It was 'cause he's white.

BOY IN WINDBREAKER: I know.

GIRL: I know. What was he doing with his car door open like that?

BOY IN WINDBREAKER: I don't know, man. [*Overlapping inaudible dialogue.*]

GIRL: When I'm in a car, I always close the door. I lock it all the times.

BOY IN WHITE CAP (*overlapping*): 'Cause you a girl.

GIRL: I be, I be afraid that, you know, I'm going to fall out or something—

BOY IN WHITE CAP: Hey, in California, you going to the store?—you leave your keys in your car, with—in the ignition.

GIRL: God, man, people are crazy all over this country, man. I don't leave my car door open.

BOY IN WHITE CAP: Well, it's true. He was in L.A., man.

JOSÉ: Like, I went to Massachusetts, you know, over the Easter vacation. And they leave their cars open with the keys inside. Are they crazy? [*Laughter.*] I was about to, you know, lock the door and everything. I was like—

BOY IN WHITE CAP: Give her the keys. Take your keys, lady. [*Laughter.*]

JOSÉ: Yeah. She was like, no, you can leave the door open. I was like, what? She was like, this ain't New York. [*Laughter.*] I know that.

BOY IN WHITE CAP: Yeah, we [*inaudible*] here, man. What happened?

GIRL: I don't know. I was crazy scared.

JOSÉ: I'd put a big alarm system in my car before I go to the store.

GIRL: And everybody buying the club now and everything.

JOSÉ: And they leave it, man. They be in the store for like ten hours. They come back. The car's still there.

GIRL: Yup.

JOSÉ: I was like, you do that over here—

BOY IN WINDBREAKER: You like working?

JOSÉ: —shit.

GIRL: In Pennsylvania—

JOSÉ: Yeah, it's fun over there, man.

BOY IN WINDBREAKER: There's too much smart people in Boston. [*Inaudible*] I thought, they're getting snotty with me, I was like, check it, what's your problem, man? I was just asking you for a question, they get snotty with me. I was like—

GIRL: In Pennsylvania, people be parking their cars and leaving them. Like, leaving them in a parking lot. And they leave their kids in the car with the car open and everything. They just leave the baby sleeping in their, whatever. Then they come back. I'd never leave my baby in the car.

JOSÉ: Remember that lady that went to court because she left her baby in the trunk?

GIRL: In the trunk? Why'd she put him in the trunk?

JOSÉ (*overlapping*): While, while—'cause she went to work, she had to go to work. She ain't find no babysitter.

GIRL: What? She left him in the trunk?

BOY IN WINDBREAKER (*overlapping*): Yeah, you didn't read about that?

49. Students discuss current affairs and having babies.

She left him in the trunk. And people heard the baby crying, so they called the cops.

GIRL: Did it die?

JOSÉ: Yeah. It wasn't really, it wasn't really the trunk. It was a trunk, but she put her—the chair, you know, the seats in the back? She pulled them down.

GIRL: Oh, so she laid it down?

JOSÉ: So, the trunk and the whole thing was, you know—

BOY IN WINDBREAKER: One.

JOSÉ: Yeah, one whole thing. And she left her baby there.

BOY IN WINDBREAKER (*overlapping*): You didn't hear about that?

GIRL: That's messed up. No, I ain't heard about that.

JOSÉ: How old was the baby? Like one year old? Two?

BOY IN WHITE CAP: How's your kid, José?

JOSÉ: My kid, he's alright. He was sick for a while.

GIRL: Oh, yeah.

JOSÉ: He had a hundred and five fever.

GIRL: A hundred and five?

BOY IN WHITE CAP: Come on, man. A hundred and six, and you dead.

JOSÉ: No, he wasn't dead. I'm saying he wasn't about to die.

GIRL (*overlapping*): Was he that sick, like he was—

JOSÉ: —he wasn't about to die, but he was really hot.

BOY IN WHITE CAP: Seriously?

JOSÉ: Yeah.

BOY IN WHITE CAP: You took him to the hospital?

JOSÉ: For Easter vacation, we went away to Massachusetts to see his grand-mother, and he got real sick. A hundred and five fever. Took him to the hospital. Every night.

BOY IN WHITE CAP: What was wrong with him?

JOSÉ: Up and down. Up and down. Nothing. Just a fever. And then they said, they found—like he had something in his throat. Some—

BOY IN WHITE CAP: A virus probably.

JOSÉ: Yeah.

FEMALE: God. How old is he?

JOSÉ: He's one.

BOY IN WHITE CAP: How many months?

JOSÉ: Fourteen months. Something like that.

BOY IN WHITE CAP: Fourteen? That's one and a half.

GIRL: A month or two. [*Inaudible.*]

JOSÉ: A year and two months.

BOY IN WHITE CAP: How old is he? A year and a half? I haven't seen that baby.

GIRL: My friend's baby.

BOY IN WHITE CAP: How old are you, José?

JOSÉ: I'm eighteen.

BOY IN WHITE CAP: Man.

JOSÉ: I'm eighteen and two months now. [*Laughter*] I'm eighteen and—I don't know. I'm about to be nineteen soon.

BOY IN WHITE CAP: And I'm going—

GIRL: Kind of—

BOY IN WHITE CAP: —[*inaudible*] a father [*inaudible*]?

José: That's—that's one thing—

BOY IN WINDBREAKER: And I remember you.

José (*overlapping*): I never imagined myself being a father.

BOY IN WINDBREAKER (*overlapping*): No, I remember you. We used to hang out with Melvin. And we was at his house, and he goes, hell, no, I'll never get a girl pregnant. And, boom, he was, was the first guy that got—I remember that.

GIRL: Yeah, man.

BOY IN WINDBREAKER: Me and Melvin used to be like—remember when you used to say this? I'm like, yeah.

José: We always used to talk about people.

BOY IN WINDBREAKER: We stayed in Melvin's house. Remember Melvin?

GIRL: Yeah.

BOY IN WINDBREAKER: No?

GIRL: Yeah.

BOY IN WINDBREAKER: We stayed at his house like until like one o'clock in the morning. We used to talk until—talk about baseball and not talk about that. One day, I kicked the rug 'cause my mom was coming. And at two o'clock, I go, my mom. They're like, boom. They were out of that house. But we used to—

José: I used to always talk about—I used to see young girls having baby. I used to say, nah.

GIRL: [*Inaudible*].

José: What the hell are you doing, man?

BOY IN WINDBREAKER: Yous.

José: And then it happened to me. But I, I didn't want to—we didn't want to keep the baby at first. And then, we had to keep it.

BOY IN WHITE CAP: Why?

José: It was too late to do anything about it.

GIRL: How you feel now?

José: When we told our parents, she was already six months.

GIRL: Six months! Damn, they didn't notice?

José: No. She ain't showing.

BOY IN WINDBREAKER: Girls don't be showing, man.

BOY IN WHITE CAP: [*Inaudible*] especially if they be wearin' them baggy clothes.

GIRL: I doubt you can get away with that.

JOSÉ: Yeah, she got away with it until she was like six months, and then after that—

BOY IN WHITE CAP (*overlapping*): How, how your parents took it?

JOSÉ (*overlapping*): —everybody was shocked.

GIRL: Yeah? They got mad at you all?

JOSÉ: No, my parents didn't get mad. I mean, they was mad, yeah. But what could they do about it?

GIRL: That's true.

JOSÉ: But her, her parents is, like, you're going to have to get married.

BOY IN WINDBREAKER: Right.

JOSÉ: Not her parents, but her grandmother. So, we did.

BOY IN WINDBREAKER: And what was they going—?

BOY IN WHITE CAP: Where's the ring, dude? [*Laughter.*]

JOSÉ: It's being repaired.

BOY IN WHITE CAP: Yeah, right.

JOSÉ: It's being made to my ho—, my size.

BOY IN WINDBREAKER: That's what you told me last year, man. C'mon. I remember you told me last year.

GIRL: Take that shit off.

BOY IN WINDBREAKER: Take that shit off me. [*Laughter.*]

JOSÉ: Shi-i-i-i-it.

BOY IN WINDBREAKER: I remember, I remember Larry got some "yo, my girl's pregnant." I was like, who?

GIRL: Yeah.

BOY IN WINDBREAKER: And then when he told me, I was like, yo, you dumb shit.

BOY IN WHITE CAP (*overlapping*): Yo, I flipped when he told me that shit, B. I flipped.

BOY IN WINDBREAKER: I remember we were talking like, wow, you stupid or something?

JOSÉ: Yes. That's something, man. I forgot—

BOY IN WHITE CAP: I didn't get—

JOSÉ: —I still can't believe I'm a parent.

BOY IN WHITE CAP: —No, 'cause you're too young, dude. You eighteen.

GIRL: Well, how you feel about it now? Like, like how do you feel about your baby and everything? Since, at first, you didn't want to keep it and all?

JOSÉ: I love my kid. And I'm, I'm proud that we, you know, we went through with it, and we had the baby. 'Cause, I don't know. It's hard to just think about not having the baby around, so . . . that's basically it. And that's the reason—I don't know about the baby—

BOY IN WHITE CAP (*overlapping*): Is it like because if you could have done something, you would have, but—

JOSÉ: —is something I—

BOY IN WHITE CAP: —now that he's here, you're—

JOSÉ: Yeah, but a baby is a life, you know, so that's—

BOY IN WHITE CAP: Yeah, like a dog. [*Overlapping dialogue.*]

JOSÉ: I know. It ain't like—I don't know. It's weird. Having a kid and then being there to see it be born.

BOY IN WHITE CAP: You saw it?

GIRL: You were there?

BOY IN WHITE CAP: You saw it come out the mother's womb?

BOY IN WINDBREAKER: Yo, that shit must have flipped you out, B?

GIRL: Did you want to faint? [*Laughter.*]

JOSÉ: Nah.

BOY IN WHITE CAP: You never seen a baby come out before?

JOSÉ: Not till that day.

GIRL: And what'd you do? You just standing there—

JOSÉ: Yeah.

GIRL: —like, all quiet?

JOSÉ: It didn't shock me until I saw the baby. The baby was one ugly little kid. [*General laughter.*]

GIRL: Damn!

JOSÉ: The baby was like an alien. I was like, what— [*laughter*].

GIRL: An alien? You're so mean.

JOSÉ: And then the doctor said, "Do you want to hold him?" I was like, "No!" He was like an alien, it seems like. They all look like this when they born, but after a while—

BOY IN WHITE CAP (*overlapping*): They come out all like purple and everything and [*inaudible*]? [*Overlapping dialogue.*]

JOSÉ: —no, I think it was, right? He was white, all wrinkled up—

BOY IN WHITE CAP (*overlapping*): How much did he weigh?

JOSÉ: Eight pounds and three ounces.

BOY IN WINDBREAKER: When I saw my nephew like an hour after being born? I was like "ahhhh." I was like—he had marks on his face, all wrinkled up.

JOSÉ (*overlapping*): He had a big conehead like this, and I was like, God!

BOY IN WINDBREAKER: —not a conehead, but it was all wrinkled and all like, you know, ahhh. Now, the kid is like—

JOSÉ: My son had a big conehead. I was like, what the hell?

GIRL: What's his name?

JOSÉ: Nico Joseph.

BOY IN WHITE CAP: Nico?

JOSÉ: Yeah. That was one experience I never forget.

BOY IN WHITE CAP: What?

JOSÉ: Seeing a baby being born.

BOY IN WHITE CAP: Let alone your baby.

GIRL: Your baby, I know, eh?

JOSÉ: But still, just any baby—

BOY IN WHITE CAP: But somebody's, but somebody, somebody else's baby, man, you got ahhhh, 'cause you see that shit come out with all that disgusting stuff. I seen that show on TV one time, B—

JOSÉ: —that, that something that you—I don't know—

BOY IN WHITE CAP (*overlapping*): Yo, I was disgusted.

JOSÉ (*overlapping*): —I think everybody should experience that.

GIRL: You think so?

JOSÉ: All men should experience it. They should be there when they—

BOY IN WHITE CAP: No, I feel like, I'm going to leave the room—

JOSÉ: —when the wife has the baby, they should be there. That's it, that's something you never forget.

BOY IN WHITE CAP: You should record it, man. Get a camcorder.

JOSÉ: She wanted me to record it—

GIRL (*overlapping*): Some people do that. They do like—[*makes gesture as if taking photographs*].

JOSÉ: —she wanted me to record it, like her friends had pictures.

BOY IN WHITE CAP: What?

GIRL: He's in there with a flash [*repeats gesture*].

JOSÉ: I know.

GIRL: C'mon, c'mon.

BOY IN WHITE CAP (*falsetto*): "It's coming."

JOSÉ: That's one thing, like . . . Filming it is all right but—

BOY IN WHITE CAP: That thing must have changed your life completely around, man, right? You still be hanging out with your friends, though?

JOSÉ: Nah. Everything's changed. My whole life has changed. I don't act like it sometimes when I'm in school, but out of school I gotta act like—

GIRL: You got to be more responsible.

JOSÉ: Yeah, I'm responsible and everything, so.

BOY IN WHITE CAP: Ah, you're still a bum with me.

JOSÉ: Everything changes.

BOY IN WHITE CAP: Yeah.

GIRL: At least, at least you are responsible about it 'cause there's a lot of guys out there don't care.

BOY IN WHITE CAP (*overlapping*): How do you support your kid, man? You got a job, right?

JOSÉ: Yeah.

BOY IN WHITE CAP: Where do you work?

JOSÉ: Ninety-second Street Y.

GIRL: Oh, you drove me to work there this summer.

JOSÉ: Yeah.

GIRL: Yeah, I'm going to be a C-I-T.

BOY IN WHITE CAP: C-I-T?

JOSÉ: They wanted me to work—

GIRL: Counselor-in-Training.

JOSÉ: —doing that, but I don't see—they don't pay good.

GIRL: No, they don't pay good at all. I'm only doing it for the experience.

JOSÉ: I'm getting a doorman job. That pays good . . . For the summer at least, until I go to college.

BOY IN WHITE CAP: What college you going—

JOSÉ: Whenever that is . . . I don't know yet.

BOY IN WINDBREAKER: You getting out of this school or you got to stay another semester?

JOSÉ: I got to stay another semester. To go to Hunter again because—

BOY IN WINDBREAKER: That's what you get for not listening to your mother. You should go tell your school.

JOSÉ: —Last year, I never went to school.

GIRL: Damn.

BOY IN WINDBREAKER: You still didn't come to school? Come to school? Nope?

JOSÉ: It was so tiring to come to school. Imagine working till all—

BOY IN WINDBREAKER (*overlapping*): Not at the beginning—

JOSÉ: I used to work till at least twelve every day—

BOY IN WINDBREAKER: Not at the beginning of, of the—

JOSÉ: Wait, wait. Let me talk. Let me talk. Let me talk. Let me finish this. I used to work till like twelve o'clock in the night, right? And then you come home and then you up because the baby, you know, they cry at all hours of the night.

GIRL: Wow.

josé: And you're always up. And then, having to come to school at eight o'clock in the morning—

boy in white cap: Hey, old man, I be dead if I go to sleep at eleven, B.

josé: I'm serious—I used to go to sleep around one—

girl (*overlapping*): You do?

josé: —or two o'clock in the morning every night and then wake up in the middle of the night to feed the baby or my wife raises shit, you know.

boy in white cap: It is your turn now five minutes later.

josé: Take turns and I was, you know, that's, that's too tiring to come to school then in the morning. So, I, I stopped coming to school after a while. I used to be too tired. And then, I don't know, during, during the summer I came to school 'cause I wasn't working over the summer. So I came to school and then, I was in. Then I came back during this, the beginning of this year. But now it's different because the baby don't get up in the middle of the night.

boy in windbreaker: He's asleep in the whole night?

josé: Yeah.

boy in windbreaker: Giving you a rest.

josé: He better.

boy in white cap: How long that lasted? That he had to be getting up every night?

josé: I don't know.

boy in white cap: I think it's the, like the first eight months, I think.

josé: Yeah, something like that, or nine months.

boy in windbreaker: Wow.

girl: First eight months?

boy in white cap: They eat at nighttime.

josé: Well, once he started walking at nine months, he, I think that used to get him real tired walking, so I guess he's used to sleep a lot—

girl: He used to walk around all the time. He's like, come on. Walk a little more. [*Cut to FS of a boy tying his shoelaces. Cut to shot of school hallway, students walking by camera. LS of two students in a classroom. Cut to CU of the one in the background, a girl reading Homer's* Odyssey *while sucking on a big lollipop.*]

GIRL: Do they always [*inaudible*]?

SECOND GIRL: We're having a reunion next Friday. [*CU of the other student, the boy with his head on his desk. Shot of man wheeling VCR and monitor on AV cart in hallway. Cut to CU of student speaking in class.*]

BOY IN PURPLE SWEATSHIRT: We saying, it's not going to be like a straight line, but it's sort of going to be like a, like a curve, sort of showing that's it going to, like, the ozone—thick, the ozone's thickness is going to decrease slowly.

TEACHER: Okay. So, you've got some things about what you think how it changes with time?

BOY IN PURPLE SWEATSHIRT: Yeah.

TEACHER: In some of the information that I've given you, is there any evidence to kind of back up how you think this is going to change? Can you get any more information on the details about how it's changing? Like, is it kind of linear? Is it kind of like this? Does it look kind of like this? I mean—see, you all kind of agree that it changed—that it decreases with time, but what about kind of how it changes with time? Can you, can you find some evidence in this stuff that you've gotten that will kind of give you more of an indication of how it's going to change?

GIRL IN BLACK CAP: Well, I can relate—I think I can relate it to the, to the thickness, the thickness versus the refraction transmission. Because if you have, if there's gonna increase like this, it's going to empty just like—I think that the time versus thickness will, you know, decrease in opposite direction the same, the same pattern though.

TEACHER: Why?

GIRL IN BLACK CAP: Let me see . . . [*Silence.*]

TEACHER: Why?

GIRL IN BLACK CAP: . . . Don't know.

TEACHER: Okay, I want some evidence here to back this up, okay? I want some, some reason, some evidence, so go through some of the materials and see if you can come up with some more details about exactly how it's changing with time. Now, that might mean making some assumptions and some approximations. That's good. Just make sure that you know when you're making assumptions, you know when you're making approximations, and that you can kind of get a sense: are they good? are they bad? You know? How good are they? You know? Like, you know, it doesn't have to be exact.

You really don't have enough information to be exact, but, you know, using what you've got, be reasonable. Okay?

GIRL IN BLACK CAP: Turn it around like this and just put [*inaudible*] [*laughs*].

TEACHER: But you have to come up with some—you have to convince me that that's a reasonable way for it to change with time. That, that how's it's changing with time is reasonable. You know, "because I like it" is not going to convince me and persuade me to buy what you're doing. You've got to back this up with something.

GIRL IN BLACK CAP: Time is going on and the thickness is increasing.

TEACHER: Well, I buy that. Okay, sure. But how is it? How is it? Is it, is it decreasing like this? Is it decreasing like this? Is it decreasing like this? Is it decreasing, you know, like this? You know, how is it decreasing? Is it decreasing like this? You know? I want more information about what's exactly going on here?

GIRL IN BLACK CAP: Alright.

TEACHER: You know? And, and, or is it decreasing like, you know, real slow or real fast? You know, there's a lot of information in here that you can give me other than just, it's decreasing. I want more information. Okay? See if you can find some more information. Okay? [*Shot of school hallway, a few students.*]

TEACHER: DC means direct current. [*Cut to FS of teacher.*] And AC means alternating. Which one has which? The battery or the, the socket has which?

BOY (STEPHEN): Direct is the socket.

GIRL: Is the battery direct?

TEACHER: Remember, the battery is direct current. Is DC. And the—

STEPHEN: And the—

TEACHER: —sorry.

STEPHEN: —socket is the—

TEACHER: And the socket is AC. It's alternating. They're two different things. Remember what the difference was between them? I told you this very early on. I tell you quick. I'm going to draw a picture. [*She moves to the blackboard.*]

BOY (*offscreen*): Is that because the one is in the series and the other one is in parallel?

TEACHER: No. It's not exactly that. It means this. [*She begins drawing on the blackboard.*] And this is zero on your oscilloscope. And remember when you did the little thing and you plugged it in? And then the sine wave always jumped up. Right? Like say, the line started on there. And then when you plug the battery up—

BOY (*offscreen*): DC is like always [*inaudible*].

TEACHER: —Right. DC always stays on one side. Rosa.

ROSA: Yeah, I know.

TEACHER: DC stays. This is positive. And this is negative down here. DC will only stay on one way. Meaning the current only goes in one direction. So that's when I write this and I go, it always goes from a negative side. That's what I mean for DC. Okay? Alternating means with—we're alternating. Something's alternating. What does that mean?

BOY (*offscreen*): Back and forth.

TEACHER: It goes back and forth. Just—I mean, think about these words as regular words that you know in English. Alternating means that sometimes the current going this way. And sometimes the current's going this way. So, if you drew on the, on the graph, if you used this guide on the oscilloscope, this is where it's going to be. Some of it's going to be positive. Some of it's going to be negative. Some of it's going to be positive. Some of it's going to be negative. 'Cause remember, positive and negative had to do with which side you on. When you switch things on an oscilloscope, when you changed it, it jumped down there when it was on the negative side.

BOY (*offscreen*): Yeah.

TEACHER: Alternating does both, back and forth. That was a hard question, José, so. It was. It was.

BOY (STEPHEN): I go. I go.

TEACHER: Go ahead. Since he knows it.

STEPHEN: Of course. Name the parts of an atom. Which part is involved in current flow?

TEACHER: Right.

STEPHEN: Parts of the atom is neutrons, protons, and electrons.

TEACHER: Yeah, yeah.

STEPHEN: And a nucleus.

TEACHER: Yeah?

STEPHEN: And the electrons are involved in current flow.

TEACHER: How? The electrons do what?

STEPHEN: They flow.

TEACHER: They do the flowing.

STEPHEN: Yeah.

TEACHER: They flow. So, the electrons actually do the flowing. Oh, alright, Stephen. [*Group applause.*] Next, next.

GIRL IN BLACK SWEATER: What is ozone? V equals I times R.

TEACHER: Which means?

SECOND FEMALE STUDENT: Voltage equals current times resistance. [*Cut to FS of student protest meeting in the school library.*]

GIRL IN STRIPED SWEATER: I think we all have a sense, I mean, the Senior Institute students that were here a little while ago, they have their own opinion, and they want to go and start fires, that's their situation. We're not involved with that. And we have already stated that this is a positive way of resolving the conflict. We are not gonna go to start fires. We are not gonna go to kick the shit out of people. 'Cause that is not, that is not what we are trying to achieve.

GIRL (*offscreen*): What are we trying to achieve?

GIRL IN STRIPED SWEATER: The point is, right, we're trying to achieve a positive way of dealing with things. We're trying to let them, we are trying to let them know how we feel about the situation. That we feel that the situation was unjust. That Rodney King was beat by police officers and he did not get a fail, a fair trial.

GIRL (*offscreen*): He wasn't on trial.

GIRL (*offscreen*): Can I say something?

GIRL IN STRIPED SWEATER: He—it's not—you don't understand. He was on trial in a sense because, you see, these po—, police officers, they were police officers. They—

GIRL (*offscreen*): The law protects them.

GIRL IN STRIPED SWEATER: —you know, the law protects them and the law has said, they have to use any means necessary. To control a situation. They have that right. But they did not have the right to control the situation the way they did because he was not defending himself.

50. A student organizes a protest about the verdict in the Rodney King beating case.

GIRL (*offscreen*): You see?

GIRL (*offscreen*): I know this.

GIRL IN STRIPED SWEATER: Rodney King, Rodney King was not defending himself in any way. That man was beat till who knows what. He lied on the floor and had cops beat the shit out of him. And we have to let people know that we don't agree with that. And if police officers are out there to protect us, why are they beating us up?

MALE STUDENT (*offscreen*): Right up.

GIRL IN STRIPED SWEATER: That's our point. And we have to stress that we do not agree with this. Does it mean that any black person or Hispanic person that's driving along in their car, that police officers have the right to take them out of their, their car and start beating the shit out of them? He was not defending himself. He didn't even hit back . . . They repeatedly took turns and beat him. At some point or another in our lives, we are going to become, we are going to come in contact with racism. With prejudice. And we have to know how to conduct ourselves and how to deal with that in a positive way. Because, you see, minorities have already been labeled as savages, as beasts, as people with—that are uneducated. What's going on in Los Angeles right now, you're proving that stereotype right. And we don't want that. Because there are intelligent minorities. And if we show people that we can deal, handle ourselves appropriately, then we can make a difference.

By killing people and by beating them up and by burning people's homes, that's not a positive method . . . And that's what we're trying to explain to, to the system. And they have to know that we are not violent people. Not all of us feel the way those—yes, we are all upset. And we are hurt.

BOY (*offscreen*): Outraged.

GIRL IN STRIPED SWEATER: And, yes, we are outraged at the situation. But we are dealing with it in a positive way. We're going down to City Hall to make a point. To make a point that we don't agree with the decision. But that we are intelligent enough to know how to deal with it. And we're not going to take violent actions against people. And that's our point. And if you truly believe in this, then you will go with us. And if you have doubts, and if you're afraid of the situation, don't go.

GIRL IN ORANGE BLOUSE: I'm saying, but if you want to organize a march that's really going to have a statement, that's really going to say something and that's going to really make your point get across, then y'all need to be more organized than having a meeting on Friday and having a march on Monday. Because that is not going to really work. You do not have real organization. Just like people are here now talking about emergency meetings and stuff like that. That's fine, you have some organization. But there's still going to be chaos.

GIRL IN STRIPED SWEATER: We understand that, but—

GIRL IN ORANGE BLOUSE: You need more time to think about this. This is a good thing that you all want to do, and I understand that y'all really feel about this. How y'all really feel about this. But if y'all going to do it right, you have to have more time. You got to think about what you're doing. You gotta have a main point. You have to have a reason for being down there.

GIRL IN STRIPED SWEATER: Well, we—

GIRL IN ORANGE BLOUSE: You have to have a position to stand and keep standing on it. You do not go down there one day and expect that to do something. You keep doing it. This is not going to go away by one march by one high school. You need more people. [*Some applause.*] More action. You need a point to stand by. You all want to do this, this is fine. Get in contact with other high schools. High schools that you know feel just the way that we do, and get them to come down there and have leadership, have structure—

GIRL IN STRIPED SWEATER: Alright, we—

GIRL IN ORANGE BLOUSE: —so you will have that.

GIRL IN STRIPED SWEATER: —we understand that, but right now, our main focus was on our school. For later on, if we do decide to have a second march, then we will take action that way. We will inform people, there is a second march. This is what's going to happen. And if you want to get other schools involved, that's okay. We've discussed basically for our school. [*Cut to shot of students in school hallway, followed by shot of students descending school stairway. Ext. shot of students coming out of school, guard at the door. High-angle LSs of CPESS, Manhattan area. Shot of New York City at night. Ext. shot of CPESS in the morning. Shot of a student coming into the school entrance, followed by a two-shot of a teacher at his desk going over a student's work with her.*]

TEACHER: If that's what you're writing about in this paragraph here, that he was an individual, and individualism was strongly encouraged in the Renaissance.

GIRL: Right.

TEACHER: Then say that. Then say—

GIRL (*overlapping*): Well, what I was trying to get—

TEACHER (*overlapping*): —that, that's an example.

GIRL (*overlapping*): —in that this paragraph was not only showing like why they might have thought that, but I was trying to get like into the next paragraph by saying, well, look at some of the stuff he did, he wasn't really a Renaissance man because everything he did wasn't based on fact. It was just on, you know, theories that he had.

TEACHER: Hmm-mmm.

GIRL: And a Renaissance man, like, he doesn't only explore, but he has, like, some facts to back up what he says.

TEACHER: Well—

GIRL: Which he didn't, really.

TEACHER: —right.

GIRL: At least I don't think he did.

TEACHER: Right. Well, see, but I think you should be clearer in each paragraph about what characteristic of the Renaissance you're talking about.

GIRL: Uh-huh.

TEACHER: And then you can give evidence—

GIRL: Well, how can I do that?

TEACHER: Okay.

51. A teacher and a student discuss her essay on Christopher Columbus.

GIRL (*overlapping*): 'Cause I have—

TEACHER (*overlapping*): One of the ways that I—right. One, one of the ways that I thought you might be able to do it was first brainstorm a list of characteristics of the Renaissance.

GIRL: Uh-huh.

TEACHER: And then maybe you could write each—this is one way of doing it, write each paragraph corresponding with the characteristic of the Renaissance and say how Columbus met or didn't meet that characteristic.

GIRL: Right.

TEACHER: So, for example, this is your introduction, okay?

GIRL: Uh-huh.

TEACHER: Then, your first paragraph deals with the characteristic of questioning. 'Cause that's curiosity or questioning. That's one characteristic of the Renaissance. So you could describe that as being a characteristic and then say how Columbus, give an example of Columbus fitting that characteristic.

GIRL: Uh-huh.

TEACHER: Then, your second paragraph deals with the second characteristic of the Renaissance, which is following an individual path. And then you could talk about how he does that.

GIRL: Uh-huh.

TEACHER: Your third paragraph might be that you said another character-istic of the Renaissance is that people had to have, as you said, evidence for things, right?

GIRL: Right.

TEACHER: They had to—it couldn't just come from some belief. It had to come from evidence. Now what, what kind of thinking is that?

GIRL: Um, I forgot what it's called. Um . . .

TEACHER: What subject do we study that we know uses that kind of thinking?

GIRL: I forgot the word . . . Um, humanism?

TEACHER: Well, that's not exactly what I'm thinking about. It's a word that begins with an S. [*Overlapping dialogue*]

GIRL: It begins with an S.

TEACHER: Well, how's about science?

GIRL: What about science?

TEACHER: Because—

GIRL: That's not what I was thinking of.

TEACHER: Oh.

GIRL: When you asked me.

TEACHER: Oh.

GIRL: What was that word that you said?

TEACHER: Secular?

GIRL: That's it. That's what I was thinking about.

TEACHER: Oh, so that's a nonreligious worldview.

GIRL: Right.

TEACHER: Okay, but I want to come back to that one. But, if you think about it, in, in science, if you believe in science, you have to see things for your-self. You have to prove it. You have to have evidence for them. You have to experiment, have, you know—

GIRL: Right.

TEACHER: —you have to have a reason for something. It's not just because God willed it. Now, what you're saying is that he didn't really always have evidence for things.

GIRL: Right.

TEACHER: So, you know, in that sense he might not have been.

GIRL: Well, like in my opinion, he was a Renaissance man. He had some of the characteristics.

TEACHER: Right.

GIRL: I just don't think he had fact.

TEACHER: Right. Alright. Alright. But I think you have to have evidence. And you could tell about some of the characteristics that he didn't have.

GIRL: Right.

TEACHER: So, I want, you know, that—the one way that I think you could go about doing it is just, you know, going through all the characteristics and then saying whether he possessed them or whether he didn't.

GIRL: Uh-huh.

TEACHER: And I would talk about secularism. And I want you to think about that one. Because is it true that he had a nonreligious worldview?

GIRL: Uh-huh. Well, not, not, not totally.

TEACHER: Right . . . right. Why?

GIRL: Well, because when he started sailing, one—like, the three things that he stated for his reason for sailing was: God, gold, and glory.

TEACHER: Right.

GIRL: So, it couldn't have been—

TEACHER: Right.

GIRL: —a nonsecular.

TEACHER: Right. So, that's—

GIRL: Secular—

TEACHER: —so that, you know, that would go, you know, you're ambivalent about whether he's a Renaissance man or not, and that certainly you should use that—

GIRL: In my opinion, I don't think he was, but there's, like you said—

TEACHER (*overlapping*): Right, okay.

GIRL: —European—

TEACHER: Okay, okay, okay.

GIRL: —That was the question that you asked.

TEACHER: The question I asked was: was he a Renaissance man? Did he charact—, did he represent the spirit of the Renaissance—

GIRL: In Europe.

TEACHER: —did he have some of the characteristics? Yes. In Europe.

GIRL: In Europe, I believe he did. Right here and now, I don't think so.

TEACHER: I see what you're saying.

GIRL: That's why it's hard for me to, like, write the paper and, like, with your point of view.

TEACHER: Well, I think—

GIRL (*overlapping*): I could write it: in Europe, I believe he would have been considered a Renaissance man. He was considered a hero at that time. I don't think he was a hero.

TEACHER: Right. Okay, alright. Alright, alright. One, one—alright, now I see where the confusion came in. I think you have to, you have to come, you have to look at it in terms of the Renaissance at his time.

GIRL: Uh-huh.

TEACHER: You have to, in the body of the paper, you have to say to what extent he represented the Renaissance at that time.

GIRL: Uh-huh.

TEACHER: Then, you can go on afterwards and say, but according to today's characteristics, today's qualifications of—

GIRL (*overlapping*): That could be my conclusion.

TEACHER: Right. That's right.

GIRL: Okay.

TEACHER: So, what you have to do is you have to go through the characteristics of the Renaissance.

GIRL: Uh-huh.

TEACHER: And to look at the extent to which he fulfilled them.

GIRL: Right.

TEACHER: And there you need, I guess my criticisms are that you need to break up each paragraph. And you also need, you also need evidence, as I said. You need more evidence drawn from his life and the things that he did to back it up.

GIRL: Uh-huh. Okay. [*Cut to CU of Paul.*]

PAUL: —this is the third shooting this week. You know, Cattarras's cousin was shot and killed. What's-his-name was shot?

DEBBIE: One of our students. Who came in this morning? Was that Cattarras?

PAUL: Cattarras.

DEBBIE: Came in this morning?

PAUL: Yes, that was—yeah.

DEBBIE: Yeah.

PAUL: And now this . . .

DEBBIE: Twenty-third precinct. I want to call to find out whether there's anything that we were worrying about, about the King's—

PAUL: Yeah. You know, Debbie, I wonder—

DEBBIE (*overlapping*): So he said that any discussion of pros and cons, I said, I don't know of any debate of that sort. There aren't any pros and cons in this story—on that subject. We should get them to understand that.

PAUL: Well, they sh—, really, I felt sure that there are a lot of policemen across the country who are outraged, too. [*Cut to shot of teacher talking at his desk with two students.*]

TEACHER: Alright, let me ask you this. Who, what is the purpose of this form that you're doing?

BOY (STEPHEN): The purpose for this trouble is that at all these discussion about the rally or, or other demonstrations, what's going on in L.A., it's only one opinion that's thrown out. And what I want to get out of this is that, okay, we have people in our school that feel one way, but, let's hear the cops, what they have to say. And, and we say that we were harassed and, you know, beat up or whatever at that rally, and we got hit, and they said it was because the cops had something against them or whatever. Wanted to, you know, but let's hear what the—we want to—the cops to say their views. And what they were trying to do. So, that's what—and plus instead of going to all these rallies, we could try to find some solution to what's going on in [*inaudible, drowned out by siren outside*].

TEACHER: What do you mean, find the solution? How?

STEPHEN: Well, what they, what they were saying yesterday at those meetings that were—

TEACHER: Which meetings?

STEPHEN: At the library.

TEACHER: Oh, yeah.

STEPHEN: The cops, well, actually, I think it was Vanetta was saying that the cops were just doing their job and that you should have a certain type of respect for the police officers and you can't be going all up in their face and things like that, but how I saw it was that it was the opposite. The cops were the one who were instigating the issue and they were all up in the people's face, and they should have knew that it was high school students and junior high school students there. And they, they weren't supposed to do that.

GIRL: There was—excuse me, there wasn't any provoking by the students? I heard, there were like girls who were, you know, like running up to police officers and threatening them like, you know, like saying they were gonna hit them and like, you know, like just saying things against the cops. Pretending to, you know, beating them up and things like that.

STEPHEN: Yeah, but cops are tr—

GIRL: I would think that would provoke an officer.

STEPHEN: —yeah, it—but cops should know better. You know? Even if somebody provokes you, if you're a police officer, you have a, you know, you're there to serve and protect. You're not supposed to be hitting thirteen-year-old girls in the face or something like that. And that's what hap—

GIRL: Is that what happened?

STEPHEN: Yeah, they hit a girl in the face.

GIRL (*overlapping*): From our school?

STEPHEN: I don't know. Was she from our school?

TEACHER: They hit a lot of kids, some of them from our school.

STEPHEN (*overlapping*): They hit a lot of kids with sticks and stuff and, you know.

GIRL: Right.

STEPHEN: That's bad.

TEACHER: You may get a pretty big audience, you know.

STEPHEN: Yeah, I know.

TEACHER: Might have to do it in the auditorium.

STEPHEN: Maybe the whole school.

TEACHER: Yeah, you might.

GIRL: Yeah. I think it would be good just to plan to have it in the auditorium. Because this is something everybody is interested in. [*Cut to shot of students in hallway walking by camera, followed by a shot of a student sleeping on sofa. Cut to LS of teachers sitting at a table in discussion.*]

DEBBIE: I want to just say that I think next year, no. 'Cause I just don't see any way to do it now. We need sort of more formally to think through the issue of how—wha—, I mean, we all have a view—a part of our role as a school is to make students feel political, their political citizenship. And we don't have any bones about that. That's not a question. That's not using kids for political agendas and, I mean, now, that's part of our responsibility. To make them powerful political actors. But there are places in that agenda which get complicated. I mean, there are borderlines between our role as helping kids be political citizens and using kids. That's the, the extreme end. Our using kids for our political agendas. And there is a lot of gray areas in between where it's not easy to always know what it is we're doing and who's doing it, and we're very busy with our agenda, so we have other things, so, sometimes we just say yes, yes. And I don't think we thought through what it is that's, that's involved. And, and Friday's event is an example to me because we hadn't the slightest idea of what's educational about Friday. And nobod—, and people, we overwhelmingly voted in favor of that proposal, without having the slightest idea who the four speakers are, who the, what these workshops are, what the educational purposes of this. It's essentially, as far as I can see, it's 'cause there was three or four kids in the school who had very strong convictions, and had a definite ideology coming from their families and their backgrounds. Much like my own when I was growing up. And we have one or two faculty members or fac—, you know, a few other adults who support them. And on the basis of that, which we wouldn't do for anything else, pedagogically. I mean, we would think through anything else with a great deal more care. We were going to have a poli—, an educational event, lasting two hours in this school, we would spend a lot of time organizing. As we would with a class. We would try to think about what the essential question, so to speak. What's we hoped to get out of it. What's the size of the group? What kind of discussion? What kind of different viewpoints? What's the argument? So, when we, when this was a parents' association, three-to-five event, I didn't have any worries about that. When it was—see, you know, now it's something in between. I mean, sort of be, you know, to, to make life safe for ourselves, I called this a PA event. But, obviously, it's not exactly a parents' association event. It's a staff-endorsed event. And I, I just think, this is not terrible. It's not the end of the world or anything. But I think there's all along whether or not we handle politics the same way we handle other education. If we think our educational approach is good, pedagogically, in classroom. That is, to have various viewpoints, to have arguments, to get kids to do some investigation. Then, it seems to me, our way of approaching getting kids politically active, it should be similar. And then, if, you know, there are a lot of other things. Bringing kids to, to meetings. I don't think there's anything wrong with that. Bringing kids to meetings. Letting them see what pol—, rights coming back and writing up different arguments. Coming to see other kinds of meetings. In a way, we, we don't think through the question of what, what kind of activities are legitimately and powerfully appropriate for a school to do to help kids see themselves as political activists. And it, you know, it's—even in terms of community service, whether there are ways in which we could use community service more effectively to make kids knowledgeable and thoughtful political activists. [*Cut to two-shot of hallway with students at classroom door.*]

GIRL (*offscreen*): That's an advantage for everything. [*Cut to four boys around a table.*]

CARLOS: I'm Carlos, and this is Mark. And we're your mediators. Before we start this, we just want to mention that the two guys want to solve this dispute. You two, you guys want to solve this. Alright, before we go on, we have to agree to these seven rules. One is, you guys already agreed to solve the problem. Another is, the stuff that happens here is confidential. It doesn't leave this room. It stays between us four. We're the only ones that know. There'll be no name-calling during the mediation. Don't interrupt each other. Speak directly to me or Mark. Be as honest as you can, so we can come to a, a good solution. And there'll be no physical fighting.

MARK: Um, what are you two names? Lev and?

BOY IN BLUE SHIRT (LEV): Lev.

BOY IN ORANGE SHIRT (ETHAN): Ethan.

MARK: Ethan. Alright, does it matter who speaks first?

CARLOS: Let's get started. You tell me what happened.

ETHAN: We were on the stairs and he said something stupid, so I gave him a gill and I, he said, you do that again and I'm gonna hit you. So I did it again. And then he chased me down the stairs. And then, he ran to me and he hit me. So I punched him in the stomach. And then, I walked through the doors and then he hit me again. And then I hit him in the head. And then, he yelled out to Tom. And Tom didn't do anything. And then we went outside. And I was standing on the steps and he grabbed my coat. And I said, don't touch me. He pulled me over and then I hit him in the face.

CARLOS: So, what you're saying is that this started inside the school and then—

ETHAN: Yeah.

CARLOS: What, when was this, during lunchtime or something?

ETHAN: This was when we were going to swimming.

CARLOS: Oh, okay. So he called you, he called you, he gave, he called you something. He called you a name.

ETHAN: No, he said something stupid.

CARLOS: Oh, he said something stupid? And you didn't like the way he said it, so you hit him?

ETHAN: No.

CARLOS: Oh?

ETHAN: I went like this on his neck.

CARLOS: Oh, alright. And then he hit you?

ETHAN: Yeah.

CARLOS: And then from there, you two got into just hitting each other back and forth, right?

ETHAN: Yeah.

CARLOS: Alright [*inaudible*].

LEV: What happened—he—first he said something about my mother. And I said something back to him. And, first of all, I mean, I don't like people gilling me anyway. And especially if he's not my friend, and he's not my friend. So, I told him, don't do it again. Or I'll hit you. And he did it again, just to get me provoked. So when we got to the stairs, I pushed him. I said, stop. And then, Youssef—Youssef's my friend, and 'cause he, he did something to, to him and then we were walking and because I pushed him, he goes and—he didn't push me, he punched me and then—so we were walking there. We was like, well, man, I would have hit him. I can't believe that, man, and they were all like, I—you should have hit him. And then, I said,

I'm—when we were getting outside the door, I pushed him on his head, and then he comes around and he hits me in my stomach. And then, I, I went back and I pulled his jacket and I ripped it off. I ripped it. But, it was, it was kind of ripped. It was like, it was old and it was—bobby pins were holding it together, so it ripped kind of easily, but—

MARK: So, what you're saying is that you were, you didn't like him playing a game with you, right?

LEV: You know, I—he, he—even if my—I don't like even my friends doing it. If someone's not my friend, I especially don't like that.

MARK: Okay, and then when he did do it to you, you told him to stop, don't do it again. Or you're going to hit him. So, and he did it again, so you hit him. And then this went on and on.

LEV: And then, wait, wait, wait. And then after we stopped, he—we went to the—they—Tom pulled us, and the teacher pulled us into the gym and they called up Mark, and then we had to go upstairs by ourselves to Mark. So, we're walking, and you know where the guard's desk is? Well, I'm walking and he's like that—when we were going out of the gym, I held the door for him. He's like, that's right, you hold the door for me. I said, I don't have to hold the door for you, but I want to, Ethan. So, we were going and I didn't hold the door for him the second time. I just held it for myself and I went by and then he steps on the back of my shoe and kicks me in my back and I—and the guard's saying, "Get back here!" And he just ran up the stairs and he, he didn't talk to her. And I didn't do anything back to him. 'Cause I didn't want to get in more trouble.

MARK: So, you said that after that problem you got pulled into the gym. Tom had called up Mark for you to go up to the office. You walked through the door. You walked through the door and you held the door open for him. And he said, that's right, hold the door for me. And then you went out to the other door and you didn't hold the door for him that time, and he stepped on the back of your sneaker and kicked you in the back and the guard called him. But he ran up the stairs.

CARLOS: How do you feel about this?

LEV: I told him to stop. I told him, no. And I, I threatened him. I said, don't or I'm going to hit you back. And he didn't listen to me. He, he wanted me to hit him. I mean, why would he do that twice, when someone's telling him that he, that they are going to do something about it if you hit them again? And he did it again. And I pushed him and I said stop.

CARLOS: Alright.

TEACHER: I just wanted to ask a question. You said he said something stupid. Could you just tell the mediators what he said, 'cause it's sort of important to know what—

ETHAN: I don't remember what he said.

TEACHER: Oh. So—but he said something that annoyed you. Is that correct?

ETHAN: It was just like something stupid. Something that didn't make sense.

TEACHER: Right. But he said that you said something about his mother. Did you say that after he said something stupid?

CARLOS: Or before?

ETHAN: I didn't say that.

TEACHER: You didn't say anything about his mother? Do you recall what he said about your mother?

LEV: Uh-huh. We were in the classroom, right? And I was talking into the fan, right, to make my voi—, you know, how the fan, if you talking to it, it makes your voice—

CARLOS: It makes your voice squeaky, yeah.

LEV: Yeah. So, right. And then he goes like this, and you know that song, "You're Never Gonna Get It"? Never, never? You know?

Carlos: Yeah.

LEV: Like. And I was just singing to myself. I wasn't singing to anybody. He's like, you're never gonna get it, Lev. You know, I was like, I was like, I was like—oh, well. And—and then, he was like, and he says something about my mother. And so I said—

TEACHER: What did he say about your mother?

LEV: I don't know. He says, I—and then he said, so I was just like—at least I have a mother. And he was like, well, so do I. And I said, no, you don't. He said, then how did I get born? And I said, your father had artificial insemination. And he goes—

CARLOS: Hmm.

LEV: He goes, that's stupid, and then he, then he gave me a gill.

TEACHER: Gave you a what?

CARLOS AND MARK (*overlapping*): A gill. That's [*inaudible*] right [*inaudible*] across the back.

CARLOS: What do you think you can do? What do you think you two guys could agree to to solve this problem?

LEV: There's a couple of things. First, it—you know, you don't—if you have—you don't be with each other and you don't have to talk to each other. Unless you absolutely have to. Unless it's about work or something. And 'cause we're not friends. So, you know, I—so we don't have to talk to each other. And also—

TEACHER: You have the same advisor, though, right?

LEV: And all the same classes.

TEACHER: Oh.

LEV: And so, we're five hours a day we have to do with each other. And [*inaudible*] but and we don't have to be friends with each other and then, and we just don't have to talk to each other and also if he says something to me or I say something to him, we ignore each other, we ignore it. And we just walk away. 'Cause that's what we had to do. We were trying to figure this out in my conference this morning.

TEACHER: Uh-huh.

LEV: And my Dad said, just ignore it. And that's it. And just—and he'll feel like, he'll look like a jerk if he's talking to nobody. I mean, he's not talking to anybody if I'm just ignoring him and he keeps talking. And he'll look like an idiot.

CARLOS: Do you agree with him? Do you—

ETHAN: Yeah.

CARLOS: Okay. You guys can ignore each other?

TEACHER: And so, what did you, do you notice what did you two choose to talk about?

ETHAN: Mothers.

TEACHER: Mothers, right? So you picked something that's kind of a hot topic, right? That you know is going to set somebody off, both of you. Correct?

ETHAN: Yeah.

TEACHER: So, I think you have to think what are the kinds of things you, you can, you say to people. And what kind of reaction it's going—people are going to have. I think the two of you need to think about those kind of things.

CARLOS: Also, you guys have five hours of class together, I'm sure you guys are not going to be enemies for the rest of your lives.

TEACHER (*overlapping*): They're not going to be able to ignore each other—

CARLOS: I know.

TEACHER (*overlapping*): It's not, being in the same class. It's not realistic. You don't need—got to be enemies. Maybe it's realistic—

LEV: Oh, I don't know. It—I understand what you're saying, but many people have this problem with him. I mean—

TEACHER: But we're not here about many people. We're here—

LEV: No, I'm saying, I'm saying, but it, it's not hard to avoid, avoid him. It's not. Unless, I mean, it's not hard to avoid him.

TEACHER: But we have the other—what about you, Ethan? . . . Because he says things that set you off, right?

ETHAN: Yeah.

TEACHER: So what are, what are—what might have been, what might have been a different way to have handled it? Let's still go back to what happened and see what might have been a different way to have handled it?

ETHAN: Just to have left him alone.

TEACHER: Do you think you would have been able to do something like that?

ETHAN: Yeah.

TEACHER: And what might have been a different way to have handled it when he, if he said something to you?

LEV: I'd ignore it and when he, when he gave me the gill, I coulda just went upstairs and told Judy or something, 'cause she told me to tell her. But when I tell Judy—

TEACHER: Uh-huh.

LEV: —or something, or when I tell Paul, I like, I get in trouble. I mean, that happened. I'll go up. And I'll tell Paul and he'll be like, not so much Judy, but Paul. And I tell him, and I told him before 'cause Reuben—remember the thing with Reuben?

TEACHER: Yes.

LEV: He was like—Paul was fine, and then Debbie came over, and Debbie

52. Student mediators help fellow students deal with their animosity (clockwise from left: teacher, mediators, students).

was like, well, I think it's your fault. I see you in here a lot, and I think it's your fault. And so, and I got in trouble and I couldn't go to, I couldn't go to recess that day. 'Cause, because I told that someone was threatening me.

ETHAN: That doesn't make sense for them to have done that to him.

LEV: So why am I going to tell people? Why am I going to tell an adult now? When I just get in trouble for telling? And then, and then Paul said today that it was gonna be, that it's like adults sometimes feel that when I go to, that I tell too much or, like, if I'm always crying, never cry wolf. But that's not—no, I always—no, I'm always crying wolf, that adults see that, but how do I know if it's not real or real? Like Reuben was just kidding, but I didn't know.

TEACHER: Right. I remember that time—

CARLOS (*overlapping*): Right.

TEACHER: —but that worked out. That's been fine with Reuben.

LEV (*overlapping*): Uh-huh.

CARLOS: I don't think it's wrong for you to go tell a teacher because if they, they encourage your school not to use violence, then I don't see what's wrong with you telling the teacher. If, if Paul or Debbie don't want to listen to you, I think that you should probably come to one of us or something. And maybe we, between us, is going to probably come back in a group if it ever happens again. And solve the problem. 'Cause if—I don't see how Debbie or Paul come off saying that it's your fault and all that stuff. That doesn't make any sense.

ETHAN: I think that they do that because, 'cause when I do, when I tell Judy, right? . . . she says, did you do something to provoke it? And then I end up getting in trouble for saying something.

TEACHER: So it must be very hard then, because on one hand, you don't want to hit the other person or get into some kind of fight, and then if you go and tell, you feel you're—

ETHAN: Going to get in trouble.

TEACHER: —you're going to get in trouble—

CARLOS (*overlapping*): [*Inaudible.*]

TEACHER: —so we need to kind of figure out a way probably maybe that the teachers and students talk about a way of, of dealing with those kind of things, right?

LEV: And if you tell, kids are like—

TEACHER: That's fine.

LEV: —you're always, you're always telling people. You're always telling grown-ups. Why can't you deal with it yourself? Are you, you always tell on other people. I'm not even gonna say anything to you 'cause you always tell. Or, like the time, when he—like a couple of months ago, he said something about my mother. And I stepped in the back of his shoe and he turned around and hit me.

TEACHER: I remember that.

LEV: Well . . . when I went and told Judy, everybody was like, oh, when I didn't do anything back, I said, stop, because I don't want to get in trouble. Everybody, my friends, they were just like, that, that's, like, stupid. I can't believe you did it. If I were you, I woulda hit him. I woulda beat him up.

CARLOS: Well, in that case, you do—you should step ahead, like. I'm not telling you what to do, but I'm sort of—this is sort of like a suggestion. You should just step ahead of him and think for yourself, because when you're in trouble your friends are not going to be around to tell you all these things. And you're going to be the one in trouble, not them.

LEV: Hmm.

CARLOS: So, if they're telling you, they're provoking you to hit somebody, it's just because they want to see a fight. They want to see you, you know, be—if you want to—like you going to win the fight. They want to see you win a fight. And everybody be like, yeah, you won. You beat that guy's butt. That, it's not worth it. You make your own judgment and, you know.

TEACHER: Well, in—maybe we can start to think about ways that we can avoid certain things because both of you know exactly what provokes the other, right? You both know, as I say, how to press each other's nutty button. Right? So, the idea, maybe instead of thinking, what do we do if the other person does something, do we tell? Do we go to mediation? Do we go to a teacher? Do we fight it out? Maybe what we need to do is step back and start a little bit earlier. What can the two of you do to stop provoking each other?

CARLOS: I think [*inaudible*]—

TEACHER (*overlapping*): You know? So . . .

CARLOS: —they said they want to avoid each other. Now, we're not—

TEACHER: Well, they're together. The thing is this: they're together five hours a day.

CARLOS: Every day.

TEACHER: So let's—we have to come up with a solution that's realistic. If you weren't on the same floor, you know?—you weren't in the same house. And you weren't in any of the same classes, and you said you were going to avoid each other, I think the—

CARLOS: I think that maybe that would be possible, but you guys see each other like every day. Four or five hours during the whole school day, you guys are with each other. So I don't think you're going to go on for the rest of your life not talking to each other and avoiding each other.

TEACHER: Mark, you were going to say something.

MARK: Since, since you're in a room together for like five hours, could y'all come up with some kind of agreement between the two of you that can, like, if anything like this were to happen again, was to happen again, could you change the outcome of it?

LEV: Uh-huh. Just, just ignore him.

TEACHER: Would you be able not to say things about his mother and father?

ETHAN: Uh-huh.

TEACHER: Would that be hard for either of you to do?

ETHAN: No.

TEACHER: So, do you think you could agree to that?

ETHAN: Yeah, but it's that he's talking about my clothes—

TEACHER: Alright, wait, wait, wait. Okay, now, would you be able to agree not to talk about his clothes?

LEV: Uh-huh.

TEACHER: Is there anything else that you talk about to him besides his mother? Think of—can you each think of the things that you do to—

LEV: It's not—I mean—

TEACHER (*overlapping*): Okay. Is that it?

LEV: —I won't talk about his clothes or anything, but it's not going to stop.

TEACHER: Well, well, let's—we'll see, right?

CARLOS: Let's just give it a, let's try to—

CARLOS AND MARK: Let's just give it a try.

TEACHER: So, neither of you are going to talk about mothers or fathers to each other, correct? Right?

ETHAN AND LEV: Right.

TEACHER: You're not going to speak about his clothes. Ethan, is there anything else that he speaks to you about that, that upsets you? . . . [*Ethan shakes his head no. To Lev*] Is there anything else that he speaks to you about that upsets you?

LEV: Nobody in my family, and don't talk about me behind my back. 'Cause I'll be . . . I'll be absent and I'll come in the next day, and he'll have said something about—

TEACHER: How do you know?

LEV: 'Cause people tell me.

TEACHER: How do you know that he said it? We, we've done this before. How do we know that some, that, you know, when somebody else comes and tells you—

LEV (*overlapping*): I ask him. I ask him.

TEACHER: And then he says he did?

LEV: Yeah.

TEACHER: So . . . would—so, okay, I'll extend it to both of you. Both of you won't talk about family members, brothers, sisters, aunts, uncles, right? Fathers.

CARLOS (*overlapping*): And not behind each other's backs. You guys just—

TEACHER: Would it be possible if you had something to say about Lev that you could say it to him? I don't mean about teasing, but I mean, if something he does that displeases you or it makes you angry, you don't like, would you be able to say it to him?

ETHAN: Yeah.

TEACHER: It's a hard thing to do, but—and the same with you, Lev, if, if Ethan does something that displeases you, would you be able to go up to him?

LEV: But, but don't you think it would turn into being like—start making fun of me? Do you think it would turn into something like that? Well, if you said, Ethan, well, it really annoys me the way you, you, you do that or something, start making fun of me, you know, it—I mean, don't you think it could happen like that? Don't you think by, by—

TEACHER (*overlapping*): Is that a bad thing to say? Is it bad to say to somebody, look, you know, it really bothers me when you talk about me. And I feel, you know, it makes me feel uncomfortable to be at school. It doesn't make me feel particularly good. And I really don't like people talking about me. If I said that to you, would—do you think that would be a horrible thing that I said to you?

LEV: I mean something else. I can't understand why would he say anything else? Like, if you have a problem with somebody or they do something or something.

TEACHER: Yeah?

LEV: And I think that would turn into an insult if you said that to them. Don't you?

TEACHER: Did you think I insulted you when I just said that?

LEV: No, but I'm talking about other things and, and, I mean, if you like—

TEACHER: Give an example, then.

LEV: I don't like the way you always, you're always bothering people and you're always doing, you're always, you're always trying to get other people in trouble.

TEACHER: Well, what's the difference between what you said and what I said?

LEV: Mine was saying about other people?

TEACHER: That's right. Did you notice I said "I"? I don't like it when you talk about me that way. I don't like the way it makes me feel. I'm not talking about you, am I? Who am I talking about?

LEV: You.

TEACHER: Right. It makes—it's a difference, right?

ETHAN: Yeah.

TEACHER: So, I'm not attacking you. It's saying about how I feel and what, you know—

CARLOS (*overlapping*): You just—

TEACHER: Not—I'm not accusing you, right? I'm not saying you started this, right? Either of you, right? So—

CARLOS: So we came to an agreement. You guys agree not to call each other names or talk about each other's mother and all the other stuff that you guys agreed to—

TEACHER: Well, you got to say all the other stuff, what it is.

CARLOS: Well—

TEACHER: We have to be specific—

CARLOS: —not talking about his clothes and he—and not his haircut or whatever. And he's not supposed to talk about your mother. Or your family. Or bother you. You two guys agree to that, right?

LEV: Yeah.

CARLOS: And that's how it's going to be. Alright?

TEACHER: Mark, I think you were going to say something?

MARK: Oh, if you do have any other problems, you can come to one of us. And we help straighten the problem out. Possibly have another mediation and sort, and congratula—

CARLOS: When you see your friends, you know, you tell them that whatever you—the conflict you two had was solved, so that prevents rumors, you know, from people going around still saying that you two guys don't like each other and stuff like that.

TEACHER: How you feeling?

ETHAN: Fine.

TEACHER: And you?

LEV: Okay.

TEACHER: The other thing is that, you know, it might be that something comes up and it might not be that you necessarily need mediation, but you're not really sure about how to handle something or, you know, how something might go, and you could find Carlos or Mark and run it by either of them, you know?

ETHAN: Yeah.

TEACHER: And, you know, they'd—

CARLOS: We'll be more than glad to help.

TEACHER: Right. And it won't be about, you know, fault or tattling or whatever. They'll just be happy to talk to you about the situation. Would you feel comfortable with that?

LEV: Uh-huh.

ETHAN (*overlapping*): Yeah.

TEACHER: You feel all right about that? [*To Mark and Carlos*] So, congratulate them—

CARLOS: Oh, yeah. You guys did a good job.

LEV: Thank you.

CARLOS: Okay. [*Shot of crowded school hallway, lots of chatter. Cut to shot of Debbie talking with student and her father.*]

DEBBIE: She should be reading a book a week. Aside from her schoolwork. She should be doing that for three hours. She should be doing, as we say, two hours work at night of school-related work. Ten hours a week. And that's why we stay open for—we're open from three to five every day. And we're open all Saturday morning. So that a student who wanted to could put in all, could put in ten hours of work under our supervision. If that's more, if that's better than what they, than going home and doing it. But the getting into the habit. And that's the difference between depending on Sonia. I want her to have the habit. That's why we keep saying, habits of work. Habits of mind. So you're just stuck with it. It's like somebody have the habit of getting up in the morning and they, brushing their teeth, if they didn't do it, they'd feel awful all day, right?

FATHER: Okay.

DEBBIE: That's what a habit is like. You just can't stop yourself. It's just part of you.

FATHER: Okay.

53. A teacher advises a student and his mother regarding college plans.

DEBBIE: That's what we want it to be. When she's studying this year about what's an American, I want her to have a habit of every time she reads a newspaper, or talks to you, does anything, she's got a habit of asking certain kinds of questions. A feeling—not feeling right till she's answered them. Of having the habit of always having a book in her hand. So, when she gets on the bus or in the subway or she's waiting for the doctor, when she's going Friday to the doctor's appointment, she should be getting a lot of work done. She should be—and if it's not even work, she should always be having a book with her. It's just a habit of always saying, "Oh, I have twenty minutes on my hand." Whipping out a book to read. She hasn't got the habit of writing in school when she does the journals. She's not serious. Doesn't put her mind to it. [*Cut to MS of teacher Shirley talking with student and his mother.*]

TEACHER (SHIRLEY): You asked about the postgraduation plan. The crucial part of that is, Tyrell says he wants to work as a detective or he wants—

MOTHER: CIA, something like that.

SHIRLEY: Which means that, my projection is for him to probably realistically apply to a school like John Jay, if he's staying in the city, to do criminology. [*Inaudible*] this is, I'm just thinking in terms of the courses that he needs. Given that, then, he needs a certain kind of a transcript to get into that school, and it has to be a fairly strong transcript. We should see all, nothing less than satisfactory. I mean, we should really push from there on, okay.

The internship, then, he will be up for an internship next fall, and what we will try to do is to get him something in an area that's related to criminology in some way, shape, or form.

MOTHER: Do they have anything, like, within the school or the institute that can more or less go over what his future goals are to where, you know, focusing on some of what his weaknesses and his strengths are? You know, in other words, just like I'm not trying to take the full judgment from him, but just like having someone to work on it besides myself, because he gives Mom a very hard time.

SHIRLEY: Sure. Sure. But that comes in part of the—

MOTHER: Advisors?

SHIRLEY: College advising, yes. And he, the good thing for you is you sort of know what you want to do, so the other part then, it's up to you to try to work towards that.

MOTHER: Because it takes a lot of reading.

BOY (TYRELL): But I don't care [*inaudible*] what she'll say—

MOTHER: In other words, what I'm saying is from what I'm reading, the reports that I'm getting, that you're getting, from what I'm reading it says reads more, needs reading, needs more reading, needs more reading. I don't know which, I do know but I'm not going to say if you're strong and you like to read, right, and in this area that you want to go to it takes a lot of reading.

SHIRLEY: Yes.

MOTHER: Criminology takes lots of reading.

SHIRLEY: Well, but you see, he is very capable. Anything he needs to do now, it's up to him. So he has to have the will and then he'll be fine.

MOTHER (*overlapping*): Exactly. So you have to do a lot of research on what this work entails, so this way you can be sure this is what you want to do before your internship.

SHIRLEY: Now, [*inaudible*], let me ask you a question. He has always said to you he'd like to do detective work, so you're hap—, comfortable with that?

TYRELL: No.

MOTHER (*overlapping*): Not really, but it's his decision and I'll respect it.

SHIRLEY: Alright. Now, are you thinking of his staying in the city for school or are you think—, you would like him away from home?

MOTHER: Of course I would—I really don't want him to leave. [*Laughter.*]

But I think it would be a good experience. I think that it would give him a sense of responsibility, and I think it would be good if he could explore going up to a campus away from home.

SHIRLEY: So you are, so you wouldn't mind then if he, if he had the opportunity to go to another part of the, you know, maybe if a state university, part of the state university outside of New York.

MOTHER: There's a group of, no, I wouldn't, there's a, there's a person or two that we associate ourselves with and they help the junior high school students within our mosque—

TYRELL (*overlapping*): High school.

MOTHER: —that we go to—the high school students and graduates, and generally it's like Plattsburgh College.

TYRELL: Plattsburgh, yes.

MOTHER: Plattsburgh.

TYRELL: And Albany.

MOTHER: Albany.

SHIRLEY: And Albany State.

MOTHER: They have, you know, and this individual has been very, very, very good, and, um—

SHIRLEY: Also, you know, we do have, we have one student this year in Albany. Did you know Francine?

TYRELL: Yes.

SHIRLEY: She's at Albany and rather liking it and doing very well, and they have a very excellent support system.

MOTHER: Yeah, because this was the same individual that I had actually set a meeting up with you for because we were going to ask what was his—he's a social worker and he did a lot of tutoring and he was going to try to set Tyrell up to where he could start focusing on what he needs to get into his college.

SHIRLEY: But it's good to know that he would be interested then in Albany and Plattsburgh.

MOTHER: John Jay is perfect.

SHIRLEY: Yeah, I thought of—

MOTHER: I agree with John Jay.

SHIRLEY: Oh, yeah. I know, I thought of it only for the subject matter, but—

MOTHER: But I think—

SHIRLEY: We would also look at Albany and Plattsburgh.

MOTHER: Yeah, because I'm also focusing on the fact that he's very comfortable in this area here, you know, in the city—

SHIRLEY: Yes.

MOTHER: —and that can be dangerous to a certain degree.

SHIRLEY: Yes.

MOTHER: You know, so if it's a new environment, it might not take as much from him entertaining himself with the other things.

SHIRLEY: Okay, I hear you. In other words, it would be nice if we had a vacation from you. [*Laughter.*] He can get sent away.

MOTHER: Well, he's been a, you know he left me for a year!

SHIRLEY: Yes, I know.

MOTHER: Because of his education.

SHIRLEY: Right. And he did well with it.

MOTHER: He went to Africa, he did perfect.

SHIRLEY: You liked it, right?

TYRELL: I didn't want to come back.

MOTHER: But it was time.

SHIRLEY: Alright.

TYRELL: It wasn't time for me. It was time for her. [*Cut to shot of school hallway with student traffic, followed by shot of school stairwell, then by shot of teacher hurrying down hallway. Cut to shot of teachers' curriculum meeting.*]

TEACHER (DAVE): I propose that since we, that we accept the idea of a literature piece as part of the exit portfolios for Eighth and Tenth, and that each division now go back and work out, decide for themselves, what that, what that means, and that we then bring it back to the full group for further discussion.

TEACHER (JOHN): I like that proposal very much. I have a feeling it may be problematic because I think the hardest problem we're going to have is agreeing across divisions, and that, so my fear is that if we decide, if we become invested in something that we decide separately from the, from, you know, from the other divisions, then that could lead to sort of harder positions and make compromise more difficult.

DISCUSSION LEADER: To respond to that, John, I think what, the process of us finding pieces that kids have already worked on and if we as a division can come to the full group after much discussion and say this is what we see as a distinguished literature piece, this is what we see as a satisfactory one, and this is what we would see as an unsatisfactory one, however we decide to do it, when we bring that concrete work, that's when the three divisions will get together and discuss what that means. But until we do that process, how can we have the discussion? Yes?

TEACHER (LORRAINE): I would say that they're two different subjects. You can mix them, but I don't think, I think that the skill that we're trying to build here in terms of looking at literature is looking at, let's say, a novel and being able to pull out symbolism or being able to trace the development of a character or something like that.

DISCUSSION LEADER (*offscreen*): Jonathan.

JOHN: My feeling is a bit different. I think I'm more in favor of sort of looser categories. Like a literature paper would be something where the kid's project is to start writing perhaps about something which we would call literature, you know, like literary texts, something we classify as fiction or poetry as opposed to a, what we would classify as a history or social studies type. And one of the reasons I sort of feel this way is because, and it relates to discussion we've had in Division 2 about sort of empowerment of students and students becoming engaged with their work, and first, to a certain extent I think that many of these categories are really arbitrary. I think, you know, in graduate schools they're increasingly being broken down, and I think, I think that we want to sort of allow students the more freedom to respond to things and develop their own ideas. And I, for one, would like to keep it loose so that I don't have to get into the position of applying certain straitjackets to kids and say this is not, this is a something else, you have to be thinking more along these lines. I'm fuzzy on this, but, you know, like so the history would be something which is, you know, about events past and that literature be perhaps something that is about, you know, texts which are usually classified as fiction or poetry or something like that, and that *how* kids go about writing about those things we, and what they, in fact, the content of their thought is, we keep pretty loose, so that they're free to really sort of engage in and empower themselves as much as possible.

DISCUSSION LEADER (*offscreen*): Okay, Dave's next, then Shirley, then Richard.

DAVE: Okay, two things, maybe three, I'm not sure. One, I think that the difference between what I heard, what John wanted to say and Lorraine said is not as far as we might think, as I, as I initially thought we might have, because what I'm heard was a connection to literary text, a looking at literary pieces, poetry and prose, and doing some investigation. And what I heard John say was he wants students to feel free to explore avenues in their own particular ways, and a part of me responds to that, but another part of me has another reaction. I have a student right now, who simply says, who doesn't yet have the, any, the self-whatever, to think he can do work, the work. And his response is, I can't do it. And it was a major moment of education when I said, you mean you can't do it yet, and he picked up and said, okay, I can't do this yet. So what I'm saying is, in my mind, we're creating broad categories. We're creating categories, and I agree, they're arbitrary, but they're there to say this one field of endeavor, this is another field of endeavor, and this is another one. Later on, or maybe at some point when you feel strong in each of those three, you won't want to keep them distinct. You may be able to put them together in some sort of sophisticated fashion that you see Toni Morrison doing or like you'll see in a graduation, a graduate program. Anyway. So that, but they don't know what the categories are. They don't know what their choices are. They don't know what it is that they can play with. And I think, and I, I really feel that as long as we keep it fuzzy so that they are free to roam, they sometimes get lost. I think there will be students who will, who will appreciate these categories, and there will be some students say basically fuck you, I'm not going to stick with these categories, I'm going to do it my own way. I think those people should be supported and strengthened, but I think it's, majority of the students want to do it but don't know where to go, and that's why I think these categories need to be in place and then individual teachers will say, you know, this is really awkward, Jim, you don't have to do it this way, when we see those students coming up against a brick wall.

DISCUSSION LEADER (*offscreen*): Okay, next come Shirley.

TEACHER (SHIRLEY): Ironically, I think that in the literature it seems to me that I, I don't want a strict alliance as I thought I did, because while it's true that you want, in a literature class, kids to understand all the forms of, all kinds of symbolism and what goes into a work, the different kinds of styles of literature, ultimately, because of the way our school is organized and even the way our grid, that rubric we use, dictates that we need to make certain kinds of connections so that if you're teaching *The Adventures of Huck*— we're teaching *Huck,* you need to connect it with the, some history, so that it's very difficult to sort of stop and say we'll only be dealing with the river as a symbol or the boys or the raft or whatever. You ultimately have to come to history. So, I see then—this is why I was arguing for kinds of what go into each of these categories, because we have to move from, we, we, in that we as a continuum where there are different kinds of things and we finally approach the ending, and ironically, the end that we approach is not the pure literature. It really is the fusion or the fuzzy line thing. So how, we need then—I think that we need to describe the literature expectation across divisions to reflect this wide, this long line of things that we need to do.

DISCUSSION LEADER (*offscreen*): Okay, next is Richard.

TEACHER (RICHARD): Well, I was thinking along the same lines. I was trying to think of examples of pieces of literature that we use in the different divisions that clearly all crossed this division that we, this boundary we've set up, like *Inherit the Wind.* So if you have a kid who's gonna analyze the play *Inherit the Wind,* they do all of the work of understanding drama as a form of literature and what that means, but they happen to be really interested in the rise of fundamentalism in the 1920s, and in your class you've talked about that and they bring in more of that to help understand, or they want to look at, whatever it is, they want to look at the character, what's his name?—the newspaper journalist and compare him to H. L. Mencken because they've, I mean—is that not—I'm just saying there are ways that kids—

FEMALE TEACHER (*offscreen*): [*Inaudible*] alright.

RICHARD: There are ways, well, I'm just saying, but so, therefore, you got a kid who's interested in journalism who then goes back and looks all about H. L. Mencken, which is different than someone who decides to write a paper about the 1920s for their history or social studies portfolio, who starts with a different series of issues that are really related much more to history, and then they happen to bring in the play *Inherit the Wind* to show their point, or in Division 1 when we do *Of Mice and Men,* you have a kid who starts with the, with the book and really analyzes the book and looks at it, but then decides they want to look at the migration of either workers from Oklahoma to the West or the migration of African-Americans from the South to the North during those time periods, which are issues that come up. And conversely, someone looks at the issue of the great migrations of the early twentieth century in the United States, and then they use *Of Mice and Men* as an example to support their social studies paper. Now, I think if we get to that point, we have really strong students. And it's, so it's just a question of saying you have to start, one, I think going back to what John was saying, one paper has to start with one set of texts or assumptions for his social studies and the other one has to start over here with literature, but they may end up being very—they won't be similar, but they may have a lot of similar information in them. I don't think that's a problem.

TEACHER (PAT): [*Inaudible*] that's the distinction you're making. Okay. But the student has to have a grasp of those basic concepts.

RICHARD: Right.

PAT: Which is why I would, I encourage us to get back to what we said we were going to do, which is to talk about what is, what should go into a literature paper, and I think to do that is not to say that we are making rigid distinctions between this is a literature paper and this is a history paper. I mean, if we understand that the end result, as someone said, is to have them be able to integrate those two categories. But they don't know, as Dave said, what goes into each one anyway, you know, then what you get this con—, some of those kind of mishmosh fusion papers, where the kids have an idea that they want to do that, but don't know what categories they should be working with. I mean, then we just, and I'm just going to go one more thing. Shirley and I went to this AP English conference back in the fall, and, you know, so what they do is give you the questions that they give on the AP English test, which to my way of thinking our students should be able to do. But actually, the difficulty most of them would have is that there are categories in there, there are—what would you call them?—things that our students have not been taught to deal with. They're just basic literary terms and issues that they have individually not had to deal with, and most of them could never do any of the, really they could never do this exam, they could not do it. And—

SHIRLEY: This is what I was thinking when we were saying, initially going to divisions and just talking out the kinds of things, the kinds of outcomes that had to be considered within the literature, which is really involving English. As I'm talking, I realize that all are English skills here, but can't divorce it. Because that has to be, that has to happen beginning with Division 1 to make those nice, high-falutin' things we want to have occur at the end possible. So that was where, I mean precisely what Pat was saying, how the kid, they gave us a piece of writing, it was about Dickens, and the guy looking at this beautiful baby. It was chock full of symbolism and if you were a good, if you had had all of that background, you could just light right into it and just have a ball. Our kids couldn't because they didn't have that. And that's what we want to be sure to have happen in these divisions now.

PAT: And a lot of the things have to do with fine distinctions in language,

54. Teachers discuss different approaches to literature in a curriculum meeting.

you know, like Shirley said, things like irony, like satire, that you have to have some familiarity with analyzing, you know, before you can do it with a larger work. Have to do it on a small level before you can do it on a larger level.

SHIRLEY: When you talk about that irony, I immediately thought to myself, well, how do we get kids to that point? And there are several steps that we can make sure happen so that what, that's what we need to brainstorm across the divisions to be sure we teach limericks, that they can have lots of fun with it, they learn to read between the lines, and that's something that you have at different stages, bringing in, until you get to the irony and sarcasm and the whole works.

JOHN: I just want to say that I think the Senior Institute has a difficult time, a much more difficult project than we in Division 1, Division 2 does, because some ways it was added afterwards and the school sort of grew and then all of a sudden we reached the Senior Institute and the Senior Institute is this key position because they're the ones that deal with reality in a certain sense. They're the ones that deal with the outside world, much more than we do in Division 1, Division 2. So in Division 1, Division 2, we're able to create this nice world, you know, that we're sort of comfortable with and we relate to each other and we, you know, we sort of interact. And then it goes up to the Senior Institute and all of a sudden you have these questions like what does an *S* mean in terms of the transcript, which kid is, you know, where are kids going to go to college, what are kids going to do with the rest of their lives, you know, how are kids going to face on the AP exam. So I think that's, those are serious issues that have to be confronted, how the school relates to the rest, to reality per se. But part of our school is also about changing what reality is, and I, so I don't, I think that we have to, we, just because the AP says something, I don't think we have to sort of say okay [*claps for emphasis*], we got to do that, because that would make us a, what I would call a traditional school. So I think we have to be reflective of that process and not be all, you know, 'cause I think we're onto something here and I don't think we need to necessarily give it up.

PAT: Well, actually, a couple of things. First of all, I'm really sorry you picked up, you know, you keep harping on this kind of AP thing.

JOHN: Well, I just don't want to make the reason why we do something is necessarily because some external body says we have to do it.

PAT: No, no. And actually, I'll explain as to the reason I brought it up is that, and Shirley probably has a different take on this than I did. When we went there, there were, I don't know, maybe seventy people, maybe fifty taking it. There was not, there were two New York public high schools represented. We were one and I think the humanity, High School for the Humanities, was the other one. All the other schools were private schools, they were suburban schools, they were schools in New Jersey, you know, Westchester County, they're all, you know, chi-chi suburbs where these kids go to school. So they get college credit for taking the AP test. Now, I mean I have no great love of the AP test, but I want to make sure that our children can at least go to college and not have to take remedial courses, reading or writing courses, and can compete on the same level with kids from private schools and suburban schools. So that that's the only reason that I brought that up. I mean, what we see in the Senior Institute, you know, I mean, I hate, I hate this, like, you know, the lower divisions and then there's the Senior Institute who deals with reality. I mean, it seems to me that all of us should be here dealing with reality from the time a kid goes to school, goes to school, we need to be preparing them for living outside of school, you know, in whatever manner we are able to do that. So that, you know, what we are faced with in the Senior Institute is kids who go away to college—for instance, I had an advisee who I thought was a very good writer. She's having a difficult time writing in college now, you know, because she's having a difficult time analyzing writing. She writes very clearly, but her writing tends to be very narrative, narrative style. She can tell a story very well. But she cannot analyze the meaning beneath it. And I feel very badly when I hear people say that, you know, because I feel there was something that I didn't do. So that she's having a hard time. You know, I feel like I'm responsible for that, you know. So all I'm saying, what I was saying, was that I think that we need to, you know, be more conscious of where, the world our kids are going into, who they're going to be competing with, that we want to, want them to be successful. If they go to college and they spend the first two years taking remedial reading and writing courses and they'll feel inadequate, then they're not going to stay in college. They're going to drop out, and then where will they be? So I just think as we think about, you know, so, you know, I mean, we don't want to, you don't want to get technical and rigid and narrow, but on the other hand, there, we want to change the world, but we also have to have, to prepare kids to live in the world at the same time. [*Cut to high-angle ext. LS of the school and neighborhood. Cut to shot of Broadway intersection with an ambulance speeding by, siren wailing. Two shots of neighborhood buildings. Cut to shot of three teachers listening to woman discussing Condom Availability Program.*]

WOMAN: We're here today to talk about condoms [*cut to CU of woman*], and part of the training that you've been going to to help prepare you for the Condom Availability Program in each of your schools includes this particular evening, which will just, one, instruct us about proper use of condoms, possible misusage and things like that, as well as let us try out the lingo and talking about it ourselves, because, as I say a lot, if we're not clear about how *we* feel about saying "condom," showing condoms, talking about condoms, or perhaps how we feel about talking to young people about it, we're probably not going to serve the program well, so that's what today is about, okay? I brought this for our talk today [*pulls out a large black dildo from her bag for demonstration purposes*]. We have a number of these. [*Some laughter.*] The most important thing about using condoms is knowing how to use them as well, as well as feeling comfortable with them, being able to talk about them. So we want to just make sure that we know how to use a condom. And, I mean, one of the things is that we want to check an expiration date on the condom package—and why don't I hand some of them out so you can look at them.

TEACHER (LORRAINE) (*offscreen*): I was told that condoms didn't have an expiration date.

SECOND FEMALE TEACHER (*offscreen*): On the box.

LORRAINE (*offscreen*): That they were on the box, yeah.

WOMAN: Well, the box, at the—these all, I'm sorry, David—I'll just pass these out—these all came in a box but they also have an expiration date on them. You should check that. You will—there are evidently two kinds of condoms that have been donated for the Board of Ed, one that is lubed—lubricated— and one that is not. You will want to ask, because if they don't have the stamped date on it you want to talk to—

FEMALE TEACHER (*offscreen*): '96.

WOMAN: —whoever's donating them, it's not helpful. But people need to be made aware that they should check the expiration date, because if they're using a condom past the expiration date, they're using something that's bound to be more risky.

SECOND FEMALE TEACHER: Is that a standard thing, as for, it could be four years old and still be good?

WOMAN: Yes, but well, it depends on where you keep them. Rubber, we all, the condom must be latex, but if latex is worn, and we say this to guys a lot, in the back pocket of a pair of tight jeans, although today they don't have to worry about that 'cause they wear the real baggy jeans—but if it's constantly rubbing up in some part of the body where it's really warm, here, you're going to wear away the material and the odds are you're going to weaken the condom as well. They're sitting in a box somewhere that's not on top of the engine of the car, they're okay, and that, that's what that is. You can have a lubricated or nonlubricated condom. This happens to be a nonlubricated condom, which is recommended for oral sex, but, and we'll do, use it for our purposes so we don't have to get all greasy. But the lubricants need to be with Nonoxynol-9, although there are pros and cons to that. There are lots of females who, and probably some males, but a lot of women claim that they get vaginal, increased vaginal infections from the chemicals in the spermicide in Nonoxynol-9. So people need to know that. Okay, so you've checked the date and you know whether or not it's lubricated. And we open the package, and we want to open the package—you can do these a little bit later, you don't have to do it right now. [*Woman demonstrates the procedure as she talks.*] You want to open the package gently so that you don't rip the condom, right? The condom unfolds only in one direction and that is often difficult, believe it or not. I know I still sometimes get confused. But you want to look at the condom to know which way it's going to roll down, because otherwise you end up unrolling it backwards and it's prone to get a nail in it, to rip, it's harder, it's more uncomfortable, therefore less likely—

SECOND FEMALE TEACHER (*offscreen*): [*Inaudible.*]

WOMAN: Huh?

SECOND FEMALE TEACHER: It almost looks like it wouldn't unroll there very easily.

WOMAN: Well, it would, very easily, but it's not easy.

SECOND FEMALE TEACHER: But it has to, it has to unroll against the skin, in a sense.

WOMAN: Yes. It's doable, and if you don't know that that's the wrong way you think that this is the way and why bother, it's too much trouble.

SECOND FEMALE TEACHER (*overlapping*): Right. Right. Right. And then you might turn it around and put it the other way and then you've already got some . . .

WOMAN: That's true, too. Yes. There's some pre-come on it and it could have HIV in it. Okay. So this is not a, this is a nonlubricated condom and if we were going to use it for sexual intercourse, I would recommend that we have a lubricant if possible, and one with Nonoxynol-9 in it, but most definitely a water-based lubricant, not a petroleum-base like Vaseline or baby oil or Jerri Curl or Crisco, which are things that are very readily available to people, and we don't necessarily think and—something just make it slippery—we don't think about what it's going to do to the latex. Water-based. You might want to put a little dab of this lubricant inside the tip of the condom, then pinch it, because you don't want air in the tip of the condom. So we put it on, we're going to roll it down. We're holding this and we're pinching out the air and we're rolling the condom down, okay, and we want to get out all of the air bubbles, if any, on the side as well, because if there's an air bubble on the side, or if there's air in the tip, when the man ejaculates, it can burst the condom, which is what a lot of people complain about, it breaks. And that's one of the main reasons why a condom might break, and using a petroleum-based lubricant will weaken the rubber and make it break. After ejaculation occurs—well, let's just stop for a second. Before ejaculation occurs, before we even put our condom on, we want to help the people be aware that you want to be aware of your partner's readiness. You don't just want to, I mean, we talk about it can enhance this issue of communication. We don't want to just rip it up, put it on, and stick it in, because we're not necessarily thinking about our partner. If our partner is very uncomfortable with it, that is going to increase the likelihood that we will not use the condom. So partner readiness is very important. Partner readiness includes a couple of things. It includes how do they feel about it emotionally? You know, do they think that you think they're a ho' or do they think that you think something bad about them 'cause you're using it, or are they not ready physically, so that they're not sufficiently lubricated that when you insert the penis with the condom, it's going to be even more uncomfortable physically. So partner readiness is an issue we want to discuss. Once the guy has ejaculated, we want to let them know that you can't kinda lounge around because two primary possible problems with the condom is slippage or leakage, and if a guy is inside a person's body with a condom on and becomes flaccid, it is likely that the condom is going to leak, because the penis is soft and not holding itself in the condom, and/or when he pulls out, will remain inside the person's body, which defeats the purpose of having a condom. So we want to, them to know that they want to pull out before they become soft. And when they pull out, either he or his partner should hold the base of the condom to prevent the condom from falling off and staying inside his partner, okay? Any questions or comments about that?

FIRST MALE TEACHER: You mentioned something that was very important there. During the whole time that this process is occurring, I would think that there's this constant communication. You mentioned about the fact about communicating with the partner, knowing when the partner is ready, asking the partner how does the partner feel about having the condom on, etcetera, etcetera. Case in point, what happens if the young man is in a situation and the young lady does not feel comfortable with the condom?

WOMAN: What do you mean, what happens?

FIRST MALE TEACHER: For example, I know when I've talked with a, a young lady, in one situation she said that she allowed her partner to use the condom, but she didn't necessarily feel comfortable doing it.

WOMAN: Uh-huh.

FIRST MALE TEACHER: And I asked, I said, well, if you're in that situation again, what would you do? Would you once again allow your partner to use a condom? She says, I don't really think so.

WOMAN: Uh-huh.

FIRST MALE TEACHER: So—

WOMAN: Well, we could discuss that now and we will also get into it later.

FIRST MALE TEACHER: Yeah.

WOMAN: But the question is, what would you tell somebody like that? What do you think you'd say, or what did you say?

FIRST MALE TEACHER: Well, I told her, I said that maybe what you need to do is to talk with your partner prior to you getting in that situation—

WOMAN: Uh-huh.

FIRST MALE TEACHER: —so that way you can express your feelings before that—

WOMAN: Uh-huh.

FIRST MALE TEACHER: —and maybe you need to get more information on the need of why you need to wear a condom—

WOMAN: Uh-huh, uh-huh.

FIRST MALE TEACHER: —to deal with the types of, the communicative diseases—

WOMAN: Uh-huh.

FIRST MALE TEACHER: —and that may help you understand why it necessitates your partner using a condom.

WOMAN: Did she talk about what made her uncomfortable? Was it physically uncomfortable, was it emotionally uncomfortable? Did she specify, or did you ask?

FIRST MALE TEACHER: She said that it felt physically uncomfortable.

WOMAN: Okay. So maybe your partner also needs to learn some things about when to insert the penis. Maybe you weren't ready. Maybe she doesn't even know it. People when they start having sex may not know these things and just do it, but they're not familiar with what makes them comfortable. I mean, girls, in particular, who are built very differently than boys, often have sex for years with never having an orgasm because they don't know what it's, they don't know what it's about, how to do it, you know, what makes it happen, and neither do boys. So those are the—I don't know what kinds of relationships you're going to have with the kids that come in, but if you're in a situation where you can get into that kind of discussion, it would probably be helpful to be as concrete in the questions that you ask as possible. Otherwise we provide an answer that is totally missing the boat, 'cause it's not that she doesn't understand the importance because of communicable diseases or sexually transmitted diseases. It may be that she's embarrassed and shy and she doesn't know how to say this doesn't feel good. You know, is this the way it's supposed to be?

SECOND FEMALE TEACHER: Am I doing something wrong?

WOMAN: Right. Am I doing something wrong? That kind of thing. And the guy might be the same situation. One thing that I didn't mention that I have to remember to mention is if a guy is not circumcised, it's very important for him or his partner to know that the foreskin must be pulled back before you roll the condom down, okay? And if you don't do that I think it leads to more discomfort for the guy and possible damage to the condom, okay? So let's just talk about the positives of why you want to put the condom on as soon as the guy is erect and distinguish between putting the condom on from having intercourse.

LORRAINE (*offscreen*): Right.

WOMAN: You put the condom on, one, because then you're [*snaps her fingers*], then you can play as long as you want and then you don't have to stop in the middle of playing, number one, it's a good reason . . . And what's another reason? Think of any other reason? What's happening even before the guy comes?

LORRAINE (*offscreen*): Pre-come.

WOMAN: There's always pre-come. And you don't want pre-come near you, because pre-come can infect you. It could also make you pregnant, but, you know, if we're talking about not transmitting HIV and we don't know who's infected and who isn't, it's . . . it's dangerous. So if you have a condom on, the pre-come is not going to be a problem for anybody. I'm supposed to read, say to you as a group that what you're supposed to do, when a student asks you for a condom, they are to receive three things from you. One is a man-ufacturer's instruction sheet and a card listing the risks of use and misuse of condoms. Actually that's two things, but that's what it says there. Now, this is the card.

SECOND MALE TEACHER (*offscreen*): And a condom.

WOMAN: And a condom, thank you! [*Laughter.*] Have you all seen this card yet?

SECOND MALE TEACHER (*offscreen*): No.

LORRAINE (*offscreen*): Isn't there a card, the one with all the diagrams on it?

WOMAN: No, that's not the card, that may be the instruction sheet that they're giving out. This is a card that discusses the risks and benefits of the use and misuse of condoms. Since I only have, happen to have one, they didn't come in the packet, I'm going to read this out loud, okay? "The, this is, the only 100 percent effective way to prevent the sexual spread of HIV and other sexually transmitted diseases is not to have sexual intercourse.

Abstinence. If you do have sexual intercourse of any kind, the only way to help protect yourself is to use a condom. The main reason a condom may *not* provide protection is because it is not used correctly. If you use condoms you can help protect yourself by reading and learning how to use them properly. The person making condoms available in your school can answer questions or can refer you to other people who can give you additional info on condom usage." The other side of the card says, "There are two reasons a condom may not protect you. One is it may break, two is it may slip and leak. Knowing how to use a condom properly can reduce these risks. If you have additional questions, you can ask the person who's making the condoms available in your school." Now, I'm bringing up these issues and I'm sure they could create a lot of anxiety and panic. There are resources out there, and in each of those rooms, wherever it may happen to be in the school, you should have resource lists for where kids can get medical attention, emotional attention, physical or psychological attention. [*Three ext. shots: a neighborhood building, a bridge, exterior of school. Cut to CU of Debbie on auditorium stage with girls' choir behind her.*]

DEBBIE: This has been a long and hard week and a particularly long and hard twenty-four hours, and we're all stirring with lots of emotions today. And we have a chance for half an hour to in a way settle in and welcome the Hazlett High School choir from Michigan. Some of you may know that this is the high school that one of our faculty members, Jennifer—where is Jennifer?—went to, and she was a member of this chorus. [*Applause.*] I shouldn't have said that because you're getting noisy again. They come to town because they're one of the very distinguished choruses, choirs, in the United States and they travel many parts around the world, and they're in New York this weekend to sing at a music festival at the Penta Hotel, where many high school choruses come, and there's a kind of judgments made about their, different aspects of their singing and musical work. So, they're nervous, they're nervous doubly. They're nervous 'cause they're coming to New York to sing in an important event. They're nervous 'cause they've come to sing to you. And they're probably nervous to be coming to New York at this difficult time. And I want to welcome them and thank you for joining us today. And let's give them a round of applause. [*Applause from students. Chorus stands on stage. Boy comes into frame.*]

BOY: Y'all can hear me? Well, I chose upon myself to come here and stand in front of stage and talk to all y'all Central Park East Secondary School students to talk about a little bit what we've been going through today. And I know from the Senior Institute that a lot of students are upset about what's

55. A student asks for calm before the guest school choir from Michigan performs.

been happening in Los Angeles and, and it bothers them a lot, and what's happening. I just wanted to tell them that nobody here's our enemy and that same way that the newspapers say and all these people that come visit us say that we have to stick together and that these people—from Michigan, right? [*laughter*]—from Michigan, not California, they're from Michigan, that what they're doing here they're doing here for us. They're not, they're not here to, to make us feel better, they're here because they like to sing and they want, they want to show what they got. And they're not our enemies either. Right here, they're nobody in this room that are enemies and, you know, doing anything drastic would just put us in a bad position and make us just like any other high school in New York City, which we're not. And, we just stick together and just stay with each other and not become enemies and show these people that we're not, we're not falling apart like other high schools in other states and other parts of the United States. [*Applause.*] I know, I know the Senior Institute is real upset and that they're real smart also, that they know violence isn't the answer and they know, you know, I know what you got on your mind and we know, but we have to do things peaceful way because we're not hiding anything from anybody. Showing, showing your anger to these people and to people in here isn't going to do nothing for none of us and [*applause*] that's it.

CHORAL TEACHER: We'd like to thank you for the opportunity to come and perform for you today. We're really honored to do that. We have read several articles in our newspapers from out of Detroit and Lansing about this school, and so it was great for us to come here and look around and see what it's all about. We're looking forward to talking with all of you after the concert about all sorts of things, including current issues. I think that you'll find that we all share a common philosophy about what's going on in our world. But first, we'd like to entertain you if we can. Our first choir in front of you, this is a combined women's ensemble made up of mostly freshmen, some sophomore, junior, seniors—ninth-, tenth-, eleventh-, twelfth-grade women—and they're going to sing two songs about love for you today. The first one is called "You Stole My Love," by Walter McFerrin. [*Piano gives chord, followed by choral performance. After first selection, cut to LS of students in auditorium applauding. LS looking down school hallway, followed by cut to MS of teacher talking to class.*]

TEACHER: First thing that you're doing is just simply presenting your policy, the policy that you have designed, that you have spent the last week or so developing. You're just going to present that. Okay? The second thing you're going to do—and there's where the fun begins—is, you're going to challenge your opposition's policy and try to figure out how to prove to us over there that your policy is better than their policy. Your goal is to prove that yours is better than theirs. Okay, alright, I made this suggestion to everyone, I'm going to make it again. While the, while this group is presenting its policy, you take notes on, on things that you think are weaknesses in their policy. Same thing is true for you. And going to be very few rules except that you should try to speak one at a time so that I can get clear notes. You should try to speak one at a time, simply so that you're all heard, but unlike when we had this censorship debate, there's no specific order, there's no particular back and forth, you're just going at it, and you're just gonna try to prove that your policy is better than theirs, and may the better policy win. Okay? Oh, we should decide on which group goes first.

GIRL IN ORANGE BLOUSE (TEAM 1): They did the coin and they got the heads. And we got tails.

TEACHER: Oh, okay, then I guess that means you're going to go first.

GIRL IN ORANGE BLOUSE (TEAM 1): Yeah.

TEACHER: You may fire when ready.

GIRL IN ORANGE BLOUSE (TEAM 1): No sick people that doesn't have a cure, like a disease-infected person, because they can spread it, they'll spread it to other people.

BOY IN GREEN SHIRT (TEAM 1): Okay, and another one is no communist,

56. The teacher explains the rules for a debate on immigration.

because they thought because they're against the government and they'll overthrow our country. And also no anarchists, so almost the same thing. And ten percent of people coming to America must work for two years.

GIRL IN ORANGE BLOUSE (TEAM 1): And no handicapped people without someone to, like, watch after them, which includes retarded and mentally ill people.

BOY IN BROWN TURTLENECK (TEAM 1): The quota is that no more than 500,000 people could come in one year, and no more than 35,000 could come in from each country.

GIRL IN BLUE BLOUSE (TEAM 2): Our policy is the SAM Act of 1992. Just in case you're wondering, SAM stands for Sarah, Adrian, and Marlene. Our policy states that 15,000 people from every nation should be allowed to enter the United States a year, but the people that will come after will be notified. All the people must pass a literacy test. They must, they then must have a, I mean, they must prove that they don't have a criminal record and they have to pass a medical exam.

GIRL IN BLUE T-SHIRT (TEAM 2): Okay, people that don't pass the literacy test will be, will get another chance at a mental ability test. This is to see if they have enough mental ability to learn how to read if they don't know how, and to support themselves and their family economically.

BOY IN WHITE T-SHIRT (TEAM 2): Any undocumented immigrant or illegal alien, alien, that comes into the country by false ID will be sent back to their country unless they're married, have unadopted children, or show that they can support themselves during the time that they came, that they came in till the time they got caught or a year after they came in the country. Refugees will not be sent back to their country. [*Applause.*]

TEACHER: Okay, now in, in any order you choose you may go at each other. Be sure to include members of the Congress. Go for yours.

GIRL IN BLUE BLOUSE (TEAM 2): Why can't handicapped people be, why don't—

GIRL (*offscreen*): Why aren't they allowed?

GIRL IN BLUE BLOUSE (TEAM 2): Yeah, why aren't they allowed?

BOY IN GREEN SHIRT (TEAM 1): Well, see, this is not for all handicapped people. It's for handicapped people that, you know, that they have no family there, they have nobody take care of them. Then they will be hopeless, you know.

TEACHER: How are you going to determine whether or not this handicapped person—

BOY IN GREEN SHIRT (TEAM 1): Not hopeless, but—

TEACHER: —can take care of themself?

BOY IN GREEN SHIRT (TEAM 1): What?

TEACHER: How you going to determine . . . how are you going to determine whether or not this handicapped person needs someone to take care of them?

GIRL IN ORANGE BLOUSE: (TEAM 1) Well, it depends if they—

BOY IN WHITE SWEATSHIRT (MANNY): Can I ask one question? Are people allowed to bring their children to the country?

GIRL (TEAM 1) (*offscreen*): Yes.

MANNY: So what if your child is handicapped?

GIRL IN ORANGE BLOUSE: (TEAM 1) The parent will take care of them.

BOY IN BLUE SWEATSHIRT (TEAM 1): The parents will take care of them.

GIRL IN ORANGE BLOUSE (TEAM 1): Not to take care of them, like watch after them, like if there's just like to be able like some people like they can't cook their own food, they can't get their own food, or they can't work, so someone has to take care of them.

GIRL IN BLUE T-SHIRT (TEAM 2): Wait, wait, wait, wait. If—

57. One of the student teams defends its proposed immigration policy.

BOY IN GREEN SHIRT (TEAM 1): If people have no arms or—

GIRL IN BLUE T-SHIRT (TEAM 2): Well, if their parents are worried they die. What happens to them after, you just going to send them back to their country, or they still allowed to stay?

BOY IN GREEN SHIRT (TEAM 1): They're allowed to stay.

GIRL IN BLUE T-SHIRT (TEAM 2): But you just said that—

BOY IN BROWN TURTLENECK (TEAM 1): Well, when you first come in, you need someone to take care of.

GIRL IN BLUE T-SHIRT (TEAM 2): But if they have, still have no arms or anything and they can't cook for themselves, they're going to have problems with that, and before you had said that they couldn't, that—

GIRL IN ORANGE BLOUSE (TEAM 1): They have to find someone to take care of them.

TEACHER: I think we're making some assumptions here that I'm not so sure, as a member of Congress, I'm just going to stand by and accept. We're making assumptions that simply because someone has no arms that they can't care for themselves. There was an incident involving child care in which a woman with no arms in the court changed the diaper of her infant child, to win custody of the child. So I mean, we're making some assumptions here that I'm not so sure we can buy into in this sweeping way. I understand why you want to restrict physically handicapped people, but I'm not so sure that I'm ready to do that. Sell me on the idea.

MANNY: They're people too.

GIRL IN ORANGE BLOUSE (TEAM 1): We're not saying that they're not people. We're just saying that some of them—

TEACHER: You're just saying they're not the kind of people we want in our country.

MANNY: Oh, so y'all don't want no immigrant handicapped people.

GIRL IN ORANGE BLOUSE (TEAM 1): Well, we didn't say that. We said that they should have someone to take care of, so that, 'cause they said before that they can't, they wouldn't let handicapped people in because they didn't have anyone to take care of them, they, 'cause they couldn't be able to have a job, or someone couldn't be able to have a job. It depends on what kind of condition they're in.

MANNY: Well, what if they know how to read and write and, I mean, not write, but what if they know how to read and speak the language but they have no arms?

GIRL IN BLUE T-SHIRT (TEAM 2): Are you going to let that just stop them? I mean, is that going to be the reason they [inaudible]?

GIRL IN BLUE BLOUSE (TEAM 2) (overlapping): Where they're smart enough to succeed in their job.

GIRL IN ORANGE BLOUSE (TEAM 1): I'm saying people that are like, I mean, that are in a wheelchair and they're like a whole part of their body is, like, not working or something. They need someone to take care of them.

TEACHER: This question of a literacy test and mental ability. Seems to me that you, that that has the same exact effect that their straightforward discussion of handicapped does. They're willing to say outright, we don't want handicapped people. Meanwhile, you're trying to pull the same thing on the sly. Well, you know, if you can read and write, well, you know, do you have the mental ability to—who decides whether or not they have the mental ability to be able to learn to read or write?

GIRL IN BLUE T-SHIRT (TEAM 2): Doctors.

TEACHER: What doctors?

GIRL IN BLUE T-SHIRT (TEAM 2): The doctors that are in where they come in, where they enter.

GIRL IN BLUE BLOUSE (TEAM 2): And they have to pass the literacy exam.

BOY IN BLUE SWEATSHIRT (TEAM 1): But how about if they don't, how about if they're not good test takers?

GIRL IN BLUE T-SHIRT (TEAM 2): What do you mean?

GIRL IN BLUE SWEATSHIRT (TEAM 2): If they can't take the test that that proves that they're not smart enough.

GIRL IN BLUE T-SHIRT (TEAM 2): No, what we're trying to do—

BOY IN BLUE SWEATSHIRT (TEAM 1): No, no, no, no, no!

GIRL IN BLUE T-SHIRT (TEAM 2): Wait, can I say something? You asked if they— [*Several voices simultaneously.*]

BOY IN BLUE SHIRT: People get nervous on tests.

GIRL IN BLUE SWEATSHIRT (TEAM 2): Yeah!

BOY IN BROWN TURTLENECK (TEAM 1): People get nervous on tests 'cause they know that if they, if they're, if they mess up the, they, they're messed up, so they get nervous.

GIRL IN BLUE T-SHIRT (TEAM 2): Can I say, try to make it, like, easier for the—we don't want them to come in and when they find out that they can't read and write and they can't get a job, we're trying to let them know that before they come in and, you know, start trying to get jobs.

GIRL IN BLUE SHIRT (TEAM 2): And if they can't, and if they come to America to succeed and they can't succeed, then why they going to come?

GIRL IN BLUE T-SHIRT (TEAM 2): What's the point? What's the point of just faking them and coming in and just having them find out that they can't get jobs?

GIRL: Alright, hold on a second. I got something for you, it's like two parts. You were the ones who said you weren't sending refugees back, right?

GIRL IN BLUE T-SHIRT (TEAM 2): Right.

GIRL: Okay, let's say if in their country they had a democracy, right, and they were, but they supported an anarchy. Would you send them back then, if they were fleeing to your country and they got persecuted for that?

BOY IN WHITE T-SHIRT (TEAM 2): 'Cause they were anarchists?

GIRL: Yeah.

BOY IN WHITE T-SHIRT (TEAM 2): No, we wouldn't. They're the ones against the anarchists.

TEACHER: Yeah, but you said that, you said that refugees would face no restrictions and these people would qualify as refugees if—she's right. These people would qualify as refugees. And now you're saying that, you know, you'd let anarchists come in. You want anarchists coming in here, disrupting our government, overthrowing our government? What kind of sense does that make?

BOY IN WHITE T-SHIRT (TEAM 2): I didn't know, I didn't know how many people would vote for anarchists here.

BOY IN BLUE SWEATSHIRT (TEAM 1): But how do you know if they are anarchists, if they just play like, in refugee?

GIRL IN BLUE T-SHIRT (TEAM 2): They have to prove to, they have to prove that they haven't committed any—what was it?—crime, that they were able to support themselves, and that they were living like normal people.

BOY IN BLUE SWEATSHIRT (TEAM 1): You said that you ain't sending *no* refugees back.

GIRL IN BLUE T-SHIRT (TEAM 2): Right. But that's—

BOY IN BLUE SWEATSHIRT (TEAM 1): You didn't say, you didn't say that they had to take the test!

MANNY: What if it was a murderer?

GIRL IN BLUE SHIRT: What if one-third of a country was—

MANNY (*overlapping*): —killed everybody.

GIRL IN BLUE SHIRT: I'm just saying, what if one-third of a country was anarchists in a country that had a democracy? You mean if one-third of that country came, and you wouldn't, you wouldn't send them back at all?

MANNY: What if he was a murderer in his country? What if he believes in killing?

GIRL IN BLUE SHIRT (*overlapping*): —they came to your country, you would send them to another country?

GIRL IN BLUE T-SHIRT (TEAM 2): Wait, wait. If they were going to face persecution if we sent them back—

GIRL IN BLUE T-SHIRT (TEAM 2): Wait. Right, if they were going to face persecution if we sent them back to their country, we wouldn't do that, okay.

GIRL IN BLUE SHIRT: But what if—

GIRL IN BLUE T-SHIRT (TEAM 2): [*Overlapping, inaudible.*]

GIRL IN BLUE SHIRT: Wait a second. Then what if they get power and they take over the American government, huh? And you're facing persecution.

MANNY: What if he was a murderer in his country? Would you let them go like that? Then they would think it's alright to kill people in the United States also.

GIRL IN BLUE T-SHIRT (TEAM 2) (*overlapping*): No, they would have, no. 'Cause we said they have to [*overlapping dialogue*]—yeah, and we said that in order to stay that they had to prove that they had not committed a crime once they've gotten here.

GIRL IN BLUE SHIRT: I got a problem with this. You're saying they won't be sent back. Let's say they're facing persecution in their country but you bring them here just to lock 'em up?

BOY IN BROWN TURTLENECK (TEAM 1): No, if they— [*overlapping dialogue*].

GIRL IN BLUE T-SHIRT (TEAM 2): —and have people spending tax dollars on these people that were facing persecution came to mess your country up and you putting them in your jails and I'm spending money for anarchists! I don't think so! [*Several voices shout at once.*]

GIRL IN BLUE SHIRT (TEAM 2): No. If they're criminal it's their fault, it's their fault.

TEACHER: Defend yourself!

GIRL IN BLUE SHIRT (TEAM 2): If they're criminals it's their fault, it's their fault, it's not our fault that they have, they have a criminal record and they will be sent to jail.

TEACHER: Okay, the question is this—

MANNY: [*Inaudible.*]

TEACHER: Wait, hold on, hold on, Manny, Manny, Manny, the question is this, okay.

BOY IN BROWN TURTLENECK (TEAM 1): Send them back [*inaudible*].

TEACHER: If they're criminals, right, why bring them in just to put them in jail? Why not leave them in their own country? [*Overlapping dialogue.*] Hold on, hold on, let me finish. Why not just leave these criminals in— Czechoslovakia? [*Overlapping dialogue.*] Yeah, but we let them in! Why let them in? [*Overlapping dialogue.*]

GIRL IN BLUE SHIRT (TEAM 2): We let them in, Ricky, because then if we just leave them going around, they'll kill people in other, in other countries.

TEACHER: What do we care about whether or not people are getting murdered in Czechoslovakia? What do we care? Why should I, why should I care about whether or not there are murderers loose in Czechoslovakia? The United States is not the world police. You know, we're not the world police.

GIRL (*offscreen*): They act like it.

TEACHER: We don't run around, we don't run around the globe arresting every criminal on the planet. [*Cut to shot of students in school hallway, one boy having angry words with a girl.*] If the Czechoslovakians can't handle their own criminals, that's their problem. [*Shot of boy going from hallway through door. Cut to CU of teacher talking with student about her writing.*]

TEACHER: That's a good sentence. "A lot of innocent people died." Okay, read this one.

GIRL: Also, some [*inaudible*] people who set fire and robbed the stores were not serious, they just wanted take advantage of the verdict.

TEACHER: So I would take out the word *of*. Also I think some people who set fire and rob the—

GIRL: Stores.

TEACHER: Stores, good . . . what do you mean they were not very serious?

GIRL: Some of them just take advantage.

TEACHER: You might want to be specific about why do you think they weren't serious, you know, that they weren't, that they really weren't unhappy about the verdict, they were just violent, they were, wanted to steal things. Okay? End your sentence there and start a new sentence: They . . . they just wanted to take advantage of the verdict. Okay, next sentence.

GIRL: It didn't, they didn't think the results will get after the affair, that would increases the hatred between whites and blacks.

TEACHER: Okay, try and tell me what you're saying there, 'cause I'm, it's a little confusing.

GIRL: Just doing what they want. They didn't think what the, whatever happened after the doing these things.

TEACHER: Okay. When you say they didn't think the result, what result?

GIRL: The result after they robbing the stores.

TEACHER: Okay, so they thought that they would get away with—?

GIRL: I don't know . . . yeah.

TEACHER: Okay. Because of this—again, you've got a very long sentence there. It makes it a little confusing where you're starting and where you end up. Okay. What is it that increases the hatred between whites and blacks? Is it the beating of Rodney King, is it—

GIRL: Yeah.

TEACHER: —the white cops getting off—

GIRL: Uh-huh.

TEACHER: —is it the violence, the burning and looting—

GIRL: Uh-huh.

TEACHER: —so perhaps you need to break this sentence up again into smaller pieces and be specific about what it is that you're, that you're talking about, okay? That was a good essay. I liked that. [*Cut to long shot of students in discussion group.*]

GIRL IN PURPLE SHIRT: It was really interesting 'cause it was also, it was about teenagers, like I was the only teenager there so they were like, everybody was like asking me questions. They said what do you think about this, it was like we're reading the papers. I was like, I mean, it was kind of like, I mean, it was kind of dumb, like the sheet that we read at first, like the boys thought it was kind of, because they spoke about his father a lot and what I see now in communities is that fathers aren't really involved with their kids anymore. Either they're not there or they just don't feel like it. And they were asking me questions, they were like, do you have friends like this or has this ever happened to you, and like, 'cause the girl, like her boyfriend left her and she thought she was pregnant. And I was like, yeah, I know kids like that. And then they started talking about how girls, like sometimes, how lot of teenage girls get into abusive relationships and stuff.

TEACHER: Can you explain that? What do you mean?

GIRL IN PURPLE SHIRT: Well alright, like—what do you mean, can I explain it?

TEACHER: What's an abusive relationship?

GIRL IN PURPLE SHIRT: It would be like a relationship like where the boy, well, he can, he can abuse you verbally or physically or sexually or whatever, and like they started off first talking about, oh well, a lot of, a lot of teenage girls seem to think that you can, like when you have a, when they have a boyfriend and he's like, well, no, you can't do this because I said so, that that's good, because it's like, oh, he's taking care of me and he's doing it because he really loves me. But in fact that's not the case. He's taking control of your life and you're giving him permission to take over certain amount of your life because, you know, just because, it's like a way of looking for affection, and they were talking about how we shouldn't be that way because a woman should have control over her own life, 'cause if she wants to go here she can go here, and if she wants to do this she can do that, you know, because a boyfriend is a boyfriend, he's not a husband or, you know, I mean, he's just not, he doesn't, he doesn't have the right to have that much control over your life. And then they got, and then they started talking about—

TEACHER: But a husband does?

GIRL IN PURPLE SHIRT: Huh?

TEACHER: But a husband does?

GIRL IN PURPLE SHIRT: No, no, I, that was a mistake, you know, like, but when you're in a marriage, I mean, you're in marriage, it's a different thing, I mean, you have to come together talk about things, you know. But anyway, so, and they were talking about how girls get, a lot of girls get into abusive relationships, and after a while they just don't know what to do because they think they have to accept things like that because that's the way that things are, because either they see their mothers being, like, you know, being beaten by their fathers when they're younger, or, you know, things like that. And like, like they were talking about how you can talk to kids and be like, you know, you can, you can show them that that's not what they have to, that's not how their life has to end up or be or whatever, you know, that girls don't have to, you know, you don't have to take that stuff from the guy and things like . . .

TEACHER: Any other, any comments from anybody else? What do you think? That was a pretty heavy day. But just in terms of, like, what you've been, you were thinking about in terms of your future or whatever kind of field you want to go in. Does this, like, does this help you at all, kind of some direction forward, some kind of ideas?

GIRL IN PURPLE SHIRT: Well, sort of, because see, before I went to the agency, I didn't really know much about, that's what, well, you know—well, now I know that I want to do something like [*inaudible*] like I can benefit like Latino people and stuff. See, I don't know exactly what that's going to be, but I know that I need to be more educated, like on issues concerning Latinos and stuff like that, because otherwise then can't help myself if I don't know what's going on with my people, and so and I want, like I want, I know, like I might even want to go into something like this, but like, like maybe a social worker or maybe somebody like Ivy Morales does, like she does training programs and—that's what she does, she does training programs. Like things like this, like I want to go into this kind of field because it's interesting and I think it's necessary. [*Cut to shot of hallway, a student and a teacher passing by the camera.*]

TEACHER: If you don't understand [*cut to girl at school drinking fountain*] that, then we need to have a conference with your advisor and your parents [*cut to two-shot of teacher and boy talking outside of classroom in hallway*], because I don't want you doing that anymore. I don't think that's unreasonable. Understand what I'm saying? You don't decide to get up and get your hat. That's very rude, and I don't treat you that way. Understand what I'm saying? If you don't, you have a real big problem. So, what are you going to do? You going to come back and sit down and do your work or are you going to fool around? You decide. You decide. You think you're being fair, you can go to Debbie and say I'm being very unfair with you . . . I'm not being unfair with you. [*Student turns and walks away out of frame right, then the teacher goes through the door back to his class. Cut to shot of Paul, teacher, and student talking.*]

TEACHER: Okay, Joanie is the volunteer. We have felt that we don't know the whole story about what's going on upstairs, and we now hear—

PAUL: Joanie, did you write this?

TEACHER: Yeah, she wrote that—

PAUL: You just wrote this? Okay. Yeah . . . ?

TEACHER: That we felt that on Thursday on the trip there was gossip going on that had some—and that note I showed you this morning, was from the trip on Thursday, and we just felt we didn't have the whole story. So we've asked some people and this and that, and here we find that there still is more, that the child has left the school and there's still more of this back forth, he said she said, and then—

PAUL: Which student has left the school?

TEACHER: JoAnne.

PAUL: JoAnne. Okay, you called Joanie, I'm sorry, you called JoAnne on Wednesday. We talked about school and everything. She told me that Ali and some other kid on the third floor called her and told her that Saffra and another girl was talking—

TEACHER: —Talking about her, and she told her cousins, and they said the cousins of the girl who's left school were going to come and jump Saffra and, okay, so now Saffra knew this Wednesday. First of all, nobody came to me to say that they had heard any of these rumors. Secondly, Saffra has not been in school since Friday, or today she's not in school. So I think that some-body has to call Saffra's mother and see if she's heard these rumors and if there's any problem from her point of view.

PAUL: Okay, I'll call.

TEACHER: Because that's a, that's a point they brought up before, but a point that we brought up, that if she ever felt threatened she had to tell us, okay. So I don't know if she's told her family, I don't know why she's out of school Friday and today.

PAUL: But Joanie, but Joanie, you, tell me, you just called JoAnne to say good-bye to her?

JOANIE: I just call her 'cause of friends and everything.

PAUL: Yeah, right.

TEACHER: See how she was.

PAUL: And she said, so Ali might know something about this, right?

TEACHER: Yes, so you might want to call—

PAUL: Right, let me call Ali, let me talk to Ali first and see if I can get any information.

TEACHER: Okay.

PAUL: Then I'll call Saffra's mother.

TEACHER: I think you need to talk to her.

PAUL: I will, I will.

TEACHER: Okay. Come back to class. Thank you.

PAUL: Thanks, Joanie.

JOANIE: You're welcome. [*Cut to FS of literature class discussion.*]

TEACHER: —you think of anything in the play that, that supports a deeper, deeper connection the two of them have?

GIRL IN TAN BLOUSE: I just wanted to say that you were talking about the issue of respect and everything and material items. I think that everybody, like a lot of people in this world, like lost all their moral values and every-thing. Like searching for this American dream. Like the dr—, like drug deal-ers and even big corporations, they don't care who they hurt. Like, they just messing up the environment and all so that they could live comfortably. And people need to think about that.

GIRL IN CHECKERED SHIRT: But I don't think it's going to get any better.

TEACHER: So, in the search for the American dream, was Lorraine Hansberry part of what, what her story is about, you're saying that you're taking it much further. Huh?

BOY (*offscreen*): It's destroying—everything.

TEACHER: The search for the American dream is destroying everything. I think that's part of her statement and what we're saying. We're taking this, this play takes place in the fifties. Fifties.

STUDENTS: Fifties.

TEACHER: And she dies in 1965, right?

STUDENTS: Yeah.

TEACHER: That's what this article just said. Now, here it's what?

GIRL IN TAN BLOUSE: In the sense that it almost destroys their family and it destroyed Walter's dignity. Almost did, when he was going to take that money instead of standing up for himself.

TEACHER: Okay. Now, it's twenty-seven years later. And a couple of you are saying that the search for the American dream has had some negative . . . stuff happen—

GIRL IN CHECKERED SHIRT: It is negative. The American dream, what is that? What people think the American dream is—I mean, for all of, all of the white family with the white picket fence and the dog, that's not how it is. I mean . . .

BOY IN BLUE TRACKSUIT: I think the American dream has changed [*inaudible*]. When America, like, had started, the American dream, when it started, used to be freedom of religion and freedom to practice what you wanted and freedom from persecution. And then the American dream was to have money and to have the, the life that you want starting with money, so to get a white picket fence and a nice house and a dog, you need money. To get land, you need money. To get your freedom at, at one time, there was money. If you were a slave, so—

TEACHER: And today?

BOY IN BLUE TRACKSUIT: Today—

GIRL (*offscreen*): You got freedom.

BOY IN BLUE TRACKSUIT: —it's pretty much money.

GIRL (*offscreen*): What money?

TEACHER: Well, I've heard two things. I've heard money is power, and greed come out of a couple of people.

GIRL (*offscreen*): And evil.

TEACHER: And evil.

GIRL (*offscreen*): They don't—

TEACHER: So which is it?

GIRL IN WHITE SHIRT: If you have a lot of money, you have a lot of power. It's like the saying.

TEACHER: So, okay. And, and how does it influence the dream then? If the dream was to get money—

GIRL IN CHECKERED SHIRT: Because, 'cause you need money to have the dream. I mean, you have to have money to get possessions and send your kids to a nice school.

GIRL IN POLKA DOT BLOUSE (*overlapping*): Without money, you ain't nobody. That's the way it is. Nowadays without money, there's—you're nobody.

GIRL IN WHITE SHIRT: You're nothing.

GIRL IN POLKA DOT BLOUSE (*overlapping*): You have nothing.

TEACHER: So, how does it fit with the, what you've been saying? That in the search for the American dream has now also had some negative effects on us.

BOY IN BLUE SWEATER: That's why it's evil—because everybody thinks with, without money, you know, you have nothing. And it's not really money, it's just what money represents, that makes it evil.

BOY IN BLUE SWEATSHIRT: Money is like the door to your dream. And the more, the more, the more that you have—

SEVERAL VOICES SIMULTANEOUSLY: The more money you get—the more money you have—the more you're going to get—the more—the more— they treat you—

BOY WEARING JACKET: I think people think it's more important than other people's lives. That's why that there's a lot of killing going on.

BOY (*offscreen*): Like drug dealers—

BOY WEARING JACKET: Like drug dealers, they want money. So they just sell drugs and have people killed for their drugs. That's why. So they can get their money. And everything.

TEACHER: So, where does the dignity come in, then, that we talked about with *Raisin in the Sun* and Lorraine Hansberry? Or does it come in?

GIRL IN CHECKERED SHIRT: We all want to be like all [*inaudible*], as much money and, you know, I—I think [*inaudible*] killed this person. No one cares now. It's all for the money—

TEACHER: So there is no dignity with all that money.

GIRL: That's why they're always saying, money is [*inaudible, overlapping dialogue*].

GIRL IN CHECKERED SHIRT: No, 'cause, 'cause when you have money, it's like everyone looks at you.

GIRL (*offscreen*): They worship you.

GIRL IN CHECKERED SHIRT: Yeah, they worship you 'cause you have money.

BOY (*offscreen*): Well, [*inaudible*] like. You have no money, you have no life.

TEACHER: Pursuing the American dream—it's never finished.

BOY (*offscreen*): There's always going to be something that you're not happy with.

GIRL IN CHECKERED SHIRT: I think that if you're happy, then that's your dream. If your dreams come true. Well, I don't think, I don't think—that that's—I think that there's—

BOY IN BLUE SWEATSHIRT (*overlapping*): The American dream's to live comfortably with a nice family and don't have to worry—

BOY IN BLUE TRACKSUIT (*overlapping*): That's not the American dream anymore. The American dream today—

GIRL (*offscreen*): No, but even if you don't have a family.

BOY IN BLUE TRACKSUIT: —the American dream today is not to have a family. The American dream today is what you *want*. [*Overlapping dialogue.*]

GIRL IN POLKA DOT BLOUSE: Right. Your dream is both: to have a career and be what you want as your dream, and also have a family.

GIRL IN CHECKERED SHIRT: Right. Because if you don't have a family, that—I mean, just 'cause you don't have a family—it doesn't mean, that doesn't mean that you—

GIRL (*offscreen*): You're not fulfilled.

GIRL IN CHECKERED SHIRT: Right. Like inside yourself. It doesn't mean that you don't have peace with yourself.

GIRL (*offscreen*): Only some people [*inaudible*].

BOY WEARING JACKET: I think that America is, like, too individualized just to have one dream.

BOY (*offscreen*): Yeah. That, that's—

BOY WEARING JACKET: Anything you want, it's just like—

BOY IN BLUE TRACKSUIT: If there's a standard that everybody pretty much has in their head, but we don't really go find them in our—the American dream isn't a unified dream. That's, that's why our culture's all mixed up. Our culture, where, where you could have your own say—there is no culture. It's our society. Our society's all mixed up, where you can have your own say and you have the right to disagree. Well, you also have the right to think differently. And you also have the right to have a different dream than, than your neighbor. Your neighbor might want money. But you might want peace and quiet. So, I don't—so in that respect, I change my mind, I don't think that there is an American dream anymore. I think that it's, it's just what you want and that's *your* American dream.

GIRL (*offscreen*): Right, right.

BOY IN BLUE SWEATSHIRT: Any way you want to live your life? Live your life. That's your American dream right there.

BOY IN BLUE TRACKSUIT: Now today, because of, you know, our ideas are so different, everybody has their idea. We tend to be selfish and think only about ourselves. That's, that's—

BOY (*offscreen*): That's the way the world is.

BOY IN BLUE TRACKSUIT: —that's why, that's why the hair spray analogy fits into that, you know. About if you buy hair spray, you don't think about the ozone. You just think about your hair. Well, if you want a job, you don't care about all the other people who apply for that job, you want that job. And if you're a particularly determined person, you'll do pretty much anything to get that job. [*Cut to shot of school hallway with sign posted, "Stop! Silent reading time. Please no other business until 9:30." FS inside classroom, followed by another view of same class. Cut to students walking in hallway past camera, followed by a cut to MS of one of the teachers in the placement meeting.*]

PAUL: Do we have anybody going to Wesleyan?

DEBBIE: Possibly. Earl.

MALE TEACHER (*offscreen*): Earl? No, because— [*inaudible*].

PAUL (*overlapping*): She thinks Earl's going to—you think he's going to choose Vassar?

TEACHER: I think he's going to choose Vassar, yeah. That's what's—my last time I talked to him.

PAUL: Well, we do have some kids going to Bard this year.

DEBBIE: Which is something new.

PAUL: Which is—we had—we did not have—

TEACHER (*overlapping*): No, we had no obligations last year to Bard.

PAUL (*overlapping*): But we have a couple this year.

TEACHER: We have several.

DEBBIE: (*overlapping*): And we have Clark. We have one for Clark.

TEACHER: And we have one for Clark, which is new. And possibly Hampshire, which is new.

DEBBIE (*overlapping*): One for Hampshire, which is new. We didn't apply there before.

TEACHER: Right.

DEBBIE: The School for Visual Arts, we have two this year.

PAUL: Right. That's new, right.

DEBBIE: We never applied anybody there before.

DEBBIE: Howard?

TEACHER: We didn't have anybody there last year. Last year we did—did we have—only been five—we probably made some applications—

PAUL: We made some applications?

TEACHER: —we probably did, but I don't think anybody chose it. I mean, I know nobody chose it.

DEBBIE: Morehouse is new.

TEACHER: Right.

DEBBIE: Where, where, where did Angela go last year?

TEACHER: Angela is in—

DEBBIE: Spelman.

TEACHER: Spelman. As is Tanya.

DEBBIE: NYU, we didn't have anybody last year, did we?

TEACHER: No. Nor applications, I don't believe.

DEBBIE: I didn't think so.

PAUL: Whose—Ian's going to NYU.

TEACHER: We have a couple of applications—

DEBBIE (*overlapping*): And Amilcar might—

TEACHER: —because Amilcar was accepted there. So he might choose that.

DEBBIE: Hmm.

PAUL: Last year we had one in Columbia. Who is doing well.

TEACHER: Right.

PAUL: We hear.

TEACHER: We hear, right. Yeah.

DEBBIE: If, if that's true, that's one of the bizarrest stories in America.

PAUL: Absolutely. [*Laughter.*]

TEACHER: But we—I tell you, some of our—[*Many voices talking simultaneously.*] We have only what? Our, our small group. Now, I'm telling you, I'm getting complaints from ones who got ours last year, not getting it this year. They're not at all happy up at Hobart–William Smith. Because they got four of our students last year. They hosted Pat up there for a, you know, she had a wonderful advisory trip up there, and they paid for everything and they were really great—

DEBBIE (*overlapping*): We have to keep remembering people for this. I mean, we should write them a profuse letter of something.

TEACHER: Well, I talked to her on the phone and I tell her how thankful— Telling them how [*inaudible*]—

TEACHER: —we are, yeah, and Pat has written back, right. She knows that. She's been very intimately connected with this—

DEBBIE: —who is—well, one of the other things we can do is we have more high schools in New York.

TEACHER: Yes. We can really connect them. And, of course, this meeting that I had, I really did, I put forth, you know, this Hobart-Williams—

DEBBIE (*overlapping*): —maybe somebody else—

TEACHER: —Smith as a good school for them. Right.

DEBBIE: They don't see us.

TEACHER: Right. It's just this one isolated school, right.

DEBBIE: So, they know that they're going to get other kids. They don't get us one year. They get somebody else. I know, but—and it might be interesting to pool the coalition school data.

TEACHER: Yes.

DEBBIE: You know, that'd be a nice thing. When this is all over—

TEACHER (*overlapping*): Yes, yes.

DEBBIE: —you have a few days to relax.

TEACHER (*overlapping*): Yes, yes. It's the same thing. We'll pool it all together and see where people are going.

DEBBIE: And see where people are going. And even publicize something about it.

TEACHER: Right, right.

DEBBIE: What we did. It looks good. It's nice. [*Counting a list*] One, two, three, four, five, six, seven, eight, nine, ten, eleven, twelve, thirteen, fourteen, fifteen, sixteen, seventeen, eighteen, nineteen, twenty, twenty-one, twenty-two. I mean, it's, it's like fifty percent of the kids are going to four-year private colleges. That's good. [*Cut to shot of woman at photocopy machine.*]

BOY: Perhaps you're just slow. [*Cut to shot of boys at computers.*] So just, so just [*inaudible*].

GIRL (*offscreen*): Y equals zero. Wait.

BOY (*offscreen*): Go. [*Cut to school hallway, Lorraine walking by camera shouting.*]

TEACHER (LORRAINE): Okay, so it's time for advisory, let's go. [*Cut to CU of student, Killiss.*]

PAUL: Killiss, I'm, I get real confused over this. I can't tell whether or not some of this you're holding back and not telling us the whole story on or some of this you're completely innocent about and just don't understand what your assignments are. I, I really get con—, I don't know if you have that feeling, too, where you do, too. But I just—I don't understand what's going on exactly.

TEACHER (BRIDGET): Well, my—well, I have a feeling. My feeling is that you know what's going on, but you're just not doing the work. Now, I could be wrong. But I think—

PAUL: Is there something to that, Killiss?

KILLISS: No.

BRIDGET: Okay, so we need to hear from you.

KILLISS: I was just saying that, that I do the work and I get, get it in.

MOTHER: Do you do all the work completely?

KILLISS: Yes.

MOTHER: And you get the complete work in?

KILLISS: Yes.

MOTHER: Okay, now you're saying, yes. Right? You have a draft of your male and female reproduction—

PAUL (*overlapping*): Oh, that's right.

MOTHER: —that you only turned in a draft. That you did not turn in a final. Right? Am I correct?

KILLISS: No, I never got that back.

MOTHER: You never got what back?

KILLISS: The male and female.

MOTHER: You never got that back?

KILLISS: No.

PAUL: How long—

MOTHER: What about the—

PAUL: Yeast.

MOTHER: —yeast inf—

KILLISS: Yeah, I, I have the draft.

MOTHER: —and you never did a final on the draft—on the re—, from the draft?

KILLISS: Right.

MOTHER: Right?

KILLISS: Right.

MOTHER: Okay. If you never did a final from the draft, how can you say Bridget did not credit you for the final for the draft? She may have—well, your name has nothing written by it, so therefore, I hate to say nothing, but this is the way that that seeing it, that's how it affects me. Okay? And so it's really nothing to me. Me, I would take it and throw it in the garbage somewhere. Okay? You know me as well or better than anyone else. And anyone listening to me should be able to understand, because I'm not biting my tongue. I'm not speaking in a language that no one doesn't understand. This is highly intolerable. How can I sit here and defend you in school and you going to play little games yourself? But feeling that you had done so well for this period, that you would not have had any Unsatisfactories, I went out and I paid eighty dollars for a first baseman's catcher's mitt. Do you think these papers warrant that?

KILLISS: No.

MOTHER: This is my last time sitting here before people, having to talk to you this way. Okay? Do you understand me clearly?

KILLISS: Yes.

MOTHER: Paul has the greatest respect for you. He has the utmost respect for your mind. Bridget has the greatest respect for you. They respect your mind. You only twelve years of age. If you choose to cry, you may go ahead and cry because, yes, you should feel sad inside. Because you are letting—you know who you really letting down? You are letting Killiss down. Because I am forty-eight years of age. I don't know how old they are. But we will be somewhere dead, and you know who's going to have to be here to look after Killiss? Killiss is. Okay? And we are trying to prepare you for today. So that tomorrow Killiss can move on and Killiss can advance. You can't ask for anything better. You can fool people, yes. But it will always show. Just like you learn. You see children having a good time, throwing rocks, throwing sticks and bricks. But in the long run, you would suffer. Well, it's the same difference here. Okay? Okay?

BRIDGET: You know, Courtney, today, for example, today he worked in class. He modeled the type of behavior I need to see all my students do. He was working on an assignment. This is maybe the first time in a long time I've seen you work on an assignment for two hours straight. Every ten minutes—

MOTHER (*overlapping*): That's hard for him, and I realize that that's hard for him.

BRIDGET: It's hard for any—

MOTHER: You know? And this is what I was—

BRIDGET: —but he did it.

MOTHER: —asking Paul.

PAUL: Yeah, it's—

MOTHER: Is it that—what is that, his mind can't focus on something that long? Yes, he'll read it and everything, but to actually sit there and work on it. Okay? Maybe—I don't know if the—for Killiss, if that, and I'm not trying to give you an out either. If that is a problem for him, okay? And maybe this is something where—like you—the example you just finished giving is what I was speaking to Paul—ask—trying to question him—

PAUL: Uh-huh.

MOTHER: —about I was using terms. And he says, just label terms, more or less. But this is what I actually mean. Okay? If this is a problem for Killiss.

PAUL: So Killiss, so Killiss really spent two hours today?

BRIDGET: Yeah, when—I mean, I saw him enough times today to know exactly what he worked on. It's still vivid in my mind, the pieces that you worked on. I have students who give me work every day, but cannot show me as much knowledge as you do. But they got *Ss* on their work. Because they're always trying. I need to see from you that you try.

MOTHER: Now, do you understand—

BRIDGET: Okay?

MOTHER: —a little bit more what she means?

BRIDGET: You give me these two: completion of work and meets deadline, and you will always pass my class . . . Alright? Those are my expectations. I, I—that's all.

PAUL: Okay.

BRIDGET: You complete your work and meet your deadlines, and you will always pass my class. The quality part you know I'm not—I'm going to challenge you on that anyway. Because that's what I do. Okay? But you will always pass when you do your work. Even when you get a job, you will always get credit for work you do.

PAUL: Do you think what's been said so far is true, or has some reality to it, Killiss? Yeah?

KILLISS: I don't know.

BRIDGET: What don't you agree with here?

KILLISS: The grade.

BRIDGET: What do you think you should have gotten?

KILLISS: A Satisfactory.

BRIDGET: Okay. Do you agree with the marks that I gave you? How would you have changed this report?

KILLISS: The participation.

BRIDGET: In class discussion?

PAUL (*overlapping*): Parti—, participation. "All Is Well."

BRIDGET (*overlapping*): Go ahead.

KILLISS: Understand, understanding concepts.

BRIDGET: Uh-huh.

KILLISS: The class activities.

BRIDGET: How would you change those? Where would—what kind of grades would you give it?

KILLISS: Major Areas of Strength.

BRIDGET: Which one? Participation in class activities?

KILLISS: Yeah.

BRIDGET: Okay.

KILLISS: And class discussions. And understanding concepts. And respect for others.

BRIDGET: So, you're saying a lot of these—three that I gave you All In Well, All Is Well, should be major areas of strength?

KILLISS: And meeting deadlines should be, and completion of work should be "Needs Improvement."

BRIDGET: Instead of a serious problem? Okay. The participation in class discussions and activities and respectful cooperation with others, I'll give you as a Major Area of Strength. 'Cause if I compare you with another kid, then that *would* be, okay? But when I fill out this report, I'm talk—, and I look— and I think in my mind, and I see Killiss Foster in my mind, I'll say participation in class discussions, yeah, All Is Well. He participates in class discussions. He's a verbal child. He's very articulate. This is what he likes to do, that's fine. So, maybe I should give you Major Area of Strength for that, though. But do you understand how I can give you an All Is Well? Meaning maybe there's something wrong with this report. But when I say All Is Well, I mean, you're doing A-OK. Okay? If you want me to give you Major Area of Strength, I have no problem with that. I will give you that. Okay? This report is an interim, interim report. In other words, if you continue to work, if you continue to give work in late or not give in work at all, I will have to give you a *U* for this semester. This is like a kick in the butt for you now. This is saying, wake up, Killiss, Bridget is not going to accept incomplete work or late work. Okay? This is what this is saying. This does not mean you are a *U* individ—, this has—this is me—in other words, I didn't want to give you any breaks. I don't know if Richard was giving you a break—

KILLISS: No.

BRIDGET: Okay? I'm not giving you a break for this report. Because this report is for me to tell you whether or not you're in trouble. And I'm telling you you're in trouble. Okay?

MOTHER: But did you also understand her and hear her well when she said, if she were comparing you with another child, she—your grading here is not on comparison with what any other child does in class. This is grading saying to Killiss only. That Killiss need—, he—yes, he does part of his homework. Or maybe he just turned in the draft. Okay? But you can do better. We respect you more. We love you more. That we don't want to see you sell yourself short. By just doing hard enough just to get by. Because we know that our little Killiss is capable of completing it to the max—to the fullest. You understand what she's saying to you? Okay?

BRIDGET: You, you—that's right. That's exactly it.

MOTHER: Do you understand? She's not comparing you with no one else in your class. No one in your advisory class. This is how she feels that you need to work for Killiss. No one else, but for Killiss.

BRIDGET: And it's going to pay off. All this—

MOTHER: Okay?

BRIDGET: —all this busting your chops, which is what I'm going to look at it now, it's going to pay off.

MOTHER (*overlapping*): It's the same difference when you—

BRIDGET: You don't think—maybe you don't feel that now—

MOTHER: —on the field.

BRIDGET: —but when June comes, when you start completing your work and meeting your deadlines, you're going to see the difference.

MOTHER (*overlapping*): And to show a comparison—

BRIDGET (*overlapping*): Maybe not today.

MOTHER: How does Michael hit the ball to you and Mikey?

KILLISS: Hard.

MOTHER: Hard. Harder than the other children, right? Well, that's the same thing—

KILLISS: I know.

MOTHER: —Bridget is doing to you.

KILLISS: —that's not right. [*Mother laughs.*]

BRIDGET: Well, then, then—wait a minute. When you were working today, Killiss, did I give you a hard time during that process?

KILLISS: No.

BRIDGET: Did I complain about the quality of the work you were giving me?

KILLISS: No.

BRIDGET: Because I believe that the quality of work you were giving me was good. Okay? And was that fair? Do you think that the way I was working with you today was in a fair manner?

KILLISS: Yeah.

BRIDGET: Was I expecting more than you could give me?

KILLISS: No.

BRIDGET: So, that's what, how I would envision it being every day for me and you.

KILLISS: No, but you, you are expecting more than what I'm trying to do.

BRIDGET: You mean, all I expect you to do is give in your work. Now, when you start giving in your work and you feel that what I say to you about your work is unfair, then we talk about that. Okay? And you let your mother know. And then your mother has some leverage, also. You say, Bridg, look, you say to your mother, look, Ma, this is the work I did. And Bridget says it's not good enough and I'm getting frustrated with that, then we will talk about it. I'm going to be very fair with you. Then, then we have something to work with, Killiss. But I have, if I have nothing from you, we have nothing to work with.

PAUL: Killiss, when we, when we think about teaching and what teachers do, we often use the metaphor of the teacher as a coach. She, Bridget wants your personal best. She's pushing you very hard. We're not going to accept less than your best. We're not going to push you. We're going to try very hard not to push you. Or make demands on you that are impossible for you.

But we're going to push you very hard so that you can give us and give yourself your personal best. That's what coaches do. And that's what they demand of people, and they push them very hard. Actually, Bridget's talk was a lot like a basketball coach, coach at halftime. Or a football coach—

BRIDGET: Uh-huh.

PAUL: —at halftime. And she's pushing very hard. And I think a lot of people resent that. And I think that you're feeling you're getting pushed real hard now, don't you? You are. We expect an awful lot of you, Killiss. And we're going to push you real hard. Killiss, you and I have had a lot of conversations together about being, about what you're going to do when you finish high school and college. You and I have thought about it. And you've told me about some of your plans. You have very high expectations for yourself.

KILLISS: What?

PAUL: You have to work very hard for them—

BRIDGET: What were you going to say?

PAUL: —to make them true.

BRIDGET: What are your plans?

KILLISS: I want to play ball and, if not, I want to be a lawyer.

PAUL: And you expect that of yourself, don't you?

KILLISS: Yes.

PAUL: So do we. It's hard, hard work. Both the ball—

KILLISS (*overlapping*): I'm not pushing myself.

PAUL: But you what?

BRIDGET: You don't push yourself?

MOTHER: You have ample time—

PAUL: I'm sorry. I couldn't—what did—I couldn't hear you. You don't push yourself, you say?

KILLISS: I'm pushing myself to the limit now.

PAUL (*overlapping*): Okay. [*Cut to two-shot of Debbie talking with student.*]

DEBBIE: Can I ask you what book you're reading right now?

BOY: I'm reading—I haven't started on the book. I just reads—

DEBBIE: What?

BOY: —through *Sports Illustrated.*

DEBBIE: Hmm?

BOY: I read through *Sports Illustrated.*

DEBBIE: You, you—

BOY: 'Cause I'm a-going downstairs—

DEBBIE (*overlapping*): —go downstairs to the library right now. Get me a book, and I'm going to give you these when you come back up with the book you're going to read.

BOY: I was going to go to public library today.

DEBBIE: Go to this one.

BOY: Alright.

DEBBIE: I can't be sure you'll do the other one. [*Cut to two-shot of teacher talking with student.*]

BOY: Anybody had a migration?

TEACHER (DAVE): What? Let me put it like this? There was—that land was empty. The land was empty. And the only way the land can be filled is if people came here. So people migrated. [*Cut to two-shot of Paul talking with teacher.*]

PAUL: Suppose the focus of the family conference on Thursday is his school? As it is a part of the family. He's acting out the family stuff in school. His school is crumbling. His schoolwork is crumbling because of the acting out of the family. [*Shot of girl at computer.*]

GIRL (*offscreen*): That [*inaudible*] my problems. Times twelve or whatever. [*Cut to three girls.*] I'm just told what I'm going—thirty-three degrees—

GIRL IN WHITE SWEATSHIRT (*overlapping*): This is the way it's laid out.

GIRL IN WHITE JACKET (*overlapping*): Wait, wait, wait, wait.

GIRL IN WHITE SWEATSHIRT: Okay. It's co-sine. Thirty-three degrees. Right. Now—

GIRL IN DENIM JACKET: Times.

GIRL IN WHITE SWEATSHIRT: This is, this is hypotenuse and adjacent, so adjacent goes on top. And hypotenuse goes on the bottom. [*Cut to shot of a boy at his desk.*] Right? And you divide. [*Cut to LS of Debbie and parents sitting at desks in a circle.*]

DEBBIE: Yeah, I want, I wanted to just—I was thinking about just telling you a little about why we organized the school this way, which I'm sure you've already heard. But I was thinking last night, which I sometimes write about that which—I'm hesitant to say with two students present—that in some ways we organize this school on the basis of what I knew as an Early Childhood Educator. 'Cause actually I'm a kindergarten teacher. And that's the only real substantial teaching experience I had was as a kindergarten and prekindergarten teacher. I had one, I had some other visions in my mind of the kind of schooling I went to myself. [*To students, who had begun to leave*] You have to find out afterwards why it's not an insult. [*Laughter.*] But you can leave.

GIRL: I have to go to the bathroom.

DEBBIE: Go ahead. [*Laughter.*] Just thinking, you were so annoyed to hear that you going to leave. I have two other images in mind. And, and often that they're—that are interesting to think about in connection with Early Childhood. One of the most powerful was the stories I'd hear about what Oxford and Cambridge were like. Two famous English universities. And in some ways, they're, they both to me seem like the same image. My image— I never went to Oxford or Cambridge, I don't know whether it's really true or not—but my image of that and my image of kindergarten are very much alike. And I think it's the years in between that worry me. That is, it's a little bit like a doctoral program. In many ways, a lot of the things, habits— that practices of this school are sort of like a doctoral program. Even the way you graduate from this school. You—we have fourteen little doctoral dissertations. We're trying to cut it back because it's a little bit too many doctoral graduation committee meetings. But many of our ideas are borrowed from the two extreme ends of the educational spectrum. The two places where we concern ourselves with what the individual's own interests, learning style, what's, what—how to engage them. In which we respect their independence, their capacity to take on serious responsibilities. It always used to seem, seem to me eerie that the kids who had been in my kindergarten, the first-grade teacher would say, you can't get him interested in anything. And I thought, well, they were very interested when they were in my kindergarten. Now, she wasn't necessarily a worse teacher than I. It was that we accepted the idea in kindergarten that we had to create an environment that would capture and engage students' interests and that we had to, as a teacher, learn about them and not by the tests we gave them on Friday, but our observation of what they were doing at work. And that developing certain attitudes and curiosity and passion for work, which we call "play" in kindergarten, is at the heart of our job. And the same thing is—I have the same vision of Cambridge and Oxford, that you have this one tutor—or advisor here whose job it is to try to figure out with you, together, what you need to do to end up being a well-educated person. And who can lay out the parameters of the kinds of things that will be expected of you in order to graduate from Cambridge or Oxford, and what lectures you might attend. What papers you ought to write. Who meets with you on a regular basis. And a few of his others, or her other students, to talk about those papers, to suggest revisions that, they could be made. A lecture that might help fill it out. Some books you might read in connection with it. But it's at those two ends that we take seriously what we know about how human beings learn, and in between we have a—we engage in a series of practices that are absolutely—conflict with everything we know about the most powerful, effective way in which human beings learn. So, in a way, when we organized Central Park East Elementary School, we tried to keep the spirit of a good kindergarten going all the way through six years. We did that for ten years, and then thought, with the help of Ted Sizer, why shouldn't we keep the same idea going all the way through high school? And, personally, in my opinion, that's what a good college is like also. And that's what a good life is like. It's finding people to have an interesting and important and powerful conversations with, and then seeing what you, else you could do to extend that conversation and carry it on again the next time you do with more facts, with more information, and in a more powerful position to think through those issues. And it's sort of this, in a way, the power of a good life is to be everlastingly involved, either internally or externally, with a terrific conversation. For which you need to know more and more in order to make that conversation go somewhere. It is certainly at the heart of what a powerful citizenry and a powerful democracy would be. And that is citizens who are in a position to carry on that public dialogue about the nature of their society, its purposes, and ways in which it could be improved. And in that sense, we have tried to design a school that will encourage that kind of habit of mind. So that it's, it's habitual, just a way you can't help but think. That every time you're in a situation, you'll say to yourself, I've got a theory about that. Or, I wonder if this is true. Or, I wonder what the connection between this is and that is. And I wonder why and how could I find it out? And isn't that a marvelous feeling? To understand it better and to be able to persuade other people or be persuaded. So, it's to create in this school from kindergarten through high school a conversation that might engage and capture students and that leads them to be more widely powerful in a larger world. Now, do we succeed? Yes and no. Just having a conversation with a seventh-grader this morning and her family who had been through our elementary school. And she had a lovely time and she enjoyed it very much, but actually, she didn't pick up that idea. She did pick up the idea that school's a nice place to be, but not that it was, that this conversation has not yet engaged her. And it's, but I do think that in talking to the graduates of our schools, in talking to our own students, and that they have begun to get that idea. It's like I've, I was thinking about my own education. The best part of my education may have well taken place sitting around the dinner table over-hearing a conversation that was carried on above my head. But which in-trigued me. And in many ways, the interage grouping, the kinds of rela-tionships we try to establish between students and faculty, are also efforts to, for kids to get a little, listen into a conversation that sometimes is being carried on above their heads. But which might intrigue them and interest them. So that's, that's the idea that we're struggling with. How to create a school that's powerful enough to turn kids on to the possible power of ideas in their lives.

[*Cut to exterior shot of school entrance. Cut to neighborhood street corner. Extreme high-angle LS of school. Extreme high-angle LS of Manhattan. End credits: Director, Producer, Editor: Frederick Wiseman. Photography: John Davey. Camera assistant: Evan Eames, Assistant editor: Victoria Garvin Davis. Assistant sound editor: Carolyn Kaylor, Editorial assistant: Andrea Lelievre, Titles: Marian Parry. Special thanks to the students, teach-ers, and parents of Central Park East Secondary School for their coopera-tion. Funding for this film was provided by: The Annie E. Casey Foundation. The Aaron Diamond Foundation. The Ford Foundation. Public Broadcasting Service. A Zipporah Films release © 1994 HSII, Inc. All rights reserved.*]

Public Housing (1997)

Public Housing, which was shot at the Ida B. Wells Housing Development in Chicago for five weeks during May and June 1996, was released the following year. The development was first built by the Chicago Housing Authority in 1941 on the city's south side and named for the African-American activist and cofounder of the NAACP who lived there. For many years the Wells Housing Project was one of the country's poorest inner-city neighborhoods, and the film documents the area before the subsequent process of gentrification began. *Public Housing* immerses us in the life of this neighborhood, showing a series of scenes involving community groups, schools, shopping, the local barbershop, mail delivery, and maintenance of the apartments. Several scenes emphasize the prevalence of drugs, unemployment, and crime—all major problems in the area—and how residents are attempting to address them. The important presence of the police is also shown, with officers making arrests, checking suspects, and assisting people. While many of Wiseman's films address racism in American society, *Public Housing* examines part of its legacy in its look at this impoverished inner-city neighborhood.

[Title on black background accompanied by the sound of a siren on the soundtrack. Quick fade-out and fade-in to extreme high-angle LS of Ida B. Wells Housing Development in Chicago, the first of seven establishing shots. The siren is audible over the first four shots of the series, all of which are high-angle LSs, and fades away in the fifth shot, the first ground-level shot of Wells. Shot of "Welcome to Ida B. Wells Homes" sign. This is followed by fourteen shots of various tenants outside, doing daily things. In one of these shots, a police car with siren wailing speeds by, and in another an ice cream truck plays "Pop Goes the Weasel." LS of building, followed by a

closer view revealing sign: "Ida B. Wells Homes Resident Advisory Council." Cut to MS of Mrs. Finner at her desk talking on the telephone.]

MRS. FINNER (*on telephone*): But it is an emergency. She's a young girl with a baby and nowhere to stay. She's going from house to house, and that's when I get involved . . . Joy, if people could go around the city and just see how many homeless people there are, how many vacancies . . . No, they, I was at the county hospital on Monday, and honestly, my heart was just aching to see people, women and men, laying around in the lobby of the hospital in the waiting room and all of these vacancies in public housing that are being tore up for the lack of people living in 'em. That's ridiculous. Just take my development, for instance, Ida B. Wells. With over two hundred and some vacancies just setting here waiting on somebody to move into 'em, and then they're going to tell me that there's a waiting list? You know, I don't mind getting up there before HUD and telling them just what I'm saying to you, because it's not fair. They want us to do a job. They want us to work for residents, which we do. You know, just take, for instance, over in the Wells Extension, the newly rehabilitated buildings. There is no way in the world that one hundred apartments should be vacant. There are, there's no reason why over two hundred vacancies are in Wells alone. There is no reason . . . No, I'm talking about those buildings over there in the Wells Extension that were just newly rehabilitated, that are just setting there. They got five-ten that really, we don't even want to go talk about five-ten, because they still have people living in those conditions because they haven't gotten them out yet . . . Okay. That was all done. That was all done. They're slow about getting the units ready for the people to live in. Those people over there have no lights, all kind of animals running in there. Nobody under the sun is supposed to live like that, and nobody under the sun should be homeless with all of these units vacant in public housing, and I think I might stand on that floor Wednesday and let them know how I feel about it . . . No, Tuesday night. I don't go to those meetings downtown. I do not go down there to six-twenty-six and waste my time setting up there hearing nothing. I'm for the residents and if I can't help my residents, I don't go where I can't help . . . Yeah, but you know what? What good is it going to do to screen people? . . . But what are you going to do with the ones, what are you going to do with the people that need housing? That's why we have all these, so—what's the need of all these social agencies? If you can't? . . . Well, they're gonna make it 'cause I'm not going, I'm not going to be one of the presidents that set back and see my residents being misused and being left because of rules. Some rules are made to bend, and when there is a woman and a baby on the street? You supposed—I would bend the rules, and I have been called down because of that, because I, for one, I care about people because you know why? I've been that route. I've been hungry, I've been homeless. Her baby's one, so, she could really get by with a one-bedroom unit that we got in here. Yeah, that's what she needs. First, I'm sorry. She needs that interview first . . . I understand, I understand your role, Joy, and if I went off, I humbly apologize, but see, I get so flusterated when I see units being torn up, windows broken out, fixtures being pulled out that causes the Authority double money to put 'em back in when, if a person moves out today and the unit is in good shape, somebody should be in there the next day. I can't seem to get anybody to hear our cry. So I guess what they want us to do is just go crazy and act crazy. I think that's what's gonna happen. Well, they're going to have to come up with a solution for Wells because I speak only for Wells. I'm not gonna let the units continually to be torn up when we've got a waiting list going out the door all the way down the street . . . Well, I don't, you know, I don't mind saying it, because you know why? C-H-A didn't hire me. Residents hired me. And I must be working for the residents. I've been in this chair for twenty years. And it just burns me up when, when I see things shouldn't be that-a-way. You know I just have to go off. And all the money, all of the money that these higherups are making in salaries and if anybody ever looked at the LAC president's stipend—they don't even call it a check—a stipend, they say you guys are crazy, but if you care about people, money is not everything. Money is not everything. Not to me it isn't . . . Uh, you can't give me the appointment today? . . . But even then, Joy, she knows she has, there's hope that she's going to get an interview. If it's a month off, there's hope that she's gonna be interviewed. When my people are hungry and there's a young baby on the street, she's a baby with a baby. That's the way I look at it. And they have nowhere to stay, going from door to door. That should not be with all of these doggone vacancies they got in public housing. It shouldn't be that-a-way. So, I'll wait to hear from you Monday at one o'clock. I'm making a notation on my calendar. One P.M. Alright. Thank you, Joy. [*Hangs up telephone, turns to girl*] Monday at one o'clock. Yeah, I will have something for you or either Tues—, Wednesday, I'll be up on that floor. They don't like for me to get up on the commissioners' floor. It shouldn't have to be. I'm taking care of your case. I said, I gave her till Monday at one o'clock to hear from her. If I haven't heard from her, then I'm going call her down there and act crazy. One o'clock. Doggone.

HOMELESS GIRL: Thank you.

58. The head of the Tenants' Council tries to get help for a pregnant girl.

MRS. FINNER: Have a nice weekend. Don't you get upset, because you have somebody fighting for you. Christ. [*Cut to LS of a woman hanging up clothesline, beginning a series of eleven shots of people outside their units or in the street. In one shot, a man stands outside building; a police car drives into frame left and the man moves out of frame right. After these shots, cut to a policeman approaching a woman on the street, the sound of his police radio audible.*]

FIRST POLICEMAN: Come here. I told you two hours ago, two hours ago, to leave this corner, didn't I? [*He looks in the hollows of fence posts in the area.*] Don't go nowhere.

WOMAN (DEBORAH PATTERSON): I'm not going to go anywhere.

FIRST POLICEMAN: 'Cause if I find anything . . .

PATTERSON: Officer, I don't have anything.

FIRST POLICEMAN: No, I ain't saying nothing. If I find anything. I'm about tired of you.

PATTERSON: Sir, you won't see my face no more, I bet you. [*Laughs.*]

FIRST POLICEMAN: I've got, I've got one, I've got one nerve left and you done got on it. I told you two hours ago to find something to do, okay? You just keep pushing me. You just keep pushing me. Now I ain't going to tell you no more.

PATTERSON: Alright.

FIRST POLICEMAN: You know what I mean.

POLICE RADIO: Ten-four. Thank you.

SECOND POLICEMAN: You have any identification on you? So how I know you live down there?

PATTERSON: I can take you up there and—

SECOND POLICEMAN: You're on the lease?

PATTERSON: Huh?

SECOND POLICEMAN: You're on the lease?

PATTERSON: Yeah.

SECOND POLICEMAN: You the leaseholder?

PATTERSON: No, I'm not the leaseholder.

SECOND POLICEMAN: Are you *on* the lease?

PATTERSON: Yes.

SECOND POLICEMAN: So if I check with the dispatcher, your name will show up on the lease? What's your name?

PATTERSON: Deborah Patterson.

SECOND POLICEMAN: Deborah Patterson. What building?

PATTERSON: Thirty-eight-thirty-three in nine-oh-six.

SECOND POLICEMAN: Thirty-eight-thirty-three in nine-oh-six? [*On police radio*] Twenty-eighty-two. [*To woman*] Nine-oh-six?

PATTERSON: Yeah.

SECOND POLICEMAN (*on radio*): Yes, can you give me some leaseholder information for thirty-eight-thirty-three South Langley, apartment nine-oh-six?

POLICE RADIO: Ten-four.

SECOND POLICEMAN: So I need to know who's on the roster? Who's on the tenant roster?

FIRST POLICEMAN: You got anything in your pockets?

PATTERSON: No, I don't have anything in my pockets, sir.

SECOND POLICEMAN: Is that a cigarette?

FIRST POLICEMAN: Let me see that bag.

SECOND POLICEMAN: Is that a cigarette?

PATTERSON: Yes, it's a cigarette.

POLICE RADIO: Twenty-eight eighty-one. Twenty-eight eighty-one. Go ahead.

FIRST POLICEMAN: You got a name on it?

SECOND POLICEMAN: Yeah, I'm checking.

POLICE RADIO (*woman's voice*): Twenty-eight eighty-one. Go ahead. [*Man's voice*] What's the status at thirty-eight-thirty-three? [*Woman's voice*] They want the leaseholder's apartment number and name, [*inaudible*] apartment number and name.

FIRST POLICEMAN: Where did you tell him you live?

PATTERSON: Thirty-eight-thirty-three Langley. Lucinda Patterson, that's my sister, she's the leaseholder.

POLICE RADIO (*man's voice, overlapping*): I'm inquiring the zone put out a few minutes ago, a large crowd of twenty to thirty people threatening to kill somebody over there.

PATTERSON: Might be Marcy Patterson 'cause that's what we call her for short.

FIRST POLICEMAN: You on the lease?

PATTERSON: I'm not sure. I suppose. He just asked me that. I told him yes. I supposed to be getting on the lease since I just moved over here to stay—

SECOND POLICEMAN (*overlapping, on radio*): Twenty-eighty-two, information.

PATTERSON: I was staying on Fifty-seventh and Ashland.

SECOND POLICEMAN: Be advised, Jason. They, like they was trying to have a gang meeting, and every time we ride through about thirty-eight-thirty-three, they'll disperse and run all over the place. So, that's probably what that call over the zone was about.

PATTERSON: I ain't in no gang. I swear.

SECOND POLICEMAN (*overlapping*): They're trying to have a gang meeting.

PATTERSON: You won't see my face no more.

FIRST POLICEMAN: I don't think I will 'cause you done ticked me off. You know. I gave you fair warning, you know. As far as I'm concerned, you don't belong right here. This is a high drug area. You know that.

PATTERSON: Right, I do. I just come up here drinking a couple of beers.

FIRST POLICEMAN (*overlapping*): You's probably dirty.

PATTERSON: No, sir. I don't have on a bra.

FIRST POLICEMAN (*overlapping*): Unless there's something about this shade tree you like or something—

PATTERSON (*overlapping*): But I can go home, very simple.

FIRST POLICEMAN (*overlapping*): 'Cause you been under it for like three hours. I know you can go home. I got no problem, you gonna go home. That's your last option.

PATTERSON: Okay.

FIRST POLICEMAN: To go home or to go to jail. Or find something else to do for the rest of the day.

PATTERSON: I truly prefer to go home.

FIRST POLICEMAN: Because you done, you done got on our nerves here. Now, we done gave you warning.

POLICE RADIO: Twenty-eight-eighty-three. It's clear.

FIRST POLICEMAN: And you better not be here tomorrow.

PATTERSON: I won't.

FIRST POLICEMAN: Whatever you do or whatever you doing, you better find a new spot for it. And you better hope he don't get nothing out of there. [*Cut to second policeman searching area.*]

PATTERSON: Not to put on me.

FIRST POLICEMAN: Don't put it on you. Yeah. Right. You wouldn't do that, would you?

PATTERSON: No, I wouldn't, sir.

FIRST POLICEMAN: You just standing up here soaking up the rays, huh?

PATTERSON: I'm ready to go home.

FIRST POLICEMAN: This is a nice spot, huh? When the last time you was arrested?

PATTERSON: 'Bout a month ago.

FIRST POLICEMAN: What was you arrested for?

PATTERSON: Theft.

FIRST POLICEMAN: What you steal?

PATTERSON: A outfit.

FIRST POLICEMAN: A what?

PATTERSON: An outfit.

FIRST POLICEMAN: You got arrested for what, uh, shoplifting? [*Cut back to first policeman and woman.*] At where? What store?

PATTERSON: Marshall Fields.

FIRST POLICEMAN: You been to jail for it yet? I mean, you been to court?

PATTERSON: It's March the 3rd. July the 3rd. What am I talking about?

FIRST POLICEMAN (*as a man approaches*): Who's greeting you, coming here?

PATTERSON: He's from right across the street.

SECOND POLICEMAN: My man, my man, let us finish doing what we're doing before you end up in jail. Okay? So, I will advise you to walk back that way for a few minutes and let us finish.

MAN: Alright!

SECOND POLICEMAN: Alright? Thank you. [*Cut to shot of a bus on the street, followed by shot of a street corner.*]

FIRST POLICEMAN: So, you got any outstanding warrants on you or anything? You go to court?

PATTERSON: July 3rd.

FIRST POLICEMAN: And when you was arrested before then, for what?

PATTERSON: Criminal trespassing.

FIRST POLICEMAN: In C-H-A? Same thing we about to get you on. How many times they arrest you for criminal trespassing?

PATTERSON: Once.

FIRST POLICEMAN: Once. You had a hard life?

PATTERSON: Really, no, I haven't. I've been had a pretty good life, but I've been off of work now going on almost a year. [*Cut back to woman.*]

FIRST POLICEMAN: You mess with drugs?

PATTERSON: No, I don't. I used to, but I went in treatment.

FIRST POLICEMAN: You lying, ain't you?

PATTERSON: No, I'm not lying.

FIRST POLICEMAN: You know you—

PATTERSON (*overlapping*): I stand up here and drink a little beer. That's about it.

FIRST POLICEMAN (*overlapping*): You, you, you out of treatment. You bettering yourself, but you still could look out for other people, right?

PATTERSON: No, that's because I lost my—look out for—I ain't looking out for nobody else and I'm struggling. How am I gonna look out for somebody else?

FIRST POLICEMAN: How old are you?

PATTERSON: Thirty-six.

FIRST POLICEMAN: Thirty-six.

PATTERSON: I've just, my furniture in storage. I just moved up on Fifty-seventh and Ashland.

FIRST POLICEMAN: So, you in some kind of drug treatment program right now?

PATTERSON: No, I just go to meetings.

FIRST POLICEMAN: 'Cause when you go to them treatments, you're not supposed to drink or nothing, right?

PATTERSON: I know. I know.

FIRST POLICEMAN: But you're drinking, which is breaking some of they rules. Right? That's just as bad as picking up the pipe, right? Far as I know, I ain't never been to treatment. I talk to people that go to that kind of stuff, though. So you might as well just pick up the pipe if you're going to drink, right?

PATTERSON: I don't think it's that bad?

FIRST POLICEMAN: You don't think it's that bad?

SECOND POLICEMAN (*on radio*): Come in, eighty-two.

FIRST POLICEMAN: You're gonna have to wake up. What did you say your name is?

PATTERSON: Deborah.

FIRST POLICEMAN: You have to wake up, Deborah. You're a pretty young lady. You still got a little beauty left in you.

POLICE RADIO: Over.

FIRST POLICEMAN: You still got a whole life ahead of you. I don't know what you're doing. I assume you somehow involved in this drug thing. Even though you're lying to me.

PATTERSON: No, I'm not.

59. Two policemen question a woman on the street.

FIRST POLICEMAN: You gonna get caught. You gonna get caught, and we're gonna lock you up.

PATTERSON: I bet you won't see my face out here.

FIRST POLICEMAN: You gotta stop it. I don't know if anybody ever told you that, but I'm going to tell you that. You gonna have to stop it. You still got a life ahead of you. You could beat these drugs, and I'm not going to give you no quick drug counseling thing, but you still got a life ahead of you. I don't want to be the one to lock you up, 'cause I still see potential in you, and I always talk to people when I see potential in them. You know, I see people— when I see you six months from now, all your teeth gonna be missing, you gonna have one eye hanging down. Half your ear gonna be bit off.

PATTERSON: I hope not, sir.

FIRST POLICEMAN: Well, that's the case. That's how it usually go.

SECOND POLICEMAN: Better get off the streets and get yourself together.

FIRST POLICEMAN: I'm gonna remember you. You gonna be my, you gonna be my special project. Every time I see you, I'm going to pull over.

PATTERSON: Alright.

FIRST POLICEMAN: You ain't gonna sell nothing. Get out of here, go home.

PATTERSON: Okay, thank you. I appreciate it.

SECOND POLICEMAN (*on radio*): Eighty-two, go.

POLICE RADIO: What number, what for?

SECOND POLICEMAN: Apartment nine-oh-six. [*Six shots of local street scenes and people in front of apartment units. Cut to exterior shot of one building, followed by FS of two exterminators working inside an apartment.*]

WOMAN: All behind my little doolie-gigs. I just put a pile of clothes in there to get, go get washed. Did y'all git them rats?

EXTERMINATOR: If not, they'll put, they'll put some poison down for you.

WOMAN: Oh, I'll be glad. I'm scared to go out my front door, I tell you. They're so fast.

EXTERMINATOR: Yeah.

WOMAN: And they get behind that back door. And I've got mine pretty good 'cause I been using this Tak, which is almost gone.

EXTERMINATOR: Yeah. Well, that's good. That works.

WOMAN (*overlapping*): Well, I've been using that, so I been doing pretty good.

EXTERMINATOR: It works pretty good.

WOMAN (*overlapping*): I'm glad I mopped my kitchen floor before y'all got here 'cause you know—

EXTERMINATOR (*overlapping*): Is that a powder or a liquid?

WOMAN: This here?

EXTERMINATOR: Yes.

WOMAN: This here is liquid.

EXTERMINATOR: Okay. If you have any powder, you know, you could put it down across the whole floor. You see. A lot of people like boric acid.

WOMAN: Yeah.

EXTERMINATOR: A lot of people.

WOMAN: It's high, too. I bought some, but I'm out now.

EXTERMINATOR: Well, a lot of people just put the powder down in the corner and that's it.

WOMAN: I'll tell you something else I got too that I've been using.

EXTERMINATOR: Let me explain this to you first.

WOMAN: Okay.

EXTERMINATOR: What you do is: before you go to bed at night, sweep and

60. A resident talks with an exterminator.

mop your floors. Then you take the powder and you put it across the whole floor, and then you go to bed. When you get up in the morning, get your dustpan and your broom and sweep up dead, the dead roaches. Put them in the toilet so their eggs won't come off. *Then* you take the powder and you sweep it into the corners. That's what you're supposed to do with boric acid.

WOMAN: Okay.

EXTERMINATOR: Now, a helpful hint if you want to. Get a very, just a pinch of sugar and put it on top of the powder.

WOMAN: Lady just told me that this mornin'.

EXTERMINATOR: Right.

WOMAN: My mom told me about the boric acid.

EXTERMINATOR: Well, it works. It works.

WOMAN: But I didn't know about the sugar till this morning. But I really don't have many roaches 'cause I got rid of 'em. But I was looking for that Chinese Chop.

EXTERMINATOR (*overlapping*): The Chop, the Chop is very good, but they say it causes skin cancer. So, you have to be careful with that. You have to use gloves when you're putting it down.

WOMAN: Uh-oh.

EXTERMINATOR: Don't put it where you're gonna be touching it at any time. Just put it in spots where, you know, you won't be touching.

WOMAN: Well, I put it all down there.

EXTERMINATOR: And if you don't, if you don't wear any gloves, don't just wash your hands, brush 'em, 'cause it gets in your skin pores.

WOMAN (*overlapping*): Okay. Oh yeah, hit my bottom of my table too. 'Cause my table—

EXTERMINATOR (*overlapping*): Okay. Well, he should put some powder up under there. Chris! Let's see, he should put some powder, 'cause see, if I put some liquid up on it, it could drop on the floor or something and get slippery. You might slip and fall. I don't want you to slip.

WOMAN (*overlapping*): Okay. See, that's why I caught myself mopping the kitchen before y'all got here. 'Cause I know you ain't supposed to mop it after y'all put the stuff down.

EXTERMINATOR: Well, at least for thirty minutes to forty minutes.

WOMAN: Oh, I thought it was two to three days.

EXTERMINATOR: Oh, no, no, no, about forty minutes.

WOMAN (*overlapping*): Okay, well, long as it's done I don't care.

EXTERMINATOR: And don't mop close to the baseboards. That's all.

WOMAN: Okay.

EXTERMINATOR: But other than that, I'm going to have him put some powder up under here because, you see, the haze, the haze will stay on, stick to the table.

WOMAN: Okay.

EXTERMINATOR: See, this stuff here will just drip down.

WOMAN: I'm glad y'all came. Now what time y'all coming next time?

EXTERMINATOR: Ah, the management will have to notify you all and notify us. They'll pass, we'll pass notices out when they want us to come out.

WOMAN: Oh, okay.

EXTERMINATOR: But it will be forty-eight hours before, you know, we get here. So you will have plenty of time to make preparations for the—

WOMAN: No, I just want to know what time y'all coming here, 'cause I'd like for y'all to come every month.

EXTERMINATOR: Oh, I wish we could.

WOMAN: You know, once you get it started and they go away, you don't want to see them back no more.

EXTERMINATOR (*overlapping*): Well, you see, it's not—

WOMAN: I like to sleep on my floor sometimes with this arthritis I got.

EXTERMINATOR (*overlapping*): Well, you see, it's not up to us.

WOMAN (*overlapping*): Yeah, I know you can't come all the time.

EXTERMINATOR (*overlapping*): It's not just up to us. Yeah, it's up to the management; it's up to the management. They have to—you know, if y'all go to the management and, you know, make out requisitions—you know, worksheets.

WOMAN: Yeah.

EXTERMINATOR: If it's enough of them, then they'll have us come out, you see, but if there's not, then they're not going to just have us come out for one apartment.

WOMAN: Well, you know what. This apartment has been broken into four different times. And I've been begging for a back screen door for about three or fo—, well, 'bout almost three years.

EXTERMINATOR: Well, what you going to have to do is stay on them.

WOMAN: I'm tired of filling out requisitions for the same darn thing.

EXTERMINATOR: I understand. See, we're just here for the infestations.

WOMAN: Yeah, well, I am glad you came.

EXTERMINATOR: Okay, well, I try to do the job—

WOMAN: Yeah.

EXTERMINATOR: —the way it's supposed to be done, you know. Because sometimes the people that come out only half-do the job.

WOMAN: I try to keep this little raggedy house clean, as much as I can.

EXTERMINATOR: Yes, ma'am. You know the main, the purpose of keeping the rodents down is to have a clean apartment.

WOMAN: I don't have no rodents. They outside. [*Both laugh.*] Thank God. I don't want them comin' in here either.

EXTERMINATOR: Okay, well, I've got to get on to the next apartment, but you have a nice day, though.

WOMAN: Okay.

EXTERMINATOR: And God bless you because you see, you know, a lot of folks, they don't care about how their houses look—

WOMAN: Well, I do.

EXTERMINATOR: —and what we are doing, you know. So, you take it easy and have a nice day and don't get too hot out here [*laughs*].

WOMAN: It'll melt off some of this fat.

EXTERMINATOR: Oh, yeah, mine too [*laughs*]. Okay.

WOMAN: Okay. You got behind my whatcha call it? [*Cut to shot of children in yard, followed by a shot of two policemen walking in street.*]

EXTERMINATOR: Exterminator man. Exterminator man. [*Cut to exterminator at the front door of a unit, dog barking.*]

WOMAN (*in apartment, through screen door*): Just a minute, [*inaudible*].

EXTERMINATOR: You want your apartment sprayed, ma'am?

WOMAN: Yes, I do.

EXTERMINATOR: Alrighty. [*Referring to lock on the door gate*] Can you get it? You want the whole house sprayed?

WOMAN (*unlocking gate*): No, just the kitchen out here and the bathroom.

EXTERMINATOR: Want some powder put in it?

WOMAN: Yes. Otherwise I can do it myself.

EXTERMINATOR: You want, you want powder put in it?

WOMAN: Yes.

EXTERMINATOR: We can put it in for you. Okay, I'm gonna spray and powder. How's that?

WOMAN: Yeah, because, I mean, I didn't move everything like they said.

EXTERMINATOR: That's okay. Don't worry about it. Let me get this for you. Watch your hands.

WOMAN: I can't take too much dust because I have asthma.

EXTERMINATOR: Okay. Hey, Logan?

LOGAN: Yeah.

EXTERMINATOR: You want to put some powder in here too. Just in the kitchen. [*Cut to LS of mailman coming down the street toward the camera and putting mail into boxes.*]

61. The Men of Wells discuss the lack of participation in community affairs.

MAILMAN: How y'all doin'? . . . Alright. [*Two ext. shots of development. Cut to shot of men sitting around a table in conversation.*]

MAN IN WHITE SHIRT AND TIE: Go to number two, where we was talking about dedication. James and myself came up with this, where we're saying that some of our positions are not being fulfilled, or our duties that we supposed to be doing. So James came over. He can elaborate to you more on number two.

MAN IN STRIPED SHIRT AND TIE (JAMES): The purpose of rule number two, dedication not being fulfilled, it's been a lack of communication throughout the community so far as different type of things that they wanted us to do within the community, such as a cleanup drive to help Chicago Housing get their feet on the map. And what happened so far as us being dedicated to that program, we was supposed to send ten guys over there to participate in the cleanup drive, and we only sent—six showed up. That's what I meant by dedication not being fulfilled. If we want, if we send ten guys over there, we want ten to show up. And if you put your name on that sheet saying that you's going to show up, we want you to be able to be a truthful man of Wells and show up with dedication.

MAN IN WHITE SHIRT AND TIE: Okay, with that I'm gonna go down to number four, where it says, what's wrong with the Men of Wells? Ah, with that, I would just like to say this. A lot of us was saying that we were going to do a little volunteering here, a little volunteering there. And, some of us have been lacking on our responsibilities, and the reason why we're doing it, I don't know. I would like for us to just talk a little bit on that. For example, some of us say we was going to work up, help with the school system up at Dolittle West. Some of us have showed up; some of us didn't show up. The reason why, you know, we don't know. Anybody who want to elaborate on that, feel free to do so.

MAN IN BLACK AND WHITE JACKET: [*Inaudible*], I guess. Well, I got somethin' to say. Well, I know I had to sign my name and I been comin' sometimes, I haven't been comin' because I have a two-year-old son. And most of the time I take care of my son alone and so, you know, I can't get up every day and, you know, and wake up and go up to Dolittle to watch other kids and, you know, not watch mine. So I think the responsibility starts at the home first.

MAN IN WHITE SHIRT AND TIE (*offscreen*): Exactly.

MAN IN BLACK AND WHITE JACKET: So I have to take care of mines before I can take care of anybody else's. So that's the reason why I haven't been comin' to some of the meetings. Some of the security guard checks.

MAN IN GREEN T-SHIRT: Well, it's—you know, that is a volunteer type of situation. You know, if you are able to make it and you got kids, you should make it. But if you have other, you know, other things to do, it shouldn't be no force type of thing or, you know, criticize somebody for not being there. I mean, some brothers show up and wants to show up, and I clap for that and stand up to that. We don't have to make it a mandatory type of situation, because a lot of people won't be able to make it different, you know, given days. Some will be able to make it, some won't. But as long as somebody from Men of Wells show up, it's showin' support for all us.

VOICE (*offscreen*): Right.

MAN IN GREEN T-SHIRT: And I appreciate the brothers that do make it, you know. I don't have kids that go to Dolittle, but I'm not saying I'm excluding myself because of that. I got other, you know, other things, you know, I have to do too.

MAN IN PINK SHIRT: Now granted we all have certain things we have to do but not—then what we have to do is choose our day.

MAN (*offscreen*): Right.

MAN IN PINK SHIRT: Know what I'm sayin'? So for the other brothers, those who are not here and myself and yo'self, we have to help pick up the slack. If Elwood have to stay home on Wednesday, whatever, then one of us need to fill that gap, you know. And I know that, first of all, that I've been one who's been lacking, but I was there yesterday and I spoke to Mr. Dumas and, you know, he was sayin' how proud, you know, of the Men of Wells he was for comin' to support. But every member has a part to play and we all accepted that role. So what we have to do is now try to get a calendar set up 'cause it is not going to end this year. Next year it's gonna kick off, and it's gonna be throughout the school year. We've just—this is a trial period for the last maybe month and a half. And you guys have done a really great job, as proved by what Mr. Dumas said. He said that he is really proud of Men of Wells, and let you guys know that he appreciates you, and his concern was that the attendance had been gettin' fewer and fewer. So we have to, like, make sure that for us who have, can't come on Monday, maybe we can make it on Friday. For us who can't make it on Wednesday might be able to make it on Tuesday or Thurs—, the individual have to pick a day, but we all should pick at least *a* day out of the week that we'll be there. And then, along with those who been comin' consistently, that means that we'll have a good, solid program goin' on and the young people appreciate it. I know that y'all been there. Y'all know, right?

VOICE (*offscreen*): Yeah.

MAN IN PINK SHIRT: You know I'm there in another capacity and them kids, man, embrace you and want to talk and hug ya. They just, they need that love. And to see some men, some African-American men from the community there, it means the world to 'em. Because some of 'em don't have no men in their home. You know, so that's a piece that's really gonna boost, you know, the group to another level and show the community where we really comin' from. So we just have to really deal, we have to deal with that. We have to, like, you know, call the members and ask, what day can you make it? And, you know, I commit myself to really making a very high effort to get away from my job and come in the mornin' and in the afternoon at least one day a week. And I let you know what day that'll be.

JAMES: When we say, what's wrong with the Men of Wells, we started out together as a strong group. And each member, in order to be strong as a group, you have to be strong for yourself. But not by missing those members, by not comin' to the meetin' and participatin' in various type of programs that we do. We just have to be strong for those individuals that's not participatin' in the program and just hope that they fall back in line.

MAN IN GREEN T-SHIRT: I know I haven't been participatin' in a lot of functions and stuff as of late. But I vowed that I will be participatin' pretty soon. There's a lot of things I've been dealin' with and I have to kind of get together because I just moved over to King Drive side. And I'm gonna participate and volunteer a lot more. And I really do speak from the heart and I say, I appreciate you brothers that do participate in a volunteer projects that we're doing. I think it's a good thing and never stop, you know. I'm sorry that I haven't been there because I have committed myself to certain things that haven't carried out the commitment, but I will kinda pick up the effort. I think we got a positive thing goin' here, and hopefully it'll get better. Not hopefully—it's gonna get better. That's it. Tell Eric when you see him, hang in there.

MAN (*offscreen*): That's right.

MAN IN PINK SHIRT: We want to help, you know, through this process any way we can, even if it's just conversation, lettin' somebody get the steam off. We want to help people move up, out, wherever they want to go, and then they gonna tell a story. They gonna say, man, that was a group in Ida B. Wells, Men of Wells, that help me move, you know? And so we ain't gonna be forgotten. And that's why we have to try to make positive impressions on people so that when they talk about us, it'll be in a positive way. You know, so that's why that part about fulfillin' our commitments and dedications is all good. If we say we gonna be there and we can't, then it's your commitment to call and say I can't be there before. You know, maybe they can contact someone else. It don't matter if it's me or whoever. It's, it's the commitment that made me say, hey man, I can't make it today. Then they can say well, man, brother Clark can't make it, who we got that might be able to? Or maybe Terry James say, well, he can't make it so I'll go. Even if they just go for a few minutes and say, look, Mr. Dumas, the guy was supposed to be here and couldn't make it. I came. I can't stay. But about ten or fifteen minutes, we show. That's what makes the difference.

MAN IN GREEN T-SHIRT: Due to the changes that's about to take place— we all know the changes with the HUD situation and the public aid situation, the membership drive might drastically go up because they gonna be a lot of things changin'. A lot of brothers wanna get right. You know, and the Men of Wells should be there to help 'em. You know, when you make a transition from this type of life to a better life, you want to have something to reach out to. And there's a lot of brothers waitin' to find out what is it that I can do to better myself in the community without havin' to go through a lot of drastic changes, you know, and participatin' in a meeting like what we doin' here—would be something that can start off in a positive manner. I mean, if you are gangbangin' or sellin' drugs or something like that, you can make that transition into bein' part of Men of Wells. And we need to accommodate the people that's goin' to be comin', because there's gonna be a lot of brothers that want to change. And we need a bigger space. We need to communicate a little better with ourselves, and some of these meetings, I mean gatherings, we give can help them.

MAN (*offscreen*): Right, and I was—

MAN IN GREEN T-SHIRT: And then we can take some of the kids to baseball games. I've only been to one baseball game in my life, one baseball game.

VOICE (*offscreen*): One?

MAN IN GREEN T-SHIRT: My uncle took me to the White Sox.

VOICE (*offscreen*): That's sad. [*Laughter.*]

MAN IN GREEN T-SHIRT: There are a lot of little kids that have never been to a baseball game before. So we can get together one day and escort some kids to a baseball game.

MAN (*offscreen*): Right.

MAN IN BLACK AND WHITE JACKET: You help somebody, they gonna help you. Because if you don't, you just sit around and say what we gonna do?, that's not gonna get nothin' done. It's time to start doing and stop saying. Everybody got lip service. That's what my boy, Tate, says all the time, lip service. He's tired of lip service; he wants to get some action. [*Four ext. shots of development, people going about daily life in the courtyards. Cut to CU of woman with baby, a crying boy on the soundtrack.*]

WOMAN: [*Inaudible*], you'd better come. [*Cut to shot of woman examining boy's injured knee. Shot of boys riding their bicycles by the camera. Cut to long take of three policemen searching three men against a wall. Cut to LS of children playing baseball in the courtyard, man in wheelchair frame right, followed by three more shots of people in the courtyard, the last showing the exterminator entering another unit as a man waters the lawn. Cut to LS of church rummage sale, people looking through boxes and tables of used clothing.*]

CROUCHING WOMAN: How you doing?

WOMAN IN GREEN SKIRT (DIANE): Alright. How you doing? Didn't know who you was bending over leaning like that.

CROUCHING WOMAN: Tell I'm bending over big.

NUN: JoAnne?

WOMAN (*offscreen*): Yes, dear.

NUN: Well, [*inaudible*]. How are you today?

WOMAN IN WHITE SWEATER: Baby, what is this? Oh, this a top.

NUN: Jeans are a dollar.

SECOND NUN: All those kinds of things are twenty-five cents.

WOMAN WITH BEADED BRAIDS: How much?

NUN: Twenty-five cents.

WOMAN IN WHITE SWEATER: Do you think that's a little too big on me?

NUN: It's a blouse.

WOMAN IN WHITE SWEATER: Because they strings at the top too, look.

BOY (*in background*): What's your name?

NUN: One, two, three, four, ten, twenty, thirty, forty, fifty, sixty. This would be—how 'bout five dollars even. Okay?

MAN: Okay. Hey, I will be right—I'm going right down the street where my cousin's at.

NUN: Oh yeah, okay, we'll see ya.

MAN: I will be right back.

NUN: Alright.

DIANE: Can I get a bag?

NUN: You sure can. Okay. I don't know if I have change. You don't have five singles, do you?

MAN: I gotta go somewhere in private. Go put on my outfit over another outfit.

NUN: We're out here every Thursday, and what you don't get, you know, what you don't see—well, you know. You're Diane, aren't you?

DIANE: Yeah.

NUN: How've you been?

DIANE (*overlapping*): Did you forget about me?

NUN: No, I didn't forget about you. I see you there.

DIANE: I've been alright. I've been alright.

NUN: Yeah? How's your house doing? You getting your furniture and everything?

DIANE: Naw, I gotta throw that away.

62. A resident talks with a nun at the church rummage sale.

NUN: Do you? How come?

DIANE: Everything just blew out because I got two TVs and the furniture is—see, I was trying to get some furniture from you, right?

NUN: Right.

DIANE: And I still got the same furniture, but it's time to go because—

NUN: Right.

DIANE: —you know—

NUN: Well.

DIANE: —the springs in the furniture—

NUN: That's right.

DIANE: —and you sit down on it—

NUN: Right.

DIANE: —and it's hurting everybody. But other than that—

NUN: Well, I have it down on paper, Diane. See, a lot of other—people have not given furniture like they did when I first started. I think everybody who knew me cleaned out and that was it. But I think now that the summer's starting, they'll be getting some more too. But you're getting too skinny.

DIANE: I know.

NUN: Are ya?

DIANE: Yeah.

NUN: Are you eating?

DIANE: Yeah, I'm eating. I eat. Just other things I gotta leave alone.

NUN: Yeah, hmm, that's right. Well, we'll pray for you too.

DIANE: I've been praying. For myself.

NUN: You'll be okay.

DIANE: I know.

NUN: We still love ya.

DIANE: I know. I've been off of it for about three weeks, though.

NUN: Oh, really? Good.

DIANE: I'm fightin' it.

NUN: Are ya?

DIANE: I'm fightin', I'm fightin'. As long as I keep going, it will be alright if I just can keep on going.

NUN: Uh-huh.

DIANE: Every time temptation come around me, I leave it.

NUN: That's right. And it's hard too.

DIANE: Yeah, it's real hard.

NUN: It's real hard.

DIANE: And I've been doin' it.

NUN: Hmm. Okay, that's pretty. Ooh, that is pretty.

DIANE: It's the only thing I see out here.

NUN (*overlapping*): Oh, wow. That's okay. You just keep coming in every— just keep coming back, you know.

DIANE: Yeah.

NUN: See, now she found some shirts and some shorts. I have a—you know, there is a lot over there, but I wasn't, I'm not into it yet. When I really get into it, you'll see all the good stuff [*laughs*].

DIANE: Yeah. So y'all school closed for the year, right?

NUN: Well, just until the twenty-first, and then it opens up again. They have school all year round now at Holy Angels.

DIANE: Yeah?

NUN: Uh-huh.

DIANE: I was gonna put my son in there, but I said, it's too expensive, I don't think I could do it.

NUN (*overlapping*): Right, that's true. There are some scholarships. But, you know, if you're really interested, just go and talk to Sister Helen, she's the principal.

DIANE (*overlapping*): I talked to one of them, and they gave me an application.

NUN (*overlapping*): Oh, did she?

DIANE (*overlapping*): I don't know who it was. But they gave me an application and stuff for my son. But I never filled it out because I didn't—the fees was too high for me.

NUN: Yeah, yeah, that's hard. Right, yeah, right.

DIANE: I really just come over here to talk to you.

NUN: I know. I like seein' you too. Okay, I'm gonna get some—oh, this must belong, this box belongs to somebody, does it? Okay, that bag.

DIANE: That bag is—

NUN: Do you have the money in your pocket? No one checked out anything yet, is that it?

WOMAN: I gave the dollar that I got to you.

NUN: Right. Oh nobody, that's what I mean, but no one else checked out. Okay.

WOMAN (*offscreen*): Oh, I had a teddy bear for him. Here it is. [*Cut to shot of man leaving rummage sale on a three-wheeled bike, followed by LS of people on the street as a police car drives by, frame left. Cut to a closer view of man in the background, sitting on a chair and staring at the ground.*]

POLICEMAN: This is what we're going to do. [*Cut to MS of policeman talking in a darkened apartment, the sound of the television, a combination of commentary and classical music, competing with his voice on the soundtrack.*] We're going to take you to the King Center first. There, they are going to take some information about you, and then they'll try to place you and try to find you a temporary shelter where you can go and stay. Then we're gonna try to get you a senior citizens home. Actually, that is what we are really trying to do. [*Policewoman turns down volume on television.*] It's gonna take a little time, so you're gonna have to be patient with us.

MAN: Good.

POLICEWOMAN: But in the meantime, the Department of Human Services gonna find a shelter somewhere else for you to go to get you up out of here for the time being. And then, after that, they'll place you in a facility of your own. But in the meantime, we'll be working ourselves to try to find a home or something else for you.

MAN: Good. Here you go.

POLICEWOMAN: You got some clothes or somethin' you wanna take wit' you?

MAN: Well, ah, yeah, take some clothes.

POLICEWOMAN: Okay, we'll get you something.

POLICEMAN: Okay, let's get everything that you really need to take with you now and we'll worry about, you know—

POLICEWOMAN: Getting the apartment secured for you. Find somewhere where they will store your belongings until you can get it to take it wit' you.

MAN: Yeah, yeah.

POLICEMAN: Because they are not gonna—see, they are gonna secure this here. They are not gonna let you stay here, you know, after today. They're gonna board this up.

MAN: Well, what I wanna do, I wanna get me, most of, all my stuff, right where I can get it stored, what I need, you know? Got a pretty good old TV there, and, uh, I don't know. I don't know.

POLICEMAN: You said, you said you had relatives.

POLICEWOMAN: Do you have any phone numbers or anything or way to get in contact with them?

MAN: Yeah, my sister.

POLICEMAN: Okay, one of 'em's—you don't have a phone, right?

MAN: No.

POLICEMAN: We can call her, okay?

MAN: Yeah . . . I don't know what is goin' on.

POLICEMAN: You goin' to the room here?

MAN: Goin' to the bathroom.

POLICEWOMAN: Here, put this card in there.

POLICEMAN: Well, this still looks pretty . . . This still looks pretty [*inaudible*].

MAN: Today, see, I need to get outta here.

POLICEMAN: What's wrong? The ceiling?

MAN: Stuff is falling.

POLICEMAN: Right, right, right.

MAN: But this is what I mean. I, like you say, you gonna, whatcha gonna do. You gonna secure it and board it up.

POLICEMAN: Right, they're gonna board it up. Where are your clothing? Your personal belongings?

POLICEWOMAN: I don't even see a bag to put it in.

POLICEMAN: See, that's gonna be a big problem. I mean, as far as storing your property. I mean, we really don't have any place, you know. And that's why I am tryin' to—

MAN: Well, what I do, right?—what I wanna do is get my little clothes and send that other stuff over there by the dumpster. I wouldn't care.

POLICEWOMAN: So what clothes are you gonna take?

MAN: Gonna take it all. [*Policeman in kitchen takes down canned goods. Old man sits on bed.*]

POLICEMAN: Where are your clothes at? Are they in the drawers?

MAN: Huh?

POLICEMAN: Where are your clothes?

MAN: In the closet.

POLICEMAN: Where?

MAN: In the closet.

POLICEMAN: Why don't you just leave all that for now and just bring what you really need with you, okay? [*Police radio in background.*] Really important things, like papers or whatever . . . Take your medicine with you. By all means, take your medicine with you . . . You can leave that. Keep that in there. Keep all that in there. That's fine . . . What type of medicine are you taking?

MAN: For arthritis.

POLICEMAN: For arthritis? . . . You all ready? Need me to carry anything? You ready?

MAN: I don't know what's happening. I don't know.

POLICEWOMAN: We can stop and get some bags. Some bags.

POLICEMAN: C'mon. Stop and—you gonna need some bags, we will come back and get these things later. [*Police radio in background.*] . . . You want your shirt down?

MAN: Yes.

POLICEWOMAN: Okay, now I'll get it down for you. [*Police and man leave apartment, police radio still audible in background. Six shots of people outside: women sitting on chairs, a woman sweeping the street, children on bicycles, a man mowing the lawn. Shot of ice cream truck going by playing Scott Joplin's "The Entertainer." Several shots of men washing cars on corner.*]

FIRST MAN (*offscreen*): So everybody need a job. I need a job.

SECOND MAN (*offscreen*): We need a job bad.

THIRD MAN (*offscreen*): Right, from the Wells Community. We made a car wash job operation. [*Seven shots of outdoor life in the development: children riding bikes, playing basketball with a milk crate as a makeshift basket, women doing their hair, man barbecuing. Cut to shot of people at HUD meeting.*]

WOMAN IN BLACK JACKET (HUD REP): You can receive training in various areas if you want to be a painter, or to do maintenance, and that kind of thing. I mean, you can receive training in all those areas to allow you to then receive monies, I guess under Section 3, Program—

WOMAN IN BLUE DRESS (HUD REP): Right.

WOMAN IN BLACK JACKET: —you know, to start your business. Because that's what, that's what Section 3 is all about. And I believe that there is a limit of what?, a hundred thousand dollars, that you can get as start-up monies to start a business. So, the resources are there, it's just that, you know, you just need to be made aware of what is available to you.

RESIDENT: I, I've been a painter for eight years, I've worked for the city, I have my own business that's set up, but my problem is getting business. You know, going out and getting a hundred thousand dollars, and I want to participate in what the change is gonna happen in public housing. You know, I want to do some of the work here. I want to contract and hire some of the residents here, 'cause that's gonna fit in with welfare reform. We're sitting in the middle of an empowerment zone, you know, and we want to take advantage of some of them situations. We want to be part of it. You know, before others come in here and we'll still be sitting on the sideline watching

63. Representatives from HUD meet with local residents.

others build up and make money on our community, and taking their economics someplace else, and they're not staying here.

WOMAN IN BLACK JACKET: More than likely, we will be, if things go well, announcing another funding round. We have twenty-five million dollars, you know, that, that, that's available to resident councils. And so, probably in the spring is when we'll be announcing, you know, another funding round. And so, you need to apply for those funds.

MAN (*offscreen*): Can I ask you one more question?

WOMAN IN BLACK JACKET: It's meant to augment, you know—

WOMAN IN BLUE DRESS: Wait a minute, but under Section 3, Section 3 requirements have to be met ongoing. I mean that's not something that's a clo—, gonna close. That's not a program with money attached to it that's gonna close at a certain time. Section 3 is a requirement that is attached to every dollar that is spent by the C-H-A.

WOMAN IN BLACK JACKET: Comp grants.

MAN IN WINDBREAKER (HUD REP RON CARTER): Comp Grants. Now, let, yeah, let me, let me add, add a little meat to that. What Section 3 says is, and I'm going to give some examples just so, of numbers, if HUD gave C-H-A money, and C-H-A was then gonna use that money to do construction at Ida B. Wells—let's say they were gonna spend a million dollars—Section 3 says that there is a specific—in the event that the com-

64. A resident expresses his concern that work should be given to local businesses.

pany that's gonna do the work is bringing on new people, hiring new folks, a certain threshold of them have to be residents, under Section 3. Any, anytime a company is getting a contract with C-H-A, and they're hiring new employees to do the work, they must have a certain percentage of them come from the resident population. We are hearing a lot of, we're getting a lot of feedback about the unions here in Chicago, and rest assured we're gonna be talking to them very shortly, because we, we have had a very good developing relationship with unions nationwide, and we don't have any reason to believe that we won't be able to do similar things here in Chicago. [*Woman tries to ask question.*] One other point. On the other issue that Beverly Harding mentioned, if you have a resident-owned business, that means fifty-one percent of that business is owned by residents of public housing, you can get a contract with C-H-A without competitively bidding. And that contract can be up to as much as five hundred thousand dollars, which means if C-H-A has work that needs to be done, up to a half million can be given to you without even competing.

RESIDENT: Yeah, I've heard this, some of this before, especially about the percentage of, that's supposed to go to residents. All of this work that's going on here, and we couldn't get a cut of it. And usually if they hire residents, it's as, because of the union problems, like you said, y'all gonna take care o' them. This usually is just a laborer, of which is only gonna be a short period of time, when we have people, and it's a labor problem, that can be carpenters, can do dry-walling, you know, those type of jobs. But they still standing on the corner, you know; they are not working. They see other people come here and work everyday, and they're still standing out here on the corner. Ya know, I hope this is, I hope it's better, I hope it's improved so we can—twenty-five million dollars and that's just a drop in the bucket. You know, but for us here in public housing, that's a lot of money that can create a whole lot of economic development for people, you know.

RON CARTER: Part of our responsibility as HUD at C-H-A is to make these rules work here. We realize that after evaluating them, things have not gone well here. That, that Chicago is somewhat behind other cities, but we're here to address those things immediately and try to put in place the mechanisms that will allow residents access to these opportunities. And, and that's our charge.

MRS. FINNER: We have a school down on Twenty-sixth and Cagney—

WOMAN FROM HUD (*offscreen*): What's, what is it?

MRS. FINNER: It's called, it's, uh, Wells [*shushing noise*] Training, I mean, no, C-H-A—

WOMAN FROM HUD (*offscreen*): Training.

MRS. FINNER: —Training Center. We send people down there, they'll call and say, send me some people, to come down there for training. And that's all they're gonna get is training. Now with the idea and the hope that they're gonna be hired.

WOMAN FROM HUD (*offscreen*): Right.

MRS. FINNER: What has happened with presidents, we've been put in the doghouse because we get a long list and send them down to the school, send them down to the school. They never get hired. They train them to death and they never get hired. This is a hardship on presidents, because everybody is looking at us. Why you send me down there if they wasn't gonna hire us? We have a program called Step Up. We have sent gobs of people down there. Two or three get hired, and they don't work a very long time. And they are qualified. The people that we send are qualified to do these jobs. Why are they not hired? The hardship comes back on us.

WOMAN (*offscreen*): And another—

MRS. FINNER: And that's been goin' on too long, too.

WOMAN IN BLACK T-SHIRT: I have another, please, ma'am. In the back of where I live, there are no lights. There have been no lights there in I don't know how long. And I frequent the back [*knocks on desk to quiet the room*] because I go across to see about my sister across the yard and stuff, and other

neighbors up and down that aisle. There are no lights, pitch black. Another
one, got another one. All along the front where I live—I live on Langley,
Thirty-eighth and Langley—they have holes this big and rats come out and
they won't even let you in the door. And I was promised that someone would
come and fill that. All along Thirty-ninth and Langley, so it's really Thirty-
eighth to Thirty-ninth.

RON CARTER: I'd like, what I like to do is take things that appear to be negative on the surface and try to turn them to a positive. First, let's talk about
the lights for a second. We all know that those lights don't break themselves,
and they're not all goin' out because they, of functional obsolescence. We
know that they're being vandalized. Well, there is a technology out there
now called Mightee-Lights that can take a nine-millimeter shell, and more
than likely it'll ricochet and—

WOMAN (*offscreen*): Hit them. That would be great. [*Laughter.*]

RON CARTER: —but they're expensive. So, as we work through your plan,
and we have identified that lights are a problem, we can look at what it would
cost to get lights in. And then we have to prioritize. Is that more important
than gettin' the door jambs fixed? Because we're only gonna have, you know,
limited resources. But, you know, we want it to be your priority. What is
your priority? Now, just, this is sorta off the, off that path, but it's still dealing with lights. We have observed in the nine or ten developments that we
have been to, that every development has lights burning during the day. We
have concluded—

MAN (*offscreen*): Stairwells.

RON CARTER: Huh? Yeah. Stairwells. Walkways. Common area lights.

MAN (*offscreen*): Buildings.

RON CARTER: Buildings, all types of situations. And we have, okay, we have
concluded that C-H-A, I mean, and we haven't done the math, we just looked
at one building at Hilliard, and we have figured out that they're burning a
thousand watts a minute during the day. Now, if you, if you do the math
on that electric bill, I suspect it might be millions, when you talk about
C-H-A-wide and the 1,400 buildings in this city, and how many are burning lights during the day. And, my suggestion was, if you got a group of
residents together who did nothing but energy conservation, you could ne-
gotiate with the Authority. They're paying millions in electric bills. If you
tell 'em, we can save you a million dollars, we'll take ten percent, you give
us a hundred thousand, we'll save you a million, that's a resident-owned

business. Very possible. That's the kind of creative thinkin' that has got to go on. Everybody says we want jobs, we want jobs. There are jobs all around us. And now that we, HUD, and C-H-A are one and we're receptive to getting jobs and businesses going, get creative. Now's the time to talk to us.

WOMAN (*offscreen*): Uh-huh.

RON CARTER: We can, I think we can start to make some of those things happen.

WOMAN IN BLACK SWEATER: I'm looking at it from the other side, I guess you would say from the management side, and it filters down to the services provided to the residents. And one of them is in the area of securing what you need, supplies and services that you need. The hassle that you have to go through to get supplies is unbelievable.

RON CARTER: Within C-H-A.

WOMAN IN BLACK SWEATER: Within C-H-A. You can order something that you need today, and if you get it—and if you really need it you better go buy it yourself, because it will be three months before you can get it through the system and this, the paperwork that's set up. So by the time it filters down, just from my department alone—I run a department—can you imagine what would happen, what happens in management trying to get supplies to meet the need of the resident. They have to go through the same system that I do to get a pen. And it, it is, it is unbelievable. Right now I'm waiting, I have been waiting, this is the fourth month, for ink cartridge for a copier that I just went out and bought myself 'cause I couldn't use the copier and I needed it. But I'm still waiting for that cartridge. That happens over and over and over and over again. It happens in the, in the departments, it happens in the management office, it happens for pens, pencils. It happens for doors and screens.

WOMAN IN BLUE DRESS: Why, what takes it so long? From your sitting there?

MAN (*offscreen, overlapping*): Paperwork.

WOMAN IN BLACK SWEATER (*overlapping*): I would really like to know what takes it so long, because there are a number, there are at least three, four levels of authorization that you have to go through before it gets to us in purchasing, maybe. And then it has to go through budget that has already been approved, for them to reapprove it. Then it comes back to purchasing to be bidded out for three bids. And by the time you go through all of this cycle, it's sitting here for two weeks, it sit there for two weeks, it sit there for three weeks. It's, you know, it's three months later and you're still waiting. Something has to be done to streamline that process in order for the people to provide a service.

RON CARTER: We are looking at every community separately. Assistant Secretary Schulner has said, look, we want to evaluate every community separately, because the needs of one community may not be consistent with the needs of another. You have to budget yourselves individually. You have to track and monitor your programs individually. So we want to give every community its own identity. And what should be happening, just as we share with the folks over at Lake Park Place, you should have a budget of what it takes to run this community. Included in that budget should be a line item for reserves and replacements to deal with capital improvement issues. Every month there should be a printed financial statement that the management gets and the residents get to show you how you did the previous month. [*Applause.*] Alright? These are the types of things we want to move towards. And eventually you all will become so expert on what it costs to run your complex that when you get that financial statement, you go, "Wait a minute, what is the problem here? Look at this water bill." And then you find out that by looking at the monthly statement there's a busted pipe underneath one of the buildings that's been running water for a month. Okay? So that's what we're trying to move toward. Now, how we get there is, is, it's gonna take a lot of effort on both our parts. This, this planning that we're doing now is, is your piece to it. We gotta get over to C-H-A and work with the staff over there and try to figure out why eighteen people got to sign a work request, or whatever the number is. Yeah, we've heard forty. So, so we're on that, and we hear you loud and clear. And, as far as public safety goes, we are looking at every community individually and we're looking at the resources within the police department, within the security contracts that exist, and then the tenant patrols, because those three things together can, hopefully, bring together healthy public safety programs . . . Now, the important thing is that because we are now here, we hope that we'll have a direct dialogue, get our local field office involved and try to help move you forward. Somewhere between your talents and your desire and our information and resources, we should be able to get this done. [*Twelve shots of people outside development, including girls in prom dresses, woman looking out the window, girl pushing baby in stroller. LS of video crew working in street, crowd of people gathered around.*]

MAN: [*Inaudible.*] So, however you look at it—

DIRECTOR: You ready? Let's, let's, let's call it; let's do it before we lose any more light.

WALKIE-TALKIE: Okay, copy.

DIRECTOR: Okay. Jeff, can we shoot?

WALKIE-TALKIE: [*Inaudible.*]

DIRECTOR: Ready. Wait. I'm gonna give you a sign. I'm gonna give you a action, okay?

WALKIE-TALKIE: You do that.

MAN: Call the action.

WOMAN: Can you move the people up? Are the people closer? They're not where they were before.

MAN: Is Maurice gonna make them go on action?

DIRECTOR: Huh?

CREWMAN: Does Maurice know to make him go on action?

DIRECTOR: Maurice?

WALKIE-TALKIE: Yes.

DIRECTOR: Make him go on action.

WALKIE-TALKIE: You call it.

DIRECTOR: Yeah. Alright. You ready?

CREW MEMBERS: Yes. Set. Yes. Yes.

WALKIE-TALKIE: When you're ready, okay?

DIRECTOR: Do not look at the camera. Okay?

CAMERAMAN: [*Inaudible*] fucking me up.

SAM: Let's go, let's go, let's go, let's go.

DIRECTOR: Alright, let's do it. You call it, Sam. Call.

SAM: Alright. Camera set?

CAMERAMAN: Yeah.

SAM: Roll camera, please.

CREW MEMBER: Camera rolling.

SAM: Speed!

DIRECTOR: Action. [*Many voices yelling "action."*] Action!

CAMERAMAN: Cut! . . . Maurice, you can't get the fucking—the traffic!

SAM: Get that traffic out of the street. Get out of the way.

CREWMAN: Get your ass out of the way.

MAN: Shut the fuck up. [*Laughter.*]

DIRECTOR: [*Laughs.*] No, that's okay. That's okay. We want it to look like that. Maurice, is camera, are talent ready? Camera two still ready? Alright, come on, Sam, come out the way.

SAM: [*Inaudible.*]

DIRECTOR: What? Alright. Maurice, talent ready.

CREWMAN: We're good, go back to one.

DIRECTOR: Call camera roll. [*On bullhorn*] Ready.

SAM: Roll camera, please.

CAMERAMAN: Camera rolling.

DIRECTOR: Action.

CREWMAN: Let's go! [*A car rolls into view, followed by many children clambering to meet the driver, who gets out of the car and is surrounded by the applauding and cheering crowd. Cut to young girl looking out a window. Three shots of people outside units in the afternoon. Shot of police car at night, accompanied on the soundtrack by a calliope version of "Pop Goes the Weasel," which carries over the next two shots of the development at night followed by three shots of the ice cream truck, source of the music, on its nighttime route. In the third shot, the truck turns a corner, revealing a store across the street, some people gathered around it. Cut to a closer view, a LS of grocery store, O.T. Food and Liquors, at night, a crowd at the order window. Cut to shot among the crowd, then behind shoppers at store window, through which they place their orders to clerks on the other side.*]

WOMAN IN HALTER TOP: Give me a soda . . ginger ale . . . And tell her to give me a bag of them Doodles right there, a bag of them Doodles. Up, down, down. One more. Right there.

SALES CLERK: And what else?

WOMAN IN HALTER TOP: What? Wait!

WOMAN IN SWEATER: Alright, a bag a Cheetos . . . Can I have a bag of Flamin' Hots then.

CLERK: Baby, I can't hear you.

WOMAN IN SWEATER: I said a bag of Flamin' Hots then.

CLERK: Baby, I can't hear you.

65. A woman orders a snack through the glass partition of a local store.

WOMAN IN SWEATER: I said a bag of Flamin' Hots. I gonna be burnin' up. [*Cut to inside store.*]

CLERK: What? Twenty-five-cent bag? [*Shouts*] Twenty-five-cent bag? Alright, why do I have to holler so much? It's against my religion. Forget this shit. Y'all can do it and tell me to stay at home. Move back that way. Watch your hand, baby. [*Cut to boy outside.*]

BOY: I want a box of doughnuts, different colors. I want a box of doughnuts, different kinds.

MAN (*offscreen*): Get that outta here. What you want? You don't want nothin'? [*Cut back to inside store.*]

CLERK: Three forty-nine, three forty-nine.

WOMAN IN PINK TOP: I want a six-pack of Miller.

CLERK: Short or tall?

WOMAN IN PINK TOP: Short.

CLERK: Who's next? [*Nine shots of clerks getting goods for customers, placing items in paper bags, White manager counting money, shoppers outside store. Shot of police cars and policemen in front of police station.*]

POLICEMAN: I mean, how long are you gonna run from 'em? Till you can pay 'em?

MAN (MICHAEL REED): Well, not at this very moment.

POLICEMAN: I guess at this point they're just lookin' to beat you up.

REED: Right. [*Cut to policeman speaking to man in front of station.*]

POLICEMAN: So, what are you gonna do?

REED: I'll just, I just want somewhere to go until I can get their money. I gotta live. I gotta live.

POLICEMAN (*overlapping*): Do you work?

REED: No. No, I do hustlin' cans and stuff like that.

POLICEMAN: That's a lot of cans, to come up with eighty dollars. I'm surprised they let you get that far in their pockets . . . Now you, you're gonna have to do somethin' or we'll be callin' an ambulance for you before the night is over if they get hold of you, 'cause you know that, right?

REED: Yeah.

POLICEMAN: If they can't get their money, they're gonna beat it out of you . . . So they just actually chased you across the street over there?

REED: Yeah.

POLICEMAN: What'd you do, go over there to try to get some more on credit?

REED: No. You know, they jus' came for me.

POLICEMAN: What did they do, come to your house?

REED: Yeah, I saw 'em. You know, I saw 'em comin', you know. I just ran out the back.

POLICEMAN: How many of them was there?

REED: Ten, twelve, thirteen, like that.

POLICEMAN: They aren't too smart, are they, they didn't cover the back door, huh? They all came to the front door?

REED: Yeah, I just happened to be lookin' out the window.

POLICEMAN: Who do you live with over there at the apartment?

REED: Well, right now, me and my wife, we separated. Me and my wife, she's separated 'cause of the drugs.

POLICEMAN: She's the leaseholder over there?

REED: No, both of us.

POLICEMAN: Both of you are on the lease? So you are legally married? She's not there right now?

REED: No, she's sep—, you know, we separated, you know.

POLICEMAN: Because of your problem?

REED: Right.

POLICEMAN: So that means you're probably behind on your rent, too, then, right?

REED: Well, one, one, one or two months. She usually take care of that.

POLICEMAN: How long you been, uh—

REED: Usin', seven years.

POLICEMAN: Seven years you been on drugs?

REED: Yeah.

POLICEMAN: Your wife hung in there for a while then, huh?

REED: Yes, she did, you know. I can't blame her, you know.

POLICEMAN: How many children?

REED: Four.

POLICEMAN: Four. She finally just had enough, huh? Decided to leave? So she's left you there by yourself?

REED: Yeah.

POLICEMAN: Don't be surprised if when you go back to the apartment, it's trashed.

REED: Yeah.

POLICEMAN: It's one of the other things that they do. Well, all I can say is you're welcome to stay here as long as you feel safe. Unless you leave the area, you know, eventually they'll catch up with you . . . How long have you lived over there?

REED: Five year.

POLICEMAN: Five years? There's nowhere you could even hide out over here. I mean—

REED: Well, I got relatives—

POLICEMAN: Well, they probably know where your relatives live, too, right?

REED: No.

POLICEMAN: No? 'Cause you don't want to get your relatives involved in this. This is, this is your problem and not something you need to bring on your relatives . . . What's your name?

REED: Michael Reed.

POLICEMAN: Michael?

REED: Reed. R-double-E-D.

POLICEMAN: Oh, how ya' doin'? I'm Sergeant Loren. I'm the midnight watch commander over here. I'll be here until six in the morning. Like I said, you're welcome to stay here. I don't know that you want to sit out here all night. Have you ever tried to go in rehab or anything and get some help for it?

REED: It's been, it's been some years, you know.

POLICEMAN: Since you've tried it?

REED (*overlapping*): It's about time, yeah. It's about time. 'Cause, you know, it had never escalated to this point, you know.

POLICEMAN: It's a hard habit to break, huh?

REED: Yeah.

POLICEMAN: Okay, Mr. Reed. I'll, I'll be in the station if you need me. Okay? Alright. [*Officer goes into stationhouse. Mr. Reed sits outside the door. Shot of parked police cars at night. Twenty-eight shots of fenced-in development balconies in daytime, some extreme LSs from outside, others from inside the balconies showing people cleaning, children skipping rope, playing. People sitting in entranceway.*]

CARD PLAYERS (*over shot of building fronts*): Hey, boy, come right back here. [*Shot of police car driving by.*] . . . That's my card . . . You gotta throw it out . . . I told you there was another card in there, man. [*Cut to shot of men standing by a car.*] Y'all didn't believe me . . . Put it at the bottom of the deck. [*Cut to shot of woman on portable phone in a car.*] It's down there now. [*Cut to men gathered around a small table on the street playing cards.*] . . . Hold on. How do you get to deal, right off the bat right there? . . . 'Cause I can, man . . . Shame on ya! Wu Tang made me do it . . . My way. The trail way . . . I ain't got nothin' over here, man . . . Trey, can I see your hand . . . What'd you get? . . . Three. I know y'all got signals— . . . I'm fucked over here . . . Better let him get some money. It's his birthday . . . Oh? . . . Come see me . . . Don't even trip, come on whip . . . Play with the Ouija board. Play with the Ouija board . . . Don't want none of this, man . . . Y'all need three of these. Y'all need three of these . . . You fucked up, nigger . . . He ain't got nothing going on . . . Nothing but a bad queen, nigger. Put it down, nigger. [*Laughter.*] . . . Don't call me nigger, shit. [*Cut to shot of woman sitting on chair eating chips.*] . . . No, eight fives . . . It's nothin'. We playin' cards. It ain't nothin'. [*Cut to shot of little children playing, a loud bang on soundtrack. Cut to police going by in all-terrain vehicles. Cut to two-shot of Mrs. Finner and policeman.*]

MRS. FINNER: I'm doing this for the good of Ida B. Wells community, and I am not going to let a handful of something-that-don't-want-nothin' come and tear what it has taken us all this time to build up.

WOMAN (*offscreen*): Okay.

MRS. FINNER: Now, if they, if they complain tonight I'm gonna have head knockers, the real ones, the real ones that don't care what they do when they come. It doesn't make sense. I have ran into a lot of problems in the twenty years that I've been president, and whatever I did has always been for the good of the community. There are a lot of things I could get, just being the president. Why should I have it if my other people can't get it? And that's how I look at life. And that's how it's gonna be. And if they think that I am afraid, you better ask them about it. Ask that young man standin' right out there how many times I've knocked him upside the head. He's a full-grown man, he can tell you.

POLICEMAN: I understand what you're sayin', but—

MRS. FINNER: But some—

POLICEMAN: Fighting violence with violence is not the answer. You can't—

MRS. FINNER: I know that, but what am I supposed to do, let them hurt somebody in my house?

POLICEMAN: No.

MRS. FINNER: Alright.

POLICEMAN: No, no. You defend yourself, but when you get somebody—

MRS. FINNER (*overlapping*): In my way?

POLICEMAN: It's not about your way. Now you know to what exten—

MRS. FINNER (*overlapping*): I was just talkin' when I said that.

POLICEMAN (*overlapping*): Okay, okay.

MRS. FINNER: I have always been able to take care of myself. And I've got three sons that never had to go out there and defend Mama. Am I right, Tony?

TONY: You got that right, Ms. Finner.

MRS. FINNER: I have always been able to talk, not violence, but when you start throwin' firecrackers at my door, you're lookin' for trouble. Am I right or wrong?

POLICEMAN: Yeah.

MRS. FINNER: Now, you all can't just sit at seven-fifty. I'm not gonna have it. And they're not goin' to wash no cars over in that corner.

POLICEMAN: Right. But you know, any of those guys that throw firecrackers or whatever—a lot of residents consider it a bothersome, but it helps when you call it in, give us a description. You know, maybe we ride around, we pick 'em up. You know, I mean, at least you're doing something as far as we recognize what's goin' on and we can come and try to do somethin' about it and we're workin' together.

MRS. FINNER: Well, I know everything you is saying is the truth. I've been a resident of Ida B. Wells for many, many years, and I've never seen it this bad. We've got a development coming across the street to our development. If I have to be a one-woman crusader to run 'em back to Meadow Park, that's where they're goin'. They're not goin' to intimidate me. I'm serious.

WOMAN: Do you think that the firecrackers is a result of the—

MRS. FINNER: It's the result of the no washing cars group. I know what it is. I know exactly what it is. So who cares? I'm not afraid. You've never seen me with a police escort, have you?

POLICEMAN: No.

MRS. FINNER: Alright, you never will. I'm not scared of them. See, they want you to fear them. But I don't have sense enough to fear nobody.

POLICEMAN: Could you do me a favor?

WOMAN: Sure.

POLICEMAN: Anytime you see them out there, whatever, just give the station a call.

WOMAN: Oh, they know, 'cause I chased them off of there today.

POLICEMAN: They're depending on—I mean, sometimes I'll be in the station and I don't know. I mean, I'm doing, like, whatever.

MRS. FINNER (*overlapping*): No, you're in the station so you won't know.

POLICEMAN: But that's what I'm saying. Call over, let me know.

WOMAN (*overlapping*): Uh-huh. Yeah, I'll let you know.

POLICEMAN: Call over, because I'll be in the station.

WOMAN: Because I told them this morning, I said, now you know you're doing—you're not supposed to be washing cars on this corner. And I know who the culprits are.

MRS. FINNER (*overlapping*): I can tell you who was washing there.

WOMAN: Uh-huh. And so—

MRS. FINNER (*overlapping*): It's not fair! Tony, do you want to see me?

TONY: Yeah. I'll come back. I'll come back.

MRS. FINNER: But you just have to take—we gotta fight fire with fire.

POLICEMAN: You fight fire with water.

MRS. FINNER: With fire.

POLICEMAN: Water.

MRS. FINNER: However.

POLICEMAN (*laughing*): You fight fire with water.

WOMAN (*overlapping*): Ms. Finner's upset right now, she's—

POLICEMAN (*overlapping*): The water is every time you see them, call. Please.

MRS. FINNER: That's every minute.

POLICEMAN: I'm, I'm—alright, then if it's every minute, I'm at the station.

MRS. FINNER (*overlapping*): Do you see that water in the street? It makes our street look bad. Paper floatin' in the water, down the street. Janitors have cleaned. And our—we have a good janitor. He cleans thorough. When I get home it looks like I don't know what. And that one, that one person in particular has defied me. His mama lives right there. You want to mess up, come down here to your mama's house and do all the messin' up you want to do, 'cause you're *not* gonna do it on Thirty-seventh Place. And I mean that. If I have to have the police come and sit there on that corner. It's not fair to the residents that are trying to keep their area clean. It's not fair.

POLICEMAN: Let me ask you this question. Concerning those kids who create a problem or create a mess in a area, does anybody report this to management? Because, I mean, as far—

MRS. FINNER: Well, Meadow Park? Meadow Park knows.

WOMAN: Besides that, it's not necessarily kids that are messing up.

POLICEMAN (*overlapping*): Isn't there some type of fine that is imposed?

WOMAN (*overlapping*): It's men, it's adults. These are grown people.

MRS. FINNER: These are grown adults.

POLICEMAN: Grown adults.

MRS. FINNER (*overlapping*): You've seen 'em. I know you rolled by there and saw him. The one guy that was washing cars out there kept everything neat. But when he started letting everybody come on that corner—

POLICEMAN: Okay.

MRS. FINNER: —to wash the car so they can get 'em a bottle. And when they finish the bottle, they just throw it down on the ground and break it. We got little-bitty kids that play out there.

POLICEMAN: Right, okay. Now, let me explain something to you. Initially, when it was happening and they were out there washing cars, it seemed like a positive activity—

MRS. FINNER (*overlapping*): It was.

POLICEMAN: —as opposed to being hanging out doin' other kind of crazy stuff. But now that it is getting out of hand, it is a problem that we are going to have to address.

MRS. FINNER: They had a big fight on that corner Saturday night. Two boys got cut. That was a family affair, but it resulted from the car wash. And they didn't give, the one individual didn't give the other individual some money, so they had a big fight. One is still in the hospital.

POLICEMAN: Each time any of you see anything, call. Call the station, okay? So I can take it that whenever there's a problem—

WOMAN: You're gonna hear about it.

POLICEMAN (*overlapping*): —I'm gonna be hearing from you.

MRS. FINNER: You're certainly gonna hear about it.

POLICEMAN: Okay. Alright. That's good.

MRS. FINNER: That's the only way we're gonna break it up. You can't close your eyes.

POLICEMAN: Exactly.

MRS. FINNER: To the real picture.

POLICEMAN: I'm in the station. I'll come out and take care of it if necessary.

MRS. FINNER: Well, I told Lieutenant Scott, I told Sergeant Brad, I told Lieutenant Evans, I'm gonna tell everybody every time I see 'em, about it.

POLICEMAN: Okay. And every time—

WOMAN: You just happened to walk in on another thing, and I got to preaching about it.

POLICEMAN: No problem, no problem. I understand. Give me a call. [*Cut to shot of seated women listening to director of Child Family Preservation Center.*]

DIRECTOR OF CENTER: Fortunately, there are those of us [*cut to director*] who do not believe that group homes and orphanages, we're not ready to accept that as the answer, yet. That's what the Child Family Preservation Center is all about. We're not ready to see families separated as the only solution. Obviously, there are times when that is the only solution. But we believe if we can work aggressively with families who are at risk, we can prevent separation from families, or separation of families. The thing that sticks out most in my mind about this cycle, about incompetent families, if you will, dysfunctional families—when I was at Cabrini Green, I was in Juvenile Court one day, supporting a mother, trying to help her keep her family together. The judge was ready to separate them. She did okay, because we came up with a crisis plan and responded to her needs, and she was okay. But the family that came up before her court call was not so fortunate. And the mother told the whole story, in my opinion, in three sentences. The judge ordered her family separated from her for the State of Illinois. Of course, she cried. The children began to cry. The separation was awful. She walked out into the outer area, and *her* mother came to embrace her daughter who had just gone through this trauma. And that mother's response to *her* mother was, "I don't need you now." She said, "I don't need you to hug me, I don't need to even talk to you. If they had taken *us* away from *you*, I wouldn't be here today." So, in four or five sentences she defined the cycle, the very sad cycle. Does she love her children? I'm sure she does. But she doesn't have a clue as to how to raise them. No support system. Her mother was about thirty-five. So she's still struggling, and I don't know what that history was. It's the cycle we are attempting to break. And that is not an easy task, and we realize that. But that's why we're here, because we don't like what people are discussing as the solution, which is separation of all families that have a problem into the foster care system, which has proved not to work very well. So, the Child Family Preservation Center is a, an at-risk family alternative. And that's what we intend to do—work with families who are at risk before they become high risk. We work with them aggressively. DCFS can't do what we're prepared to do. It's impossible for them to do, and give the attention to families that's required. What's it gonna do? We hope, solve a lot of problems. We also are counting on the services that are already here, because that was one of the reasons Ida B. Wells was selected, and that's why you're here. Because there was enough backup service to support what it is we're doing. Because we have to have a referral service and a networking service in order to—networking agreement, in order to make the care plan for the families work. [*Three ext. shots of development: first and last of buildings, the middle shot of a woman working in a garden patch. Cut to shot inside an apartment, an elderly woman preparing cabbage at kitchen table.*]

PLUMBER: Do you have a mop I can use, miss? Excuse me, do you have a mop I can use, miss? A mop?

WOMAN (Miss Cheatham): Right there.

PLUMBER: Yes, ma'am.

MISS CHEATHAM: There's water all in that room.

MAN: Yeah, I see it on the floor in there. [*Plumber mops bathroom.*]

PLUMBER: Miss Cheatham? Miss Cheatham? I gotta go get a part to fix the sink with and I'll be right back.

MISS CHEATHAM: You'll be right back?

PLUMBER: Yes, ma'am.

MISS CHEATHAM: Okay.

PLUMBER: I should be back in about ten or fifteen minutes.

MISS CHEATHAM: Oh, just shut the door—

PLUMBER: Okay, I'll close the door.

MISS CHEATHAM: —when you go out. [*Woman continues to sit at table and cleans greens. Cut to shot of plumber coming back into room.*]

PLUMBER: Hey, Miss Cheatham? Miss Cheatham? I'm back. Okay? [*Cut to plumber working on sink in bathroom.*]

MISS CHEATHAM (*on telephone*): Uh, who is it? Oh, Leah? Does that mean you's on your way? . . . No? . . . You're a little tired? . . . Don't know when you're coming, huh? . . . No? No . . . I ain't doin' so hot . . . You don't know now when you're coming, huh? [*Plumber puts away tools and wipes down sink.*]

PLUMBER: I'm finished. I'm all done. Miss Cheatham? I say I'm all done with the leak in there.

MISS CHEATHAM: I don't understand.

PLUMBER: I repaired the leak that was coming from the face bowl in the bathroom.

MISS CHEATHAM: Uh-huh.

PLUMBER: Yeah, I'm all finished. So, this is the, where you sign the, uh—

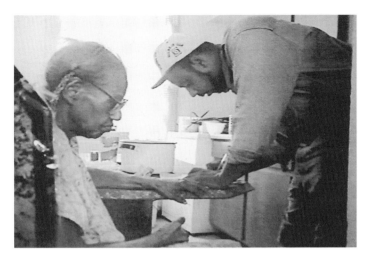

66. The plumber prepares his work order for a tenant.

MISS CHEATHAM: I don't write.

PLUMBER: Okay. Do you have somebody here that can write?

MISS CHEATHAM: I'll make an X.

PLUMBER: Was that your grandson that was just here?

MISS CHEATHAM: Huh?

PLUMBER: Was that your grandson?

MISS CHEATHAM: This hand is all asleep.

PLUMBER: Huh?

MISS CHEATHAM: This hand is all asleep.

PLUMBER: Oh, okay, I understand.

MISS CHEATHAM: I don't write.

PLUMBER: Oh, okay. I understand. [*To young man in house*] Could you sign this for—it's your grandmother, right?

BOY: Uh, nah. I'm looking for my mother. My mother be over here watchin' her.

PLUMBER: Oh, okay. She said she was having a problem with her hand. [*To Miss Cheatham*] So I'll just leave the copy wit' you that the work was done. Okay? [*Plumber fills out form.*] You want to put this copy up? Huh? I'll just put the copy up here on top of your refrigerator, okay?

MISS CHEATHAM (*overlapping*): Yes.

PLUMBER: Okay. Have a nice day, Miss Cheatham.

MISS CHEATHAM: Have a nice day. I've got to go to get that water up.

PLUMBER: Well, I got most of it up. It should dry up. Alright, take it easy.

MISS CHEATHAM: Good day. [*Six shots outside development, including girls jumping rope, woman walking dog, children playing.*]

POLICEMAN: They're starting to run this way. Stop them over there on your side, Somerville. [*Policeman running, camera following.*]

MAN IN RED SWEATSHIRT (*as policeman runs past him*): I didn't do nothin', man. I'm innocent.

POLICEMAN: Come here, dude. Come here.

SECOND MAN (HUGH TOMLIN): What happened, sir? I just came from across the street there. I mean, I just came from across the street.

POLICEMAN: What's your name, man?

TOMLIN: Hugh Tomlin, sir.

POLICEMAN: Where you stay at?

TOMLIN: Pardon me?

POLICEMAN: Where you stay at?

TOMLIN: I stay right there at 74 Langley, sir. Oh, I'm sorry.

POLICEMAN (*searching man*): You got anything on you, man?

TOMLIN: No sir.

POLICEMAN: What is this?

TOMLIN: Those are Tylenol 3s with codeine, sir. I take those for my asthma.

POLICEMAN: You got any prescription for those?

TOMLIN: I don't have the prescription bottle with me, no sir.

POLICEMAN: You got anything on you, man?

TOMLIN: No, sir. I'm telling you the truth.

POLICEMAN: Hold this.

TOMLIN: I'm telling you the truth. I got no reason to lie to you at all.

POLICEMAN: You ain't got no drugs, no nothin'?

TOMLIN: No sir. I just got off of work.

67. A policeman frisks a suspicious man.

POLICEMAN: Hold your wallet. Turn around . . . Spread your legs. [*Two policemen search the two men.*] . . . Turn around, dude. So where's your ID?

TOMLIN: Right there.

POLICEMAN: Who you work for?

TOMLIN: I can show you right now, sir.

POLICEMAN: Who you work for?

TOMLIN: Allied Security.

POLICEMAN: Allied Security. Where you work at?

TOMLIN: I work at—

POLICEMAN: Now, look at this, man. How bogus does that look to you, with a picture that comes off the ID?

TOMLIN: Wait a minute. I will show you another piece of identification, sir.

POLICEMAN: You know, this could be anybody's.

TOMLIN: No, I understand that. Three-forty-six, forty-four, one-six-one-eight, and also have my voter's registration card right here.

POLICEMAN: Yeah, see this. Okay. Because this right here, this isn't any good, either. These metal ones are no good.

TOMLIN: That's what I heard.

POLICEMAN: Right. You gotta have, you gotta have a real—

TOMLIN (*overlapping*): I applied for a new one.

POLICEMAN (*to other officer*): Hey, you see anything over there, man? [*To other man being searched*] Put your hands on the wall and shut, shut up. Stand over here, chief. Don't you, don't you guys go nowhere. Did they find anything over there, man?

SECOND POLICEMAN: Not yet.

POLICEMAN: Y'see, you's were the first two I saw fadin' when I came up.

MAN IN RED JACKET: No, we came straight across—

POLICEMAN: Oh, man, everybody got, everybody got, an excuse, dude. Everybody got an excuse.

TOMLIN: I'm not trying to give no excuse. I'm tellin' you exactly where we came from. We just got off the bus on Thirty-ninth and, and Cottage, Oakwood and Cottage, and came across Oakwood. We came across Mancini, we come through that lot, and we came straight through here, and that was it, sir. Honestly.

POLICEMAN (*overlapping*): Uh-huh. And, like I said, everybody got a story, man. You guys are saying the truth, then you just happen to be in the wrong place at the wrong time.

MAN IN RED JACKET: That's what it got to be!

POLICE RADIO (*male voice*): There's about five hundred police cars out here. (*Female voice*): Ten-four. We'll send a car out there to see what's going on.

POLICEMAN: Ah, it's too late to ride that way anyway.

SECOND POLICEMAN: You want to?

POLICEMAN: Okay, if we clear up and find out what's happenin'. Man, you stay on Seventy-second, dude. You shouldn't even be over here, man. I could lock you up right now for criminal trespass of state-supported land.

TOMLIN: I understand that.

POLICEMAN: What's this, now?

TOMLIN: This is a slip, a piece of paper that I had to pay, okay, when I had a problem with the judge over there—

POLICEMAN: Okay.

TOMLIN: —and I was told, because of the fact that they had issued a warrant, I had to go down to the Daley Plaza to pay the thirty dollars to reopen the case, and I was told to keep this piece of paper on me at all time in case the warrant should come back up.

POLICEMAN: It's probably gonna come back up.

TOMLIN: To show that I've already been, okay, that I have already been for that. And I can show you proof of that, because I went yesterday to pay the restitution of the one-sixty-two, a hundred and sixty-two dollars, and I'm on three months supervision. Okay? I just had the card yesterday. I contacted this young lady right here, on Fifty-first Street. [*Police radio in background.*]

POLICEMAN: Well, I'll tell you this, if you pop up hot, we're going to have a unit transfer you to Fifty-first Street and you explain it to them. Because, you know, I can't do nothin' about it right here and now. I'm lettin' you know that now.

TOMLIN: I understand that, sir.

POLICEMAN: You know. We just had somebody earlier on one of these and he came back. He had popped a warrant.

SECOND POLICEMAN: Yeah, he cleared.

POLICEMAN: They cleared him?

SECOND POLICEMAN: He cleared.

POLICEMAN: So what do you want to do?

SECOND POLICEMAN: You can let him go. Give him back his card and paper and stuff, and, uh, everything is cool.

POLICE RADIO (*female voice*): Twenty-eight A-D.

POLICEMAN: Well, what was this for, anyway?

TOMLIN: That was for, that's where my driver's license got stolen. I was coming from work, and my pocket was picked, and that's the slip that I have—

POLICEMAN: Well what, what did you, what did you get in, what'd you get this for?

TOMLIN: Okay, this was for theft, sir.

FIRST POLICEMAN: Theft of what? What'd you steal?

TOMLIN: I had cashed someone's traveler's checks.

POLICE RADIO (*male voice*): Ten-four.

POLICEMAN: Ten-four. Go find you some business, man.

TOMLIN: Thank you very much, sir.

POLICEMAN: And don't be around here no more. I'm tellin' you now, you don't stay over here, you don't live here, don't be over here. If you're caught over here again the next time, I'm locking you up for criminal trespass on state-supported land. Is that understood?

TOMLIN: Yes, sir.

POLICEMAN: Thank you.

TOMLIN: Thank you. Thank you very much.

POLICEMAN: Where'd they go? Do you know where they went, man?

SECOND POLICEMAN: They out.

FIRST POLICEMAN: They out? Okay, we're out of here. [*Two shots of an ambulance going down a neighborhood street. Long take of people hanging out on the sidewalk. Eight shots of neighborhood scenes, including two women sharing a bottle, a man in a motorized wheelchair, and a boy running away from the police. Ext. shot of hair salon. Twenty-three shots inside hair salon of men and women getting their hair done and facials, and of the cosmeticians and barbers, as rap song "Born to Die" plays on salon sound system. Two ext. shots of the salon, followed by three ext. shots of neighborhood scenes, followed by LS of building with sign: "Wells Medical Center." Cut to another view of building. Cut to CU of drug counselor interviewing client.*]

DRUG COUNSELOR: You live with your family?

MAN: Yes.

DRUG COUNSELOR: How many people are in the household beside you and your wife?

MAN: Six of us.

DRUG COUNSELOR: Six?

MAN: Six of us.

DRUG COUNSELOR: And, plus you and your wife, or does that include—

MAN: Plus me and my wife.

DRUG COUNSELOR: So, there are eight of you altogether? What would you estimate the annual family income to be? I mean, how much—how do y'all pay the bills?

MAN: I get a SSI check. She get a aid check. And then I got a daughter work at the airport and she get a SSI check. We kinda manage offa those.

DRUG COUNSELOR: So, then, what we are looking at is, what, maybe eleven hundred a month. Four hundred, four hundred, and three hundred?

MAN: Yeah, eleven or twelve hundred a month.

DRUG COUNSELOR: Okay. So, altogether we are looking at about fifteen hundred, I mean about fifteen thousand dollars a year?

MAN: Right.

DRUG COUNSELOR: Okay. And do you have any health insurance at this time?

MAN: No.

DRUG COUNSELOR: On the last job you had, how long did you keep it?

MAN: The last job I had, I kept it for twelve years.

DRUG COUNSELOR: How many times have you been arrested as an adult?

MAN: About six or seven times.

DRUG COUNSELOR: How many times you been convicted?

MAN: Twice.

DRUG COUNSELOR: And what were you convicted of, man?

MAN: Huh?

DRUG COUNSELOR: What were you convicted of?

MAN: Same charges.

DRUG COUNSELOR: Delivery?

MAN: Yeah. I think it was possession. It was supposed to be possession.

DRUG COUNSELOR: Was it possession or possession with intent?

MAN: Possession with intent, I think.

DRUG COUNSELOR: You didn't sell the Man no dope?

MAN: No, I didn't sell the Man no dope.

DRUG COUNSELOR: Okay. And what did you get on that?

MAN: Three years.

DRUG COUNSELOR: Three years probation?

MAN: Yeah.

DRUG COUNSELOR: You ever do any heroin?

MAN: No.

DRUG COUNSELOR: Any Carache?

MAN: No.

DRUG COUNSELOR: You ever buy any methadone on the street?

MAN: No.

DRUG COUNSELOR: You ever do any Dilaudin, the Ts and blues?

MAN: No.

DRUG COUNSELOR: You ever do any other opiates, like morphine, or China white, or codeine for fun?

MAN: No.

DRUG COUNSELOR: We talkin' about recreation use here. Alcohol. How old were you the first time you drank enough to get buzzed?

MAN: Sixteen.

DRUG COUNSELOR: And at what point did you start to drink seriously? That is, rela—, more seriously than, than any previous time before that?

MAN: I can't remember 'cause I did it.

DRUG COUNSELOR: Well, at some point or another, you started drinking regularly or more frequently than any other time. About what age was that, did that happen?

MAN: Well, I was—well, lemme see. A couple years ago. I was thirty-nine. I had a son born and I just went out and got drunk 'cause I couldn't get there. I wasn't there when he was born and I just went out and got drunk. You know. From there I—downhill from there.

DRUG COUNSELOR: So at thirty-nine years old, you started gettin' serious about alcohol, and you had not seriously drank before then.

MAN: Right.

DRUG COUNSELOR: Is that correct?

MAN: Right.

DRUG COUNSELOR: Okay. Now, how frequently were you drinking when you, when shit started to go downhill? Were you drinking every day?

MAN: Every day.

DRUG COUNSELOR: What would a day's drinkin' be?

MAN: Whiskey, beer.

DRUG COUNSELOR: How much?

68. A man is interviewed by a drug counselor.

MAN: Maybe a fifth a day.

DRUG COUNSELOR: Okay, are we talking about a fifth of whiskey?

MAN: Yeah, we talkin' about a fifth of whiskey.

DRUG COUNSELOR: Um . . . would you drink any beer with that?

MAN: Yes.

DRUG COUNSELOR: How much?

MAN: Maybe four or five—forty ounces.

DRUG COUNSELOR: Are we talkin' 'bout in addition to or either/or?

MAN: Either/or.

DRUG COUNSELOR: So you would either drink a fifth of whiskey or a four or five—or forty ounces?

MAN: No, no, this is together.

DRUG COUNSELOR (*laughing*): This is together, okay. Um . . . you ever drop any pills to get loaded?

MAN: No.

DRUG COUNSELOR: Never. None of any kind? No Valium, no Zanax, no Elavils, no Adavans, no sleeping pills, no reds, blues, trees, no nonbarbiturate sedatives, no 'ludes, no pills of any kind?

MAN: No.

DRUG COUNSELOR: What about some uppers? You ever do any, any stimulants? No white crosses? No brown bombers, no black beauties, none of that?

MAN: No, sir.

DRUG COUNSELOR: Okay. You ever took any crank or crystal? That's methamphetamine?

MAN: No.

DRUG COUNSELOR: Mostly a biker thing. We gonna talk about some girl here. Powder, cocaine. How old were you the first time you was nice to your nose?

MAN: Okay, well, the first time I put cocaine to my nose was—I was maybe about twenty-three.

DRUG COUNSELOR: And at what age did, did your use of powder peak? That is, at what point—

MAN: That was—

DRUG COUNSELOR: —were you tootin' more powder than any other time?

MAN: That wasn't a problem. I just did that every once in a while.

DRUG COUNSELOR: What's once in a while? You talkin' about once a week, once a month?

MAN: Right, whenever I got wit' some friends of mine and they was doin' it. I was tootin' some cocaine.

DRUG COUNSELOR: Well, on average, how frequently did that happen?

MAN: Maybe twice a month.

DRUG COUNSELOR: Okay, so twice a month you bumped into somebody with a bag?

MAN: Right.

DRUG COUNSELOR: Would you buy?

MAN: No.

DRUG COUNSELOR: Okay, you bumped into somebody who was holding the bag?

MAN (*overlapping*): With a bag, right.

DRUG COUNSELOR: Okay. And you never used powdered cocaine any more frequently than that, right?

MAN: That's right.

DRUG COUNSELOR: Did you ever take any powder and cook it up so that you could smoke it?

MAN: Yes.

DRUG COUNSELOR: Okay, what did you use to cook it up with?

MAN: Baking soda.

DRUG COUNSELOR: Baking soda?

MAN: Right.

DRUG COUNSELOR: And how old were you the first time you did that?

MAN: I was a—what?, about a year afterwards.

DRUG COUNSELOR: So we're talking about twenty-four?

MAN: About twenty-four years old.

DRUG COUNSELOR: Okay. You never used ether or grain alcohol to cook up your dope?

MAN (*overlapping*): No.

DRUG COUNSELOR: Okay. You been up here at, behind crack for what, fifteen years?

MAN: About fifteen years.

DRUG COUNSELOR: Essentially the only thing that you really got a problem with is crack. But you got enough problems with crack—

MAN: Yeah?

DRUG COUNSELOR: Yeah, I mean you got a *serious* problem with crack.

MAN: I got a real serious problem with the crack.

DRUG COUNSELOR: You ever have any trouble with your nose when you were tootin' powder?

MAN: No.

DRUG COUNSELOR: Um, did you ever decide you was just gonna chill?

MAN: Yeah.

DRUG COUNSELOR: How old were you when you gave chillin' out your best shot?

MAN: Couple o' years ago. I chilled for two years.

DRUG COUNSELOR: So you were clean for two years?

MAN: I was clean for two years.

DRUG COUNSELOR: You think you got a drug problem?

MAN: Huh? Yes, I do.

DRUG COUNSELOR: Why do you think you have a drug problem? How has having the drug problem affected your life? What has it cost you?

MAN: It cost me from—a lot of time from being with my family, and 'cause I never, I never been like this. Even though I've used this drug for fifteen year, now lately I'm out two and three weeks at a time, and that's night and day here, and I never did that. You know, stay away from my family like that.

DRUG COUNSELOR: It has caused you to abandon your family?

MAN (*overlapping*): Right. Really just, totally neglect my family.

DRUG COUNSELOR: Um . . . What, what else are the things that doin' this to a—the way that this dope has impacted your life?

MAN: Okay. I find, I find myself now, you know, like late at night, if I don't have, if I don't spent a little money on maybe doing little carpentry jobs or whatever, there is a service station around my neighborhood that I go up, and I pump people gas and that's something that I, I don't, I don't catch— these drugs got me out here doin' things that I wouldn't normally do. Pumpin' gas for a quarter or whatever I can git in order to git these drugs, that ain't me. So that's why I know I got a problem.

DRUG COUNSELOR: So, so I think that what I hear you saying is that your self-respect has suffered as a result of doing these drugs—

MAN: Right.

DRUG COUNSELOR: Is that right?

MAN: Right.

DRUG COUNSELOR: Um . . . do you think that you'd've had these cases, this case, if you hadn't been done—out there and y'all trying to chase them rocks down?

MAN: No, I would not.

DRUG COUNSELOR: So that amongst the other ways it has affected your life is that, that your criminal, your involvement with the criminal justice system is related to your drug addiction? Is that right?

MAN: Right.

DRUG COUNSELOR: You think you need treatment?

MAN: Yes.

DRUG COUNSELOR: Why? I mean, what, what is it that you want treatment to do for you? What do you expect from treatment?

MAN: I want to, I wanna be able to know how to handle this thing that I got. You know, just like it slipped into my life, I wanna know how to let it slip right back out of it, you know?

DRUG COUNSELOR: So that, that what you wanna learn is how to regain control of your life?

MAN: Regain control of my life.

DRUG COUNSELOR: You the only person who can do that, you know.

MAN: Right.

DRUG COUNSELOR: I mean, there is no way that we can wave any magic wands and suddenly make you alright and cool.

MAN (*overlapping*): I want, I wants to. *I* wants to.

DRUG COUNSELOR: Alright.

MAN: But I just gotta—I wants to know how.

DRUG COUNSELOR: Cool.

MAN: You know?

DRUG COUNSELOR: Okay. Good. I'm glad to hear you sayin' that because everybody wants to be someplace.

MAN: Right.

DRUG COUNSELOR: Not everybody wants to get there.

MAN: Right.

DRUG COUNSELOR: Have you ever been the victim of violence and/or abuse, be it physical, emotional, or sexual, either as a child or as an adult?

MAN: Wait a minute, okay, now we—

DRUG COUNSELOR: Now we gettin' to the trauma.

MAN: We gettin' to the trauma part of it. Yes, I got hit on the head with a bat.

DRUG COUNSELOR: How old were you when you got hit?

MAN: I was, I was, that was in '88.

DRUG COUNSELOR: So we are talkin' about seven years ago.

MAN: Seven years ago.

DRUG COUNSELOR: You were thirty-three years old.

MAN: I was thirty-three.

DRUG COUNSELOR: Why, why were you hit on the head with a bat?

MAN: I was goin' into this, what they call a smokehouse and, you know at this particular time, there were some more guys that wanted what they wanted. So. And they, and so they, well, they thought that I was the guy that was sellin'. You know how the guys are?

DRUG COUNSELOR: Yeah.

MAN: This guy gettin' more money than I am and I'm a close this part down. So—but they thought—they got the wrong guy. They thought I was the guy that was sellin' the coke.

DRUG COUNSELOR: Were these, were these guys who were people who were dealing, or were they just rock stars who were lookin' for some money to get loaded on?

MAN: They was dealin'. They thought I was the guy—

DRUG COUNSELOR: So they thought they was dealin' with the competition?

MAN: Yeah.

DRUG COUNSELOR: Um . . . and how badly were you hurt?

MAN: Yeah, well, I was in a coma for, like, two days.

DRUG COUNSELOR: So you mean you were unconscious for two days?

MAN: I was unconscious for two days. Whatever they wanna call that.

DRUG COUNSELOR: Yeah. You lucky you walked from that one, guy.

MAN: Yeah.

DRUG COUNSELOR: And now talk to me about your back. How did that happen?

MAN: I was goin' into—

DRUG COUNSELOR: First of all, how old were you?

MAN: I was—it was last year. I was forty, uh, thirty-nine. I was goin' into a rock spot—

DRUG COUNSELOR: Uh-huh.

MAN: —and this guy asked me, when you come out, would you give me a bump of your—

DRUG COUNSELOR: Rock.

MAN: —your rock.

DRUG COUNSELOR: Right, right.

MAN: I told him no, I don't have anything for you. I don't even know nothin' about ya.

DRUG COUNSELOR: Uh-huh.

MAN: So I turned and walked off and— [*Makes hitting gesture with hand.*]

DRUG COUNSELOR: So you were knocked—

MAN: Cut me with a box cutter.

DRUG COUNSELOR: So he didn't even attempt to rob you? You know, all, all he was, was just resentful because you refused to share—

MAN: I refused to share my, my rock.

DRUG COUNSELOR: Yeah. It's bad enough that you belong to a group of people, the only group of people in the whole industrialized world whose life expectancy has fallen in the last ten years. That is, the black males that are the only group in the whole industrialized planet whose life expectancy has fallen in the last ten years. Without you subjecting your stuff to incidents like these.

MAN: Yeah.

DRUG COUNSELOR: That's counseling; this is diagnosis. Alright, listen. I have to—at this point, this assessment isn't over. But at this point, I have to tell you that I have to find you ineligible because the law says that if you are charged with delivery, you are ineligible for our program, but that's up to the judge. But I am finding you acceptable for Path Services. I think that you're sincere in your desire for treatment.

MAN: Yes, I am.

DRUG COUNSELOR: And I think you need it.

MAN: Yes, I do.

DRUG COUNSELOR: And to the extent that I can exert some control, I'm gonna urge that you get it, but that's ultimately up to the judge, okay?

MAN: Right.

DRUG COUNSELOR: And clearly the judge wanted this option at his disposal before he sentenced you or he would not have signed the court order. Okay? Hey, good luck, [*inaudible*].

69. The drug counselor speaks with an addict.

MAN: Alright, thank you.

DRUG COUNSELOR: Yeah, okay.

MAN: Have a nice day.

DRUG COUNSELOR: You take care.

MAN: I sure will. [*Cut to LS behind woman at computer in an office. Cut to shot of women sitting around a table listening to career counselor.*]

CAREER COUNSELOR: Last week we talked about a lot of things that you—

VOICE (*offscreen*): —last month, I'm sorry. We talked about a lot of things. You all remember. I'm just gonna review that briefly. We talked about public aid.

WOMAN (*offscreen*): Yes.

CAREER COUNSELOR: We talked about the new cuts. We also talked about all the programs that are going on, that aren't going to be here after these cuts come in December. Alright? We talked about taking advantage of the programs that we have now, because after this, these new legislations start, you won't have these programs. So have you all been giving any thought to what you're gonna do now that you see public aid is gonna be cut? Now that you see these programs are gonna be cut and you got a short time to get yourselves together? Have you all thought about and thought about the things that you wanna do? Plans for the future. Nikki?

70. A job counselor meets with some local residents.

NIKKI: I'll be working. I said, I get the newspaper every Sunday, send out my resume.

CAREER COUNSELOR (*overlapping*): Well, what do you do—what do you do every day?

NIKKI: What do I do every day?

CAREER COUNSELOR (*overlapping*): What's a typical day for Nikki?

NIKKI: Open up the newspaper, look at the job ads.

CAREER COUNSELOR: When you get up in the morning, what do you do?

NIKKI: Wash my face, brush my teeth.

CAREER COUNSELOR (*overlapping*): I'm not trying to put you on the spot, it's just . . . What do you do during the day?

NIKKI: Nothing. Just roam around the house. Sit on the park bench.

CAREER COUNSELOR: Hang.

NIKKI: That's it, [*inaudible*] with the TV. I go on a couple of job requests and then I just go back into the house.

CAREER COUNSELOR: Job ain't gonna come to you.

NIKKI: I know. I go lookin', I go lookin'.

CAREER COUNSELOR (*overlapping*): But mostly you just hangin'.

NIKKI: No, not really. I've been out of work for about a month now. A whole month. I worked a whole year. I've been out of work for a whole month now.

CAREER COUNSELOR: Okay. Anybody else been thinking about what they gonna do? Now, ladies that haven't gotten to that point, that have told me that they have a plan, it's gotta be something stoppin' you from doin' that. What is it?

NIKKI: I don't wanna work for five dollars or five-fifty. I ain't got no kids. I can't move. 'Cause I'm not makin' enough money. If I move, I ain't gonna have 'nuff money for the food, the gas bill, the lights, and the rent. I ain't got no kids. I can't live. I'm stayin' wit' my sister.

WOMAN (*offscreen*): I understand what she's saying.

NIKKI: I can't make it. I can't work for five dollars.

CAREER COUNSELOR: Okay, you can't work for five dollars.

NIKKI: I can work for it, but I got skills. I mean I got skills, but I can't work for five dollars. I'm just usin' myself up. I ain't got no—I have to wait to income tax time come to move. You move to an apartment, you need about a thousand dollars.

WOMAN (*offscreen*): You gonna be home.

CAREER COUNSELOR: Well, what do you have money for?

NIKKI: I don't have money for nothin'.

CAREER COUNSELOR: You got money for somethin'.

NIKKI: I don't have money for nothin'.

CAREER COUNSELOR: Yes, you do. You know what you got money for? You got money for a, a, a cute little jogging outfit. Your hair is layed to the nines.

NIKKI (*overlapping*): I got this from the booths that be outside, and I'll be shoppin' wit' them. I ain't been to the store in a year.

CAREER COUNSELOR: Well, somebody fried that hair.

NIKKI: Free.

CAREER COUNSELOR: You paid for it.

NIKKI: Free.

CAREER COUNSELOR: One way or the other it got paid for.

NIKKI: No.

CAREER COUNSELOR: It wasn't free.

NIKKI: A lot of people just got skills.

CAREER COUNSELOR: A lot a people got skills.

NIKKI: And they'll do it.

CAREER COUNSELOR: But don't you trade skills for another skill?

WOMAN: Yeah.

CAREER COUNSELOR: Aha, aha.

NIKKI: But see, I can't move. I don't want five dollars, though. I don't want five dollars.

CAREER COUNSELOR: You don't want it. But can you afford—but can you really afford to say what you want and what you don't want at this stage in the game? I mean, do you understand what I'm saying? Can you really afford to say, "Yeah, I work but, but I ain't doin' it for five-fifty—

WOMAN (*offscreen*): Not for five-fifty.

CAREER COUNSELOR: "When somebody knock on my door for ten-fifty, I will get with them. But for five-fifty I ain't gonna do nothin. I'm just gonna hang for right now with the five-fifty." Now if—now I ain't tryin' to be funny or anythin' but it's like—

NIKKI: I tell you, ain't nobody offerin' no more than five-fifty.

WOMAN (*offscreen*): I'll work for five-fifty.

WOMAN (*offscreen*): Would you take five-fifty for six months until you find somethin better?

WOMAN (*offscreen*): Seven dollars.

WOMAN WITH HAIR IN BUN: I'd work for five-fifty because, okay, you made—you gonna start makin' five-fifty, but that's probably—you not—if you gonna stay there, I'm sure you gonna advance.

WOMAN WITH SHORT HAIR: You bring some skills and qualifications that you git, then you're gonna get a raise.

WOMAN WITH HAIR IN BUN (*overlapping*): You have a problem going to work? I'll take it.

WOMAN WITH NECKLACE: Go to work every day, be on time every day, and you show some stability and at one place, you know. Like you say, you bring a skill to the table, you might be somebody's supervisor. Okay?

WOMAN WITH HAIR IN BUN (*overlapping*): Because when I was working at Presbyterian St. Luke's, I was just supposed to be a day worker, for three weeks, and I ended up being there for eight years. So you can't say well, I can't work for five-fifty, because you don't know what the future holds.

CAREER COUNSELOR: You know we doin' this because we want you all to know that if a plan isn't clear, we can still help you make one. 'Cause I'm gonna tell y'all. I will be very honest with you. I was talkin' to my boss the other day and I said, you know what? If there aren't any changes made real soon, when these cuts come, in December of what, what is it, '96? '98?

WOMAN (*offscreen*): '98.

CAREER COUNSELOR: I'm not working at Ida B. Wells.

WOMAN (*offscreen*): It's gonna be crazy.

CAREER COUNSELOR: It's gonna be like a war zone.

WOMAN (*offscreen*): Yeah, it is.

CAREER COUNSELOR: I'll be very honest with you. I said that. [*Eleven shots of various neighborhood street scenes, including liquor store, empty lots, someone selling clothes out of a truck.*]

FIRST POLICEMAN: C'mere, put you hands on the car. Get your hands on the car. Get your hands on the car. Spread 'em out, dude. Where's the refrigerator at? [*Cut to policeman frisking two men.*]

MAN IN GREEN SHIRT: That wasn't no housing refrigerator.

FIRST POLICEMAN: Where is the refrigerator at?

MAN IN GREEN SHIRT: That wasn't no housing refrigerator.

MAN IN BURGUNDY JACKET: That wasn't no housing refrigerator.

FIRST POLICEMAN: Yeah, okay.

MAN IN GREEN SHIRT: I show you where it's at.

FIRST POLICEMAN: Yeah, okay. Yeah, okay.

MAN IN GREEN SHIRT: That wasn't no housing refrigerator.

SECOND POLICEMAN: Spread your legs. Spread your legs.

MAN IN GREEN SHIRT: The refrigerator . . . wasn't no housing—it was given to us, right there.

FIRST POLICEMAN: Where'd it come from, then?

MAN IN GREEN SHIRT: It wasn't no housing refrigerator.

FIRST POLICEMAN: Where did it come from?

MAN IN GREEN SHIRT: I got it from my cousin.

FIRST POLICEMAN: Where?

MAN IN GREEN SHIRT: She told me I could sell it.

POLICEMAN: Where's it at? Where's it at?

MAN IN GREEN SHIRT: It's down there.

FIRST POLICEMAN: In the yellow house down there.

MAN IN BURGUNDY SHIRT: That ain't no housing refrigerator . . .

MAN IN GREEN SHIRT (*overlapping*): You think we woulda took that refrigerator all the way down here like that?

FIRST POLICEMAN: Who's wit' you? Who's wit' you?

VOICE (*offscreen*): What's that?

MAN IN BURGUNDY JACKET (*offscreen*): It's down there.

FIRST POLICEMAN: Where that yellow house is at?

MAN IN GREEN SHIRT: Yeah.

FIRST POLICEMAN: When the numbers are ran on this refrigerator, whose refrigerator is it?

MAN IN GREEN SHIRT: It ain't no housing refrigerator—

MAN IN BURGUNDY JACKET: Somebody just set it in the incinerator on the fourth floor. We took it out of the incinerator, and we sold it.

POLICEMAN: Yeah, first we was just talkin' to you, and you just told me you got it from your cousin.

MAN IN BURGUNDY JACKET: Right, man. That's right. Because I thought it was a housing refrigerator, but he told me it wasn't.

MAN IN GREEN SHIRT: They was just gonna leave it there and throw it out anyway, so we got it. That ain't no housing refrigerator. It ain't, no sweat. We ain't worried about gettin' a housing refrigerator.

POLICEMAN: Okay, alright, okay, okay. [*Police scanner, inaudible.*] You got it?

MAN IN GREEN SHIRT: The guy said [*inaudible*]. Ain't no housing.

FIRST POLICEMAN: It's housing.

THIRD POLICEMAN: Ten-four. [*Policemen proceed to handcuff the two men.*]

MAN IN GREEN SHIRT: Why don't you go on in and lookin' at that old 'frigerator? That's not no housing 'frigerator.

FIRST POLICEMAN: It's a housing refrigerator.

MAN IN GREEN SHIRT: No it's not. Man! You boys go in and look at the 'frigerator. That's not a housing—

FIRST POLICEMAN: They already in there!

BOTH MEN: But it's not a housing refrigerator. That's not a housing refrigerator!

FIRST POLICEMAN (*overlapping*): You all wait out here and I'll come back with the car.

SECOND POLICEMAN (*overlapping*): Okay.

MAN IN GREEN SHIRT: Okay, but that's not a housing refrigerator right there. Straight up. That's not the housing refrigerator.

FIRST POLICEMAN (*overlapping*): Just lean on the car. Just lean on the car.

MAN IN GREEN SHIRT: No. Okay, go ahead. I'm leaning on it.

FIRST POLICEMAN: Okay.

MAN IN GREEN SHIRT: But that is not a housing refrigerator. [*Voice on police scanner, inaudible.*] That ain't no housing refrigerator, man. Straight up. It's not a housing refrigerator.

MAN IN BURGUNDY JACKET: C'mon, man. What the fuck?

SECOND POLICEMAN: Just lean forward.

FIRST POLICEMAN: Just lean forward.

SECOND POLICEMAN: If you move back, you're gonna get hurt.

MAN IN BURGUNDY JACKET (*overlapping*): But the cuffs hurt, man.

SECOND POLICEMAN: Well, that's what I am trying to fix.

MAN IN GREEN SHIRT: Yeah, they're trying to fix it—right! Hey, that's not a housing refrigerator. We wouldn't go through all that.

FIRST POLICEMAN (*overlapping*): Police said it was a housing 'frigerator. They said cuff 'em.

MAN IN GREEN SHIRT: Oh, y'all didn't check it yet?

FIRST POLICEMAN: They checked it.

MAN IN GREEN SHIRT: It's not a housing refrigerator.

FIRST POLICEMAN: You can tell me all you want to tell.

MAN IN GREEN SHIRT: That is not a housing refrigerator. We wouldn't even took that mothafucker. It was in the incinerator. We wouldn't have even took the mothafucker out from the incinerator if it wasn't no housing refrigerator.

SECOND POLICEMAN: You know what? There is no sense in talking. Look forward.

MAN IN BURGUNDY JACKET: I am.

SECOND POLICEMAN: There is no sense in talking about right now.

MAN IN GREEN SHIRT: Well, I want to—I was just asking. Did they really check the numbers, because that ain't no housing refrigerator. It ain't no housing refrigerator.

MAN IN BURGUNDY JACKET: Right, it's not a housing refrigerator, man. Sure the hell ain't.

MAN IN GREEN SHIRT (*overlapping*): We know this.

SECOND POLICEMAN: So what should we do? Should we just turn you loose right now?

MAN IN GREEN SHIRT: For what? Alright, that's what I'm saying. He can go talk to them. Yeah, that's what I am talkin' 'bout.

SECOND POLICEMAN (*overlapping*): Alright, that's what we'll do then.

MAN IN GREEN SHIRT: Yeah.

FIRST POLICEMAN: Yeah. We gonna do what you tell us to do.

MAN IN GREEN SHIRT: Not we. I ain't saying it like that. I'm just saying uh, uh—

FIRST POLICEMAN: Yeah.

MAN IN GREEN SHIRT: —you know, just go down and talk to them peoples because it's not a housing refrigerator.

FIRST POLICEMAN: Okay.

MAN IN GREEN SHIRT: Okay.

FIRST POLICEMAN: I ain't gonna talk to nobody.

MAN IN GREEN SHIRT: Well, you ain't got to. I'm sorry, you ain't got to—

MAN IN BURGUNDY SHIRT: That's what I'm saying. What kind a numbers did they run on it? Y'all ran some numbers?

MAN IN GREEN SHIRT: Ain't no numbers on the mothafucker. That's an old-ass 'frigerator. It ain't even housing. [*Eight shots of neighborhood street scenes: traffic, children playing baseball, abandoned cars, people relaxing outside, a small child throwing a piece of metal against a brick wall. In the eighth shot, an angry woman slaps one of her two young children and argues with a man who tries to restrain her.*]

WOMAN (*to man*): Let me go before I knock your ass out. [*Slaps girl in the face. To man*] Bitch, you know when I catch you, I'm gonna fuck yo' ass up.

MAN: Nice language for a lady.

WOMAN: Get the goddamn kids out of my mothafuckin' face. [*CU of young girl in diaper left alone as the woman chases the man out of frame right. Four shots of different views of development exterior. Shot of sign on building: "Grandmother's Sewing Circle, 533 East 38th Place." Three shots of women sewing.*]

WOMAN IN HAIRNET: This is gonna be some piece when I get through with it.

WOMAN (*offscreen*): Yeah, you tell them.

WOMAN IN HAIRNET: Give me the scissors.

WOMAN (*offscreen*): Who? Who needs the scissors? Who needs the scissors?

WOMAN IN GREY PRINT TOP: Yeah. Gimme scissors . . . Hey, go girl.

WOMAN (*offscreen*): [*Inaudible.*] Cut it, like, on an angle.

WOMAN IN BLUE SMOCK: I can't even see without my glasses.

WOMAN IN FLOWER PRINT DRESS: Don't let everybody know you blind.

WOMAN IN BLUE SMOCK: Hey, I can't—I ain't ashamed to let 'em know I can't see.

WOMAN IN PRINT DRESS: How low?

WOMAN IN BLUE SMOCK: I'm not ashamed to let 'em know I need glasses.

WOMAN IN PLAID (*offscreen*): Turn around here.

WOMAN IN PRINT DRESS: Look, I'm tryin' to see 'bout how low, where them pockets should be, yeah . . . Think that's gonna be too low?

WOMAN IN PLAID: Think that's too low, yeah.

WOMAN IN PRINT DRESS: It's too low.

WOMAN IN PLAID: Bring it a little higher.

WOMAN IN PRINT DRESS: What I gotta do is make a shawl. Got enough material to make a shawl, or a hat.

WOMAN IN HAIRNET: It's gonna look kinda nice, maybe.

WOMAN IN BLUE SMOCK (*threading needle on sewing machine*): Oh I got it, I got it, I got it, I got it. Eee—eee—eee, I got it. There it is. There it is.

WOMAN IN PRINT DRESS: So, so you not gonna go tonight, right?

71. One member of the sewing circle discusses her patterns.

WOMAN (*offscreen*): Me?

WOMAN IN PRINT DRESS: Yeah, to the ball game?

WOMAN (*offscreen*): Unless you take me.

WOMAN IN PRINT DRESS: You not goin' on the bus? Well, I'm not driving, so you just won't be goin'. As you know, I don't have an automobile.

WOMAN IN HAIRNET: What's that long thing there for? Cap and a thing to go with it?

WOMAN IN PRINT DRESS: Oh no, that's a scarf that go over—oh, you didn't see this outfit. I thought you saw it.

WOMAN IN HAIRNET: This?

WOMAN IN PRINT DRESS: Here, I'll show you. See, this is trimmed in this. This is the scarf. I saw this at an African, African um—

WOMAN IN HAIRNET: Yeah, that looks pretty.

WOMAN IN PRINT DRESS: I saw it at an African thing. I told the lady, I said, how'd you make that? She said, you put foam in— [*Woman puts on hat.*]

WOMAN IN HAIRNET: You look right fine.

WOMAN IN PRINT DRESS: Oh, just gorgeous, I know. Hmm! [*Laughter from other woman.*] Ain't no need for tellin' me. I know it.

WOMAN IN HAIRNET: I like it, though.

WOMAN IN PRINT DRESS: Yeah, it's pretty, isn't it? But they didn't have any more material.

WOMAN IN HAIRNET: You shoulda made a whole outfit like that.

WOMAN IN PRINT DRESS: They didn't have any more material like this. I went all the way to Ford City, and they didn't have it in then. And now, I love to drive to Ford City. I don't know when I will be back out there. They'll have it whenever I go back because it'll be forever. I don't like to go that far.

WOMAN IN HAIRNET: Who made this one?

WOMAN IN PRINT DRESS: I made this for Mom.

WOMAN IN HAIRNET: For who?

WOMAN IN PRINT DRESS: Mom.

WOMAN IN HAIRNET: Whose mom?

WOMAN IN PRINT DRESS: My mom!

WOMAN IN HAIRNET: Oh.

WOMAN IN PRINT DRESS: I ain't got but one.

WOMAN IN HAIRNET: Yeah, that's pretty.

WOMAN IN PRINT DRESS: Yeah, I learned how to make these buttonholes. I did all that . . . and then I gotta put ruffles on there, then I'm through with that one. Ms. Williams did that. I didn't do that.

WOMAN IN HAIRNET: Oh. It looked like a—it, it's a dress. I like this one. Who'd ya make this one for?

WOMAN IN PRINT DRESS: For me.

WOMAN IN HAIRNET: Hey, you got somethin' in the pocket. What is it?

WOMAN IN PRINT DRESS: Pins. I'm going to—when I take the pins out, the ruffles are just pinned there. I gotta sew 'em.

WOMAN IN HAIRNET: Oh.

WOMAN IN PRINT DRESS: I can throw 'em back in that pin thing.

WOMAN IN HAIRNET: How'd you get these ruffles so even?

WOMAN IN PRINT DRESS: Well, I didn't do it on a machine. I did it by hand.

WOMAN IN HAIRNET: Looks nice. [*Two ext. shots: a building, a person gardening. Cut to shot of two policeman walking through courtyard.*]

BOY: What's up, man?

POLICEMAN: How ya doin'? [*Boombox playing.*] That's the real music. That ain't no electronics. [*Three shots: children at front door of unit, CU of boom-box in window, LS of people barbecuing, the music carrying over on the soundtrack. Cut to shot of the two policemen walking in courtyard away from camera.*]

POLICEMAN: Yeah, here we are. Once we go all the way through, then we'll check and do the [*inaudible*] of the basement. [*Cut to shot of one girl chasing another, arguing.*]

FIRST GIRL (*overlapping*): What you mean, what? I wish I had bust yo' mouth—keep running. Oh, it's a joke?

SECOND GIRL: No, it wasn't.

FIRST GIRL: I'll tell you what. Keep runnin', keep runnin'.

POLICEMAN: Tell one of them what's up.

FIRST GIRL: I'm gonna fuck you up. I'm gonna kick you mothafuckin' ass when I get my hands on you. [*In far background, the two girls continue arguing. The first girl picks up a bottle out of a dumpster and continues after the other girl. The two policemen rush into frame left.*]

POLICEMAN: Hey, hey, hey, hey, hey, hey. C'mere, you. Okay, c'mere. Put the bottle down. Put the bottle down. Put the bottle down.

GIRL: Don't put your hands on me. Yo' hands. Don't put yo' hands on me. [*Cut to eight shots of neighborhood scenes, including two of children in public swimming pool, boy on bench, children on swings, man gardening, boys playing basketball. Eighth shot is of a building exterior, followed by a cut to MS of girl reading.*]

GIRL (SHAQUIA) (*reading from newspaper*): "Parental abuse phenomenon stems from lack of control at home. A kid bombs his parents with artillery shells because an erroneous fear of a parental attack was resented. Seconds from progress of a parental abuse case. In another case, a child asked his parents if he could go outside, and the father said no. The child then proceeded to beat up both parents. When you hear about abuse, you usually think of parents abusing children. Whether it was mental or physical abuse, you've heard the stories. But what would you—but would you believe, in some cases, it's the child who's actually abusing the parent? It doesn't happen as much as its reverse, with a one in ten chance, but it does happen. Both mental and physical abuse. And just as in child abuse cases, you can't help but ask yourself the same question: why? Why would someone want to abuse his or her parents? Well, surely someone, some wise-guy teens, could give some answers to that, but this is serious. And what parent would allow their child to

72. A girl reads from a newspaper story about abusive family relationships.

abuse them? Have these families forgotten the simple fact that the parent is over the child, the head of the household regardless of any situation?"

MAN: Hold up. Trina?

TRINA (*continuing*): "Let's focus on why. Researchers find this problem has its beginnings with the parent not having control. So the child feels he can do as he wishes. Once this is set in a child's mind, it's hard to change. Then when parents try to discipline the child, he retaliates. So in a sense the child becomes the boss over the parent. The child's internal anger of not having the opportunity to be a child builds up, and the abuse escalates from there. This anger at oneself is also an excuse used by parents who abuse their children. In some of the reported cases of teens abusing parents, it has occurred in single-parent homes. But it's still no stranger in two-family homes. Usually the child will see one parent hitting the other. With the child having this example and no other discipline, the child does what he or she's seen. Unless or until it's stopped, it can become routine. After reading the research and conducting interviews, it seems that discipline and morals begin at, in the home. If there is no discipline in the home, or if the child abuses his or her parents, then in all reality he or she is not free to be a child at all, and in most cases, both abusers and abused suffer because of the conflict."

MAN: What do you guys think of that?

BOY (*offscreen*): It's weird.

GIRL (*offscreen*): Strange.

GIRL (*offscreen*): It's true.

MAN: Why is it weird?

GIRL IN BLUE T-SHIRT: Because when you think about it, you don't think about it. Like they said, you don't think about the kids beating up on the parents. You think about the parents beating on the kids.

MAN: Alright, and why is it that you think it to be true?

GIRL IN BLACK TOP: Because some kids, they don't have no self-control. And they mamas or they daddies, they are raisin' 'em to have none, so they just do what they want.

MAN: Okay, so, you think that a kid have to be out of control in order to beat their parent?

GIRL IN WHITE T-SHIRT: (NICOLE): Uh-huh.

GIRL: Yeah.

BOY: I don't think so.

MAN: Nicole?

NICOLE: Naw, they just beat up like on one of those cartoon shows, like rabbit beat up on the mouse or the mouse, the little people beat up on the big kids, the little mouse beat up the big cat. So they think they can do it.

MAN: So they might be influenced by television shows or something they saw?

NICOLE: That's one.

MAN: Shaquia?

SHAQUIA: It's not that they out of control. It's like sometimes the parent give their child a little bit too much freedom. And they say, well, I can do what I wanna do. Can't nobody tell me what to do, and I could beat you anyway, so I, ain't no need of you tryin' to stop me.

MAN: What kind of a parent do you think allows their child to beat them? Or is it that they can't do anything about it?

GIRL IN BLACK T-SHIRT: Some of 'em might just—can't do nothin' about it. Better call the police or somethin'.

SHAQUIA: It was, it's like, it's like some parents, they sound weird, but some parents are actually scared of their children. Because I know this boy where his father is actually scared of him, and his father let him do what he wanna do and run over him and leave out of the house when he wants to and come in when he wants to and not go to school if he don't want to. So it's like they just scared of him.

MAN: Anybody else know somebody who, kids who—scared of their kids?

NICOLE: Some people, like, you know, their mothers and their fathers be deceased and their grandma watchin' over them. You know, when they—some grandmamas ain't—some grandmamas have control over their kids. But, you know, my grandma put me up her lap and beat me with a swatter, a fly swatter. But some old people just can't do that. You know, they probably try to just do this. You know when they walk out the house, they ain't sayin' a word behind them because, you know, they probably ain't got no authority over them.

MAN: Okay, Dominique.

DOMINIQUE: Sometimes they parents might beat them and they feel like they get to beat 'em back.

MAN: Alright. That's a good—

GIRL (*overlapping*): I was about to say that.

MAN: That's a point too, that maybe—and I think the article did refer to that in a way, but it said from the point that the parents might fight each other and the child has been raised seeing violence, so that's what they know. So they think that that is the way to get, of gettin' their way, that they react by jumping on their parent when they can't get their way. But what's right? What would be the right way to handle that for all parties involved?

SHAQUIA: I think instead of just going at the hand, you should calm down a little bit. I know some situations, they just get out of hand. You feel like you just hit 'em right off the bat. So sometimes if you feel like you could just really, really, at your, at your top temper, you can just feel like you gonna kill 'em, you should just sit down and think about it or talk about or something. Because you—like after you killed them, you be like, I miss my baby when all you shoulda just cooled down a little bit and just talk about it a little later on. [*Several shots of bulldozers razing a building intercut with shots of people watching. Two shots of building exteriors. Cut to shot of several women listening to birth control counselor.*]

BIRTH CONTROL COUNSELOR (*baby crying in background throughout scene*): Well, nowadays we want our young girls to know about condoms. Rubbers, at that time, you know what, rubbers theoretically were a man's thing. [*Cut to counselor.*] Men used them when they went into service, you know it was like, the man uses this when he goes to service to protect himself. And he uses it when he goes out there creepin', you know, to protect himself. Whereas now it's a universal thing. Everybody uses the condom. Women are expected to have condoms. We came up with a little condom purse. It's like we can carry our condoms around and still have style and class.

WOMAN IN PLAID TOP: Oh, let me see that. [*Laughter.*]

BIRTH CONTROL COUNSELOR: And you know, at Expo—we did a table at Today's Black Woman Expo—and this one lady, she's developed an underwear that has a little pocket where you keep your condom. But, in other words, the idea of the condom is a universal thing now. You know, it's like, me and my daughter were sittin' on, on the bus one day fillin' the purses because I had this order. And we were trying to fill 'em before—and a policeman got on, he was like, you let your daughter touch those? I'm like, why wouldn't she touch it? And then when I think about it, at my age, I wouldn't, I didn't even know what they were. [*Laughter.*] Much less—they were those things that were way back in the drugstore, and you didn't even pay any attention to them. Besides being excellent for AIDS protection and STDs, the condom originally was a birth control device. When you were pregnant and if you didn't want to get pregnant—I mean, if you were married and you didn't want to get pregnant—and you are having sex, you use the condom. That's basically all you had. Well, a condom is—

WOMAN (*offscreen overlapping*): Stop it.

BIRTH CONTROL COUNSELOR: —still a very good birth control device, ladies. Especially when you add the use of spermicide to it. You take a little spermicide. Where's my little Woody? Oh, here he is over here [*picks up dildo*]. Now here's my little condom . . . sample over here. We did a poster, and I do believe I brought it, of quality of condoms, and Silk is the highest rated condom in the country right now. So keep that in mind. Trojan, which used to be one—is very low, is very low because the material that Trojan is used out of— that's why Trojan is always—remember, they used to break. They still do!

WOMAN IN PLAID TOP: Yeah, that's how I got pregnant, with Trojans.

WOMAN (*offscreen*): 'Cause it's just a name.

BIRTH CONTROL COUNSELOR: And condoms will break. Okay, from different times. But Trojans have one of the highest incidents of breakage, just in general, not because they've been stored improperly or whatever. These come lubricated, and they come with Noxinol-9 and without, with just lubricant. Because, a lot of times, people are finding that they are allergic to the Noxinol-9 ingredient. The Noxinol-9 and lubricant are two separate things, okay? Some lubricants have Noxinol-9, some lubricants don't. So even if, if, you know, your mate or if you are allergic to the Noxinol-9, you can get a lubricant that does not have that ingredient. And what Noxinol-9 is, is the ingredient that right now is the best for killing the AIDS virus.

WOMAN (*offscreen*): Oh, okay.

BIRTH CONTROL COUNSELOR: That does not mean that if I have sex with a person who has AIDS, and we use Noxinol-9, I will not get AIDS because it will kill it. It has a better chance of killing a lot of it, but you can still get AIDS. Okay? But it, on the average, Noxinol-9 is that ingredient that kills the AIDS virus faster than anything else that is going on out here, on contact. Okay? Always demonstrate the proper usage of a condom. Okay? One of the things—always remember that the penis is erect. You cannot put a condom on a nonerect penis, ladies, I'm sorry, it doesn't work, okay? The penis must be erect. Okay? When you take a condom out of the package, one of the things that's changed—Trojans, when you take it out of the package, it's flat across there. One of the things they've done is they've given— that little imprint right there, the part that points up. That's real important for you to pay attention to because, for one thing, that point should always be able to stick up and you should be able to roll the condom down.

WOMAN (*offscreen, overlapping, to her crying baby*): Shhh. Shhh.

BIRTH CONTROL COUNSELOR: Not the other way around, because if so, you're putting the condom on inside out and your spermicide is inside and is doing you no good. Try and keep that in mind. When you put the spermicide in, whether you're, you're putting it on or whether he's putting it on, make sure that he starts at the tip of the penis with the condom rolled up. You do not unroll the condom and then put it on. Then it's like this, straight out. And then try to put it on because you have a bigger chance of breakage, okay? And it's also much more uncomfortable. And they gives you like, they gives you more of those excuses. You know, like, "Oh, it's too hard," "I don't like it." No, you start just like this and then you roll it. You simply roll it on. Even though this is fake, on the real thing, it works even easier. Because you roll it on.

WOMAN (*offscreen, to crying infant*): Shut up!

BIRTH CONTROL COUNSELOR: If it's not rolling on like this, check it because more than likely it is inside out and it's like rolling from the inside, and that means you also have no spermicide on the outside, okay? When you insert, when finish inserting the penis, that little point that I showed you, that area should be open on the end of the penis. The condom should never fit all the way down on the penis like this, where there is no room on the end of it. Because during ejaculation that can give that condom a bigger chance of breakage. Okay? It can also give it a bigger chance of coming out through the back. And one little drop, one little tiny drop of sperm, ladies, contains over a thousand sperms, okay?, of semen, contains over a thousand sperm, okay? So one little drop can get you! You want to be real careful . . . One of the things they've come out with in the nineties, ladies, because we have a lot of, a lot of people, a lot of men, give us reasons why they don't like condoms: y'know, they're too tight, they don't feel like the real thing, I don't like it, it breaks, whatever. Well, if you have run into that case, it's just like, but I want to use a condom. I wanna use it. I can't use a condom. We have the female condom, ladies. This is called the Reality. I'm gonna pass it around, and I'm gonna use my little book over here to explain it to you. But this is the Reality condom. This is new. This is the female condom, and the way that it's used is: it has a little ring. You see that little ring up at the top? It feels kind of like the outside of a diaphragm and basically you take it and it's inserted. And this is a diagram of how it looks. It's inserted into the vagina and it goes up and it covers the cervix just like a diaphragm did.

WOMAN IN WHITE T-SHIRT: It be that big?

BIRTH CONTROL COUNSELOR: That's it.

WOMAN IN WHITE T-SHIRT: I wanna see it.

BIRTH CONTROL COUNSELOR: That's it. And it looks—it's like, wow, it's so big and it hangs out of the vagina like this.

WOMAN (*offscreen*): Like what?

WOMAN (*offscreen*): That hard thing?

BIRTH CONTROL COUNSELOR: It hangs out.

WOMAN (*offscreen*): No, it hangs on out.

WOMAN (*offscreen*): That hard thing—

BIRTH CONTROL COUNSELOR: Now the part on the inside, that's a little ring because that makes it fit around your cervix. Okay?

WOMAN (*offscreen*): So you tellin' me—

BIRTH CONTROL COUNSELOR: Uh-huh, and the only thing that hangs out is the opening part.

WOMAN (*offscreen*): This part here? So it won't fit all the way in?

BIRTH CONTROL COUNSELOR: Right, no, the whole thing does not go in. It literally hangs out, and it's supposed to.

WOMAN (*offscreen*): So, what's a man gonna say when he sees that thing hangin' out?

BIRTH CONTROL COUNSELOR: Well, well, I mean, what is his—I mean, think about it now. What is he gonna say?

WOMAN (*overlapping*): He gonna say—

BIRTH CONTROL COUNSELOR (*overlapping*): He's gonna say, well I want it, or I don't. But at least now you got a choice because it used to be, you gotta put this on. Okay? But the point of it is it gives you a little bit more leverage. If I'm a woman and I say, listen, I have to have a condom to use. You're the man and you say, I'm not gonna use it—then I'm gonna, well, I have my own. And if he don't want to use it, then cool, let's go play tennis. You know? But the point of it is, that's what it's about. It's about giving yourself a little bit more power. Y'know, 'bout giving—in other words, you've got to at least start the conversation, and for a lot of us, it's hard to even get that conversation going. Because, you know, we get that "Well, don't you trust me? If you trust me, you wouldn't be tellin' me to use a condom. I told you I'm not, I'm not messin' around with nobody else." And that's well and fine, but do I really want to put my life on the line when we talk about things like AIDS, or do I want to put the life of a child that I might not be ready for right now into, you know, into this friction? If I know I'm not ready for that, then maybe it's for me. And then if he doesn't want to use it, we got somethin' to talk about. Why not? Don't you care about me? Don't you care about my concerns? Aren't you concerned about me possibly having a baby that we can't take care of? Aren't you concerned about me possibly getting an infection that maybe you don't know you have right now?

WOMAN IN BLUE SHORTS: Why all the women's protection got all them hard rings and stuff?

BIRTH CONTROL COUNSELOR: We need them 'cause we want to hold them in place. See, men, they're erect, so they have something to hold this condom on to. We, basically—if you just put it in there—

WOMAN: We have nothin' to hold it.

BIRTH CONTROL COUNSELOR: Right, and the whole thing of this, why you usin' this, is you want to protect your cervix. [*Various shots of people outside development, including woman beating throw rug against a brick wall, man putting tire into car trunk, children playing, people walking. Various shots of people outside at a party, dancing to music. People watching. Two shots of neighborhood in late afternoon. In the first, a police car drives by. Cut to Police station parking lot at night. Cut to CU of moon (three-quarters).*]

73. A guest speaker discusses the danger of drugs with local schoolchildren.

Cut to ext. shot of entrance to "Resident Advisory Council." Cut to MS of Mrs. Finner at her desk.]

MRS. FINNER (*on telephone*): Oh Booker, you just the one I wanna see, talk to. Why, I have the toilets at 3726 Cottage Grove, which is a food site, where Mr. Maja came in and wrote the site manager up. The toilet has not been taken care of. It's stopped up. It has not been taken care of. Why hasn't the lock—somebody came out and change the lock on the door, so both site managers can have a key? . . . I don't know. Uh-huh. . . . Booker, don't play with me. I don't wanna get no more upset than I am already. Would someone please write the work order? [*Cut to ext. shot of entrance to Resident Advisory Council. Several shots of a barbecue, two men grilling and others lining up for food.*]

MAN: My brother, would you cut that steakburger in half too? [*Shot of people lined up at snack truck. Cut to ext. LS of Abraham Lincoln Center, followed by shot of boys and girls in room dressed in similar "Kid's Day 1995" T-shirts listening to drug counselor.*]

DRUG COUNSELOR: Only thing—I don't have a lot of time today because I gotta go and bury my friend. [*Cut to counselor.*] His funeral is at ten o'clock today. And you know, it was something real, real sad 'cause it was five of us. I'm gonna write the names down of these guys. I need y'all to see this to really understand what I went through. It was five of us. It was David, which was me. It was Larue, Carl, Fred, and oh, man . . . Donald. Thank you. Alright. This is a real quick life, okay. When I drove around the corner to see their mamas, I got messed up 'cause Larue is serving his second sentence. Now mind you, all of us, when we were fifteen, were A students. I was at Linbloom Technical High School, Larue was at Harland, Carl was at Leo, Fred was at Harland, and Donald was at Linbloom with me. Donald was All-State in basketball; Fred was just a genius. Carl was a basketball and baseball player. Larue was a baseball player. I ran track and played baseball and basketball. By the time we got to our senior year, we had all tried something. But when I went around to their mamas' house, Larue was in Danfield on his second sentence in jail or maybe his third. Larue has, possibly has, AIDS. He's in a wheelchair and can't walk. He was walking two and a half months ago. He never stopped shootin' dope. Carl is dead. I'm goin' to his funeral today. Fred might have AIDS. He's shootin' dope now too. I last saw Donald—he might have AIDS. He was shootin' dope. He's got a master's degree in education and is homeless and can't nobody find him. Everybody started out doin', and I'm alive. Okay? I'm kickin'. Look at that. Got muscles and stuff. I was pushin' weights yesterday. I was eatin' iron on the weight bench yesterday. Man, I was pumpin' weights yesterday. Felt good, too. Every one of 'em started out drinkin' and smokin'. The two gateway drugs in the world that people say won't hurt you. It won't hurt to take a drink. It won't hurt to take a smoke. This stuff will kill you. Black children and adults are allergic to alcohol, tobacco, and other drugs, 'cause every time we do it, we end up in the same boat—addicted. And we have a hard time gettin' out, and there's addicts in every community in the world. It's people in Wells that's still here when I was here, 1967, got three generations of kids that ain't moved off zero. Their daddy is still on the corner drinkin'. Pisses me off, and I have to say that word. Makes me mad. It makes me mad that I had to bury a friend of mine. Do y'all see this? I'm only forty! [*Bangs his chest.*] These guys started at your age. If you are doin' it, I advise you to stop. If you are thinking about doing it, trust me. Is there a guarantee you won't be a dope fiend at forty? Is there a guarantee that you won't be walkin' around wit yo'—a girl walkin around wit' yo' T-shirt tied in a knot on one side with lipstick half way over yo' face talking about "want a date?" with the spandex tights on. I call them skisac atteracts [*laughter*] 'cause that's what they look like, a new animal. And I hate to say it, but that's what they look like and that's what happens. Because I cannot get wit' black women sacrificing themselves at the age of fifteen, to get a rock. Are y'all with me? Check? [*Cut to LS of Lincoln Center. Thirteen shots of people on street, including children playing, a bag man, a parked police car, liquor store, Baptist church, two men on a motorcycle, woman sitting on a chair. LS of woman sitting on steps in front of building. Cut to CU of YWCA sign: "Coretta Scott King Child Development Center. Pre-School Program." Another shot of woman on steps. Shot of woman bringing a boy into building. Cut to inside building, LS of children playing. Boy playing by himself.*]

TEACHER: No, that's mine . . . Winston, give that back to him. Thank you. That's yours. This is mine. Now you go get a paper and write . . . [*Cut to teacher and boy.*] Okay, you gonna put 'em in order by size. Okay, you gotta take all of the cards first and you gotta lay 'em out. You take a good look at 'em. Where's the big, big flower pot at? Where's the big, big flower pot? Show me the pot.

BOY: Right here.

TEACHER: Very good. So it's gonna be the first flower pot. Okay, *now* where's the big flower pot?

BOY: Right here.

TEACHER: Very good. So it's gonna be number two. *Now* where's the big flower pot?

BOY: Right here.

TEACHER: Let's see. Take a good look at that. Take a good look. Look at the three flower pots that are left. Where's the big flower pot that's left?

BOY: Right here.

TEACHER: Very good. Now show me another big flower pot.

BOY: Right here.

TEACHER: Okay, now where's the little bitty flower pot?

BOY: Right here.

TEACHER: Very good. Very good. Okay, now this time you gonna do it all by yourself. Can you do it again? C'mon, you can do all these cards now. Let's try the trucks. You love trucks. What color is that truck?

BOY: Yellow.

TEACHER: Yellow.

BOY: And black.

TEACHER: Yellow and what other color?

BOY: Black.

TEACHER: Okay, now find a big, big truck for me. Find a big truck.

BOY: Right here.

TEACHER: Oh, take a good look at it. Take a good look at those trucks. Where's the big, big truck at?

BOY: Right here.

TEACHER: Alright. That's truck number one. Okay, now where's the big truck at?

BOY: Right here.

TEACHER: Oh, take a good look at it. Take a good look. That's a tricky one. Where's that big truck at?

BOY: Right here.

TEACHER: Alright, that's truck number two. Now take a good look. Where's the big truck at? Where's the big truck?

BOY (*overlapping*): Right here.

TEACHER: Very good. Truck number three. Now where's the big truck at now?

BOY: Right here.

TEACHER: Alright. And where's the little bitty truck?

BOY: Right here.

TEACHER: Very good. Give yourself another hand. You did a good job. C'mon, do one more set of cards for us. [*Cut to another teacher with children.*]

GIRL (*reading cards*): X.

BOY: You got a X, Paris.

SECOND TEACHER: Very good, Paris.

CHILD: Y.

SECOND TEACHER: Does anyone have a Y?

GIRL: No, I don't.

CHILDREN: A.

TEACHER: What letter is this, Duponté?

BOY: Oh, I had a Z.

BOY: Oh.

CHILDREN: Q.

SECOND TEACHER: Very good.

GIRL: Bingo!

SECOND TEACHER: Very good. Let's move on. Okay, she has bingo. You can get a—

KENYA: M! Bingo!

SECOND TEACHER: Very good, Kenya.

THIRD TEACHER: What is this? What color is this? The bluuue, okay. What color is this? What color is this?

BOY: Green.

THIRD TEACHER: Greeeeen! And you have on green socks.

BOY: Green!

THIRD TEACHER: Yeah, it's green. What color is this one?

BOY: Red.

THIRD TEACHER: Red. Good, Kendall. What color?

BOY: Bluuue!

THIRD TEACHER: Noooo!

BOY: Orange!!

THIRD TEACHER: Orange.

BOY: It's orange!

THIRD TEACHER: Orange. You want the orange? Very good. What color?

GIRL: Yellow!

THIRD TEACHER: Yellow! Who needs a yellow?

BOY: Me. [*Shots of children playing with soapy water. A boy paints. Two children playing. A child puts colored pegs in holes.*]

PUPPET: Is it nice to sell drugs in our neighborhood?

CHILDREN: Nooo!!!!!

PUPPET: Nooo! What does drugs do to boys and girls and men and women? [*Cut to CU of puppet speaking to children.*]

GIRL: Make you die.

BOY: Die.

PUPPET: Eventually it will make you die. But also what does it make you do?

GIRL: Sick.

PUPPET: It makes you sick. It makes you lose your mind. You start doin' things—excuse me. I hear talking out there, boys and girls. This is very important. You start usin' drugs, it makes your mind poison.

GIRL: I know that.

PUPPET: Did you know that?

CHILDREN: Yeah!!

PUPPET: Will you be usin' drugs?

BOY: No!!

BOY: No, I see.

WOMAN: Shhh!

PUPPET: When you see people in our neighborhoods selling drugs, what are you gonna go?

GIRL: Call the police.

CHILDREN: The police.

PUPPET: Call the police. What is my name?

CHILDREN: Mr. Officer.

PUPPET: And we gonna do good in the—

CHILDREN: 'Hood!

PUPPET: Alright! Put your hands together. [*Children clap along.*] Down with dope. Up with—I can't hear you.

CHILDREN: Hope!

CHILDREN: Down with dope; up with hope. Down with dope; up with hope.

PUPPET: We gonna do good in the—

CHILDREN: 'Hood!!

PUPPET: In the 'hood, okay? We have to take care of our own community because if we don't do it, nobody else will. Bye, boys and girls.

CHILDREN: Bye, Mr. Officer! Bye. [*A record plays "Chug-along-choo-choo" as children play along. Ext. shot of same woman waiting on steps. Nine shots of neighborhood street scenes. Two ext. shots of Kennedy King College. Cut to LS of audience gathered to listen to Ron Carter.*]

MAN: Put your hands together. Former NBA player, now with HUD, Ron Carter. [*Applause.*]

RON CARTER: I'm a-bring it; I'm a-bring it. But I'm a-bring it correct. [*Clap.*] We got the shot of a lifetime. Alright. Now hear me, because I'm comin'

74. A HUD representative shares his ideas with the people of Wells.

correct from the heart. We got the shot of a lifetime. [*Clap.*] My office is one of five offices within a department. I will give away from my office three hundred million dollars this year. A brother [*applause*] born, born and raised in the projects. Born and raised, alright? Went to college, did the basketball thing, went to the pros, left the pros to be in this business. To come home. I coulda made much more money building housing in Beverly Hills, which I was doin' with Magic and James Worthy and Norm and all my boys, but I wasn't doin nothin' for my people. And C-H-A was goin' downhill back then. So I came home. My boss is a Latino woman. Her boss is a brother. His boss is a brother, and his boss is a Latino man, and his boss is the president. We go from me—from you, to me, to the president, and it ain't nothin' but minority people. We got the shot of a lifetime. Right now. Alright. Here's how the game works. The State Street corridor from Hilliard to the Hole is a two-hundred-million-dollar business. Don't y'all go nowhere. [*Applause.*] Alright. What, what we need to be doin' is takin' care of our own. Alright? Now, let me show you how we gonna do that. I'm gonna lay it out there, and then y'all gonna tell me how we gonna make this work. Let's just take Robert Taylor Homes. I had hoped to have some visuals, but I couldn't—I was tied up in meetings and couldn't get to my paperwork to bring it to you. But Robert Taylor Homes has an operating budget. We, HUD, my office in Washington, pays the C-H-A thirty-five million dollars a year to run Robert Taylor. Thirty-five million. So when y'all walk out your doors in the mornin' and say man, I need a job, there's jobs all around you. The second you walk out the door, there's a job waitin' right there in front of your front door. When I look at the budget—I'm a-, I'm a-show it to you. Then I'm a-show you how to get to it. And then I'm [*clap*] a-get in, stand in the gap as HUD, and help to get you there. You can climb all across me gittin' to that job. [*Applause.*] Alright, alright? When you look at the budget for Robert Taylor Homes, there are line items on that budget. One of 'em is elevator maintenance. You know how much they spent on elevator maintenance last year? One point two million dollars. Y'all ride 'em, I know y'all can fix 'em. [*Applause.*] One point two million dollars. Brother, can't you start a elevator repair company? I know you can. Can't you hire all my brothers down here to fix them elevators for one point two million? That's a job. That's a job. Now check this out. If you start a elevator repair company, and it is fifty-one percent owned by residents, the executive director of the housing authority can give you a contract for a million dollars without going to bid. He ain't got to ask nobody. He can cut a check for a million because you a resident. So why don't y'all have a elevator company?

MAN IN AUDIENCE: 'Cause we [*inaudible*].

CARTER: Okay. Next line item. Utilities. How much does Robert Taylor spend on utilities? I don't know. But let's guess. Considering the lights are burnin' twenty-four-seven every time I look at one of 'em high raises—it's seven o'clock, it's high noon, and the lights is on. Am I lyin'?

AUDIENCE: No.

CARTER: So I'm guessin' three million. Electric bill gotta be three million dollars. Here's another business. I call it the Robert Taylor Homes Energy Conservation Company. We spent three million dollars on electricity. You go down to Kevin Marxman of the C-H-A who, by the way, is a brother, who, by the way, is the deputy assistant secretary at HUD. Kevin, you spent three million last year. I bet we can cut your electric bill by a million dollars if you give us twenty-five percent. That's two hundred and fifty Gs. All you gotta do is get up at six and turn the light out. So I could do this all night.

WOMAN: Yeah!

CARTER: I could do this all night.

WOMAN: Yeah!

CARTER: We gotta go from all this—this is great talk now. Now this brother's standin' up here tellin'—this is great rap. How do we make this happen? Well, step number one is, y'all got to go back and talk to the rest of the brothers. Y'all know that there's a hard-core thing goin' out there. And let's get real again. Drugs ain't new. Alright? When I grew up in the 'hood, when I grew up in North View Heights in Pittsburgh, they was sellin' drugs then too. But you know what the difference was? The brothers that was doin' that had respect for their community. They wasn't cuttin' deals on the side of the building like this. [*Applause.*] It was behind closed doors. I never had to see that.

MAN (*offscreen*): That's right!

CARTER: My mama never had to see it, my grandmother never had to see it, and the babies never had to see it. [*Applause.*] It ain't correct. I can't police that away. We can put a hundred thousand cops in Robert Taylor, all they gonna do is lose. We can't police that away. Y'all got to make it right. Y'all gonna make this work. It's time for men to step up and be leaders. So what I'm saying is, now we have got to build a machine. I tell ya, I got an African brother, a dear friend of mine from Nigeria. He came here broke. Multimillionaire. Seven years. He said, "Ron, I love America." [*Laughter.*] He said, "Money is fallin' out the sky." He said, "The only rule is you can't catch it wit' your hands, you got to build a basket." What he means is you got to form a company. So we gonna form businesses. So this is how we get this thing rollin'. I got a master's degree in business. I got a master's degree in finance. I'm gonna get with Dr. Adams, we gonna start holding classes. We gonna start showin' you brothers how to form businesses. 'Cause let me tell you somethin' about when you form your own business, ain't no application. [*Applause.*] Ain't nobody gone tell you, you can't do this because you have a felony arrest record. We can, we can work this now and start to form businesses. I can get Nike and Coca-Cola and IBM and people like that that make investments in the 'hood if they believe that we will take care of their investment. It gets down to that. Alright? So what I'm trying to say is, in two weeks I'll talk to Gil, we'll start with the first session. Let's pack this house. And what I will do is come and I will begin to show you how to set up your business. I'll work with Dr. Adam Stand. We will begin to develop the curriculum, but y'all have to make the commitment, because the only ones that can do it is you brothers, man. You know, the brothers and sisters that are out there. Yeah.

[*Exterior shot of Kennedy-King College. "Turkey in the Straw" coming from ice cream truck offscreen, playing over credits. Black screen before credits: Director, Producer, Editor: Frederick Wiseman. Photography: John Davey. Camera assistant: Lawrence Dobbs, Assistant editor: Victoria Garvin Davis. Production coordinator: Karen Konicek, Sound mix: Rick Dior. Editorial as-*]

sistants: Carolyn Kaylor, Siobhan Dunne, Leslie May-Chibani; Production assistant: Annie B. Smith, Titles: Marian Parry, Type design: Jean Evans. Special thanks to the residents and staff of the Ida B. Wells Housing Development and the Chicago Housing Authority for their cooperation and assistance. Funding for the film was provided by the John D. and Catherine T. MacArthur Foundation, Public Broadcasting Service, Corporation for Public Broadcasting, the Joyce Foundation. A Zipporah Films Release © 1997 Housing Film, Inc. All rights reserved.]

Filmography

The Cool World (1964; b&w, 104 min.)
Screenplay by Shirley Clarke and Carl Lee
Adapted from the novel by Warren Miller and the play by Warren Miller
    and Robert Rossen
Photography: Baird Bryant
Sound: David Jones
Music: Mal Waldron
Producer: Frederick Wiseman
Director and editor: Shirley Clarke

Titicut Follies (1967; b&w, 83 min.)
Director, producer, editor, sound: Frederick Wiseman
Photography: John Marshall
AWARDS
First Prize, Best Documentary, Mannheim Film Festival, 1967
Best Film Dealing with the Human Condition, Festival dei Popoli, Florence,
    1967

High School (1968; b&w, 75 min.)
Director, producer, editor, sound: Frederick Wiseman
Photography: Richard Leiterman

Law and Order (1969; b&w, 81 min.)
Director, producer, editor, sound: Frederick Wiseman
Photography: William Brayne
AWARDS
Emmy, Best Documentary, 1969
Award for Exceptional Merit, Philadelphia International Film Festival, 1971

Hospital (1969; b&w, 84 min.)

Director, producer, editor, sound: Frederick Wiseman
Photography: William Brayne

AWARDS

Emmy, Best Documentary, 1970
Emmy, Best Director, 1970
Catholic Film Workers Award, Mannheim Film Festival, 1970
Dupont Award for Excellence in Broadcast Journalism, Columbia University
    School of Journalism, 1970
Red Ribbon, American Film Festival, California, 1972

Basic Training (1971; b&w, 89 min.)

Director, producer, editor, sound: Frederick Wiseman
Photography: William Brayne

AWARDS

Award for Exceptional Merit, Philadelphia International Film Festival, 1971

Essene (1972; b&w, 89 min.)

Director, producer, editor, sound: Frederick Wiseman
Photography: William Brayne

AWARDS

Gabriel Award, Catholic Broadcasters Association, 1972

Juvenile Court (1973; b&w, 144 min.)

Director, producer, editor, sound: Frederick Wiseman
Photography: William Brayne

AWARDS

Silver Phoenix, Atlanta International Film Festival, 1974
CINE Golden Eagle Certificate, 1974
Dupont Award for Excellence in Broadcast Journalism, Columbia University
    School of Journalism, 1974
Emmy nomination, Best News Documentary, 1974

Primate (1974; b&w, 105 min.)

Director, producer, editor, sound: Frederick Wiseman
Photography: William Brayne

Welfare (1975; b&w, 167 min.)

Director, producer, editor, sound: Frederick Wiseman
Photography: William Brayne

AWARDS

Gold Medal, Special Jury Award, Virgin Islands International Film Festival, 1975
CINE Golden Eagle Certificate, 1975

Best Documentary, Athens International Film Festival, 1976
Ohio State Award for Excellence in Broadcasting, 1977

Meat (1976; b&w, 113 min.)

Director, producer, editor, sound: Frederick Wiseman
Photography: William Brayne

Canal Zone (1977; b&w, 174 min.)

Director, producer, editor, sound: Frederick Wiseman
Photography: William Brayne

AWARDS

Golden Athena Prize for Best Feature, Athens International Film Festival, 1978

Sinai Field Mission (1978; b&w, 127 min.)

Director, producer, editor, sound: Frederick Wiseman
Photography: William Brayne

Manoeuvre (1979; b&w, 115 min.)

Director, producer, editor, sound: Frederick Wiseman
Photography: John Davey

AWARDS

CINE Golden Eagle Certificate, 1980
Best Documentary, Festival Internacional de Cinema, Portugal, 1980

Model (1980; b&w, 129 min.)

Director, producer, editor, sound: Frederick Wiseman
Photography: John Davey

AWARDS

CINE Golden Eagle Certificate, 1981

Seraphita's Diary (1982; color, 90 min.)

Director, producer, editor: Frederick Wiseman
Screenplay: Frederick Wiseman
Photography: John Davey
Sound: David John

AWARDS

Honorary Mention, Festival dei Popoli, 1983
Gold Special Jury Award, Houston Film Festival, 1983

The Store (1983; color, 118 min.)

Director, producer, editor, sound: Frederick Wiseman
Photography: John Davey

Racetrack (1985; b&w, 114 min.)
Director, producer, editor, sound: Frederick Wiseman
Photography: John Davey

Blind (1986; color, 132 min.)
Director, producer, editor, sound: Frederick Wiseman
Photography: John Davey

AWARDS
Honorary Mention, American Film and Video Festival, California, 1987

Deaf (1986; color, 164 min.)
Director, producer, editor, sound: Frederick Wiseman
Photography: John Davey

Adjustment and Work (1986; color, 120 min.)
Director, producer, editor, sound: Frederick Wiseman
Photography: John Davey

Multi-Handicapped (1986; color, 126 min.)
Director, producer, editor, sound: Frederick Wiseman
Photography: John Davey

Missile (1987; color, 115 min.)
Director, producer, editor, sound: Frederick Wiseman
Photography: John Davey

Near Death (1989; b&w, 358 min.)
Director, producer, editor, sound: Frederick Wiseman
Photography: John Davey

AWARDS
L'Age d'Or Prize, Royal Film Archive, Belgium, 1989
International Critics Prize, Berlin Film Festival, 1990
Media Award, Retirement Research Foundation, 1990
Broadcast Media Award, American Association of Critical Care Nurses, 1990
DuPont Award for Excellence in Broadcast Journalism, Columbia University
    School of Journalism, 1991

Central Park (1990; color, 176 min.)
Director, producer, editor, sound: Frederick Wiseman
Photography: John Davey

AWARDS
CINE Golden Eagle Certificate, 1990

Aspen (1991; color, 146 min.)
Director, producer, editor, sound: Frederick Wiseman
Photography: John Davey

Zoo (1993; color, 130 min.)
Director, producer, editor, sound: Frederick Wiseman
Photography: John Davey

>   AWARDS
>   Mayor's Prize, Yamagata International Documentary Film Festival, 1993

High School II (1994; color, 220 min.)
Director, producer, editor, sound: Frederick Wiseman
Photography: John Davey

Ballet (1995; color, 170 min.)
Director, producer, editor, sound: Frederick Wiseman
Photography: John Davey

>   AWARDS
>   Golden Gate Award Certificate of Merit, San Francisco International Film
>   Festival, 1996

La Comédie-Française, ou L'amour joué (1996; color, 223 min.)
Director, producer, editor, sound: Frederick Wiseman
Photography: John Davey

>   AWARDS
>   Competition Jury's Special Prize, Yamagata International Film Festival, 1997

Public Housing (1997; color, 200 min.)
Director, producer, editor, sound: Frederick Wiseman
Photography: John Davey

>   AWARDS
>   Jury Award, L'Age d'Or Prize, Royal Film Archive, Belgium, 1998
>   Prix du Cinéma de Recherche, Grand Prix, Vue sur les Docs, International
>   Documentary Film Festival, Marseilles, 1998

Belfast, Maine (1999; color, 248 min.)
Director, producer, editor, sound: Frederick Wiseman
Photography: John Davey

>   AWARDS
>   Mayor's Prize, Yamagata International Documentary Film Festival, 1999
>   Documentary Award of Bayerischer Rundfunk, Munich Documentary Festival,
>   2000

Domestic Violence (2001; color, 196 min.)
Director, producer, editor, sound: Frederick Wiseman
Photography: John Davey

AWARDS

Silver Hugo Award, Chicago Film Festival, 2001

Domestic Violence 2 (2002; color, 160 min.)
Director, producer, editor, sound: Frederick Wiseman
Photography: John Davey

La Dernière Lettre (2002; b&w, 61 min.)
Director, editor: Frederick Wiseman
Photography: Yorgos Arvanitis, A.F.C.
Starring: Catherine Samie, sociétaire de la Comédie-Française
Producer: Frederick Wiseman, Pierre-Olivier Bardet
Written by Vassili Grossman
Sound: François Waledisch

Personal Awards
Gold Hugo Award, Chicago International Film Festival, 1972
Personal Achievement Gabriel Award, Catholic Broadcasters Association, 1975
John Simon Guggenheim Memorial Fellow, 1980–81
John D. and Catherine T. MacArthur Foundation Fellow, 1982–87
Great Director Tribute and Award for Continuing Directorial Achievement in the
    Documentary Field, USA Film Festival, 1984
Chevalier de l'Ordre des Arts et des Lettres, 1987
Louis Hazam Award, Washington Film and Video Council, 1987
Award for Excellence in Documentary Filmmaking, Virginia Festival of American
    Film, 1998
Humanitarian Award, Massachusetts Psychological Association, 1990
Career Achievement Award, International Documentary Association, 1990
Peabody Award for Significant and Meritorious Achievement, 1990
The Rosenberger Medal, University of Chicago, 1999
Commandeur de l'Ordre des Arts et des Lettres, 2000
Irene Diamond Life-Time Achievement Award/Human Rights Watch, 2000
Yale Law Association Award of Merit, 2002
Full Frame Documentary Film Festival, Career Award, 2002
HOT DOCS Canadian International Documentary Film Festival, Lifetime
    Achievement Award, 2002
Dan David Prize Laureate, 2003

Honorary Degrees

Doctor of Humane Letters, University of Chicago, 1973
Doctor of Humane Letters, Williams College, 1976
Doctor of Fine Arts, Lake Forest College, 1991
Doctor of Humane Letters, John Jay College of Criminal Justice, 1994
Doctor of Fine Arts, Princeton University, 1994

Bibliography

Ames, Elizabeth. "Fred Wiseman's Candid Camera." *Horizon* 24, no. 9 (September 1974): 62–66.

Anderson, Carolyn. "The Conundrum of Competing Rights in *Titicut Follies.*" *Journal of the University Film Association* 33, no. 1 (Winter 1981): 15–22.

———. "The *Titicut Follies* Audience and the Double Bind of Court-Restricted Exhibition." In *Current Research in Film: Audiences, Economics, and Law,* vol. 3, edited by Bruce A. Austin, 189–214. Norwood, NJ: Ablex, 1987.

Anderson, Carolyn, and Thomas W. Benson. "Direct Cinema and the Myth of Informed Consent: The Case of *Titicut Follies.*" In *Image Ethics: The Moral Rights of Subjects in Photography, Film, and Television,* edited by Larry Gross, John Katz, and Jay Ruby, 58–90. New York: Oxford University Press, 1988.

———. *Documentary Dilemmas: Frederick Wiseman's Titicut Follies.* Carbondale: Southern Illinois University Press, 1991.

Arlen, Michael. "Frederick Wiseman's 'Kino Pravda.'" *New Yorker,* April 21, 1980, pp. 91–101.

Armstrong, Dan. "Wiseman's *Model* and the Documentary Project: Towards a Radical Film Practice." *Film Quarterly* 37, no. 2 (Winter 1983–84): 2–10; rpt. in *New Challenges for Documentary,* ed. Alan Rosenthal, 180–90. Berkeley: University of California Press, 1988.

———. "Wiseman's Cinema of the Absurd: *Welfare,* or 'Waiting for the Dole.'" *Film Criticism* 12, no. 3 (Spring 1988): 3–19.

———. "Wiseman's Realm of Transgression: *Titicut Follies,* the Symbolic Father, and the Spectacle of Confinement." *Cinema Journal* 29, no. 1 (Fall 1989): 20–35.

———. "Wiseman and the Politics of Looking: *Manoeuvre* in the Documentary Project." *Quarterly Review of Film Studies* 11, no. 4 (1990): 35–50.

Arnold, Gary. "*Law and Order.*" *Washington Post,* March 7, 1970, p. C6.

———. "Frederick Wiseman's *Primates.*" *Washington Post,* December 5, 1974, pp. B1, B15.

———. "Wiseman's *Welfare:* Compelling Case Study." *Washington Post,* September 24, 1975, pp. C1–C2.

Atkins, Thomas R. "American Institutions: The Films of Frederick Wiseman." *Sight and Sound* 43, no. 4 (Autumn 1974): 232–35.

———, ed. *Frederick Wiseman*. New York: Simon & Schuster, 1976.

———. "Frederick Wiseman's America: *Titicut Follies* to *Primate*." In *The Documentary Tradition*, 2d. ed., edited by Lewis Jacobs, 536–50. New York: Oxford University Press, 1979.

Bamber, Martin. "*Basic Training*." *Senses of Cinema*, no. 25 (March–April 2003), available at http://www.sensesofcinema.com/contents/cteq/03/25/basic_training.html.

Barnouw, Erik. *Documentary: A History of the Nonfiction Film*. New York: Oxford University Press, 1974.

Barsam, Richard M. *Nonfiction Film: A Critical History*. New York: Dutton, 1973.

———. "American Direct Cinema: The Re-Presentation of Reality." *Persistence of Vision*, nos. 3–4 (Summer 1986): 131–56.

Bassoff, Betty Zippin. "*Welfare*." *Social Work* 20, no. 6 (November 1975): 498.

Benson, Thomas W. "The Rhetorical Structure of Frederick Wiseman's *High School*." *Communications Monographs* 47 (1980): 233–61.

Benson, Thomas W., and Carolyn Anderson. "The Rhetorical Structure of Frederick Wiseman's *Model*." *Journal of Film and Video* 36, no. 4 (Fall 1984): 30–40.

———. *Reality Fictions: The Films of Frederick Wiseman*, 2d ed. Carbondale: Southern Illinois University Press, 2002.

Berg, Beatrice. "'I Was Fed Up with Hollywood Fantasies.'" *New York Times*, February 1, 1970, sec. 2, pp. 25–26.

Boodman, Sandra G. "A Look at the End of Life." *Washington Post*, January 16, 1990. [*Near Death*]

Bordwell, David, and Kristin Thompson. *Film Art: An Introduction*, 7th ed. New York: Knopf, 2003. [*High School*]

Bourne, Geoffrey H. "Yerkes Director Calls Foul." *New York Times*, December 15, 1974, p. 33.

Boyd, Malcolm. "*Essene*." *New York Times*, November 12, 1973, p. 17.

Boyum, Joy Gould. "Watching Real Life Problems." *Wall Street Journal*, October 1, 1973, p. 3. [*Juvenile Court*]

Bradlow, Paul. "Two . . . But Not of a Kind." *Film Comment* 5, no. 3 (1968): 60–61. [*Titicut Follies*]

Bromwich, David. "Documentary Now." *Dissent*, October 1971, pp. 507–12.

———. "Unsentimental Education." *New Republic* (September 9–19, 1994), p. 39. [*High School II*]

Brown, Les. "Scientist Angrily Cancels TV Discussion of *Primate*." *New York Times*, December 7, 1974, p. 59.

Campbell, J. Louis III. "'All Men Are Created Equal': Waiting for Godot in the Culture of Inequality." *Communications Monographs* 55 (1988): 143–61.

Campbell, J. Louis III, and Richard Buttny. "Rhetorical Coherence: An Exploration into Thomas Farrell's Theory of the Synchrony of Rhetoric and Conversation." *Communication Quarterly* 36, no. 4 (Fall 1988): 262–75. [*Welfare*]

Canby, Vincent. "The Screen: *Titicut Follies* Observes Life in a Modern Bedlam." *New York Times*, October 4, 1967, p. 38.

Cass, James. "*High School.*" *Saturday Review,* April 19, 1969, p. 57.

Cholodenko, Alan. "'The Borders of Our Lives': Frederick Wiseman, Jean Baudrillard, and the Question of Documentary." *International Journal of Baudrillard Studies* 1, no. 2 (July 2004), available at http://www.ubishops.ca/baudrillardstudies/vol1_2/cholodenko.html.

Colby, Ira. "*Titicut Follies* Revisited." *Social Work* 37, no. 5 (September 1992): 389.

Coleman, John. "Long Look." *New Statesman,* November 1975, pp. 589–90. [*Welfare*]

Coles, Robert. "Stripped Bare at the Follies." *New Republic,* January 20, 1968, pp. 18, 28–30.

———. "Senses and Sensibility." *New Republic,* August 29, 1988, pp. 58–60. [*Deaf and Blind.* series]

Combs, Richard. "*Model.*" *Monthly Film Bulletin* 48, no. 567 (April 1981): 73.

Corry, John. "TV: *The Store,* a Wiseman Film." *New York Times,* December 14, 1983, p. C34.

———. "Wiseman Examines Racetracks." *New York Times,* June 4, 1986, p. C26.

Covington, Richard. "The *Salon* Interview: Frederick Wiseman." *Salon,* March 12, 2005, available at http://www.salon.com/weekly/interview960826.html.

Crain, Jane Larkin. "TV Verite." *Commentary* 56, no.6 (December 1973): 70–75.

Cunningham, Stuart. "The Look and Its Revocation: Wiseman's *Primate.*" *Australian Journal of Screen Theory,* nos. 11–12 (1982): 86–95.

Curry, Timothy Jon. "Frederick Wiseman: Sociological Filmmaker?" *Contemporary Sociology* 14, no. 1 (January 1985): 35–39.

Denby, David. "Documenting America." *Atlantic,* March 1970, pp. 139–42; rpt. in *The Documentary Tradition,* edited by Lewis Jacobs, 2d ed., 447–82. New York: Hopkinson and Blake, 1972. Also rpt. in *Nonfiction Film: Theory and Criticism,* edited by Richard Barsam, 310–14. New York: Dutton, 1976.

———. "Taps." *New York,* October 4, 1971, p. 69. [*Basic Training*]

———. "The Real Thing." *New York Review,* November 8, 1990, pp. 24–27.

———. "Women and Children." *New Yorker,* February 11, 2002, p. 92. [*Domestic Violence*]

DeVries, Hillary. "Fred Wiseman's Unblinking Camera Watches How Society Works." *Christian Science Monitor,* May 1, 1984, pp. 25–27.

Dowd, Nancy Ellen. "Popular Conventions." *Film Quarterly* 22, no. 3 (Spring 1969): 28–31. [*Titicut Follies*]

Eames, David. "Watching Wiseman Watch." *New York Times Magazine,* October 2, 1977, pp. 96–102, 104, 108.

Edelstein, David. "Taking a Time-Tested Approach to a Cruel Reality." *New York Times,* March 16, 2003, p. 38. [*Domestic Violence*]

Ellis, Jack C. *The Documentary Idea: A Critical History of English-Language Documentary Film and Video.* Englewood Cliffs, NJ: Prentice-Hall, 1989.

Ellsworth, Liz. *Frederick Wiseman: A Guide to References and Sources.* Boston: G.K. Hall, 1979.

Faucher, Charles A. "The Kids of *High School.*" *Media and Methods* 6, no. 1 (September 1969): 54–55.

Featherstone, Joseph. "*High School.*" *New Republic,* June 21, 1969, pp. 28–30.

Feldman, Silvia. "The Wiseman Documentary." *Human Behavior* 5 (February 1976): 64–69.

Ferguson, Gretje. "The Unflinching Eye of Frederick Wiseman." *American Cinematographer* 75, no. 1 (January 1994): 75–77.

Freedman, Samuel G. "Showing a Harrowing World but Not How It Got That Way." *New York Times,* November 30, 1997, sec. 2, pp. 37, 40. [*Public Housing*]

Friedenberg, Edgar Z. "Ship of Fools: The Films of Frederick Wiseman." *New York Review of Books,* October 21, 1971, pp. 19–22.

Fuerst, J. S. "*Public Housing.*" *Commonweal* 125, no. 7 (April 10, 1998): 11.

Fuller, Richard. "'Survive, Survive, Survive': Frederick Wiseman's New Documentary *Basic Training.*" *Film Journal* 1, nos. 3–4 (Fall/Winter 1972): 74–79. Rpt. in *Frederick Wiseman,* edited by Thomas R. Atkins, 103–12. New York: Simon & Schuster, 1976.

———. "*Primate.*" *Films and Filming* 21, no. 6 (March 1975): 37–38.

Geduld, Harry M. "Garbage Cans and Institutions: The Films of Frederick Wiseman." *Humanist* 31, no. 5 (September/October 1971): 36–37.

Gill, Brendan. "The Current Cinema." *New Yorker,* October 28, 1967, pp. 166–67. [*Titicut Follies*]

Goodman, Walter. "Hands That Could Launch the Missiles." *New York Times,* August 31, 1988, p. C22.

Graham, John, and George Garett. "How Far Can You Go?: A Conversation with Fred Wiseman." *Contempora* 1, no. 4 (October/November 1970): 30–33. Rpt. as "There Are No Simple Solutions." *Film Journal* 1, no.1 (Spring 1971): 43–47. Also rpt. in *Frederick Wiseman,* edited by Thomas R. Atkins, 33–45. New York: Simon & Schuster, 1976.

Grant, Barry Keith. *Voyages of Discovery: The Cinema of Frederick Wiseman.* Urbana: University of Illinois Press, 1992.

———. "'Ethnography in the First Person': Frederick Wiseman's Titicut Follies." In *Documenting the Documentary: Close Readings of Documentary Film and Video,* edited by Barry Keith Grant and Jeannette Sloniowski, 238–53. Detroit: Wayne State University Press, 1998.

Halberstadt, Ira. "An Interview with Fred Wiseman." *Filmmakers Newsletter* 7, no.4 (February 1974): 19–25. Rpt. in *Nonfiction Film: Theory and Criticism,* edited by Richard M. Barsam, 296–309. New York: Dutton, 1976.

Handelman, Janet. "An Interview with Frederick Wiseman." *Film Library Quarterly* 3, no. 3 (1970): 5–9.

Hatch, Robert. "Films." *Nation,* October 30, 1967, pp. 445–46. [*Titicut Follies*]

Hecht, Chandra. "Total Institutions on Celluloid." *Society* 9 (April 1972): 44–48.

Hedges, Chris. "Excavating the Memories of a Generation's Horrors." *New York Times,* May 27, 2001, sec. 2, p. 5. [*La Dernière Lettre*]

Hill, David. "High School Reunion." *Education Week* 14, no. 1 (September 7, 1994): 32. [*High School II*]

Hill, Logan. "Pushing the Envelope." *New York* 34, no. 22 (June 4, 2001): 117. [*La Dernière Lettre*]

Hockman, William S. "*Essene.*" *Film News* (September 1973), p. 24.

Holland, Patricia. "Taking Time." *New Statesman,* November 20, 2000, pp. 45–46.

Horn, Miriam. "Shining a Light on Their Follies." *U.S. News & World Report,* April 12, 1993, p. 20. [*Titicut Follies*]

Janis, Eugenia, and Wendy MacNeil, eds. *Photography within the Humanities.* Danbury, NH: Addison Rouse, 1977.

Janssen, Peter A. "The Last Bell." *Newsweek,* May 19, 1969, p. 102. [*High School*]

Jones, Kent. "First Look: *Domestic Violence.*" *Film Comment* 37, no. 4 (July/August 2001): 14–15.

Kael, Pauline. "*High School.*" *New Yorker,* October 18, 1969, pp. 199–204. Rpt. in Kael, *Deeper into Movies,* pp. 19–24. Boston: Little, Brown, 1973. Also rpt. in *Frederick Wiseman,* edited by Thomas R. Atkins, 95–101. New York: Simon & Schuster, 1976.

———. "The Current Cinema." *New Yorker,* January 31, 1970, pp. 74–76. Rpt. in Kael, *Deeper into Movies,* pp. 101–102. Boston: Little, Brown, 1973. [*Hospital*]

Kirtz, Bill. "Acclaimed Filmmaker Doesn't Like to Play 'Gotcha.'" *Christian Science Monitor,* August 24, 2001, p. 19.

Kleinman, Arthur. "The American Medical Way of Death: Do Not Go Gentle." *New Republic,* February 5, 1990, pp. 28–29. [*Near Death*]

Knight, Arthur. "Cinema Verite and Film Truth." *Saturday Review,* September 9, 1967, p. 44. [*Titicut Follies*]

Kramer, Chuck. "Fred Wiseman's *Primate* Makes Monkeys of Scientists." *New York Times,* December 1, 1974, sec. 2, pp. 1, 31.

Le Péron, Serge. "Cinema Independant Americain: Fred Wiseman." *Cahiers du Cinéma,* no. 303 (September 1979): 41–49.

———. "Wiseman ou le cinéma Americain vu de dos." *Cahiers du Cinéma* 330 (December 1981): 43–49.

Levin, G. Roy. *Documentary Explorations: 15 Interviews with Film-makers.* Garden City, NY: Anchor/Doubleday, 1971.

Lewis, Caroline. "*Juvenile Court.*" *Monthly Film Bulletin* 41, no. 485 (June 1974): 129.

———. "*High School.*" *Monthly Film Bulletin* 41, no. 487 (August 1974): 177.

———. "*Essene.*" *Monthly Film Bulletin* 41, no. 488 (September 1974): 198.

———. "*Welfare.*" *Monthly Film Bulletin* 43 (March 1976): 65.

Lewis, Jon. "The Shifting Camera Point of View and Model of Language in Frederick Wiseman's *High School.*" *Quarterly Review of Film Studies* 7, no.1 (Winter 1982): 69–77.

Lopate, Phillip. "Composing an American Epic." *New York Times,* January 23, 2000, pp. 11, 26.

Lucia, Cynthia. "Revisiting High School: An Interview with Frederick Wiseman." *Cineaste* 20, no. 4 (October 1994): pp. 5–11.

Macdonald, Dwight. "*The Cool World.*" In *Dwight Macdonald on Movies.* Englewood Cliffs, NJ: Prentice-Hall, 1969, pp. 323–27.

McKay, Jim. "A Discussion with Frederick Wiseman, Part 1." *IndieWIRE,* Dec. 18, 1997, available at http://www.indiewire.com/people/int_wiseman_frdrk_971218_1.html.

———. "A Discussion with Frederick Wiseman, Part 2." *IndieWIRE,* Dec. 19, 1997, available at http://www.indiewire.com/people/int_wiseman_frdrk_971219_2.html.

McWilliams, Donald E. "Frederick Wiseman." *Film Quarterly* 24, no. 1 (Fall 1970): 17–26.

Mamber, Stephen. *"High School." Film Quarterly* 23, no. 3 (Spring 1970): 48–51.

———. *Cinema Verite in America: Studies in Uncontrolled Documentary.* Cambridge, MA: MIT Press, 1973.

———. "Cinema Verite and Social Concerns." *Film Comment* 9, no. 6 (November/December 1973): 8–15.

———. "One Man's *Meat.*" *New Republic,* December 4, 1976, pp. 21–22.

———. "The New Documentaries of Frederick Wiseman." *Cinema* (L. A.) 6, no.1 (n.d.): 33–40.

Maslin, Janet. "Frederick Wiseman's *Near Death.*" *New York Times,* October 7, 1979, pp. 11, 13.

Meehan, Thomas. "The Documentary Maker." *Saturday Review of the Arts,* December 1972, pp. 12, 14, 18.

Mitchell, Elvis. "Battering Begins. The Police Come. It All Starts Again." *New York Times,* January 30, 2002, p. E1. [*Domestic Violence*]

Morgenstern, Joseph. "It Don't Make Sense." *Newsweek,* February 9, 1970, pp. 85–86. [*Hospital*]

———. "Probing the Kafkaesque World of Welfare." *New York Times,* September 21, 1975, sec. 2, pp. 1, 25.

Moss, Jesse. "Interview: A Master's Unflinching Eye: Wiseman Returns with *Domestic Violence.*" *IndieWIRE,* Jan. 29, 2002, available at http://www.indiewire.com/people/int_Wiseman_Fredrik_020129.html.

Nichols, Bill. "Fred Wiseman's Documentaries: Theory and Structure." *Film Quarterly* 31, no. 3 (Spring 1978): 15–28. Revised as chap. 7 of Nichols, *Ideology and the Image.* Bloomington: Indiana University Press, 1981.

Nicholson, Philip, and Elizabeth Nicholson. "Meet Lawyer-Filmmaker Frederick Wiseman." *American Bar Association Journal* 61, no. 3 (1975): 328–32.

O'Connor; John J. "The Film Is about Killing." *New York Times,* October 3, 1971, sec. 2, p. 17. [*Basic Training*]

———. "TV: Strong Wiseman Documentary on Monastery." *New York Times,* November 14, 1972, p. 94.

———. "TV: *Primate,* A Study by Wiseman." *New York Times,* December 5, 1974, p. 124.

———. "Wiseman's *Welfare* is on Channel 13 Tonight." *New York Times,* September 24, 1975, p. 91.

———. "Wiseman's Latest Film Is Another 'Reality Fiction.'" *New York Times,* November 7, 1976, p. 26. [*Meat*]

———. "TV: Wiseman Captures the World of Modeling." *New York Times,* September 16, 1981, p. C26.

———. "Capturing the Essence of Art, in Sweat and Genius." *New York Times,* June 26, 1995, p. C14. [*Ballet*]

———. "Acting, Love and Play at a Very Old Institution." *New York Times,* August 31, 1996, p. 11. [*La Comédie Française ou L'amour joué*]

Peary, Gerald. "Boston: A New Hub for Filmmakers." *American Film* 6, no. 8 (June 1981): 20–24, 64.

———. "Frederick Wiseman Interview." *Boston Phoenix* (March 1998). Available at http://www.geraldpeary.com/interviews/wxyz/wiseman.html.

Poppy, Nick. "Frederick Wiseman." *Salon*, March 28, 2002, available at http://archive .salon.com/people/conv/2002/01/30/wiseman.

———. "Stalking Shadows: Frederick Wiseman on *The Last Letter*." *IndieWIRE*, Feb. 10, 2003, available at http://www.indiewire.com/people/people_030210wiseman .html.

Price, Michael. "*Titicut Follies*." *Senses of Cinema*, no. 19 (March–April 2002), available at http://www.sensesofcinema.com/contents/cteq/01/19/titicut.html.

Pryluck, Calvin. "Ultimately We Are All Outsiders: The Ethics of Documentary Filming." *Journal of the University Film Association* 28, no.1 (Winter 1976): 21–29. Rpt. in *New Challenges for Documentary*, edited by Alan Rosenthal, 255–68. Berkeley: University of California Press, 1988.

Rapfogel, Jared. "The Birth, Life, and Death of a Nation: A Portrait of Frederick Wiseman." *Senses of Cinema*, no. 19 (March–April 2002), available at http://www .sensesofcinema.com/contents/01/19/wiseman.html.

———. "Out of Time: *The Last Letter*." *Cinemascope*, no. 14 (Spring 2003): 77.

Rayns, Tony. "*Basic Training*." *Monthly Film Bulletin* 41 (November 1974): 246–47.

Rice, Eugene. "*Essene*: A Documentary Film on Benedictine Community Life." *American Benedictine Review* 24, no. 3 (1973): 382.

Rice, Susan. "The Movies: *Hospital*." *Media and Methods* 6, no. 7 (March 1970): 14.

Rich, Frank. "A Sunny, Nightmare Vision." *Time*, October 10, 1977, p. 103. [*Canal Zone*]

Richardson, Elliot. "Letters: Focusing Again on *Titicut*." *Civil Liberties Review* 1, no. 3 (Summer 1974): 148–49. Rpt. in *Frederick Wiseman*, edited by Thomas R. Atkins, 67–69. New York: Simon & Schuster, 1976.

Rifkin, Glenn. "Wiseman Looks at Affluent Texans." *New York Times*, December 11, 1983, pp. 37, 44. [*The Store*]

Robb, Christina. "Focus on Life." *Boston Globe Magazine*, January 23, 1983, pp. 15–17, 26–34.

Robinson, David. "A Slanted, Cruelly Middle-Class-Debunking Film." *Phi Delta Kappan* 51, no. 1 (September 1969): 47. [*High School*]

———. "Apes and Essentials." (London) *Times*, January 10, 1975, p. 11. [*Primate*]

Rose, Daniel Asa. "Frederick Wiseman Takes His Camera to the Races." *New York Times*, June 1, 1986, pp. 29, 38.

Rosenberg, Karen. "*The Store*." *Nation*, December 17, 1983, pp. 642–43.

Rosenblatt, Roger. "Frederick Wiseman's *Welfare*." *New Republic*, September 27, 1975, pp. 65–67.

Rosenthal, Alan, ed. *The New Documentary in Action: A Casebook in Film Making*. Berkeley: University of California Press, 1972.

———, ed. *New Challenges for Documentary*. Berkeley: University of California Press, 1988.

Russell, Cristine. "Science on Film: The *Primate* Controversy." *Bioscience* 25, no. 3 (March 1976): 151–54, 218.

Sarris, Andrew. "*The Cool World.*" *Village Voice*, April 23, 1964. Rpt. in Sarris, *Confessions of a Cultist: On the Cinema, 1955–1969*, pp. 135–36. New York: Simon & Schuster, 1971.

———. "Films." *Village Voice*, November 9, 1967, p. 33. [*Titicut Follies*]

Schickel, Richard. "The Sorriest Spectacle." *Life*, December 1, 1967, p. 12. [*Titicut Follies*]. Rpt. in *Film 67/68*, edited by Richard Schickel and John Simon, 246–48. New York: Simon & Schuster, 1968. Also rpt. in *Frederick Wiseman*, ed. Thomas R. Atkins, 91–93. New York: Simon & Schuster, 1976. Also rpt. in *The Documentary Tradition*, 2d ed., edited by Lewis Jacobs, 459–61. New York: Norton, 1979.

———. "A Verite View of High School." *Life*, September 12, 1969. Rpt. in *Film 69/70*, edited by Joseph Morgenstern and Stefan Kanfer, 209–11. New York: Simon & Schuster, 1969. Also rpt. in Schickel, *Second Sight: Notes on Some Movies, 1965–1970*, pp. 155–59. New York: Simon & Schuster, 1972.

———. "Where Misery Must Be Confronted." *Life*, February 6, 1970, p. 14. [*Hospital*]

Schwartz, Richard A. "Frederick Wiseman's Modernist Vision: *Central Park.*" *Literature/Film Quarterly* 23, no. 3 (1995): 223–28.

Sheed, Wilfred. "Films." *Esquire*, March 1968, pp. 52, 55. [*Titicut Follies*]

Sidel, Victor W. "*Hospital* on View." *New England Journal of Medicine* 285, no. 5 (January 29, 1970): 279.

Slavitt, David R. "*Basic Training.*" *Contempora* 2, no.1 (September/February 1972): 10–11.

Snyder, Sharon, and David Mitchell. "The Visual Foucauldian: Institutional Coercion and Surveillance in Frederick Wiseman's Multi-Handicapped Documentary Series." *Journal of Medical Humanities* 24, nos. 3–4 (December 2003): 291–308.

Sourian, Peter. "Television." *Nation*, October 15, 1977, 181–82. [*Canal Zone*]

Spotnitz, Frank. "Frederick Wiseman." *American Film* 16, no. 5 (May 1991): 16–21.

Steele, Robert. "*Essene.*" *Film News*, September 1973, p. 24.

Sullivan, Patrick J. "'What's All the Cryin' About?': The Films of Frederick Wiseman." *Massachusetts Review* 13, no. 3 (Summer 1972): 452–59.

———. "*Essene.*" *Film Quarterly*, 27, no. 1 (Fall 1973): 55–57. Rpt. in *Frederick Wiseman*, edited by Thomas R. Atkins, 113–20. New York: Simon & Schuster, 1976.

———. "Frederick Wiseman's *Primate.*" *New Republic*, January 25, 1975, pp. 30–32.

Sutherland, Allan T. "Wiseman on Polemic." *Sight and Sound* 47, no. 2 (Spring 1978): 82.

Swartz, Susan. "The Real Northeast." *Film Library Quarterly* 6, no. 1 (1972–73): 12–15.

Sweet, Louise. "*Canal Zone.*" *Sight and Sound* 47, no. 1 (Winter 1977–78): 59–60.

"Talk of the Town." *New Yorker*, October 5, 1981, p. 41. [*Model*]

"Talk of the Town." *New Yorker*, October 24, 1988, pp. 31–32. [*Missile*]

"Talk of the Town: New Producer." *New Yorker*, September 14, 1963, pp. 33–35.

Tarratt, Margaret. *"Juvenile Court." Films and Filming* 19, no. 11 (August 1974): 43–44.

———. *"Meat." Films and Filming* 23, no. 9 (June 1977): 42–43.

Taylor, Charles. *"Titicut Follies." Sight and Sound* 57, no. 2 (Spring 1988): 98–103.

Tuch, Roland. "Frederick Wiseman's Cinema of Alienation." *Film Library Quarterly* 11, no. 3 (1978): 9–15, 49. [*Meat*]

"Viewpoints: Shooting the Institution." *Time*, December 9, 1974, pp. 95, 98.

Vineberg, Steve. "In Familiar Corridors, An American Vision of Despair." *New York Times*, August 26, 2001, sec. 2, p. 23. [*High School*]

Wakefield, Dan. "American Close-Ups." *Atlantic*, May 1969, pp. 107–108. [*High School*]

Walker, Jesse. "Film Reviews: *The Cool World*." *Film Comment* 1/2, no. 2 (Spring 1964): 51–52.

Waters, Harry F. "Wiseman on Welfare." *Newsweek*, September 29, 1975, pp. 62–63.

———. "Inside a Shopping Shrine." *Newsweek*, December 19, 1983, p. 81.

———. "A Stiff Dose of Intensive Care." *Newsweek*, January 22, 1990, p. 52. [*Near Death*]

Weiler, A. H. "Wiseman to Make 'Yes Yes, No No,' First Fiction Film." *New York Times*, December 6, 1974, p. 78.

Weisman, Mary-Lou. "Neiman-Marcus, the Movie." *New Republic*, December 31, 1983, pp. 25–26.

Westin, Alan. " 'You Start Off with a Bromide': Conversation with Film Maker Frederick Wiseman." *Civil Liberties Review* 1, no. 2 (Winter/Spring 1974): 52–67. Rpt. in *Frederick Wiseman*, edited by Thomas R. Atkins, 47–66. New York: Simon & Schuster, 1976.

Wilson, David. *"Meat." Monthly Film Bulletin* 44, no. 520 (May 1977): 102–103.

Wiseman, Frederick. "Lawyer-Client Interviews: Some Lessons from Psychiatry." *Boston University Law Review* 39, no. 2 (Spring 1959): 181–87.

———. "Reminiscences of a Filmmaker: Fred Wiseman on *Law and Order*." *Police Chief* 36, no. 9 (September 1969): 32–35.

———. "Wiseman on *Juvenile Court*." *Journal of the University Film Association* 25, no. 3 (1973): 48–49, 58.

———. "Letters: Focusing Again on *Titicut*." *Civil Liberties Review* 1, no. 3 (Summer 1974): 149–51. Rpt. in *Frederick Wiseman*, edited by Thomas R. Atkins, 69–73. New York: Simon & Schuster, 1976.

———. "A Filmmaker's Choices." *Christian Science Monitor*, April 25, 1984, p. 30.

———. "What Public TV Needs: Less Bureaucracy." *New York Times*, November 27, 1988, pp. 35, 42.

———, et al. "Letter to the Editor." *New England Journal of Medicine* 322, no. 22 (May 1990): 1605–6.

———. "Dialogue on Film." *American Film* 16, no. 5 (May 1991): 16–21.

Wolcott, James. *"Welfare* Must Be Seen." *Village Voice*, September 29, 1975, p. 126.

———. "Blood on the Racks: Wiseman's *Meat*." *Village Voice*, November 15, 1976, p. 95.

———. "Television and Its Discontents: Wiseman's Panamania." *Village Voice,* October 10, 1977, p. 45.

———. "Adrift in Cheekbone Heaven." *Village Voice,* September 11, 1981, p. 67. [*Model*]

Wolf, Susan M. "*Near Death*—In the Moment of Decision." *New England Journal of Medicine* 322, no. 3 (June 1990): 208–209.

Zimmerman, Paul D. "Shooting It Like It Is." *Newsweek,* March 17, 1969, pp. 134–35.

Zoglin, Richard. "Let the Music Go Inside of You." *Time,* June 20, 1988, p. 64. [*Deaf and Blind* series]